Beards and Texts

Beards and Texts

Images of masculinity in medieval German literature

Sebastian Coxon

UCLPRESS

First published in 2021 by
UCL Press
University College London
Gower Street
London WC1E 6BT

Available to download free: www.uclpress.co.uk

A CIP catalogue record for this book is available from The British Library.

ISBN: 978-1-78735-223-0 (Hbk.)
ISBN: 978-1-78735-222-3 (Pbk.)
ISBN: 978-1-78735-221-6 (PDF)
ISBN: 978-1-78735-224-7 (epub)
ISBN: 978-1-78735-225-4 (mobi)
DOI: https://doi.org/10.14324/111 9781787352216

For PWC, a true reader

Contents

List of figures

List of abbreviations

ABäG	Amsterdamer Beiträge zur älteren Germanistik
BHVB	Bericht des historischen Vereins Bamberg
BSB	Bayerische Staatsbibliothek
DVjs	Deutsche Vierteljahrsschrift für Literaturwissenschaft und Geistesgeschichte
DVN	Deutsche Versnovellistik des 13. bis 15. Jahrhunderts, edited by Klaus Ridder and Hans-Joachim Ziegeler
FMLS	Forum for Modern Language Studies
FS	Festschrift
JEGP	Journal of English and Germanic Philology
JOWG	Jahrbuch der Oswald von Wolkenstein-Gesellschaft
LB	Landesbibliothek
LCI	Lexikon der christlichen Ikonographie
LiLi	Zeitschrift für Literaturwissenschaft und Linguistik
LMB	Landesbibliothek und Murhardsche Bibliothek
MGH	Monumenta Germaniae Historica
MGH Auct. Ant.	Monumenta Germaniae Historica: Auctores antiquissimi
MGH Dt. Chron.	Monumenta Germaniae Historica: Deutsche Chroniken
MGH LL	Monumenta Germaniae Historica: Leges (in Folio)
MGH LL nat. Germ.	Monumenta Germaniae Historica: Leges nationum Germanicarum
MGH SS	Monumenta Germaniae Historica: Scriptores (in Folio)
ÖNB	Österreichische Nationalbibliothek

PBB	Beiträge zur Geschichte der deutschen Sprache und Literatur
PL	Patrologia Latina, edited by Jacques-Paul Migne
SBPK	Staatsbibliothek zu Berlin Preußischer Kulturbesitz
SSMLL	Society for the Study of Medieval Languages and Literature
UB	Universitätsbibliothek
ZfdA	Zeitschrift für deutsches Altertum und deutsche Literatur
ZfdPh	Zeitschrift für deutsche Philologie

1
Beards and texts, texts and beards

Most fundamentally, this book is concerned with the role played by references to beards in medieval German literature, and with the different forms and functions such references take in a variety of text types and vernacular literary traditions as they evolved from the mid-twelfth to the early sixteenth centuries. Such an investigation derives its legitimacy from the peculiar (and pretty much universal) cultural-historical significance of the beard as a – if not *the* – pre-eminent 'natural' symbol of masculinity. From a literary-historical point of view it seems pertinent to enquire how this notion translated into literary practice. Two inextricably linked objects of study emerge. For just as literary texts from the past may serve as a rich source of historical ideas concerning beards, so the beard, by virtue of its longstanding connotations of virility, authority and wisdom, can be used to measure developments in vernacular literature itself. It follows that the emphasis throughout this book will be on textual detail. Indeed, its main chapters stand and fall by the close readings they contain. For that reason this book is not overtly theoretical, although it has been written with a mind to several underlying issues.

Preliminary observations

The status of literary references to beards – for that matter the status of literary evidence per se – is of course up for debate. In the most general terms, the relationship between literature and the culture that produces it is complex and dynamic. As has been frequently observed, literary texts are shaped by and respond to their cultural environment, which may be understood to consist of any number of social practices, norms and ideals, imaginary notions and codified bodies of learning and knowledge.[1] For many of the texts under discussion here the cultural context in question is that of the courts of the higher nobility, for whom literature served as a source of entertainment, a means of instruction (whether in moral-didactic issues, social ethics or religious ideas) and as a relatively sophisticated form of self-representation. That said, medieval courtly literature was not merely a receptacle for cultural content; it generated this cultural content also, helping to create and reiterate the images the nobility chose to define itself by.[2]

Medieval courtly society evidently had a number of media at its disposal when it came to expressing its own values. Yet literature seems to have enjoyed a special status. Statues of leading noblemen and noblewomen stood as enduring reminders of courtly lives well lived; however, as Joachim Bumke has pointed out, in matters of fashion, for instance, courtly poets were better placed to respond to the changing demands and predilections of their audiences.[3] More significantly for us, literature's very discursivity facilitated the integration of (textual) material from other cultural domains. Prevalent social norms could be upheld in literature but they could also be treated with ironic detachment. With fictional narrative some poets exercised their imagination to focus on the extraordinary, although such fictionality, delimited by the wishes and mental horizons of their audiences, was never entirely unconstrained.[4] For this reason Rüdiger Schnell's distinction between fictional content in the foreground of such texts (love scenes, battles, dialogue, descriptions) and the perceived reality and veracity of the concepts underpinning such content is a helpful one.[5]

All literary texts are documents of their time. Still, the position they occupy within their cultural context is in part dependent on their literary make-up. Chronicles do not as a rule function like comic tales, for example. Different literary traditions or, in the loosest sense, genres privilege different modes of presentation and reveal a preference for certain literary strategies and poetic devices. Certain types of content, certain narrative structures and motifs may conform to the culture of the day and may thus be subject to change in accordance with text-external social developments. But this is not always the case. Some types of content go unchanged for centuries.[6] More often than not (and especially in the twelfth and thirteenth centuries), the telling of a story in literary form actually constituted a retelling, a translation-cum-adaptation of a Latin or an Old French source text.[7] Thus, a number of divergent forces shaped literary work of this kind, including fidelity to source and truthfulness, generic conventions, the expectations of the new target audience, and the next poet's inventiveness, rhetorical expertise and determination in pursuing their own thematic agenda. Even for deceptively straightforward issues like the external appearance of narrative figures, we must assume that poets took into account both text-external and text-internal factors when going about their business.

It is tempting to treat medieval literature as a window through which we may – if we look hard enough – catch a glimpse of past cultural reality, of how women and men actually thought, felt and behaved. However, it is just as important, if not more so, to bring to light what makes these literary texts so literary.[8] Narrative or poetic detail is not just culturally coded, which is to say, indicative of the cultural codes at work in society at large. It is not just derived from other source texts or established discourses (theological, legal, medical); it exercises numerous functions within the text itself, whether this be a matter of theme, structure or characterization.[9] The impact, both emotional and intellectual, which such detail may have had on recipients is closely related to the question of how or on what level it is being relayed, as part of the objective account of an omniscient narrator, as part of a more obviously subjective narratorial commentary, or as spoken, directly or indirectly, by the figures themselves.[10] There is in fact no reason to doubt that in some literary works these text-internal functions were the poet's primary consideration. More to the point, it is entirely feasible that in some literary works the symbolic and poetic significance of beards was writ large in spite of prevailing social practices and attitudes.[11]

For many pieces of medieval German literature, the contexts that we know most about are literary on the one hand, and on the other pertain to the manuscripts in which these works are preserved.[12] The search for medieval literary meaning therefore entails a close reading of the relevant material in its immediate narrative or poetic context (the text in question as a whole), as well as a comparative analysis of the principal source (where possible) and a review of the broader literary traditions with which the individual work is associated. Further nuances may be gleaned from manuscript variants, as well as from the emergence of differing redactions of one and the same work or even new versions.[13] Where texts were received in collective manuscripts, the themes that spoke out to the readers or listeners of any one work may have, on occasion, been determined by its co-texts.[14]

The miniatures contained in illustrated codices represent another form of contextualization, albeit a very different one, not least because these pictures – which usually, but not always, belong to a second or third phase of reception – deploy iconographic motifs such as beardedness in their own way. Aside from their decorative and representative functions, most miniatures illustrate the accompanying text without necessarily being subservient to it. Miniatures can provide a commentary; they can heighten the text's impact at certain points, modify textual content or develop it differently.[15] Whereas the narration of detail pertaining to visual appearance (visualization) in any medieval text is almost always intermittent and subject to other poetic or narrative demands, miniatures simply had to provide concrete visual detail.[16] Artists had no choice but to decide, for instance, whether male figures were bearded or beardless, quite apart from what (fashionable) garments or headgear they should be wearing. More often than not, the resulting images had little to do with beard-specific detail from within the text, being a product rather of the established iconographic motifs and schemes at their disposal. An amply illustrated codex could thus feature numerous bearded figures, far more than the literary text its miniatures were accompanying.

One such book of beards is the Berlin/Krakow codex, dateable c. 1220, of Priester Wernher's *Maria* (apocryphal account of Mary's life up to birth of Jesus), which contains an array of beard motifs, denoting sexual maturity (Joachim),[17] old age (Joseph),[18] rulership (fols 60r (Augustus), 79v (Herod)), wisdom (80v), mastery of a craft (50v) and years of imprisonment (76v). The generational scheme (for groups of three men) of beardless, cropped beard and long beard, as noted by Bumke for the Three Kings (83r), is also used throughout.[19] The special interest taken in beards is attested above all by the miniature on fol. 73r (Figure 1.1), where a bearded figure of the artist's own conception – one of the shepherds outside Bethlehem – clutches his beard and declares in astonishment, by means of a speech scroll: 'Als grise so mir min bart ist. so vernam ich ditze wunder nie mere' / 'As grey as my beard is, I have never heard of such a marvel'. Unlike many of the other speech scrolls in this manuscript (the earliest known vernacular German codex to feature this device) this utterance is not based on lines found in the *Maria*-text.[20] Over and above Priester Wernher's narrative depiction of this scene (4192–225), the all-too-human response of bewilderment in the face of divine intervention is thus conveyed by the artist, for maximum affective impact, through the visualization of gesture and speech.

One thing that image and text, or art and literature, do have in common is that they both represent ideals far more neatly than is possible in messy reality,[21] allowing for the clearest of clear-cut distinctions between closely related phenomena and conditions, such as the difference between being clean-shaven, a relative concept throughout the Middle Ages, and being bearded. It is more than likely that this artistic amplification, as it were, applied in fact to other aspects of courtly culture and social interaction. The importance of the body as sign in a society still

Figure 1.1 Four shepherds behold a golden ring around the sun (Priester Wernher's *Maria*). Krakow, Bibl. Jagiellońska, Berol. mgo 109, fol. 73r. Public domain.

dominated by face-to-face communication – by gesture, bodily self-discipline and appearance – is thus especially palpable in courtly literature, where this very principle is simultaneously subjected to critique.[22] Likewise, as perfectly summed up by Beate Kellner and Christian Kiening, other kinds of knowledge concerning the body were not so much reiterated in the literary texts of the day as refashioned in accordance with literature's own 'Modi von Rhetorizität, Figuralität, Symbolizität und Narrativität', with its own 'Sprechweisen und Gattungen'.[23]

Bodies were and still are *commonly* perceived to be carriers of meaning in respect of gender and sex,[24] with hair playing an important role in the representation of male and female identity. In turn, medieval literary images of women's and men's bodies give us a measure of insight into the 'collective memories and fantasies of medieval people' concerning gender.[25] In this context beards might be considered by some to be a particularly significant body part, especially – if not absolutely exclusively – in terms of masculinity. Of course, to advocates of modern performative theories of gender (in the wake of Judith Butler), literary references to the body, to differences in physiology between men and women as referenced by literary texts, are only of interest in so far as they support readings of gender as an unstable category.[26] Scholars of this persuasion tend to insist that the meaning of gender is quite separate from biology, that the categories of female and male are constructed primarily through language or through being repeatedly performed.[27] Literary beard references which belie the purported attempts of medieval poets to 'feminize' their male protagonists are thus liable to be passed over in silence[28] or deliberately read against the grain in search of 'auffällige "Leerstellen", die Brüche und Widersprüche markieren'.[29] The following study offers an alternative to such ideological literary interpretation, albeit one which also seeks to benefit from the methodological gains made by studies of gender and masculinity. Thus, we will explore the possibility that medieval poets referred to beards not just to underline the differences between men and women (patriarchy) but to distinguish between men, beards being potentially expressive of 'masculinist' interests,[30] of male hierarchies, and of more than one understanding of masculinity. It remains to be seen whether the use of beard imagery to profile masculinity was always as monologic or monolithic as some critics might suspect.[31] All literature constructs through language and this applies to every literary portrayal of gender irrespective of whether it questions or indeed upholds the notion that gender difference is a natural one.

Medieval beards: medieval meanings

Poets did not start from scratch when it came to the meaning(s) of beards in their texts; rather they relied upon certain very basic and obvious ideas, ideas with which their listeners and readers too would have been familiar. Setting lived experience and social knowledge to one side, this shared understanding is also likely to have been shaped by exposure at first, second or even third hand to the discursive domains of religion, medicine and law. Vernacular evidence pertaining to beards in these more specialized contexts is relatively sparse; yet enough of it survives to suggest that vernacular poets and their audiences might well have been influenced – on occasion and to varying degrees – by these bodies of knowledge, even if they were not necessarily always aware of it.[32]

For longevity and continuity nothing comes close to the affirmation of bearded masculinity in Christian homiletics and scriptural exegesis from the writings of the Church Fathers onwards.[33] If, in principle, the beard could be seen as a marker of physical maturity, as a means of distinguishing sex and as a beautifully manly feature (Lactantius),[34] so its symbolic significance, with reference to the Scriptures, proved compelling. Thus St Augustine's commentary on Psalm 132 (133), and more specifically on the outstanding image of Aaron's anointment and the precious unguent running down over his beard,[35] was destined to become one of the most widely received theological beard references throughout the Middle Ages: 'The beard signifies the courageous; the beard distinguishes the grown man, the earnest, the active, the vigorous. So that when we describe such, we say, he is a bearded man'.[36] One such bearded hero, according to Augustine, was the martyred St Stephen;[37] and most (if not all) medieval exegetes followed suit by equating Aaron's beard in the first instance with the Apostles, men of exceptional fortitude and faith.[38] The unguent itself was commonly understood to symbolize the Holy Ghost or Divine Grace, which at first poured down onto Christ (the head) before running over his Apostles (the beard).[39]

The Old High German rendering of Psalm 132 by Notker the German (Notker Labeo; d. 1022) reiterates Augustine's interpretation.[40] Several centuries later the ripple effect of such exegesis is just about discernible in the vernacular *Christherre-Chronik* (c. 1244–87; incomplete), a chronicle of universal (Old Testament) history, where the poet openly borrows the beard reference from Psalm 132 when recounting Moses's anointing of Aaron, which results in a far more detailed description than the one actually given in Leviticus (8: 12).[41] These words of the Psalmist, the chronicler tantalizingly concedes, 'have multiple meanings' ('Bezeichenunge hant so vil' 18119) which would take too long to explain. More inventively, at the outset of Konrad von Heimesfurt's account of Mary's Assumption (*Unser vrouwen hinvart*, c. 1225) the poet, only too mindful of his awesome responsibility, draws on the central image of the same Psalm to convey his desire to please God and benefit the world, comparing his humility with the unguent running down 'through Lord Aaron's beard' ('durch des hern Aarônes bart' 52–3). This is a far cry from the salve of vanity, Konrad maintains (47–50), alluding to another Psalm in the process ('oleum autem peccatoris non inpinguet caput meum' / 'let not the oil of the sinner fatten my head' 140: 5).

The symbolic significance of hair and beards was expounded further in discussions within the Church concerning tonsuring and shaving.[42] Bruno of Segni (d. 1123) sought to inspire others by distinguishing between spiritual and physical fortitude, between the monk's inner beard (which should be allowed to grow) and his outer one (which is shaved).[43]

For Sicard of Cremona (d. 1215), shaving allowed monks to look like boys, a demonstration of humility and innocence that would help them gain entry into heaven.[44] By this time the Cistercian abbot Burchard of Bellevaux (d. 1163) had already penned an entire treatise on the subject (*Apologia de barbis*), in which he sought to pacify a group of disgruntled lay brothers by praising them for their beards.[45] These were, he reassures them, a sign of distinction, strength, maturity, wisdom and piety, although it was also important for them to understand why monks proper shaved and were tonsured. In heaven there would in any case be no more shaving or cutting of hair, and they would all be adorned with resplendent white beards.[46]

In spite of its very specific purpose Burchard's *Apologia de barbis* is widely regarded as an important document for the history of beards, a rare example of 'barbilogia' (III, 432) as Burchard the 'Barbilogus' (Preface, 3) puts it. Not only does it constitute a study in beard symbolism from a churchman's point of view, it contains information on contemporary beard fashions, as well as several different approaches to categorizing beard growth. Of course Burchard's reflections on the cleanliness (*sermo* I), 'composition' (II) and nature (III) of beards draw heavily on biblical passages, some of his favourite topics being Aaron's beard (anointed and pure), the leprous (subject to ritual purification), David's beard (covered in spittle) and the prophet Ezekiel (shaving in despair).[47] Being something of a literary scholar, Burchard also submits the Vulgate and his other sources to close textual analysis,[48] and he firmly distinguishes between those events in the Bible which actually happened (David did play the madman to escape capture) and those with purely symbolic meaning, such as the leprous beards in Leviticus (13: 29–34; 14: 8–9): 'nemo enim unquam vidit barbam leprosam' / 'for no one has ever actually seen a leprous beard' (III, 1209).

Conducted exclusively in Latin, these beard debates and others like them would largely have remained a closed book for most laymen and laywomen across Europe. However, some of the ideas formulated therein must have entered broader circulation. That vernacular sermons may have played a role in this is suggested by a text attributed to the Franciscan preacher Berthold von Regensburg (c. 1220–72) which centres, ostensibly, on the theme of leprosy (sermon VIII: *Von der ûzsetzikeit*). All young priests, Berthold declares, must learn to diagnose where the person in their care is diseased, whether in their hair, flesh, skin or, in true Leviticus fashion, 'an dem barte' / 'in their beard' (111,32–5). To suffer sickness in the beard, he subsequently reveals, is to be guilty of sins of the tongue,[49] some seventeen of which are counted (115,38–118,2), including lying, cursing and mocking. Many of the sins listed are everyday ones, more relevant and less heinous to Berthold's listeners perhaps than heresy, which was the standard exegetical interpretation of leprosy of the beard.[50] The telling association here appears to be that between beard and mouth, and so, as with all of the other body parts and sins expounded in this sermon, applicable in principle to both men and women.[51] Indeed, in another version of the same sermon Berthold voices his criticism of certain bad-mouthed women in expressly these terms: 'aber der frouwen dâ ze dorfe ist mêr ûzetzic umbe den bart, dan anderswâ'/ 'but the women [out] there in the villages, they are more diseased around the beard than [women] anywhere else' (119,4).

It is possible that Berthold's reference to the symbolic beards of peasant women was calculated to raise a laugh.[52] But no matter how unnatural, suspect or even monstrous female beardedness was perceived to be throughout the Middle Ages,[53] no matter how many times Isidore of Seville's somewhat circular definition of the beard was faithfully copied out ('Our forefathers named the beard, *barba*, because it is proper to men, not to women'),[54] in religious contexts the *notion* of the female beard could be understood altogether more positively. Bishop Bruno actually prefaces his thoughts on the inner beards of monks by recognizing that female saints, who are so much stronger than normal men in spirit, fully deserve to be called 'bearded'.[55] Moreover, on the basis of a short chapter (13) in Book IV of Gregory the Great's *Dialogues* (c. 595), a certain widow by the name of Galla came to be venerated for her steadfast refusal to get married, even when warned by doctors that unless she did, she would grow a beard through 'excess of heat'.[56] Unperturbed, according to Gregory at least, Galla insisted on becoming a nun, confident in the knowledge that Christ did not love her for her outer beauty. A lot is made of St Galla's beard in the *Apologia de barbis* (III, 83–135).[57] Although Burchard classifies this beard growth as 'contra consuetum cursum naturae' / 'contrary to the normal course of nature' (III, 106), he even recommends that Galla's virtuous indifference to it should serve as an example to lay brothers who fear being ridiculed for their natural lack or thinness of beard (III, 120–7).

Unlike the miraculous beard growth of several late medieval female saints whose chastity is saved by the extraordinary transformation in their appearance,[58] Galla's physical 'deformity' is presented as having a physiological, medically cogent reason.[59] Burchard supplies further commentary: it is on account of women's 'natural inborn coldness' ('ingenitam naturaliter frigiditatem' III, 108) that they do not normally grow beards; but occasionally it can happen (by an accident of nature), this being as shameful to a woman as it is for a man to remain beardless (III, 111–15). Medical knowledge concerning men's heat and their (greater) ability to produce hair and beards from their superfluities was famously codified elsewhere in the mid-twelfth century by Hildegard of Bingen in her *Causae et curae*.[60] It is not until the first half of the fourteenth century that we find the same scientific observations being made in the vernacular. Book I of Konrad von Megenberg's *Buch der Natur* (c. 1350) contains a chapter on beards (I.9: 'Von dem part'), which provides a digest of contemporary medical opinion: the human beard is a sign of the male sex ('mannes gesläht' 2); like hair it grows from (internal) superfluities ('überflüezzichait' 3); the hotter the man, the more vigorous the beard growth; some women have a beard above the mouth, and this is due to their (unusually) hot nature; natural eunuchs cannot grow a beard; and any man who is capable of growing a beard ('partochter' 10) will, if castrated, lose beard and manly courage and 'become womanly in spirit' ('vnd gewinnet ainen weipleichen sin' 11–12).

Scientific discourse such as this explained and rationalized what everyone already knew: beard growth was a visible sign of virility and physical maturity. This common understanding of male physiology had very real social consequences, as reflected in charters and legal texts of various kinds. Giles Constable informs us that (according to their written constitutions) certain monasteries in the eleventh and twelfth centuries only admitted laymen who had enough of a beard ('tantum barbae') to be shaved off as part of the ritual of tonsure.[61] By the same token, according to the later thirteenth-century *Schwabenspiegel*, a legal compendium in the vernacular, in cases where the age of male child oblates was in doubt, puberty (the age of fourteen) was to be ascertained by examining the boy's body: 'It should be felt above his mouth below the nose: if any hair growth is found there, that counts as proof'.[62] The time-honoured principle of beardedness as a measure of a man's age, and thus also of his legal status as an adult, is similarly formulated in a secular context in the *Sachsenspiegel*, the early thirteenth-century vernacular law book most likely composed by Eike von Repgow (c. 1220–35): 'In respect of any man whose age is unknown: if he has hair in his beard and down below and under each arm, then it should be known that he has come of age'.[63] There can be little doubt that in certain circumstances beardlessness was 'socially disabling'.[64] The concomitant respect shown to bearded men, the protection afforded to their beards, something that might almost be regarded as a definitive feature of traditional Germanic law,[65] was covered expressly by legal statute in the mid-twelfth century. In the *Landfrieden* issued by Frederick I (Barbarossa) in 1152 anyone found guilty of pulling out the hair or beard of another man had to pay his victim ten pounds.[66] The same type of law is evinced for the fifteenth century by the ordinances compiled in 1433 within the city of Bremen.[67] As we shall see, there is plenty of literary and artistic evidence to suggest that throughout the Middle Ages swearing by one's beard continued to be perceived as especially forceful.[68] The striking illustration of an astonished (elderly) shepherd in the early thirteenth-century Krakow codex discussed above (Figure 1.1) is a case in point.

The ideas upon which these various discursive references to beards were based, and which the latter indeed sought to consolidate, evidently held sway over a long period of time. Their longevity is further testified to by the high number of relatively stable beard-related topoi which are to be found, both in Latin and in the vernacular, in a wide range of literary contexts. Because beards were understood in terms of sex and gender, and thus also in terms of human nature, masculinity and social relations, they almost inevitably come ideologically loaded. For the same reason, observations concerning beardedness and beardlessness could be extremely tendentious.[69] In clerical and monastic writing, well-rehearsed arguments for and against beards were often put vehemently and with recourse to the same kinds of derogatory images. Critics of fashionable shaving habitually condemned the practice as morally suspect; smooth cheeks and a chin denuded of its manly hair represented nothing other than the vile attempt to look like a woman or even a hermaphrodite.[70] On the other hand, and depending on who was wearing them, long beards could always be denounced as misleading, as a false sign, and no guarantee of wisdom or piety,[71] leading to various derisive insults, the most widespread by far being that of the goat comparison.

Already a commonplace of satirical poetry in late antiquity,[72] from a medieval perspective the derogatory goat comparison was effectively authorized by St Jerome, who characterized false holy men as sporting 'goat-like beards' ('hircorum barba') and poured scorn on one of his opponents (Jovinianus) by declaring him to be a sinful goat whether he chose to remove his beard or not.[73] Jerome's view of beards and goats was famously cited at the Council of Worms (858–67) in defence of the Western clergy's practice of shaving (which had been met by Greek Orthodox incredulity).[74] Religious controversy of a different kind is a feature of Burchard of Bellevaux's own enthusiastic discussion of goats (*Apologia de barbis* III, 219–322). The abbot begins harmlessly enough with natural science (both male and female goats have beards; goats are bearded at birth) and religious symbolism (sin and man's bestial state; wisdom and Redemption), but ends by justifying why Jews are often mocked as goats: their long, dangling beards prevent the 'truth' from entering their hearts.[75]

Not all such jibes were so bitterly serious, however. Goat comparisons are ubiquitous in vernacular literature in a variety of narrative contexts (see Chapters 4 and 5). Moreover, light-hearted aphorisms and fables, several of which had Greek and Roman antecedents, continued to be transmitted throughout this period.[76] Odo of Cheriton's early thirteenth-century fable of the dispute between two sheep (one white and one black), an ass and a goat is outstanding in this respect, with these animals standing for different monastic orders and their misguided pretensions to superiority: the idiotic goat (signifying both Grandimontensians and Cistercian lay brothers) thus prides itself on the length of its beard ('barbam prolixam').[77] From the songs of Eugene II, archbishop of Toledo (d. 657) to the 'facetiae' of the sixteenth-century German humanist Heinrich Bebel (d. 1518), goat quips came to lead a life of their own as examples of admirable wit.[78]

Courtly culture: beards and shaving

Beards were commonly understood in the Middle Ages to be quintessentially masculine, but beyond that their cultural significance varied considerably, as different groups within medieval society subscribed to different ideals in relation to beardedness and shaving.[79] Ideals are not quite the same as historical or material realities. Even in the ecclesiastical sphere, with its established tradition of tonsuring and its extensive codification of rules concerning hair and beard growth, not least in opposition to the beard-friendly Greeks, beards were far from uncommon among higher churchmen as befitting their seniority and doubtless also their age.[80] In addition, the conditions of being bearded and shaven were probably more relative than we tend to imagine. By the mid-thirteenth century Cistercian monks, who were shaving more frequently than most, were required to do so 26 times a year.[81] The attractiveness of the clean-shaven ideal, wherever it arose, must have been enhanced by the fact that in this period, for most adult men, it was so difficult to maintain.

In respect of the laity, courtly society was particularly susceptible to changes in fashion, which for noblemen necessarily involved deciding what to do with their beard. This was not just a matter of means. Cultural refinement was an aspiration shared by the nobility across medieval Europe, who had a vested interest in setting themselves apart, not least by clothing (and sumptuary laws) and the length of their hair.[82] As far as beards were concerned this aspiration seems to have translated itself into the widespread practices of shaving and beard-trimming until older age.[83] That being said, the local influence of leading individuals and their personal preferences cannot be ruled out, and collective tolerance for beards certainly fluctuated over time, with the fourteenth century most especially witnessing a resurgence in the fashion for beards (in various styles) at many courts including those in southern Germany.[84]

Some of the earliest literary evidence pertaining to courtly shaving is 'German' in origin although penned in Latin.[85] In the second half of the eleventh century the Benedictine monk Otloh of Sankt Emmeram (in Regensburg) chose to illustrate worldly vanity with the story of a nobleman who fails an ordeal by water (and thus is found guilty of a crime he did not commit) because he shows contempt for God's laws by shaving his beard 'as if he were a cleric'.[86] Although the nobleman swears never to let a razor come near his beard again, he soon changes his mind, believing he can get away with it on a technicality: 'Verily, I made no [such] promise in respect of a knife'.[87] God's retribution, however, is swift and terrible: the nobleman's enemies capture him and gouge his eyes out. Otloh is most dogmatic: 'no layman should shave his beard'.[88] A rather more humorous approach is adopted in the (fragmentary) 'epic' poem known as the *Ruodlieb* (c. 1040–70), which was most likely composed in the Benedictine monastery of Tegernsee.[89] Here, the monastic poet undermines the masculinity of his protagonist, having presented him in entirely laudatory terms up to this point, when depicting Ruodlieb's ablutions before a banquet: the heroic knight removes his facial hair so very thoroughly, the poet sardonically comments, it was impossible to tell whether he was 'a cleric or a woman or a beardless schoolboy, so delightfully girlish was his face'.[90] When both clerics and laymen shave disorder threatens, as the two no longer look wholly different, thus giving rise, in Robert Bartlett's terms, to an error in the 'symbolic grammar' of hair.[91] This new-found desire to shave seems indicative of the rise of an increasingly self-confident secular culture, against which some churchmen were still railing towards the end of the eleventh century.

Conversely, and should the circumstances require it, monastic critics were also perfectly capable of launching vituperative attacks on young noblemen who had long hair and beards. In the first half of the twelfth century fashionable Anglo-Norman society aroused the ire of the Benedictine monk and chronicler Orderic Vitalis in his *Historia ecclesiastica* (completed c. 1141).[92] Castigating young men at court as both effeminate and licentious for their absurd shoes and outrageous garments, Orderic denounces them further for their 'little beards'. If in the past long beards always used to be worn 'as an outward mark of [their] penance, or captivity, or pilgrimage', these days, Orderic expostulates, courtiers' beards are the 'tokens of their filthy lust', these courtiers being no different to 'stinking goats'.[93] Later on, the logic of this polarizing argument leads to a re-evaluation of shaving as manly, as something soft young gallants refrain from doing for fear of scratching the faces of their mistresses with their bristly stubble.[94]

By the end of the twelfth century such overtly critical voices from without courtly culture seem to fall silent.[95] Instead, commentary on courtly fashion and observations concerning the appropriateness of shaving, beards and long hair in general become a feature of satirical poetry in the vernacular as it developed in the course of the thirteenth century. In one of his strophes the 'Sangspruchdichter' Reinmar von Zweter (active c. 1225–50) derides a society in which monks and knights have lost sight of who they are and what they should look like. He sees 'Hâr unde bart'/ 'Hair and beards' aplenty that are fit for the monastery but they are not being worn by true monks ('Ton' II, 129: 1–3). Neither truly one thing nor another, these new kinds of men leave him at a loss: 'von hovemünchen unt von clôsterrittern kan ich niht gesagen' / 'I simply don't know what to say about [these] court monks and monastery knights' (129: 6).[96] Several decades later the fashion among Austrian nobility of wearing their hair (and beards) long like Hungarians gives repeated cause for complaint in the work of a certain Seifried Helbling (composed c. 1282–1300).[97] One of several unusual dialogues the poet purports to have with his hilariously outspoken servant takes place in a bathhouse, where the latter proves his worth by calling for someone to tidy up his master's hair and shave his beard.[98]

On occasion shaving is considered remarkable enough to be deemed worthy of mention in a chronicle. In Ottokar von Gaal's *Steierische Reimchronik* (c. 1310), in a section concerning the Bohemian king Ottokar's ongoing conflict with certain leading Austrian noblemen (c. 1269), the abject physical condition of the latter on being released from imprisonment is described primarily in terms of their facial hair: 'mit spannelangen berten / für den kunic kômens al gemeine' / 'with span-length beards they all went before the king' (10049–50). Only one Ulrich von Liechtenstein makes a point of acting as if he has suffered no inconvenience at all, presenting himself as entirely fit for court: 'sînen bart het er geschorn / und niwe kleider an gestrichen' / 'he had shaved and hurriedly put on new clothes' (10056–7). The king is suitably impressed and congratulates him publicly. Ulrich's performance reveals a cultural norm that would otherwise be passed over in silence; the ordinary is rendered extraordinary by virtue of the circumstances in which it takes place. In another text from around 1300, one which claims to tell the true story of Thuringian landgrave Louis the Pious's participation in the Third Crusade, Louis is praised for his determination to live up to the courtly ideal even as he is dying of illness: 'sunder nâch lust hielt er sich, / der sûzgemuoter, wol gebôrn, / sînen bart abe geschorn' / 'instead he bore himself as if he were joyful, the sweet-tempered, high-born man, with his beard shaved off' (*Kreuzfahrt des Landgrafen Ludwigs des Frommen* 7724–6). Such shaving may be understood to express defiance on Ludwig's part, not just as an individual but as a representative of Western Christian courtly culture in conflict with the (bearded) heathen East.[99]

In more obviously fictional texts the courtly norm of shaving, or of keeping a trim beard, is rendered visible by moments in stories which showcase its transgression. One such 'informative fissure', as this kind of plot point has been called,[100] is found in Hartmann von Aue's *Gregorius* (c. 1185), when the poet draws attention to the good sinner's abject physical condition and appearance after twenty years spent chained to a rock in the sea (see Chapter 3). Another occurs in the fragmentary Merlin narrative *Der Rheinische Merlin* (c. 1250), when the king's steward tries to outwit Merlin by visiting him in disguise: 'Hei leis sinen bart stain / Inde wandelde sin ouercleit' / 'He grew his beard and changed his outer garment' (70–1). This ruse clearly only makes sense if the court official is normally shaven. The practice of shaving may otherwise be alluded to *ex negativo* by the description of mourning noblemen: 'ir hâr und ir berte lanc, / ungeschorn und ungetwagen' / 'their long hair and beards, unshaven and unwashed' (*Wigalois* 9116–17). To do penance is to punish and neglect oneself: in Konrad von Würzburg's romance *Partonopier und Meliur* (c. 1260) the protagonist becomes so full of self-loathing and despair that he locks himself away and allows his beard, nails and hair to grow 'unshorn'.[101] For the same reason pilgrims are almost invariably imagined to be bearded.[102] In fact, any extended period of time spent away from court – often envisaged as the experience of wilderness – is likely to be marked by beard growth.[103] Shaving duly belongs to the process of a knight's rehabilitation upon returning to civilized society.[104]

Literary testimony to the fact that even courtiers who shaved were not always going to be free of some beard growth is harder to find. This reality is obliquely referred to in the *Frauendienst*, a first-person narrative by Ulrich von Liechtenstein (d. 1275), which is to say by the same individual whose act of shaving is lauded in the *Steirische Reimchronik*. This pseudo-autobiographical account of Ulrich's trials and tribulations as a courtly lover includes an extensive account of a journey he undertakes dressed up as Lady Venus (complete with false tresses). On one flirtatious occasion he lifts his veil high enough to receive the kiss of peace from a lady (537,8), whereupon she exclaims in mock surprise: 'wie nu, ir sit ein man?' / 'What's this? You're a man?' (538,2) – a 'revelation' of gender identity, which arises from Ulrich being unshaven and unable to shave rather than from the fact that he is sporting a full beard (on his chin).[105] Elsewhere, awareness of the everyday reality of male facial hair shapes the idiosyncratic retelling of Achilles's seduction of Deidamia which is found in Jans von Wien's *Weltchronik* (composed c. 1270). Determined to disguise himself as a maiden but concerned that his beard growth might give him away, the young hero is advised by his guardian and tutor, the centaur 'Schiro', to rub a special medicinal root ('wurze' 14583) around his mouth, which will prevent even the tiniest of beard hairs from appearing.[106]

Courtly familiarity with shaving is further evinced by a number of idiomatic expressions. In his poetic treatment of chivalric duties (*Aufgaben des Rittertums*) Der Stricker (active c. 1220–50) criticizes the knight who hears others speak ill of God and yet refrains from objecting, content instead to sit in silence 'als man im sinen bart scher' / 'just as if he were having his beard shaved' (191). A shaven appearance is all well and good and any knight can have this done, the poet seems to be implying, but some things (the religious side of chivalry) are more important and more challenging.[107] A different kind of failure is at stake in *Die Heidin*, a later thirteenth-century tale about a Christian knight's pursuit of a heathen queen who is no less clever than beautiful. Apparently no match for her wits, the red-faced knight is described accordingly: 'er saz, als im wer geschorn / der bart ane schermesser' / 'He sat there just as if he had had his beard shaved without a razor' (version IV: 1374–5). Some things really are easier than others, although in this case the knight eventually has a bright idea of his own and wins his prize.

On a different textual level, idiomatic reference to shaving occurs in the speech of narrative figures ('Figurenrede') too. In Wirnt von Grafenberg's Arthurian romance *Wigalois* (c. 1210–20) the last foe to be faced, a rash and brutal knight by the name of Lîôn, is openly contemptuous of Wigalois as a threat: 'sîn zorn unde sîn gerich / ist mir als daz boeste hâr / daz ie man von im geschar' / 'His anger and his vengeance are as feeble in my eyes as the most pitiful hair he has ever had shaved' (10176–8). What would appear to be a slight on Wigalois's manhood simultaneously sheds more light for us on the status of shaving in a chivalric context. There is little sense here of the age-old suspicion that shaving is somehow effeminate. Instead, Lîôn is casting aspersions on the vigour of Wigalois's beard growth, having made the assumption that even such a weakling as Wigalois shaves. It is perhaps telling that when Wigalois's messenger returns with Lîôn's defiant response, the latter's words are subtly altered and in turn rendered less provocative or offensive to Wigalois. Lîôn, it is reported, cares about as much for all of the knights assembled (together with Wigalois) as he does for 'daz boeste hâr / daz ie man von im geschar' / 'as the most pitiful hair that he [Lîôn] has ever had shaved' (10320–1). This time the antagonistic hyperbole attributed to Lîôn takes as its point of reference Lîôn's own beard and the (many?) years he has been shaving.

More often than not, it would seem, secular courtly literature perpetuated the notion that noblemen of a certain age should shave (more frequently) or at the very least trim their beards. If anything, illustrated manuscripts of such literature tended to reinforce this message. The famous Codex Manesse (Heidelberg, UB, Cpg 848, ('Grundstock') c. 1300), for instance, contains numerous colourful author portraits featuring for the most part beardless or clean-shaven men engaged in all sorts of courtly activities.[108] Where they occur, beards typically signify age difference or various types of authority (kings, fathers, masters).[109] Indeed, this 'Minnesang' collection is opened by the strikingly majestic picture of Emperor Henry VI (fol. 6r), who is portrayed, in good Hohenstaufen tradition, as a full-bearded (brown-haired) ruler, crowned and seated on his throne, sceptre in hand.[110] In the context of courtly culture, however, even an emperor's image could be subjected to a makeover. The rough-and-ready picture of Henry VI which opens a slightly later and more modest collection of love songs, the 'Weingartner Liederhandschrift' (Stuttgart, HB XIII 1, c. 1300–25), subscribes to an alternative thematic programme. Here the seated emperor is without beard (fol. 1r), unambiguously conforming to the figure type of the golden-haired, beardless gallant that recurs throughout the codex.[111]

Literariness

Reading references to beards and shaving for cultural norms is one approach, but it hardly does justice to the literariness of any single text, the investigation of which brings its own set of questions. One of the earliest, if not *the* earliest, known beard references in secular (vernacular) literature occurs in the *Kaiserchronik* (shortly after 1152?), in an episode which characterizes the rule of Charlemagne (Karl der Große). The beard in question does not belong to Karl but rather to a chaplain sent ahead to Karl's court by the blinded Pope Leo (who has fled Rome and is in dire need of his brother's assistance): 'er wainte alsô harte, / daz im daz pluot uber den part ran'/ 'He was weeping so hard, the blood ran down over his beard' (14451–2).[112] The priest's beardedness, an exceptional condition, may well serve as a sign of the arduous journey he has been on, and Karl immediately assumes that he is a 'pilgrîme'/ 'pilgrim' (14455) who has suffered some wrong. A beard soaked by tears of blood, however, represents something more. It introduces a highly dramatic moment, lending poignancy to a turn of events so painful that the priest can hardly put it into words.[113] The priest's face, we understand, lends weight to his odd request (for Karl himself to seek out the priest's fellow 'pilgrim'), and there is also the sense that it prefigures that of Leo, whose appearance is only really described in terms of its drastic effect on Karl when the two first meet.[114] Considering that the *Kaiserchronik* chronicles the lives of 55 emperors and kings, it is perhaps extraordinary that this should be the only beard reference in the text – and yet it is. Such detail would seem to be largely incompatible with the grand scale of this particular historiographical project. Other chronicles find more space for it.

Generic observations aside, the literary analysis of references to beards (and beardlessness) necessarily involves interpretation of their thematic significance in the immediate narrative or poetic context. In some cases, especially when beards are alluded to in more than one passage, this significance extends to the work as a whole. For this reason it is important to recognize what form beard references take, which figures are being foregrounded (social and literary types, role in plot) and at what points in the work in question such beardedness is drawn to the audience's attention (structural implications). Any, or all, of these factors may have constituted more of a priority than socio-cultural 'realism'.

In general we cannot help but observe that medieval (narrative) literature is highly selective in terms of the visual detail it provides recipients.[115] Audiences were thus frequently obliged to fill in the gaps and build up mental images for themselves by drawing on other resources, whether this be social experience in general (adult men grow beards), specialist learning (theological, medical, legal) or generic awareness based on the knowledge of certain literary traditions (bachelor knights are beardless).[116] Very often the particulars we do get are conventional, with figures conforming to type. This is not to deny that there were other poets – like Wolfram von Eschenbach (see Chapter 3) – who trod their own path. Received wisdom tells us that this is a symptom of the dubious status of individuality in this period,[117] when even in the visual arts (where facial likeness was more readily achievable) portraiture was dominated by norms and ideals rather than actual physical idiosyncrasies and perceived imperfections.[118] Be that as it may, the widespread use of types facilitated the collective reception of this literature; listening to these texts was at its heart a social activity designed to strengthen the group identity of the audience. Furthermore, no matter how formulaic or conventional many (but by no means all) visual particulars may appear to us, the fact that they are included at all is often significant: such visualization, it turns out, was a reliable means of drawing attention to a moment or a scene marking the beginning or the end of a sequence of action.[119]

The most formalized descriptions of figures are those which follow the guidelines of medieval Latin handbooks of rhetoric. The device of *descriptio personae* gave poets the opportunity to expand upon their received material, finding new ways to say the same (old) things.[120] Full-blown laudatory descriptions of this kind tend to work downwards from head to toe, attributing to each physical feature a quality normally associated with beauty (hair like gold, skin like ivory, lips like roses). This rhetorical scheme dovetails with the bigger idea that outer appearance mirrors moral character, that beauty is the outward manifestation of virtue.[121] In theory at least, detailed descriptions of beauty were considered more appropriate with reference to women than to mature men,[122] since men were to be defined rather by their actions.[123] In literary practice, however, this distinction was not always upheld. From late antiquity onwards it was not unusual for chroniclers to pen portraits of outstanding rulers.[124] Emperor Frederick I (Barbarossa), for instance, is glorified in this way by Rahewin, who rounds off the final book of the *Gesta Frederici* with a flattering description of the emperor's person – referring among other things to his 'barba subrufa' / 'reddish beard' (IV, 86) – and personal conduct.[125] As is so often the way with these verbal portraits, much of the detail here (excepting the colour of Friedrich's beard) is recycled from somewhere else and is thus not particular to this individual.[126] Nevertheless, for Rahewin it probably represented the final piece in the jigsaw, ostensibly allowing the reader to get to know the emperor as a mortal man, having been told all about his great deeds.

Another literary set piece used to foreground male appearance is that of the collective review, consisting of a series of thumbnail sketches at a single narrative juncture. In accordance with their principal Latin source (the spurious eyewitness account attributed to Dares the Phrygian) medieval French and German retellings of the Trojan war (Benoît de Sainte-Maure, Herbort von Fritzlar) line up the principal Greek and Trojan actors in this way, offering their respective audiences a veritable 'who's who' before battle is joined.[127] Dares, medieval storytellers repeatedly told their audiences, compiled all of these details during a truce when he had the opportunity to visit many of these men in their tents. An equivalent passage is to be found in the Old Norse *Thidrekssaga* (c. 1250), in which a 'gallery' of bearded Germanic heroes is presented approximately halfway through the text.[128] This collection of heroes is ostensibly motivated by a banquet hosted by Thidrek. Its underlying function is revealed, however, by the fact that two of the heroes portrayed (Sigurd and Sifka) are not even in attendance. The same device has an expositional function in the 'General Prologue' of the *Canterbury Tales*, where Chaucer takes considerable pains, by means of more detailed descriptions, to characterize his cast of pilgrims and storytellers at the outset.[129]

In principle, the more rhetorically accomplished such descriptions, the less integrated they are in their narrative context. The term 'portrait' is a telling one, conveying something of the tableau-like character of these passages. It is no coincidence that poets sometimes took the shortcut of likening a figure (in its appearance) to a painting.[130] Other kinds of reference are more fleeting, but they are also more dynamic, being embedded in the course of events, forming part of the action itself. Such embedding can take the form of a ritualized or symbolic gesture conveying contemplation, anger, or distress and grief.[131] In the so-called *Rappoltsteiner Parzifal* (dated 1331–6), when King Karade learns of the misfortune of his presumed son Karados, his anguish is plain for all to see: 'er roufte sin hor und den bart' / 'He tore at his hair and beard' (5202). Alternatively, detail pertaining to appearance may crop up quite unexpectedly, as determined by an extraordinary incident, such as when Parzifal, later in the same text, fights a devil: 'er brande Parzefalen, wissent daz, / die ougbrouwen und darzuo sinen bart' / 'He burned Parzifal, know this [for a fact], his eyebrows and his beard as well' (31469–70). In the interests of narrative economy beards need not have been mentioned already as an attribute of the figure in question. References such as these may either confirm recipients in their assumptions (kings are bearded) or take them by surprise (Parzifal is bearded?!). Unexpected references to a protagonist's beard growth later on in their story can also serve to illustrate the passing of time.

A different kind of embedding occurs when aspects of appearance are verbalized in the direct and indirect speech of the narrative figures themselves. In first-person narratives this would seem to be an entirely natural development, an inventive means of gaining an external view of the narrator-cum-protagonist which would otherwise be denied to the listener or reader. Beard references of this type are especially provocative in dialogue with a female antagonist. Ulrich von Liechtenstein's *Frauendienst* contains one notable instance of this (see above), as does Dante's *Divine Comedy*, when Beatrice mockingly questions (the shaven?) Dante's courage: 'alza la barba' / 'now raise your beard' (*Purgatory* XXXI, 68).[132] In third-person narratives male characters may refer to their own beards in exclamatory fashion ('Shame on my beard!'),[133] or when making an oath, such utterances being akin to verbal gestures in lieu of or as a complement to an actual gesture: 'So mir dirre min bart'/ 'I swear by this beard of mine'.[134] By the same token, one figure may pass comment on the appearance (and beardedness) of another.[135] This device lends itself to tendentiousness, such as when the (bushy-bearded) Green Knight dismisses Arthur's court contemptuously as 'berdlez chylder' / 'beardless boys' (*Sir Gawain and the Green Knight* 280). Employing direct speech like this enables the poet to present a clash of values for his audience's consideration without revealing his own hand. A rather different effect is achieved in texts where the same set of (traditional) values is endorsed by all voices, including that of the author-narrator.[136] In terms of narrative economy, drawing attention to one figure's appearance via the speech of another simultaneously thematizes the act of perception involved. In cases of mistaken identity, where women are wrongly believed to be young – beardless – men, or vice versa, the humorous effect is enhanced by the speaker's misinterpretation of the evidence of their own eyes.[137]

Appearance in general – and beardedness more specifically – is most obviously meaningful in relation to main protagonists. But the distribution of such detail in the first place between figures of primary and secondary importance can be quite unpredictable. On the one hand, protagonists are left 'blank' surprisingly often. Typically understood to be handsome or beautiful from the outset, their particulars often go unremarked beyond the odd formulaic reference. James A. Schultz has even identified a tendency for narrative poets (c. 1200) to avoid sexual differentiation (by means of references to beards or breasts) when it comes to communicating erotic attractiveness.[138] Within poetic schemes like this, changes in appearance may nevertheless be considered noteworthy, especially when used to dramatize thematic developments. Thus, in Konrad von Würzburg's tale of male friendship, *Engelhard*, it is only in the context of affliction (when one of the two handsome protagonists – Dietrich – is struck down by an awful disease) that recipients are given any actual physiological detail: 'im wurden hâr unde bart / dünn unde seltsaene' / 'His hair and beard grew thin and abnormal' (5150–1). No sooner has Dietrich been restored miraculously to health than his description reverts to type: 'der vil süeze jungelinc' / 'the sweetest young man' (5676).

On the other hand, it is not uncommon for secondary figures, including those who only play a role in one episode, to be introduced with reference to physical features which tend to emphasize age, beauty or ugliness.[139] In Heinrich von dem Türlin's Arthurian romance *Diu Crône* (c. 1230), for example, the most detailed descriptions in the text belong not to Gawan (the protagonist) but to Blandachors, an elderly host who embodies elegant courtliness in old age,[140] and to a hideous squire whose whiskers and sparse beard growth are dripping with pus,[141] a miniature study in repulsive ugliness.[142] Such apparently extraneous detail enables the audience to come to a quick judgement as to the relative status of these secondary figures (for the purposes of positive and negative identification respectively), although by no means every secondary figure in the text receives such treatment. It also lends colour to one or two of Gawan's many encounters and adventures, while the protagonist himself is handed over to the audience members, as it were, who are free to imagine him as they see fit. Recipient engagement with Gawan would therefore seem to rest primarily on the ideals he represents and on his actions.[143]

Diu Crône is just one text; but it should alert us to the fact that medieval narrative strategies, especially in longer texts, are not always easy to unpick. Offering a convincing explanation as to why the physical appearance (or beard) of one figure should be described and not that of another can prove tricky. To a degree the functionality of beard references in shorter texts such as 'Mären' is easier to pin down, not least because the principle of narrative economy is normally so very evident here. Two strategies in particular stand out. (1) Description as exposition, where the protagonist is clearly identified as such at the start of the story by the attention paid to his physical appearance: beardless (and courtly); first beard growth (and sexual maturity); ugly (yet virtuous).[144] (2) 'Dramatic' effects, where the protagonist's beard is thematized at a crucial moment in the story: wicked daughters kiss their elderly father's beard in a false show of affection; young nobleman returns home but goes unrecognized (because of his beard); knight's hair and beard are turned grey by a terrifying experience.[145] These techniques are of course to be found in other literary forms too.

The essence of narrative, which is to depict actions and events successively, allows meaning to develop and accrue over the course of a story. Some types of work are extremely episodic. However, by virtue of repetition any single narrative detail can grow in symbolic significance. As Harald Haferland and Armin Schulz emphasize, these narrative symbols ('Erzählsymbole[n]') were used by poets as a way of making abstract ideas or complex arguments more concrete, more comprehensible for their audiences.[146] Designating this kind of narration 'metonymisches Erzählen', Haferland and Schulz make a virtue out of the elliptical tendencies of much medieval literature. And this basic point remains valid irrespective of whether we too want to view metonymy as the defining characteristic of pre-modern thought.[147] The more familiar the perceived association (crown/kingship), the more immediately thought-provoking and affecting such narrative detail could be for listeners. Given the wealth of secondary meanings that beards had, it should come as no surprise that certain poets throughout the German Middle Ages did choose – in spite of everything else – to draw particular attention to this aspect of male appearance.

Some texts are evidently more beard-friendly than others, which might lead us to conclude that some story materials were more conducive than others to representations of beardedness. In medieval works which espoused an aggressively 'masculinist' ethos the beard was always liable to function as the perfect heroic metonym. Certain Old French *chansons de geste*, not least the *Chanson de Roland* (see Chapter 2), are prime examples of this. The same goes for the Castilian epic *El Poema de Mio Cid* (c. 1200), where the glorifying principle of 'the greater the beard, the greater the man' is realized across all textual levels in respect of the titanic Campeador by means of epithets, descriptions, defiant gestures, the hero's own words, and the words of others.[148] For sheer pogonophilia, nothing else really comes close, which is not to say that the same heroic approach to beards does not make itself felt at times in vernacular German texts too.[149] Following Simon Gaunt's discussion of gender and genre (with reference to Old French literature), one wonders just how decisive plot type was when it came to the poetic interest invested in female and male figures.[150] As will become clear from our study of a wide range of texts, beard references could be used to thematize relationships not just between men and other men (fathers and sons, kings and other kings, lords and vassals, masters and apprentices), but also between men and women (lover and beloved, husbands and wives, fathers and daughters). Furthermore, literary beards are not necessarily a sign of a preoccupation with masculinity for masculinity's sake. At times the poetic depiction of beards evinces to striking effect a concern with humanity.

Contents and approach

In order to develop a better understanding of how and why medieval German poets referred to beards, the following study is organized around close readings of a number of paradigmatic literary works or textual milestones. That is to say, each of this book's four main chapters takes as its starting point one particular work or body of lyric poetry, in which beards, beardedness and beardlessness play a prominent role in respect of certain key themes and issues: majesty and rulership (Chapter 2: Pfaffe Konrad's *Rolandslied*); masculinity and humanity (Chapter 3: Wolfram von Eschenbach's *Willehalm*); wisdom, teaching and learning (Chapter 4: 'Sangspruchdichtung'); and laughter and comedy (Chapter 5: Heinrich Wittenwiler's *Ring*). Each chapter contextualizes its milestone work by taking into account cognate material of various kinds, such as sources or later versions of the same story, manuscript transmission and miniatures, and further notable instances of a specific beard motif or type of beard reference from the same period. The chapters are arranged in rough chronological order, although it will on occasion prove necessary to trace interpretative lines backwards as well as forwards.

The headline themes and issues which are investigated here do of course overlap, and thus these chapters are designed to complement each other. Critical discussion of the literary representation of bearded majesty and bearded humanity is ongoing throughout the book (and not just restricted to Chapters 2 and 3). Similarly, the distinction between didactic and comedic approaches to literary beards implied by the chosen topics of Chapters 4 and 5 is not a strict one; the boundaries between these two interests, if they exist at all, are rather more fluid. The interdependence of the beard's various connotations and poetic treatments is epitomized by literary portrayals of arguably the single most important beard in the Middle Ages, that of Jesus Christ. Chapter 6 therefore comprises a short review of the different ways poets from across a wide range of text types drew attention to this emblematic feature of Jesus's face and to the different effects (emotive – instructive – comedic?) involved.

Given that the beard's most fundamental meanings remained intact from the twelfth century (and long before that) to the later fifteenth century (and long after that), the varying uses to which beard motifs were put can also help to shed light on changes in the workings of vernacular literature as it expanded and diversified over the centuries. That said, this remit sounds grander than the author of this project would like. When we focus on a single motif or set of motifs, it is easy to forget that many of the works in question consist of numerous meaningful details. Doing literary beards justice involves recognizing that they invite special but unexaggerated assessment.[151]

Notes

1 Müller, *Höfische Kompromisse*, 6–41; Schnell, 'Text und Kontext', 2008, 97–8.
2 Müller, 'Einleitung', VII; Schnell, 'Text und Kontext', 2008, 138.
3 Bumke, *Höfische Kultur*, 203.
4 Haubrichs, 'Bilder, Körper und Konstrukte', 1995, 31; Müller, 'Literarische und andere Spiele', 2004, 294.
5 Schnell, 'Recht und Dichtung', 2011, 21.
6 Schnell, 'Text und Kontext', 2008, 98.
7 Worstbrock, 'Wiedererzählen und Übersetzen'.
8 For the crux of this debate see Schnell, 'Kulturtheorien und Lektürepraxis', 2016.
9 An exemplary analysis of this kind is offered by Schnell, 'Narration und Emotion', 2014.
10 For more on these narrative levels see Barthel, *Empathie, Mitleid, Sympathie*, 57–80.
11 Clark, 'Fashionable beards', 2014: 'Although Westerners had little compunction with shaving their faces in actual practice, Western beards in literature retain a similar depth of symbolic meaning to Eastern ones' (98).
12 See also Reuvekamp, 'Hölzerne Bilder', 2014, 116.
13 Bumke, 'Autor und Werk'.
14 Vetter, *Textgeschichte(n)*, 57–95.
15 Manuwald, *Medialer Dialog*, 20–49.
16 Manuwald, *Medialer Dialog*, 163–4.
17 The only literary reference to Joachim's beard growth prepares us for his marriage to Anna: 'Als er zweinzic iar alte wart / unt im chume ersprанch der bart' (*Maria* D, 337–8). Joachim is beardless in the miniatures until he gets married (fol. 8v); thereafter he is consistently portrayed with a cropped, jawline beard (9v, 10v, 15r, 16r, 17r, 18r, 19v, 21v). The manuscript can be viewed online: https://jbc.bj.uj.edu.pl/dlibra/doccontent?id=159362. Accessed 4 March 2021.
18 Joseph is characterized by his (grey) beard at two points in the text: on his first appearance as an unwilling 'suitor' for Mary's hand ('sin bart was im lanch vnd gris' 1882), and when he is appalled to learn of Mary's pregnancy ('Der grise mit dem barte' 3009). In the miniatures he is represented by the same (long-bearded) figure type throughout (fols 34r, 53r, 63r, 78r).
19 Bumke, *Höfische Kultur*, 202–3. The generational template is used as early as fols 27r (strangers greeted by Mary) and 37v (temple priests).
20 Henkel, *Lesen in Bild und Text*, 36–62.
21 On the manipulability of visual representations of hair see Jolly, 'Cultural representations'.
22 For just one of the many influential publications by Horst Wenzel in this area see 'Hören und Sehen. Zur Lesbarkeit von Körperzeichen in der höfischen Literatur'.
23 Kellner and Kiening, 'Einleitung: Körper – Kultur – Literatur (1200–1800)', 2009, 5.
24 Easton, 'Gender and sexuality'.
25 Chinca, 'Women and hunting-birds', 199.
26 As exemplified by Moshövel, *Effemination*, 13–54.
27 Sieber, 'Gender studies'.
28 See Kinney, 'The (dis)embodied hero', 55–6. A more measured approach is adopted by Weichselbaumer, *Der konstruierte Mann*, 259–65.
29 Moshövel, *Effemination*, 420.
30 Lees, 'Men and *Beowulf*', 130.
31 For monologic (and dialogic) constructions of gender see Werthschulte, 'Erzählte Männlichkeiten', 269.
32 Reuvekamp, 'Hölzerne Bilder', 2014, 130.
33 Constable [and Huygens], 'Introduction', passim.
34 *De opificio Dei* VII (PL 7, col. 33). Cf. also Augustine, *De civitate Dei* XXII, 24, 4 (PL 41, col. 791).
35 'sicut unguentum optimum in capite quod descendit in barbam barbam Aaron quod descendit super oram vestimentarium eius' / 'Like the precious ointment on the head, that ran down upon the beard, the beard of Aaron, which ran down to the skirt of his garment' (Psalm 132: 2).
36 *Enarrationes in Psalmos* CXXXII, 7: 'Barba significat fortes; barba significat juvenes, strenuos, impigros, alacres. Ideo quando tales describimus, barbatus homo est, dicimus' (PL 37, col. 1733).
37 'Ex illa barba erat Stephanus sanctus' (PL 37, col. 1733).
38 Constable [and Huygens], 'Introduction', 75–7.

39 As exemplified by Rhabanus Maurus, *De Universo* VI, 1 (PL 111, col. 152).

40 'CHRISTVS ist sacerdos . also aaron uuas . unde houbet sînero ecclesie. Ab imo ran spiritus sanctus in apostolos . die sîn bart sint . uuanda sie gomelîcho an imo uuâren . unde ne-hein leîd ne-forhton umbe in ze lîdenne' (500,13–16).

41 *Christherre-Chronik*: 'Daz heilige olei er im goz / Vf sin houbit daz ran / Vf den bart dem reinin man / Als an dem salter noch stat / David da von gesprochin hat. / Als daz salb daz da schone / Ran zu tal Aarone / Von dem houbite in den bart / Vnd vurbaz ran nach sinir art / Biz an sinis cleidis ort' (18108–17).

42 Constable [and Huygens], 'Introduction', 70–5.

43 *Expositio in Leviticum* XIX (PL 164, col. 444).

44 *Mitrale* II, 1 (PL 213, col. 59).

45 For a summary of the *Apologia* see Constable and Huygens, 'Introduction', 137–49.

46 Cf. *Apologia de barbis* III, 1490–1592. The notion of spectacularly white hair, as revealed by Burchard himself, is taken from the Book of Revelation (1: 14).

47 For a table of all the relevant references see Burchard, *Apologia*, ed. Huygens, 225–6.

48 For instance, in *Apologia* I, 116–23 Burchard homes in on the repetition contained within Psalm 132: 2: 'sicut unguentum optimum in capite quod descendit in barbam barbam Aaron'.

49 For an overview see Casagrande and Vecchio, *I peccati della lingua*.

50 Cf. Rupert of Deutz, *In Leviticum* II, 25 (PL 167, cols 812–13).

51 Berthold pushes the metaphor to its limits when he goes on to discuss the 'leprosy' afflicting men and women in respect of clothing (118,3–121,6) and housing (121,7–122,39).

52 In this sermon Berthold has already mocked men who grow their hair long for being like women: 'Pfî dich, Adelheit, mit dînem langen hâre' (114,30–1).

53 Bearded women thus belong to the numerous marvels of the world listed for Otto IV by Gervase of Tilbury (c. 1215): *Otia imperialia* II, 4; III, 76. Cf. also Ulrich von Etzenbach, *Alexander* 22074–7. The figure of a monstrously ugly wild woman, with whiskers down to her feet, is used for comic effect in the heroic epic *Wolfdietrich* (version A: 471,3).

54 *Etymologiae*: 'Barbam veteres vocaverunt, quod virorum sit, non mulierum' (XI, 1, 45).

55 'Unde et sanctas mulieres, quae plerumque animi fortitudine viros superant, rectissime barbatas dicere solemus' (PL 164, col. 444).

56 'Huic autem cum valde ignea conspersio corporis inesset, ceperunt medici dicere quia nisi ad amplexus viriles rediret calore nimio contra naturam barbas esset habitura, quod ita quoque post factum est' (PL 77, col. 340).

57 Burchard even explores why Gregory used the plural 'barbas' to refer to Galla's beard (III, 90–102), suggesting that it conveys the fullness and density of her beard growth ('pleniberbis') (III, 127–35).

58 See Wallace, 'Bearded woman, female Christ', 2014.

59 The same story is told a century later by Jacobus de Voragine in his *Legenda Aurea*; see Moshövel, *Effemination*, 147–9.

60 Cf. I, 38; II, 59; II, 149; III, 176. See also Cadden, *Meanings of Sex Difference*, 181–3.

61 Constable[and Huygens], 'Introduction', 61–2.

62 'Man sol im grîfen an den obern munt unde der nasen: vindet man dâ kleinez hâr, daz ist ein geziuge' (L27). Hidden hair ('under die vohsen', 'ob sîner geschäfte') counted as well. The text of the *Schwabenspiegel* is taken here from Jones and Jones, *The Oxford Guide to Middle High German*, 583.

63 'Welchiz mannes alder man nicht en weiz, hat her har in dem barte unde nidene unde under itlichem areme, so sal man wissen daz her zu sinen tagen komen iz' (I, 42).

64 Hopwood, 'Highlighting hair', unpublished dissertation, 172.

65 Cf. *Lex Frisionum*: 'si granonem ictu percussam praeciderit, duobus solidis conponat' (XXII,17); *Leges Alamannorum*: 'Si enim barba alicuius non volentem tunderit, cum 6 solidis conponat' (LVII,30). Other medieval legal traditions preserve similar rulings; see Hopwood Griffiths, 'Self and society', 40–1.

66 *Landfrieden* (of 1152): 'Si quis alium ceperit et absque sanguinis effusione fustibus percusserit vel crines eius et barbam expilaverit, decem libras ei, cui iniuria illata esse videtur, per compositionem impendat et iudici viginti libras persolvat' (§4).

67 'unde sleyt he ene ok, edder knuppelt ene, edder toge ene by deme barde ofte haren, wert he dar umme beclaget dat he dat hebbe ghedan myt vorsate, unde en wil he dar nicht vor sweren, den vorsat schal er der stad beteren myt twintich marken' (I,106 II).

68 Constable [and Huygens], 'Introduction', 64–5; Schmidt-Lornsen, 'Der Griff an den Bart'.

69 Emphasized by Platelle, 'Le problème du scandale', 1975, 1083–9.

70 The same line of insulting argument is found in texts ranging from the second century (Clement of Alexandria, *The Instructor* III, 3) to the sixteenth (Valerian, *Pro sacerdotum barbis*). In his *Apologia de barbis* Burchard compares fashionable (lay)men who shave their beards but keep their moustaches to monstrous hermaphrodites (II, 57–60).

71 Burchard presents this sentiment as a vernacular saying ('illud vulgare proverbium'), before rendering it in Latin: 'In barba non iacet sapientia' (III, 689–90).

72 Cf. Lucian: 'If you think that to grow a beard is to acquire wisdom, a goat with a fine beard is at once a complete Plato' (LCL 85: 276–7).

73 *Epistula* XXII, 28 (PL 22, col. 413); *Adversus Jovinianum* II, 21 (PL 23, col. 316).

74 *Responsio Episcoporum Germaniae Wormatiae Coadunatorum*: 'De hoc quod reprehendunt cur barbas nostri clerici radunt, respondemus cum beato Hieronymo, quia si sanctitas est in barba, nullus sanctior est hirco' (PL 119, col. 1212).

75 Burchard further degrades his target by describing how their beards are typically covered in grease (the antithesis of the holy ointment of true Christian faith) (III, 314–19). Later in the *Apologia* Burchard cites the goat jibe as an example of malicious ridicule (III, 1153); evidently Jews were the exception to this rule.

76 Cf. Phaedrus, *Fables* IV,9, where a fox tricks a bearded goat into taking its place at the bottom of a well. In the version of the fable contained in Heinrich Steinhöwel's Latin-German *Esopus* (first printed c. 1476) the fox adds insult to injury with reference to the goat's beard: 'Wärest du mit so vil wyshait begabet, als mit vil hares dyn bart gezieret ist, so wärest do nit in den brunnen hinab gesprungen' (nr 100, p. 246).

77 Odo of Cheriton, 'De contentione Ovis albis et Ovis nigre, Asini et Hirci' (*Fabulae* nr 52).

78 Cf. Eugene of Toledo, *Carmina* 89, 4: 'Si barbae sanctum faciunt, nil sanctius hirco' (MGH Auct. Ant. 14, 266); Heinrich Bebel, *Fazetien* I, 30.

79 A comprehensive overview is given by Constable [and Huygens], 'Introduction', 85–130.

80 Constable [and Huygens], 'Introduction', 113–14.

81 Constable [and Huygens], 'Introduction', 117. The first Cistercians only shaved seven times a year; see Platelle, 'Le problème du scandale', 1975, 1073.

82 Friedman, 'Hair and social class', 137–43.

83 Bumke, *Höfische Kultur*, 201–3.

84 See also Jennings, 'Chaucer's beards', 1978, 364. The trend for long(er) beards at court leaves a mark on German literature in the fourteenth century, not least in the poetry of Heinrich der Teichner (see Chapter 4).

85 See also Platelle, 'Le problème du scandale', 1975, 1073–6.

86 *Narratio Othloni de miraculo quod nuper accidit cuidam laico*: 'quasi clericus' (PL 146, col. 243).

87 'pro novacula vero non promisi' (PL 146, col. 244).

88 *Narratio Othloni*: 'quod scilicet nemo laicorum radere barbam debeat' (PL 146, col. 244).

89 For more on this text's critical attitude towards its worldly content see Braun, *Studien zum Ruodlieb*, 41–4.

90 *Ruodlieb*: 'Barbiciam scabit, quod non pilus unus ibi sit. / Quod tam nemo vafer sit, qui discernere possit, / Clericus an mulier inberbes an esset alumnus, / Est tam iocundae tam virgineae faciei' (XIII: 1–4).

91 Bartlett, 'Symbolic meanings of hair', 1994, 44.

92 Orderic's furious commentary on courtly fashion is principally located in VIII, 10.

93 'Olim penitentes et capti ac peregrini usualiter intonsi erant, longasque barbas gestabant: indicioque tali penitentiam seu captionem uel peregrinationem spectantibus pretendebant. Nunc uero pene uniuersi populares cerriti sunt et barbatuli: palam manifestantes specimine tali quod sordibus libidinis gaudeant ut foetentes hirci' (VIII, 10).

94 This observation is attributed to the bishop of Seez on the occasion of his dramatic intervention (with a pair of scissors) at the court of Henry I (XI, 11).

95 Platelle, 'Le problème du scandale', 1975, 1083.

96 Cf. also Reinmar von Zweter II, 128: 1–3, where ecclesiastical beards are connoted with avarice and greed. See Lauer, *Ästhetik der Identität*, 191–2, 244–5.

97 *Seifried Helbling* XIV: 14–16; I: 225; III: 226–8. Cf. also the references to Hungarian warriors in Ottokar von Gaal's *Steirische Reimchronik*: 'die mit den langen berten' (16236); 'mit iren langen berten' (26386).

98 'nû dar, her scheraer, / strîchet scharsach unde schaer, / ebent hâr und scheret bart!' (III: 77–9). See also Wolf, *Kunst zu lehren*, 108–9.

99 Constable [and Huygens], 'Introduction', 97; Bartlett, 'Symbolic meanings of hair', 1994, 47–8; Phillips, 'Race and ethnicity'.
100 Bartlett, 'Symbolic meanings of hair', 1994, 59.
101 'den bart, die negel und daz hâr / liez er niht abe schrôten' (9700–1).
102 Cf. Gottfried von Strassburg's *Tristan*: 'die wâren gote gebaere, / getaget unde gejâret, / gebartet unde gehâret, / alsô die wâren gotes kint / und wallaere dicke sint' (2624–8).
103 Cf. Gottfried's description of Rual's condition after his lengthy search for Tristan: 'von unruoche was sîn hâr / an houbete unde an barte / verwalken alsô harte, / als ob er wilde waere' (*Tristan* 4004–7).
104 Cf. Herbort von Fritzlar, *Liet von Troye* 1168–9; *Rappoltsteiner Parzifal* 6773–4; *Karl und Ellegast* 1798.
105 Linden, *Kundschafter der Kommunikation*, 108–12; Moshövel, *Effemination*, 440–1.
106 'liebez kint mîn,/ strîch sie umb den munt dîn,/ dise wurz also guot,/ und habe des deheinen muot,/ daz dir nimmer dhein haerlîn/ wahset ûz dem bart dîn' (14589–94).
107 Vogt, *Ritterbild und Ritterlehre*, 83–90.
108 https://digi.ub.uni-heidelberg.de/diglit/cpg848. Accessed 6 March 2021.
109 Cf. fols 8r, 10r, 124r, 158r, 213r, 323r, 383r, 407r.
110 Kellermann, 'Die körperliche Inszenierung des Königs', 2001, 168–70.
111 http://digital.wlb-stuttgart.de/purl/bsz319421317. Accessed 6 March 2021.
112 In a Latin epic poem dated to 800–10, Leo appears to Karl in a dream with his eyes and face covered in blood, his tongue hacked out (*Karolus Magnus et Leo papa* 368–71).
113 'Nider cniet dô der êwart, / vil kûme gesprach der daz wort' (14459–60).
114 Only the intervention of Karl's men stops him from falling over in shock (14486–96).
115 Müller, 'Visualität, Geste, Schrift', 2003, 127.
116 Stock, 'Figur', 192; Reuvekamp, 'Hölzerne Bilder', 2014, 113.
117 Gerok-Reiter, *Individualität*, 1–22.
118 Kartschoke, 'Erkennen und Wiedererkennen', I, 2–5.
119 Manuwald, *Medialer Dialog*, 163–4.
120 Brüggen, 'Körperschönheit', 395.
121 Bumke, *Blutstropfen im Schnee*, 15–27.
122 Hence the established topic of female hair (in literature); see Rolland-Perrin, *Blonde comme l'or*.
123 Cf. Matthew of Vendôme's *Ars versificatoria* (c. 1175): 'Amplius, in femineo sexu approbatio formae debet ampliari, in masculine vero parcius' (I, 67). An exception to this rule can be made for handsome young men, Matthew concedes (I, 68).
124 Kartschoke, 'Erkennen und Wiedererkennen', I, 22–3.
125 'His person is well proportioned. He is shorter than very tall men, but taller and more noble than men of medium height. His hair is golden, curling a little above his forehead. His ears are scarcely covered by the hair above them, as the barber (out of respect for the empire) keeps the hair on his head and cheeks short by constantly cutting it. His eyes are sharp and piercing, his nose well formed, his beard reddish, his lips delicate and not distended by too long a mouth. His whole face is bright and cheerful. His teeth are even and snow-white in colour. The skin of his throat and neck (which is rather plump but not fat) is milk-white and often suffused with the ruddy glow of youth; modesty rather than anger causes him to blush frequently. His shoulders are rather broad, and he is strongly built. His thighs, supported by stout calves, are proper and sturdy' (translation by Charles Mierow).
126 Rahewin's model was Apollinaris Sidonius's famous description of the Visigothic king Theoderic II (d. 466): *Letters* I, 2.
127 Dares, *De excidio Troiae historia* XII–XIII; *Roman de Troie* 5093–582; *Liet von Troye* 2889–3298.
128 Coxon, 'Heroes and their beards', 2018, 33–4.
129 Lumiansky, 'Benoît's portraits', 1956, 431–8; Jennings, 'Chaucer's beards', 1978, 366–8.
130 Cf. the reference to Siegfried in the *Nibelungenlied*: 'Dô stuont sô minneclîche daz Sigemundes kint, / sam er entworfen waere an ein permint / von guotes meisters listen' (B 286,1–3).
131 Schnell, 'Gefühle gestalten', 2016, 593, 603–5.
132 Shoaf, 'Dante's Beard', 171–8.
133 As found in several thirteenth-century medieval Welsh tales, known collectively as *The Mabinogion*, including *Peredur Son of Evrawg* (p. 229), a reworking of Chrétien's *Perceval*. Wishing shame on another's beard is also a standard (literary) curse in these texts; cf. *Owein* (Luned denounces Owein, p. 209); *Peredur* (old man curses lion kept as gatekeeper, p. 236).

134 As uttered by the elderly Nestor, outraged by Priam's offer of compensation, in Herbort von Fritzlar's *Liet von Troye* (2024). This furious outburst is subsequently reported back to Priam by his envoy (Antenor): 'Nestor der alde man / Grein mich an vnd schutte sin bart' (2087–8).

135 See also von Matt, ... *fertig ist das Angesicht*, 198–200.

136 Müller, *'Episches' Erzählen*, 197–242.

137 Cf. the myth of Karl's victory over a heathen force without having to strike a blow, as recounted in the *Sächsische Weltchronik* (c. 1230). The episode revolves around the erroneous report given to the Saracen king by his scouts as Karl approaches with an army of young women (all his warriors having been killed): 'Herre, wi hebbet de alden geslagen, de iungen sin na gekomen; si willet wreken ire aldermen; si sint alle ane bart, dicke umme ire bruste, wol geschapen to wige, du ne macht mit in nicht vechte; gif dich an Karles gnade unde wirt cristen' (151,26–8).

138 Schultz, 'Bodies that don't matter', 93–4.

139 The narrative functionality of secondary figures is explored in most depth by Dimpel, *Zofe im Fokus*. See also Schnell, 'Gefühle gestalten', 2016, 585.

140 *Diu Crône*: 'Natûr wolt in sô bewarn, / daz alters reht dâ kûm schein / an im, wan an disen zwein, / an bart und an hâre: / diu zwei het zewâre / ein graewe übergangen, / diu was aber bevangen / mit reitziere wîze. / die het er mit vlîze / ze strenen gewunden, / mit golde gebunden' (6875–85).

141 *Diu Crône*: 'Über bart und über gran / diu nezze ime al zît ran, / dar under was diu hût geblaet. / ime stuont der bart, als er gesaet / waere ûf sîn wange; / er was von gedrange/ niht nâch der dicke gestalt, / man het ine allen wol gezalt. / dar zuo was er wol vinger lanc / und hât niergent einen gelanc / niht mêre denn ein scharpfe âl' (19677–87).

142 For ugliness and individuality see Kartschoke, 'Erkennen und Wiedererkennen', I, 2.

143 Reference to Gawan's beardedness is made (only) in the speech of a foe who threatens to tear the helmet from his head: 'wan sol ichz iu ziehen ab, / daz tuon ich sô ungewar, / daz beidiu bart unde hâr/ mir mit alle volget' (6294–7).

144 *Unser Frauen Ritter* 110–11; *Der Mönch als Liebesbote* A, 47–50; *Das Auge* 16–17.

145 Rüdeger der Hinkhofer, *Der Schlegel* 1072–5; Augustijn, *Der Herzog von Braunschweig* 889–90; *Ritter Gottfried* 344–6.

146 Haferland and Schulz, 'Metonymisches Erzählen', 2010, 11, 23. For balance see also Müller, 'Einige Probleme', 2013, 19–40.

147 Kropik, 'Metonymie und Vormoderne', 2012, 85–95.

148 Bly, 'Beards in the *Poema de Mio Cid*', 1978, 16–24.

149 Cf. the depiction of the elderly Wate slaughtering the enemy in the decisive battle in *Kudrun*: 'mit grisgramenden zenden zehant huob er sich dar, / mit schînenden ougen, mit ellenbreitem barte' (1508,2–3).

150 Gaunt, *Gender and Genre*. Gaunt deals with *chansons de geste*, for example, under the rubric of what he calls 'monologic masculinity' (22–70).

151 Engagement in literary analysis of this kind is neatly summed up by Rolland-Perrin, *Blonde comme l'or*: 'c'est entrer dans les textes par la petite porte' (9).

2
Beards and majesty: Pfaffe Konrad's *Rolandslied*

Der kaiser erzurnte harte
mit ûf gevangem barte.

Pfaffe Konrad, *Rolandslied* 8771–2[1]

The significance of the beard as a natural symbol of masculinity and authority is nowhere more apparent than in the portrayal of kingship in medieval visual and plastic arts in general and, more particularly, in manuscript miniatures of the High Middle Ages. The sixteen pen-and-ink pictures of enthroned emperors and kings contained in an early twelfth-century codex (Cambridge, Corpus Christi College, MS 373, (Würzburg?) c. 1114–25) as illustrations for an anonymous (Latin) chronicle of imperial history, represent a stunning example of how beards and beardlessness could be used to differentiate at a glance between rulers.[2] Thus a virile-looking Charlemagne ('Karolus magnus') with a typically Carolingian winged moustache (fol. 24r) is followed by his beardless son, Louis the Pious (28r).[3] The Ottonian dynasty makes for interesting viewing too. The artist changed his mind in respect of Henry I (40r), adding a longer beard and moustache to what was initially a lightly bearded face. Otto the Great, arguably a more dominant personality than his predecessor, is accorded a suitably magnificent stranded beard and moustache (42v) – Ottos II (47r) and III (48v), by contrast, are beardless – and the same type of beard elevates the standing of the last in the line, the saintly Henry II (51r).[4]

It seems quite logical therefore that the first of our textual milestones should come as early as the second half of the twelfth century, when a vernacular tradition of secular narrative was emerging which reflected the interest of noble patrons and audiences in the history and deeds of great emperors and kings. In literature as in art the representation of the king's body always pointed to something greater than itself,[5] although the means by which this common purpose was achieved could vary tremendously. This was a period of rapid literary development and experimentation. As far as literary images of bearded majesty are concerned, not only do we find several types of reference in operation, but we can also trace how different versions of the same text viewed the same beard(s). It should be noted, moreover, that some kings attracted more beard-specific attention than others.

Pfaffe Konrad's *Rolandslied*

Pfaffe Konrad's *Rolandslied* (c. 1170–85) is a reworking of the Old French heroic epic the *Chanson de Roland* (c. 1100). It tells the famous story of Charlemagne's complete victory over the Saracens in Spain following the treacherous annihilation of the Franks' rearguard and the death of Charles's valiant nephew Roland.[6] Composed by an otherwise unknown 'phaffe Chunrât' / 'Konrad the priest' (9079) under the illustrious patronage of Duke Henry the Lion and his wife Matilda, daughter of King Henry II of England, the German *Rolandslied* offers a version of events characterized by religious zeal which is sustained in no small part by the glorification of Charlemagne (Karl der Große) as Holy Roman Emperor rather than as the defender of 'sweet France'.[7] The *Rolandslied* is also something of a pogonographic tour de force. It contains thirteen beard references in total; the next-'best' German text of this period – *König Rother* (c. 1140–70) – has six. Moreover, the sole complete manuscript of the *Rolandslied* (Heidelberg, UB, Cpg 112), from the end of the twelfth century, is illustrated with 39 pen-and-ink drawings, more than half of which feature beards of some description.

It is important to realize at the outset that the thematic content of the *Rolandslied* as a crusading epic has several major implications for the way in which the story is told. First, since the work is inspired by an inviolable belief in martyrdom and the righteousness of militant Christianity, practically all narrative detail serves an ideological purpose. Most typically this leads to straightforward polarization: heathens are 'des tiuveles kint' / 'children of the devil' (60) and hell-bound, whereas Christians will be received in heaven. Just occasionally one and the same attribute is interpreted variously depending on the context: hence, joyful, worldly pastimes are roundly condemned as sinful folly in respect of heathens

(285–90) yet are worthy of praise when they are alluded to, rather unexpectedly perhaps, as a feature of Karl's splendid court (643–74).[8]

Secondly, the narrative is concerned almost exclusively with the words and deeds of men. Only two female characters of note appear – Brechmunda, the heathen queen of Saragossa, and Alda, Roland's grieving widow – and they do so fleetingly, towards the end of the work, in order to provide a final confirmation, if any were needed, of the power of God's grace.[9] Consequently, details pertaining to physical appearance are primarily a function of the characterization of male figures, both heathen and Christian, and are weighted accordingly. Thus, the massed ranks of the enemies of the Franks are mostly 'übel getân' / 'hideous' (6346), or monstrous ('an dem rücke tragent si borsten sam swîn' / 'Their backs are covered with bristles like pigs' 8046) or bizarre, like the heathen king Zernubele whose hair is so long it reaches down to his feet (2696). When, exceptionally, a handsome heathen king makes an appearance (3727) the narrator is quick to point out that his beauty is (merely) of the kind that finds favour with ladies at court: 'harte minnôten in die frouwen' / 'The ladies loved him very much' (3730). The audience is left in no doubt that true beauty reflects inner virtue, as is the case with Archbishop Turpin who, in the course of the first battle, inspires the outnumbered Franks to even greater heroism: 'mit scoenem antlütze, / sîn herze was liuter unt gar, / er fuor von scar hin ze scar' / 'Handsome of face, his heart was pure and without fault; he rode from group to group' (3900–2). The fact that Genelun, the wicked Frank who betrays Roland and the Twelve Peers to their deaths, is so very handsome makes him infernal in the eyes of the author-narrator: 'sîn antlizze was hêrsam. / sîn varwe, diu bran/ sam die liechten viures flammen' / 'His face was magnificent. His complexion burned brightly like the flames of a fire' (1658–60).[10]

The epitome of charismatic beauty is reached with the Emperor Karl whose face is so glorious (683, 692), his eyes so radiant (686–7), that he cannot be mistaken for anyone else. Indeed the duplicitous heathen ambassadors sent by King Marsilie to parley are as blinded by the emperor as by the midday sun: 'mit volleclîchen ougen / ne mochten si in nicht gescouwen' / 'They were unable to look at him without lowering their gaze' (693–4).[11] Much has been made of Karl's majesty, both in terms of the themes of the *Rolandslied* and as a perfect literary example of courtly society's visual culture of representation.[12] But this rather sublime image of kingship occurs early on in the story. In the course of the subsequent action Karl's self-composure is severely and repeatedly tested. His regal serenity soon vanishes once the heathen emissaries have delivered Marsilie's (misleading) offer, and a war of words breaks out between Roland and Genelun as to what the Franks should do next:

> Der keiser zurnte harte.
> mit gestreichtem barte,
> mit ûf gewunden granen
> hiez er die phacht vüre tragen. (1154–7)
>
> The emperor became very angry: stroking his beard and twirling his whiskers he had the [book of] law brought before them.

This portrayal of Karl is no less stylized than in the earlier scene, but it is of a fundamentally different order. Disturbed in his majesty by righteous anger, Karl is forced to restore order and rebuke both parties ('ir stet mit unzüchten' / 'Your behaviour is unseemly' 1158). Karl's beard is not described as part of a rigid tableau; rather it is brought to our attention gesturally, as Karl wordlessly invokes his own body even as he has the written basis of his authority produced for all to see. This distinctive gesture connotes strong emotion (anger), although it still seems very controlled.

Karl is not the only bearded figure in the *Rolandslied*. The first beard to be mentioned belongs to Marsilie's cunning old advisor, Blanscandiz: 'sîn bart was im gevlochten, / alsô er ze hove wole tochte'/ 'His beard was braided, as befitting a man of the court' (427–8).[13] Although this beard is an entirely appropriate attribute for an elderly counsellor, its courtly braids emphasize a preoccupation with worldly values far removed from the spiritual ideals of the Franks and their emperor.[14] When Blanscandiz swears by his beard – 'sô mir dirre mîn bart, / wir zestoeren sîne herevart'/ 'I swear by this beard of mine, we shall destroy Karl's campaign' (505–6) – his confidence in Marsilie's victory is so obviously mistaken that the value he sets by his beard comes across as vainglorious. Shortly afterwards (within a thousand lines or so) the same formulaic expression is put in the mouth of Genelun when he swears ('sô mir dirre mîn bart' 1646) that he will make the Twelve Peers pay for electing him to deliver Karl's ultimatum to Marsilie. This duplication may have underlined the affinity between the two as prospective co-conspirators. On the other hand, perhaps it is symptomatic of a broader assumption that many of the men in this story are bearded.

The argument between Roland and Genelun represents the first of several moments of crisis for Karl, in which he responds initially with a beard gesture of one kind or another. The emotions involved vary, as does the extent to which his conduct marks him out as an exceptional individual. When the scale of the disaster at Ronceval is first discovered by the Franks, the sense of collective grief is too great to describe, the poet declares (6963–4), before he homes in on the emperor's distress: 'der kaiser brach ûz sîn bart' / 'the emperor tore out his beard' (6965). Falling to the ground (6966) and beating his chest (6968), he laments the young (beardless?) men he has lost, the 'kint des rîches' / 'children of the empire' (6976). When, the next day, it comes to taking care of the slaughtered rearguard, the grief of one and all is conveyed by means of the same drastic gesture: 'bî hâre unt bî barte / liten si grôz ungemach' / 'By tearing at hair and beard they gave vent to their distress' (7524–5). Against this backdrop Karl's sorrow is dramatized by something more extraordinary, by a miracle: the rock on which he weeps tears of blood is still wet 'ienoch hiute' / 'even today', or so the poet claims (7564–7).

In the context of the decisive second battle, Karl and his men quickly put their sorrow behind them. Now the mood is characterized by heroic defiance, as already suggested perhaps by Karl's body language upon hearing the brazen demands of Paligan, the heathen emir: 'Der kaiser begonde den bart straichen' / 'The emperor began to stroke his beard' (7651). Before a blow has been struck, Karl issues an order which allows his warriors, outnumbered as they are, to demonstrate their solidarity as a body of men:

> der kaiser hiez si ir barte
> ûz vorne ziehen.
> daz tet er in ze liebe,
> den Karlingen ze ainem zaichen,
> dô ez scain über ir gewâfen. (7940–4)
>
> The emperor ordered them to display their beards; he did this for their sakes so that the Franks would have a sign to go by, one that would be visible over their armour.

In their time of greatest need the Franks identify themselves for and with Karl by revealing their beards in battle, collectively asserting their superiority as fighting Christian men. Unlike Alexander the Great's legendary orders to his Macedonians to shave off their beards before the battle of Gaugamela (331 BCE),[15] Karl's remarkable instruction has nothing to do with military strategy: it is a symbolic gesture of defiance, albeit one that goes unanswered. At no point in the ensuing battle do the heathens reciprocate or even comment upon this most striking aspect of their enemies' appearance. In the *Rolandslied* there is little sense of a beard competition between Christians and Saracens; the beards on display become emblematic of the close relationship between Karl and his men. As the author-narrator explains, just as Karl was moved to act like this out of love for his people, so the Franks came to adopt this practice in loving memory of him as their emperor: 'dar nâch flîzten sich iemer alle Karlinge / dem kaiser Karle ze minnen' / 'Thereafter all the Franks always did this out of their love for the Emperor Karl' (7945–6).

The final beard gesture attributed to Karl comes in the last episode of the *Rolandslied*, the trial of Genelun. Once again it serves to put the spotlight on Karl as emperor, moved to anger by the weakness of those around him, when the traitor's powerful kinsmen argue that he should be pardoned: 'Der kaiser erzurnte harte / mit ûf gevangem barte' / 'The emperor grew furious, clutching his beard [in his fist]' (8771–2). Indeed, Karl's emotions (anger, fear, joy) run high during the ensuing trial by combat, in which Roland's unlikely champion eventually decapitates Genelun's man; none are mentioned thereafter in respect of Genelun's gruesome execution. However conventional or formulaic this last beard reference may be,[16] it too allows a particular profile of the emperor's emotions to emerge more clearly, drawing the audience's attention to the difficulty Karl has in carrying out his God-given mission and in fulfilling the role he is expected to play as king.[17]

From what we have seen so far, one principle seems clear enough: in Konrad's text beard references tend to underscore the role played by individual figures at specific moments in the story. Karl's prominence in the narrative is reflected quite straightforwardly by the fact that his beard features throughout the work (from the start of the trouble at his court between Genelun and Roland to Genelun's trial). At the same time we should recognize that Karl is the only ruler in the *Rolandslied* to be foregrounded in this way. Irrespective of how contemporary audiences might have visualized King Marsilie or the Emir Paligan, any beardedness on the part of the latter is left unmarked in the actual text. The focus on Karl is such that even when Marsilie is described as losing his temper, and the same stock phrase is used – 'Marsilie erzurnte harte' / 'Marsilie grew furious' (5207) – with the possibility of another 'harte'–'barte' rhyme, the poet harks back to Karl (in the words of Marsilie), rather than electing to present the figure of the heathen king himself in more detail: '"Karl mit sînem grawen barte / hât menigiu rîche betwungen"' / ' "Karl the grey-bearded has conquered many a kingdom"' (5208–9).

Songs of Roland

Before we take the thematic analysis of the German *Rolandslied* too far, we should remind ourselves that it is a reworking of an Old French

Chanson de Roland. To put Pfaffe Konrad's work into some perspective, it is therefore necessary to check the French material which the German poet most likely had at his fingertips. His exact source is unknown to us today, but critics are agreed that it must have been very closely related to the oldest extant *Chanson de Roland* (the so-called Oxford version, found in a manuscript dated c. 1125–50).[18] This will be our primary point of reference, although we shall also cast an eye over later versions of the French text (preserved in manuscripts from the late thirteenth century onwards), which provide us with further insight into the beard-specific interests at work in the French epic Roland tradition.

Analysis of the Oxford *Chanson de Roland*, a text of around 4,000 lines, reveals just over thirty references to beards.[19] Beardedness characterizes named individuals and groups of men alike, both Christians and heathens. Beard references take the form of heroic epithets and feature repeatedly in the oaths sworn by various figures.[20] Beards are even subject to demeaning acts of violence, as when Ganelon is taken into custody by Charlemagne's cooks: 'Icil li peilent la barbe e les gernuns, / cascun le fiert quatre colps de sun puign' / 'They pluck hair from his beard and moustache; each one strikes four blows at him with his fists' (1824–5).[21] In this world populated by bearded warriors one figure stands out, and that is of course the (French) king and emperor Charlemagne, to whom two-thirds of the references apply. From the moment King Marsile's emissaries catch sight of Charles, the image of his bearded majesty dominates the text: 'la siet li reis ki dulce France tient. / Blanche ad la barbe et tut flurit le chef, / gent ad le cors e le cuntenant fier' / 'There sits the king who holds sweet France. / White-bearded and hoary-headed, / his body fit, his expression fierce' (116–18). The very whiteness of Charles's beard is a constant refrain, an epithet for him used by friend and foe alike.[22] As the external manifestation of his authority and great age, it lends him the aura of an Old Testament patriarch.[23] At the same time this beard is the focus of most if not all of Charles's gestures, as expressive of deep thought (when Roland assumes charge of the rearguard at Ganelon's suggestion), grief (at Roland's death) or anger (as Baligant's army approaches).[24] When he rides into battle, he does so with his beard on proud display: 'Mult gentement li emperere chevalchet, / desur sa bronie fors ad mise sa barbe' / 'The emperor rides magnificently, / his beard spread out on his coat of mail' (3121–2). Inspired, his Franks do the same: 'pur sue amor altretel funt li altre: / cent milie Francs en sunt reconoisable' / 'for love of him, the others do the same, / marking a hundred thousand of them as Franks' (3123–4), something which does not go unnoticed by the heathens themselves (3318–19).[25] Baligant even responds in kind, thereby proving himself to be a foe worthy of facing Charles in single combat: 'Li amiraill ad sa barbe fors mise, / altresi blanche cume flur en espine; / cument qu'il seit, ne s'i voelt celer mie' / 'The emir spreads out his beard / as white as the hawthorn flower; / whatever is to be, he does not wish to hide' (3520–2).

The (poetic) interest in Charles and his beard continues to the very end of the work, the very last lines of which appear to signal a new beginning. In the Oxford *Chanson de Roland*, no sooner has Ganelon been executed (and Bramimonde baptized) than Charles is visited by the angel Gabriel with word of another arduous mission to save Christians from heathen persecution (3991–8). What is surprising is the bearded emperor's response to this new holy call to arms: '"Deus! dist li reis, si penuse est ma vie!" / Pluret des oilz, sa barbe blanche tiret' / '"God," says the king, "how painful my life is!" / He sheds tears, pulls on his white beard' (4000–1). There is evidently no end to Charlemagne's life of service to God.[26] Notwithstanding his earlier displays of strength and leadership, the text concludes, quite remarkably, on a note of sorrow, weariness and even self-pity.

There can be no doubt that the proliferation of beard references in this Old French text is in part due to their status, in many cases, as formulaic units within an established poetic repertoire of archaic expression and epic diction which sought to evoke an older tradition of oral storytelling.[27] This same repertoire continues to characterize the other versions of the *Chanson de Roland* that are preserved in later manuscripts. If anything, the Roland text known as V4 (Venice, Biblioteca Nazionale Marciana, 225, c. 1320–45), as well as the very closely related redactions C (Châteauroux, Bibliothèque municipale, ms. 1, c. 1275) and V7 (Venice, Biblioteca Nazionale Marciana, ms. Fr. Z. 7, no later than 1320), contain even more relevant material.[28] In this later phase of written transmission a number of other stock figures are explicitly bearded,[29] the foremost of these being Roland himself who – even in his death throes – is subjected to a particularly vile attack by a wicked Saracen: 'Prist ella in ses pung, a Rollant tira sa barbe' / 'Seizing the sword, he pulled Roland by the beard' (2438). It is not inconceivable that later versions such as V4 preserve older material, and it has been suggested that precisely this reference to Roland's whiskers was suppressed in the Oxford version.[30] Be that as it may, it is quite obvious that this scene was regarded as unmissable by other redactors, who sought to enhance it in one way or another.[31]

As far as Charlemagne's beard is concerned, later songs of Roland tend to feature more of the same epithets and more of the same utterances and gestures, although none of the other known versions of the *Chanson* ends as the Oxford text does. The very last reference to Charlemagne as a bearded king in the Franco-Italian text V4, for instance, serves instead to emphasize his triumphant majesty when Ganelon is found guilty.[32] Other 'new' details shared by C and V7 include the fashionable enhancement of braiding for Charlemagne's beard, as revealed by his preparations for the second battle.[33] More importantly still, in these twin redactions Charles's glorification as a bearded king begins in the very first line of the text: 'Karle li rois, a la barbe grifaigne, / set anz toz pleins a esté en Espaigne' / 'King Charles of the daunting beard / has been in Spain for a full seven years' (1–2).[34] The impact of this strategy is accentuated by the use of the adjective 'grifaigne' / 'daunting' which is unparalleled in this whole body of (French) material. In V7 its effect is compounded by a historiated initial which contains 'the figure of a bearded and crowned Charlemagne on a field of gold, wearing a pink garment and a blue cloak'.[35]

What becomes quite apparent is that Pfaffe Konrad's *Rolandslied* contains significantly fewer beard references.[36] This may have something to do with the unequivocally literary status of this material in a German context, for this reworking is obviously even further removed from the oral tradition that gave rise to the *Chanson*. The formulaic diction and the metrical needs of the latter, which favours set phrases such as 'ki la barbe ad florie', or, even more fundamentally perhaps, the various combinations of 'barbe' with the adjective 'blanche' or 'canue', were clearly not Konrad's concern.[37] The fact that Konrad retains some beard references (such as Blanscandiz's oath),[38] while reworking or even introducing others (such as Genelun's oath), suggests that he recognized the thematic potential of this aspect of male characterization and looked to harness it in his own way. The prejudicial reference to Blanscandiz's courtly braids (427–8) would seem to be a prime example of this approach.[39]

Remaining faithful to his source early on, Konrad is evidently content to translate the beard epithet of an otherwise insignificant heathen who is listed as one of Marsilie's barons: thus, 'Guarlan le barbét' / 'Guarlan the bearded' (65) becomes 'Gerglant mit deme barte' / 'Gerglant the bearded' (574).[40] By comparison Konrad's strategy in respect of Charles/Karl can only be described as radically selective, with at best a quarter of the references to the emperor's 'barbe' and 'gernuns' (in the Oxford version) making the cut. The emotional profile that thereby emerges for Karl in the *Rolandslied* is a markedly different one, being more narrowly concentrated on righteous anger. There is no room here for the image of the weeping and weary Charles that concludes the Oxford version (4000–1).

Similarly, detailed descriptions of Karl's (hair and) beard are conspicuous by their absence in the German. Marsilie may call the emperor a greybeard ('Karl mit sînem grawen barte' 5208),[41] but otherwise Karl's beard is visualized primarily with reference to gesture. As a result the *Rolandslied* dispenses with the beard aesthetic that is such a distinctive feature of the *Chanson*, where the beards displayed by Charles, his veterans and even his foe Baligant are as white 'cume neif sur gelee' / 'as snow on ice' (3319), 'cume flur en avrill' / 'as an April flower' (3173) or 'cume flur en espine' / 'as the hawthorn flower' (3521). In the *Chanson de Roland* in fact the ideal of heroic masculinity, embodied by battle-hardened veterans, largely transcends partisanship for the Franks on the part of the epic poet.[42] In the German version the religious and moral agenda remains paramount. There can be no sense of physical or heroic compatibility between Karl and Paligan, between the Christian warriors and the heathen enemy, just as there can be no suspicion of Karl and his men vaunting themselves. The focus is on why they reveal their beards, not what those beards look like.

A book of beards

In one important respect Pfaffe Konrad's *Rolandslied* is unrivalled anywhere in Europe as a twelfth-century document of pogonographic interest: its earliest complete manuscript (Heidelberg, UB, Cpg 112, c. 1200) is densely illustrated, containing 39 pen-and-ink drawings featuring numerous bearded figures.[43] These images represent the earliest extant cycle of illustration for Charlemagne epic in any vernacular.[44] They are pre-dated only by the iconographic tradition associated with the Latin *Pseudo-Turpin* (first composed c. 1140), which exerted tremendous influence throughout the Middle Ages across all visual media from the lid panels of the 'Karlsschrein' to the stained-glass windows of Chartres Cathedral.[45] Certain very specific scenes were thereby established as canonical, not least Charles's dream-vision of St James, or rather when the (bearded) saint appears to the (bearded) emperor in his sleep to call him to Spain. The striking thing about the pictures of the *Rolandslied* is that they appear to have been a feature of the work's transmission from the very beginning,[46] devised specifically for this German work by an artist (or artists) whose technique, not least in the sketching of beards, evinces a certain English stylistic influence.[47]

Most of the drawings in Cpg 112 relate to their immediate narrative context.[48] The appearance of the figures seems to be inspired by the text's themes but realized more often than not on the basis of established iconographic types or motifs which were subject to further variation for reasons that are not always transparent to us today. The upshot of all of this is that more bearded individuals appear in the pictures than are explicitly referred to in the text. Thus, in the manuscript's very first drawing (fol. 5r), in which Archbishop Turpin baptizes a Spanish heathen, Turpin is bearded while his deacon and other helpers are not. This beard motif could simply denote superiority (age, office). Alternatively it may stress the archbishop's masculinity and heroic credentials in spite of his ecclesiastical office; after all he is the only churchman to do any actual fighting.[49] On fol. 5r the heathen (fighter?) undergoing baptism, representing the mass conversion at this point in the text (351–60) is also given a jawline beard that is not substantially different to Turpin's. In other words, the heathen's beard is not a marker of otherness. Indeed, throughout the cycle of drawings heathen figures are no more or less likely to be bearded than Christians. When fighting in full armour both sides look identical; helmets almost always cover faces and the odd suggestion of beard growth over the ventail can be found in respect of both Christian (41v) and heathen (93v) warriors.

The outstanding iconographic beard motif in the codex is that of bearded kingship, which for the most part recurs independently and without supporting narrative detail. This principle is evident as early as the top of fol. 5v, where an image of Karl's majesty – bearded, sceptre in hand, seated on throne – adds flesh to the bones of the author-narrator's summary of the power he wields in most of Spain (361–4). Karl's patriarchal and august status is conveyed by the length of his beard; and his beardedness is rendered more emphatic by the beardlessness of his sword-bearer and the two other figures in attendance (as representative of his court). This visualization of Karl's majesty is then countered at the foot of the facing page (6r) by an illustration of King Marsilie, who is characterized by a closely cropped beard, in audience with the elderly Blanscandiz. Whereas Blanscandiz's long beard (akin to Karl's in fact) is explicitly prompted by the text (425–8), the depiction of Marsilie appears to be determined by the general iconography of kingship and the desire to construct an opposition to Karl worthy of the name.[50] There are a number of such drawings for Marsilie (29v, 32v, 49v, 52r), and the same fundamental model is also used for Paligan (102r, 109v) and other heathen kings (again without any supporting textual detail). Irrespective of Pfaffe Konrad's negative characterization of these enemy kings, in terms of visual representation there is clearly an artistic strategy of equivalence at work here, providing the basis for unfavourable comparison with Karl.

The pre-eminence and dominance of Karl in the work is reflected in the number of drawings involving him. There are eleven in total, his beard being on display in nine, with a plot-determined pattern of distribution around the first twenty and the last ten pages of the manuscript. To the modern reader one aspect of this arrangement is slightly disconcerting, and that is the variation in Karl's appearance, most specifically in his style of beard. Although the first three drawings of Karl (fols 5v, 8v, 19r) present him with a long or patriarchal beard, elsewhere the dreaming (41v) or grieving (43v) emperor looks no different to the cropped-bearded Marsilie or Paligan, before reverting to long-bearded type, most obviously on fol. 119r (the very last drawing). There is no obvious reason for this fluctuation. One plausible explanation is that it is the by-product of a less than straightforward process of illustration and manuscript production, in which the artist(s) drew directly on extant older models for some of the images (patriarchal type) and worked from a template of their own design for some of the others (cropped-beard type).[51]

Certain complexities in the treatment of Karl also arise from the fact that his beard, as we have seen, is a theme in the text itself, relating above all to gesture and emotional display. This interest is evident in a number of the drawings, although the relationship between image and text on this point varies quite considerably, evincing (at least) three modes of representation.

1. Re-contextualization. The drawing on fol. 8v (Figure 2.1) shows Karl grasping his beard as he listens to Blanscandiz delivering Marsilie's request for peace; another bearded figure (normally identified as Genelun) also seems to be speaking. Unusually, this image does not illustrate its narrative context in any straightforward sense but would seem to be proleptic, for at this point in the text Marsilie is still issuing instructions to his ambassadors as to what they should offer Karl (587–624). Karl's gesture too is difficult to read: the reception scene proper features no such response on Karl's part, unless we view this iconographic motif as a means of visualizing his silence and deep thought (731, 771–3), a connotation, we should note, which is to be found in the text of the Oxford *Chanson de Roland* (214–16, 771–3). Alternatively, it is entirely possible that the artist was inspired by the first reference in Konrad's text to Karl's beard (1154–6), which involves him clutching his beard in anger at Roland's war of words with Genelun. Rather surprisingly, this scene is not illustrated in Cpg 112. It is not inconceivable that the picture on fol. 8v is the result of a desire to retain the emperor's gesture while re-contextualizing it in order to render the Christian king's reception of the treacherous heathen embassy all the more dramatic.

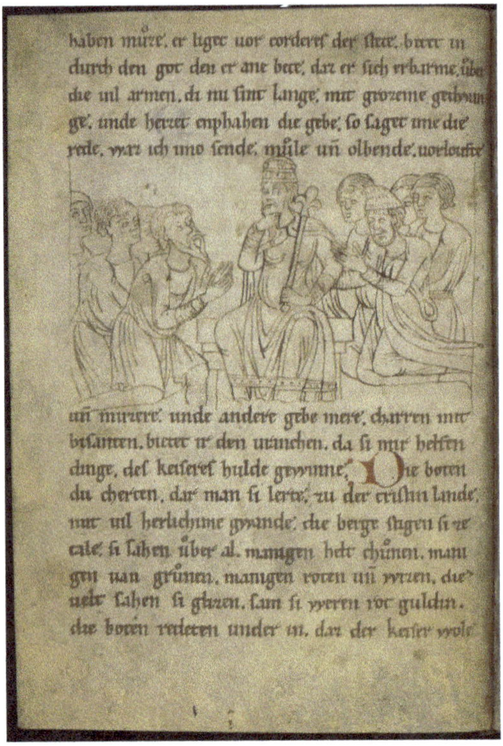

Figure 2.1 Karl receives Marsilie's emissary Blanscandiz and others (Pfaffe Konrad's *Rolandslied*). Heidelberg, UB, Cpg 112, fol. 8v. Public domain.

2. Re-emphasis. On fol. 108v (Figure 2.2) Karl is portrayed in full armour and on his knees praying before the decisive second battle begins. Unlike on fol. 98r, another image of Karl(?) praying, on fol. 108v the emperor's beard is on show over his ventail. The emphasis on Karl's bearded piety at this juncture is quite striking given that this same phase of the literary narrative features two beard-specific gestures on Karl's part: his angry response to Paligan's messengers (7522–5) several pages earlier and – in the last lines of text on fol. 108v itself – his instruction to the Franks to display their own beards (7940–6). The visual focus here is trained instead on Karl as a pious king, identifying him amid the faceless ranks of his armed and helmeted men, leading them in prayer. The same re-emphasis seems to be at work elsewhere in the codex on fol. 117r, where Karl and his men enter Saragossa in triumph and are received by Brechmunda. Here too only Karl's beard is on show and once again there is no

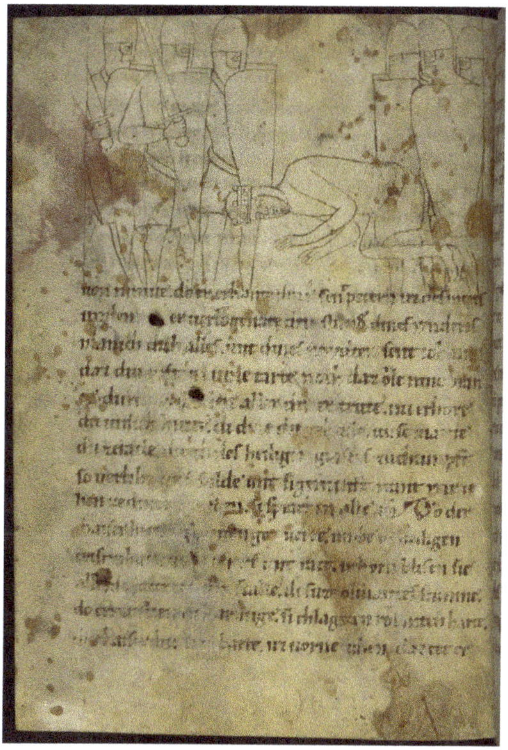

Figure 2.2 Karl prays before battle (Pfaffe Konrad's *Rolandslied*). Heidelberg, UB, Cpg 112, fol. 108v. Public domain.

equivalent line in the actual German text, although this is a standard detail in the transmission of the *Chanson de Roland*: 'Fiers est li reis a la barbe canue, / e Bramimunde les turs li ad rendues' / 'The white-bearded king is fierce / and Bramimonde surrendered the towers to him' (3654–5).

3. Convergence. On fol. 119r (Figure 2.3) Karl is shown grabbing his beard in anger during Genelun's trial when the traitor's powerful kinsmen intercede on his behalf. The final image in the manuscript directly correlates to the beard reference in the text at this point (8771–2): indeed, it is just possible to make out the word 'barte' at the end of the line above the drawing. Thus here, finally, image and text converge in respect of Karl's beard, heavily underlining the emperor's emotion and his unexpected predicament before justice can be achieved. This beard motif is contextualized further by the portrayal of the other figures in the scene. First and foremost, Karl's

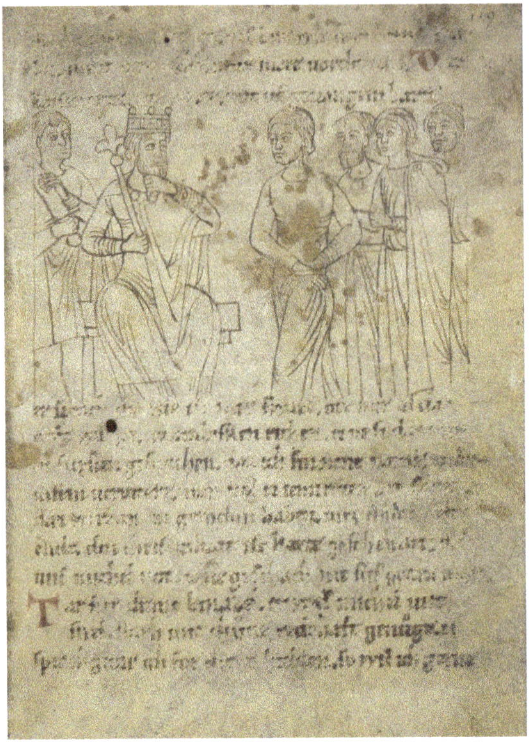

Figure 2.3 Karl responds angrily during Genelun's trial (Pfaffe Konrad's *Rolandslied*). Heidelberg, UB, Cpg 112, fol. 119r. Public domain.

regal status is upheld by the fact that his beard is longest. Genelun's beard growth is youthful by comparison, which in turn renders his treason all the more perfidious.[52] The pairing of a beardless (younger) man with a bearded older man behind Genelun may be iconographic shorthand for Genelun's kin as a whole or it may denote the two champions in the judicial combat to come: Binabel the strong (8785–7) vs Tierrich the weak (8877). Regardless of the identity of the other bearded and beardless figures in question, this picture is quite typical of the cycle as a whole in that Karl is the only one who is shown to gesture – with his beard – in this fashion.

The drawings in the *Rolandslied* are characterized by their relatively simple and sketchy execution. Their technical qualities (or deficiencies) are put into some relief by several later Anglo-Norman illustrated manuscripts of other *chansons de geste*, in which the beards of Charles and others receive special artistic attention.[53] The miniatures in one copiously illustrated codex of *Fierabras* (Hanover, Niedersächsische LB, MS IV 578, c. 1275–1330), for instance, are remarkable for the exaggerated volume and length of all the beards on display.[54] Here we get a sense of an epic world dominated by larger-than-life heroes with massive beards that simply cannot be contained by their chain-mail coifs even as they ride out to do battle (Figure 2.4). Against the background of this Anglo-Norman tradition of epic iconography as it evolved in the course of the thirteenth century, the Heidelberg *Rolandslied* would appear to be representative of an earlier, embryonic phase of beard illustration still marked by inconsistencies and idiosyncrasies.

In the context of manuscript production in Germany quite specifically, this *Rolandslied* codex is one of several relatively early manuscripts of vernacular literature to feature cycles of miniatures. Two of these share the same layout and balance between text and image, with fairly basic drawings interrupting otherwise continuous text: the *Altdeutsche/ 'Millstätter' Genesis* (Klagenfurt, Landesarchiv, Cod. GV 6/19, c. 1200),[55]

Figure 2.4 The Franks ride out to meet the enemy (*Fierabras*). Hanover, Niedersächsische LB, MS IV 578, fol. 80r.

and Priester Wernher's *Maria* (Krakow, Bibl. Jagiellońska, Berol. mgo 109, c. 1220).[56] A third, altogether grander, codex (Berlin, SBPK, Mgf 282, c. 1220–30), for another secular text, Heinrich von Veldeke's *Eneasroman*, contains more complex and carefully executed pictures that cover the entire page.[57] To an even greater extent than the Heidelberg *Rolandslied* perhaps, the manuscripts portraying biblical events (Klagenfurt, Krakow) are packed full of images of bearded figures (patriarchs, kings, wise men, old men). The Berlin *Eneasroman* by comparison is dominated by beardless (younger) warriors and knights (whether Aeneas or Turnus, Trojans or Rutulians). All four manuscripts share certain iconographic motifs and scene types, not least that of the (bearded) enthroned ruler, in audience with others (beardless and bearded) and often with a (beardless) sword-bearer at his back.[58] It is symptomatic of the modernizing, courtly stylization at work in the *Eneasroman* codex that Latinus, the king of the Latins, when portrayed in this way is either beardless (fols 57r, 57v) or evinces jawline beard growth (34r (i), 64r (i)) that is worlds away from Karl's patriarchal beard in Cpg 112. In the Krakow manuscript the Emperor Augustus too is given a similarly minimalist beard (60r) unlike those of all the other rulers featured, whether Herod (79v, 80v, 85r, 88v, 89r), or two of the Three Kings (82r, 82v, 83r).

Most tellingly, two of these other German manuscripts also include images of beard gestures. In the Berlin *Eneasroman* codex an older man (or authority figure of some kind?) of Carthage grabs his own beard with his right hand as he observes Aeneas and company approach the city gates (fol. 6v (ii)).[59] That this beard grasp signifies a proper gesture, conveying amazement or thoughtfulness perhaps, is suggested by the immediate narrative context, where the author-narrator emphasizes the extraordinary visual impression made by the Trojans and above all by the handsome Aeneas (686–728). As we have already had occasion to observe (Chapter 1), the Krakow *Maria* manuscript contains the remarkable image of an astonished elderly shepherd, holding his beard (in his right hand) and swearing by it (Figure 1.1), a pictorial detail that far exceeds the corresponding text. Notably, several pages earlier the same gesture of consternation is assigned to Joseph as he and Mary's two midwives behold the ass and the ox kneeling before Christ's crib (fol. 70r), a highly condensed iconographic translation of Priester Wernher's more general description of this very moment.[60] What is striking about Pfaffe Konrad's *Rolandslied* by comparison is that, although various figures explicitly swear by their beards in this text, only Karl's beard gestures are represented visually (8v, 119r; Figures 2.1 and 2.3); only the bearded emperor is privileged in this way. Across all three manuscripts, then, the same basic iconographic motif is used to convey a range of varying context-specific emotions, from amazement and consternation (thoughtfulness), to bewilderment, to anger.

Re-imagining beards

In the course of the thirteenth century Pfaffe Konrad's *Rolandslied* provided the impetus for another work, Der Stricker's *Karl* (c. 1215–25), which was to become one of the most widely transmitted texts of the German Middle Ages, effectively supplanting the earlier version.[61] Famous for offering a more 'modern' courtly retelling of Pfaffe Konrad's work and providing an account of Karl's life as a whole, this later text also pays very close attention to beards. In fact, of the eleven beard references in *Karl*, only six go back to the *Rolandslied*, and several of these instances are revised in quite telling ways. The beardedness of the elderly heathen advisor Blanschandiez is a case in point, with Der Stricker cutting back on all references save for the very first one: 'im was gevlohten sin bart' / 'his beard was braided' (1006) = *Rolandslied*: 'sîn bart was im gevlohten' (427). The key thing to note here, however, is that Blanschandiez is no longer primarily defined by his cultivated beard. This aspect of his appearance is only referred to by Der Stricker's narrator after his credentials as a wise counsellor at court have been emphasized (1001–5). Only the faintest echo of Pfaffe Konrad's hostility towards all-too-worldly courtly fashion (for older men) remains.[62]

As far as the figure of Karl is concerned, the emperor is no longer portrayed angrily clutching his beard at court, whether in response to Roland's unruly argument with Genelun, or during Genelun's trial. The first reference to Karl's beard actually occurs in Marsillies's outburst upon hearing that the (first) battle seems to be going against him: 'Er begunde klagen harte. / er sprach: "Karl mit dem barte,/ dem kunde niht widerstân"' / 'He began to lament greatly. He said: "Nothing can stand in the way of Karl the bearded"' (6187–9). Gone is the attribute of 'grey' as found in the corresponding line in the *Rolandslied* ('Karl mit sînem grawen barte' 5208); the Christian king's beard is thereby associated less with age and mortality than with power and strength.

In this context it seems entirely appropriate for Marsillies to tear out his own beard at the loss of so many of his men: 'an hare und ouch an barte / roufte er sich vor leide' / 'In his distress he tore at his hair and at his beard too' (6646–7), which is the first of several additional beard references in Der Stricker's version which are probably derived from the French *Chanson de Roland* tradition. And Karl is shown reacting in exactly the same way upon hearing the superhuman if somewhat futile blast the doomed Roland gives on his horn: 'den bart er weinende uoz brach' / 'Weeping, he tore the hair from his beard' (6991). In this latter instance, one might imagine, not only are the vicissitudes of war reflected once more in the condition of the king's beard, but, in this dramatic moment at least, a symbolic link is established between Karl's beard and Roland, hitherto his most important warrior. In the *Rolandslied*, in comparison, Karl performs this highly demonstrative expression of grief and distress at the sight of *all* the bodies of the slaughtered rearguard.

References to beards play an even more prominent role in the second battle, starting once again with Karl's response to Baligan's envoys: 'do begunde der keyser den bart / harte zornliche streichen' / 'At that the emperor began to stroke his beard in great anger' (8832–3). The emotional register of this gesture is, rather unusually, left unspecified in the *Rolandslied* ('Der kaiser begonde den bart straichen' 7651). Der Stricker fills this lacuna, spelling out Karl's anger in the face of the enemy in order to banish any lingering doubts: this is the heroically defiant emperor, not the distraught one.

The depiction of the battle itself cuts between two different beard motifs. First, there is the 'new' figure of a certain Richard of Normandy, who embodies the loyalty and bravery of Karl's veteran soldiers. Before a sword is drawn Karl himself pays tribute to Richard's abilities which remain undiminished, the emperor emphasizes, 'swi dir daz har unt der bart / vor zweinzech jaren gra si' / 'although your hair and beard were grey twenty years ago' (9020–1). During the battle this same Richard then performs prodigious feats – 'swie gra im doch der bart was' / 'for all that his beard was so very grey' (9682) – which is interpreted by the author-narrator as a sign of God's grace (9678–81). Secondly, we are invited to imagine the magnificent sight of Karl in all his bearded glory: 'er hiez im ziehen sinen bart / durch des halsperges ringe' / 'He had his beard pulled out from beneath his chain mail' (9234–5). When he asks his men 'wîe im daz zeichen zaeme' / 'how this display suited him' (9237), they are so impressed that they decide of their own accord to emulate him (9238–9). Nor is their collective beardedness forgotten once the battle has been won, for it is 'bi den berten' / 'by their beards' (10312) that the Christian dead are recognized.

Even more than was the case in the *Rolandslied*, beards thus come to represent the bond between Karl and his men, named and unnamed, becoming a sign of the affection and esteem in which they hold one another. But with Der Stricker's greater lucidity comes a more pronounced sense of historical perspective. In a textual variant found in several manuscripts the author-narrator takes it upon himself to explain that beard display (in battle) as a Frankish custom only lasted 'unz man die barte begunde schern' / 'until men started to shave their beards' (9240a). Der Stricker, it would seem, is acutely aware of the norms of contemporary courtly culture, including shaving, and their French origins. Heroic beardedness is apparently no longer self-explanatory to his audience of (fashion-conscious?) noblemen and noblewomen; in their eyes ebullient beards en masse may well have represented something archaic, an image of masculinity confined to the past.

Der Stricker's reworking of the *Rolandslied* generated its own images and cycles of illustrations. As a work of high cultural status his *Karl* was transmitted together with Rudolf von Ems's *Weltchronik* (c. 1240) – or chronicle of biblical history – in at least two luxury manuscripts and decorated with the finest gold-leaf illuminations: St Gallen, Kantonsbibl., Vadslg Ms 302, c. 1300; and Berlin, SBPK, Mgf 623, c. 1320–30 (fragmentary).[63] As far as the images of Karl's bearded majesty in the St Gallen codex are concerned, a principle of courtly stylization is quite apparent from the very outset. Not only does Karl have fair hair and a fair beard (Part II, fol. 3v),[64] but the courtiers who surround him (including his sword-bearer of course) are uniformly young and beardless. By contrast the heathens are generally characterized by their long beards (6v, 35v, 50v, 62r, 66r, 71r). Even a cursory look at the illuminations of the (preceding) *Weltchronik* makes clear just how differently Karl is portrayed. In comparison to the leading grey-bearded figures of the Old Testament, Karl represents something rather less aged and rather more 'glorious'.[65] The same point is made even more emphatically in the Berlin fragment of the *Weltchronik* (twenty extant miniatures) and *Karl* (three extant miniatures), where the colouring of Karl's long hair and full beard as fair or golden – as opposed to grey or white – appears unique to him.[66]

The transmission of *Karl* in the fifteenth century continues to feature pictures, albeit less opulent ones, and the use of the beard motif varies still more.[67] In the freestanding titular miniature (fol. 1v) of an early fifteenth-century manuscript (Hamburg, Staats- und Universitätsbibl., Cod. ms. germ. 19, c. 1400–30) Karl is cast very much in the role of white-bearded patriarch with his long locks, moustache and flowing beard.[68] Robed in a splendid red gown, towering crown on head and sceptre in hand, Karl is portrayed in his august majesty as he receives a holy sword from a (beardless) angel. Such characterization is all the more remarkable in the literary context of Der Stricker's *Karl* itself, in which there is not a single reference to the emperor as white-haired or white-bearded.

By contrast the extensively illustrated codex produced in Diebold Lauber's workshop in Hagenau in the 1440s (Bonn, UB, S 500, c. 1443–4) features a bushy-bearded, golden-haired Karl alongside many other bearded figures.[69] In terms of artistic design the beards here are of the same type as in certain other Lauber manuscripts of works such as Konrad Fleck's *Flore und Blanscheflur* (Heidelberg, UB, Cpg 362, c. 1442–4) and Wolfram von Eschenbach's *Parzival* (Vienna, ÖNB, Cod. 2914, c. 1440–3). However, whereas in the latter beards are reserved as an attribute of the older men encountered by the young (beardless) protagonists Flor and Parzival, in the Lauber *Karl* most of the figures in most of the drawings have golden-yellow beards; this rule even extends to Roland and Olivier, such as when the artist portrays the moment at which Roland finally sounds his horn (fol. 137r).[70] Once again, decisions such as these have little to do with specific narrative detail but are instead indicative of the iconographic models used, revealing perhaps a general understanding that this kind of story material, rather like the events depicted in the Old Testament, is ancient history of the most authoritative kind. Translated into the formulaic visual language of the Lauber workshop, the result is a set of images of surprising homogeneity: the beards of Christians and heathens are more or less the same, and the figures of Marsilie (42v, 49v, etc.) and Baligant (220r) are drawn on the basis of the same template of bearded majesty as Karl.

Other kings, other beards

Setting Charlemagne to one side, Pfaffe Konrad's *Rolandslied* was by no means the only text in the second half of the twelfth century to uphold the basic connotation of majesty that attaches to beardedness, although by definition the motif of the king's beard is not utilized in portrayals of decidedly youthful, unmarried rulers.[71] Several of these other German references to bearded kingship are shared with Old French and Latin works too, necessitating a similarly comparative approach.

The motif arguably occurs in its purest form in the most overtly fictional of all narrative works: the twelfth-century French and German beast epics concerning Reynard the fox: *Roman de Renart* (the first branches date from c. 1175); *Reinhart Fuchs* (c. 1180). In both French and German traditions the mischievous fox incurs the wrath of the lion-king (Noble/Vrevel) who swears – 'par ma barbe' / 'by my beard' (*Roman de Renart* VI: 415), 'sam mir min bart' / 'by my very beard' (*Reinhart Fuchs* 1476–7) – that he can tolerate it no longer. These half-lines represent the perfect point of convergence for several very longstanding and interconnected ideas: lion as bearded animal, lion as majestic, kings as bearded. The exact effect of the lion-king's oath, however, would seem to differ in context. In the first instance, King Noble appears to be modelled on the figure of Charles from contemporary *chansons de geste* such as the *Chanson de Roland*, and this impression is strengthened in another branch (X) with another, practically intertextual, beard reference: 'Nobles sousleve les gernons, / Si regarde toz ses barons' / 'Noble, with a wave of his whiskers, casts his eye over all his barons' (1539–40). At the same time, beards in the French text represent the next step in the anthropomorphization of several other animals, whether naturally whiskered (Ysengrin the wolf, and Hersent, his wife) or not (Tiecelin the crow).[72] In the German, by contrast, only the lion is presented – by means of his angry oath – as bearded. And if this did indeed summon up, for the German audience, an image of Karl der Große, as opposed to that of any other famously bearded German king (such as Frederick I, otherwise known as Barbarossa), it would doubtless have served only to underline the status of King Vrevel ('Outrage') as a tyrant, fully deserving of the nasty end he meets.[73]

No matter how formulaic the evocation of swearing by one's beard – or indeed pulling the hairs out of one's beard in sorrow – both the status of the figure of the king and the symbolic potential of the king's beard may have compounded the effect of such moments.[74] Nor is it out of the question that the same beard gestures that were meant to elicit recipients' sympathy in respect of 'good' kings elicited antipathy and Schadenfreude in the case of 'bad' ones (see also Chapter 5). Furious yet frustrated beard gestures are most typically assigned to kings worthy of derision, such as the heathen king Cosdroas in the German Heraclius legend of c. 1200, who foolishly believes he can prevent Heraclius from retrieving the True Cross. Although the heathen ruler swears 'bî sînem barte' / 'by his beard' (Otte's *Eraclius* 5178) that Heraclius must hang, it is Cosdroas himself who forfeits his life (and has his head chopped off). Somewhat less formulaic, and so less predictable perhaps, is another embedded reference to bearded kingship in this same text. Thus, the Roman emperor Focas, a positive ruler figure, is miraculously protected from fire by the small stone presented to him by Eraclius (as a lad) 'sô daz im nie besenget wart / weder hâr noch der bart'/ 'so that neither his hair nor his beard was singed' (1269–70). As is so often the way in medieval narrative, Focas's beardedness is mentioned solely in passing. Indicative of a priori assumptions about what kings should look like, it only becomes noteworthy in the extraordinary circumstances of this one episode.[75]

In principle the beard of any non-youthful king may be brought to the audience's attention as and when required. Nevertheless, certain German kings and emperors were associated more closely with their beards thanks to certain very specific anecdotes. Initially written up and transmitted in works of Latin historiography, these beard-related stories came to form part of vernacular literary tradition too. In *Heinrich und Kunegunde*, composed c. 1201 by one Ebernand von Erfurt, the saintly lives of Emperor Henry II and his wife Cunigunde were made accessible to a lay audience for the first time (in the wake of Cunigunde's canonization in 1200). The text takes delight in numerous miraculous occurrences, not least when shortly after his death Henry visits his stubbornly wicked brother, Bishop Bruno of Augsburg, in his sleep, in order to warn him not to pursue his plan to destroy Henry's beloved diocese of Bamberg. Bruno is amazed by Henry's sorrowful and wretched appearance and especially by one side of the dead emperor's face: 'in dûhte, wie im were / ûz geroufet sîn halber bart' / 'It seemed to him that half of his beard had been torn out' (2612–13). When Bruno asks who had the temerity to do such a thing to him, the emperor replies (of course): '"du hâst ez selbe mir getân"' / '"You're the one who has done this to me"' (2625). This is just one of several dream-visions that punctuate the work and serve to emphasize Henry's sanctity.[76] The symbolism of the king's body in Henry's visitation to Bruno is quite outstanding, however. Bruno's strategy of despoiling what Henry has bequeathed to God is visualized as a violent attack on the king's person: the king's bequests are a matter of personal faith or piety and of state and thus they should be as inviolable as the beard on his face, the natural symbol of his majesty.

Ebernand's account of this miracle closely follows that of his Latin source, Adalbert of Bamberg's *Vita Heinrici II. imperatoris*, a hagiography written (in 1145) for Henry's canonization in 1146. Here too the emperor's beard 'is torn out on one side' ('ex una parte depilata' II, 1, 811–12). In fact the anecdote was probably first penned by Frutolf of Michelsberg (d. 1103), who uses it in his chronicle of world history (*Chronicon universale*) to draw particular attention to Henry II as the saviour of Frutolf's own diocese of Bamberg.[77] Frutolf's work in turn became more widely known in the revised form given to it shortly afterwards by Ekkehard of Aura (d. 1126) in his *Chronica*.[78] This historiographical tradition bore fruit elsewhere in the vernacular in the first German chronicle in prose, the *Sächsische Weltchronik* (version A, c. 1230), where we find a slightly amended account of Henry's miraculous visitation. Now the king appears 'mit half geschorenen barde' / 'with half of his beard shaved [off]' (170,17), which we might regard as an attempt to restore some dignity to the saintly king's person. It is not inconceivable that wordplay is involved here too, as 'scheren' / 'to cut, to shave' also has the idiomatic meaning of 'to fleece, to steal from'.

Another point of difference in the *Sächsische Weltchronik* is that Henry II is actually the second German king to be distinguished by a beard anecdote of sorts, the first being Otto I ('the Great').

As Otto is about to leave Milan to quell an uprising in Germany a woman appeals to him for justice, having been the victim of rape. Otto promises that he will deal with the matter upon his return to the city, something which the woman doubts in spite of his assurances. One year later when back in Milan Otto duly summons the woman in order to keep his word, only now she protests that she is happily married to the man who had raped her: 'De koning sprach do: "Sem Otten bart" – also swor he io, – "he mot miner barden smecken"' / 'Then the king said: "By Otto's beard!" – [for] that was his customary oath – "he must taste my axe!"' (164,18–19). Thus, the chronicler notes drily, the woman was given the justice she no longer wanted (164,19).

This episode too is derived from Latin historiographical tradition, most likely from another source such as the *Annales Palidenses* (c. 1182–97).[79] For two Ottonian rulers, among all the many emperors and kings on show in the *Sächsische Weltchronik*, to receive such literary treatment is quite striking; and one wonders whether some meaningful contrast was intended.[80] If the miracle of Henry's visitation is testimony to his piety and sanctity as an instrument of God, the crowning achievement as it were of the Ottonian dynasty, Otto I, Henry's most illustrious predecessor, is remembered as an imperious king in and of this world, whose power was not to be called upon lightly and who dispensed justice without compromise.[81] The ambiguous characterization of Otto is, if anything, heightened by the wordplay in the Low German of 'bart' / 'barden' (drawing his oath and his verdict closer together), which seems quite heartless in context – the equivalent nouns in the Latin do not work like this ('barbam' / 'bipenni'). On the other hand, the notion that Otto was in the habit of swearing by his beard is central to both Latin and vernacular renderings. The alienating use of third-person self-reference ('Sem Otten bart' / 'per barbam Ottonis') accords the oath the status of a more or less institutionalized gesture,[82] a gesture, moreover, which is performed in conjunction with an irrevocable decision and the wielding of absolute power. In comparison with Henry II, the close association of Otto I with his beard can hardly be said to serve an encomiastic function. Further evidence of Otto's difficult reputation is found in another Latin twelfth-century work, Godfrey of Viterbo's *Pantheon* (1187). Here the anecdote chosen for an even more obviously tyrannical Otto I involves the latter having his beard plucked by a courageous knight (XXIII, 29).[83]

Arthur?

But what of the most famous medieval king of all? What of the legendary King Arthur? Rather bizarrely, references to Arthur's beard in the German Arthurian romance, as it emerged in the latter part of the twelfth century – and from about the same time as Pfaffe Konrad settled down to work on his *Rolandslied* –, do not exist. This is all the more astounding when we consider the first fully fledged literary treatment of Arthur, as found in Geoffrey of Monmouth's *Historia Regum Britannie* (c. 1136), which includes an account (in reported speech) of Arthur's victory over a brutal ogre called Ritho:

> Ritho had turned the beards of the kings he had slain into a cloak and had dispatched instructions to Arthur to shave off his beard carefully and send it to him, so he could place it above the rest, to reflect Arthur's preeminence over other kings. Otherwise, he challenged Arthur to a duel, to the victor of which would go the cloak together with the beard of the vanquished. Arthur won the duel and took Ritho's beard and the trophy, but had never, as he said, subsequently met Ritho's equal.[84]

The story of Ritho's gruesome cloak of beards, the threat the giant represents to Arthur's rulership, depends for its effect upon the fundamental association of kingship and beardedness.[85] In the idiom of heroic hyperbole to take another king's beard is to strip him of his power and his kingdom in the most brutal and demeaning fashion. To offer up one's own beard is to perform a gesture of humiliating self-abasement, and as such it is a course of action that Arthur utterly rejects.[86] There are no other references to Arthur's beard in the *Historia Regum Britannie*, but that does not matter.[87] This isolated episode works on the assumption that at this later stage of his life and his career as king and conqueror (of the world) Arthur must be bearded. Thus it functions as part of a broader narrative strategy that puts the spotlight on King Arthur's qualities as a man of great valour and unflinching strength. Arthur, we should remind ourselves, duly takes possession of the giant's own beard as well as his cloak of beards.

The adventure of the cloak of beards is retained in Wace's Old French translation of Geoffrey's text, the *Roman de Brut* (1155), where Arthur's ferocity is, if anything, made more explicit: 'Les pels out, la barbe escorea' / 'He flayed him and stripped off his beard' (11589).[88] However, there is no comparable episode in the subsequent literary tradition of Arthurian romance instigated by Chrétien de Troyes, which was received with such enthusiasm at German courts via the works of Hartmann von Aue and Wolfram von Eschenbach. Against the background not just of the Geoffrey–Wace tradition but also of the *chansons de geste*,[89] Chrétien takes the radical step of refraining from any description of King Arthur at all. In his very first Arthurian romance, *Erec et Enide* (c. 1170), there is something programmatic about the characterization of certain groups of men invited to Erec's wedding by Arthur. Whereas King Ban of Ganieret brings only young squires with him, some two hundred in number, who have 'ne barbe ne grenon' / 'neither beard nor whiskers' (1926), King Quirions of Orcel is accompanied by two hundred older men 'the youngest of whom was one hundred years old; their hair was as white as snow, for they had been alive for a long time, and their beards reached down to their belts' (1936–9).[90] In stark contrast to *chansons de geste* a perfect balance is struck here between the representation of beardless youthfulness and the whitebeards, whose exaggerated old age borders on parody. Arthur himself, by contrast, remains quite 'faceless' throughout, as if to describe him would be akin to diminishing his ideal status.

The German Artûs in Hartmann's *Erec* (c. 1180) is featureless too. In other respects, however, Hartmann is not afraid to go his own playful way. The extensive list of knights at the court of Artûs includes a certain 'Defemius a quatre barbes' / 'Defemius of the four beards' (1693), which is an extraordinary, ludicrous even, beard-based epithet, whose impact on the German audience as something both exotic and courtly was no doubt amplified by the fact that it is in French (although this line is not to be found in Chrétien's text).[91] In respect of the guests at Erec's wedding Hartmann largely dispenses with the complementary retinues of beardless youths and bearded ancients. His symmetrical arrangement of five young and five old kings is based primarily on a detailed description of their garments and bearing.[92] Within this scheme Hartmann recycles and modifies the beard reference as found in Chrétien: in the German text 'der bart snêvar' / 'snow-white beard[s]' (2081) which hang down as far as their belts now serve as the signal characteristic of the three-hundred-strong following of the first of the old kings (a certain Jernîs von Riel), the youngest of whom, the narrator exclaims, was 140(!) years old (2085). Here as elsewhere in *Erec* the representation of courtly perfection extends to beautiful old age;[93] yet as far as chivalric deeds are concerned the narrative remains focussed on Erec 'der junge man' / 'the young man' (18).

Not a single reference to the bearded majesty of Arthur can be found in Chrétien's other romances such as *Yvain* (c. 1170–5) and *Perceval/ Conte du Graal* (before 1190?). First and foremost, beard references in these two texts appear in the context of descriptions of exceptional ugliness or otherness. In *Yvain* the hideous peasant encountered by Calogrenant has a 'Barbe noire, grenons tortiz' / 'a black beard, tangled moustache' (305–6);[94] while the very first beard to be mentioned in *Perceval* belongs to the hideous damsel who berates Perceval in front of the Arthurian court: 'Et si ot barbe come bous' / 'and she had the beard of a goat' (4630).[95] Hartmann adheres to this principle in his *Iwein* (c. 1200), making even more of the unkempt (red) hair, beard and eyebrows of the wild man in the forest (432–6, 444–6). Wolfram von Eschenbach, on the other hand, picks up on Chrétien's further use of beardedness and beardlessness in *Perceval* as a means of differentiating between older and younger men, and takes this strategy to a whole new level in his *Parzival* (c. 1200–10) – as discussed in more detail in Chapter 3. Wolfram's approach is exemplified by Book VII of the German text, where manifestly younger kings (such as the headstrong Meljanz of Liz), rather than older ones, are presented in these terms: 'der künec mit kusse enpfangen wart, / unt zwên ander künege âne bart' / 'The king was welcomed with a kiss, as were two other beardless kings' (395,17–18).[96]

Across these various French and German courtly romances the absence of descriptive detail in respect of Arthur is remarkable. It is tempting to view such an approach as symptomatic of the mythical timelessness surrounding this king in Chrétien's model of Arthurian narrative, which could not be further removed from the historicity of Charlemagne or the biographical structure to the Arthur section in Geoffrey (and Wace). Perhaps the ideal nature of Arthur's rulership was such that actual physical descriptions of the king, or even just details pertaining to his age, were not required. The drastically reduced role Arthur plays in these romances – again in stark contrast to Arthur as a man of action in Geoffrey and Wace or the countless labours of Charles in the *chansons de geste* – means that Arthur is rarely if ever directly involved in episodes whose extraordinary circumstances would allow for an exceptional reference or two to his hair and beard. Instead Arthur stands immutable at the head of an idealized court which represents the point of departure and return for youthful male protagonists on adventure.[97]

As far as German manuscript miniatures of Arthur are concerned, such as those preserved in the transmission of Wolfram's *Parzival*, artists evidently made their own decisions concerning Arthur's appearance. Two main types of figure emerge. In manuscripts such as Munich, BSB, Cgm 19 (c. 1228–36)[98] and Berne, Burgerbibl., Cod. AA 91 (dated 1467),[99] Arthur is portrayed as beardless and youthful, the embodiment of curly-locked, clean-shaven courtliness, and surrounded by other beardless knights.[100] Elsewhere, in three codices produced by the Diebold Lauber workshop (c. 1439–46), known as *Parzival* 'm', 'o' and 'n',[101] Arthur appears as the typical bearded king once more. In 'm' and 'o' he represents a perfect vision of golden-bearded majesty.[102] In 'n' (Heidelberg, UB, Cpg 339) Arthur is characterized as very much older by virtue of his grey-white locks and a bushy grizzled beard (fol. 113r), emphasizing his wisdom and experience as opposed to the beardless Parzival's 'tumpheit' (youthful ignorance and naivety).[103] It turns out that medieval images of Arthur, in the German manuscript tradition at least, are rather more diverse than we might have expected and certainly more varied than the evidence as we have it for Charlemagne. The figure of Artûs was open to interpretation in ways that that of Karl was not.

Conclusion

Literary references to bearded majesty in the latter part of the twelfth century were evidently not restricted to Charlemagne, yet the sustained and repeated portrayal of Karl and his beard in Pfaffe Konrad's *Rolandslied* is outstanding in the vernacular German context. The prime position of this work is further enhanced by codex Cpg 112 (c. 1200) with its cycle of miniatures in which the bearded Karl plays a leading role. This first German *Rolandslied* reworks Old French *chanson de geste* material, but Pfaffe Konrad's text was itself received by later poets, giving rise not least to Stricker's *Karl*. Karl's beard remained an important motif throughout these various processes. References to it are embedded in the narrative action in the form of gestures (and emotional responses) and the utterances of various figures. Such embedding is very much a characteristic of the epic *chanson de geste* tradition, to which Konrad too was obviously indebted. Twelfth-century Latin texts tended to use alternative literary devices and strategies (tableau-like portrait, dream-vision) in accordance with historiographical and hagiographical traditions, constructing an image for Karolus that bordered on the supernatural; see Appendix I. Just as in the various versions of the *Chanson de Roland*, Karl's beardedness in the

Rolandslied is taken seriously, and this respectful strain continues in Stricker's Karl narrative too, all of which stands in marked contrast to certain later *chansons de geste* which poke fun at this famed aspect of Charles's appearance; see Appendix I. At the same time Pfaffe Konrad clearly adopted a selective approach to beard referencing (judging by the Oxford *Roland*), concentrating above all on the figure of Karl – the beards of the heathen rulers Marsilie and Paligan are never mentioned – at times of crisis when the emperor's emotions are running high. In rudimentary fashion Pfaffe Konrad's references to Karl's bearded majesty thus simultaneously raise the issue of the king's humanity.

Notes

1 'The emperor grew furious, clutching his beard [in his fist].' All translations of Pfaffe Konrad's *Rolandslied* are my own.
2 https://parker.stanford.edu/parker/catalog/rg420yp8320. Accessed 6 March 2021. See also Dale, 'Imperial self-representation', 2011.
3 Dutton, *Charlemagne's Mustache*, 3–42.
4 A comprehensive overview of this iconographic tradition is given by Schramm, *Die deutschen Kaiser und Könige in Bildern*.
5 Kantorowicz, *King's Two Bodies*, 42–86.
6 Bastert, *Helden als Heilige*, 78–85.
7 See also Chinca, 'Konrad's *Rolandslied*'.
8 Gerok-Reiter, 'Der Hof als erweiterter Körper des Herrschers', 84.
9 Brechmunda is converted and endowed with remarkable wisdom (8646–58), while Alda's wish to remain unmarried (8707–11) is heard by God, and no sooner does she finish her prayer to the Virgin Mary than she expires and is duly buried as a saint (8726–8).
10 Elsewhere the author-narrator draws on proverbial wisdom ('all that glitters is not gold') to contain the threat posed by Genelun's appearance (1956–60).
11 Richter, 'Das Hoflager Kaiser Karls', 1973; Knappe, *Repräsentation und Herrschaftszeichen*, 236–44.
12 Wenzel, 'Repräsentation und schöner Schein', 197–202; Kellermann, 'Die körperliche Inszenierung des Königs', 2001, 172–3.
13 Blanscandiz acquires the pseudonym of 'der alte mit deme barte' / 'the old man with the beard' (917; 2151) in the build-up to the conspiracy with Genelun.
14 For braided beards as a fashion for older men at court see Bumke, *Höfische Kultur*, 202. The elderly bishop who addresses Karl on behalf of his princes, in some ways Blanscandiz's counterpart, cuts a rather different figure: 'er linte über sîne krucken / mit sînen grawen locken'/ 'grey-locked as he was, he leant over his crutch' (1252–3).
15 Alexander's legendary explanation for this order is recorded by Plutarch as one of the Macedonian's most notable sayings: 'Don't you know that in battles there is nothing handier to grasp than a beard?' (*Moralia* III: Alexander nr 10). See also Oldstone-Moore, *Of Beards and Men*, 38–41.
16 See Schmidt-Lornsen, 'Der Griff an den Bart', II, 790–3; Küsters, 'Klagefiguren', 25–31; Bouillot, 'La chevelure: la tirer ou l'arracher'.
17 For 'emotional profiling' in medieval narrative see Schnell, 'Gefühle gestalten', 2016, 564.
18 Bastert, *Helden als Heilige*, 83.
19 Owen, 'Beards in the *Chanson de Roland*', 1988; Oldstone-Moore, *Of Beards and Men*, 80–1.
20 Cf. the three oaths sworn by Charles: 'par ceste barbe e par cest men gernun' (249); 'Par ceste barbe que vëez blancheier' (261); 'Par ceste barbe dunt li peil sunt canuz' (3954). Cf. also the oaths of Blancandrin: 'Par ceste meie destre / e par la barbe ki al piz me ventelet' (47–8), and Oliver: 'Par ceste meie barbe' (1719).

21 This is dealt with more concisely by Konrad: 'daz har si im zerouften; / si halslageten in genuoc' (6119–20).

22 Heathens: 970–1 (Margariz of Seville); 2605–6 (Bramimonde); 3316–19 (Baligant); 3503 (Gemalfin). Roland: 2307–8; 2333–4; 2352–3.

23 For Charles as another Abraham see Brault, *The Song of Roland*, 51–2, 95.

24 Cf. 771–3; 2414–15; 2930–2; 2943–4; 2982–6.

25 The Franks are thus collectively presented as veterans. Whether this detail was meant to evoke greater sympathy on the part of recipients is open to question; see Moroldo, 'Le portrait dans la chanson de geste [Part I]', 1980, 401–4.

26 See Brault, *The Song of Roland*: 'Suddenly Charles is no longer Abraham: he is Job in his tribulation' (337).

27 For a thorough review of this topic, which has dominated research on the *chanson de geste*, see Bastert, *Helden als Heilige*, 11–58.

28 Total number of beard references in V4: 34; C/V7: 49.

29 V4: Naimes (158, 703); Marsilio (385). C/V7: Naimes (277; 1136; 6150); Marsilie (757).

30 Short, 'Roland's final combat', 1970, 140–55.

31 The assault on Roland's beard is repeatedly referred to in C/V7: 4124–6; 4128–31; 4137–8; 4143–4. Elsewhere (Paris) the Saracen even declares his intention before the attack: 'Par Mahomet qui fait croistre l'erbiage, / je vos trairai les grenons de la barbe' (2587–8).

32 V4: 'En la cort sist Carlo a la barba florie' (5874).

33 'Par la ventaille fait les cordals sachier / de sa grant barbe, que il ot fait trecier' (5254–5).

34 The first line in the Oxford version reads: 'Carles li reis, nostre emperere magnes'.

35 *La Chanson de Roland*, ed. Duggan, vol. II, Part III, 21.

36 As observed already by Knappe, *Repräsentation und Herrschaftszeichen*, 246 n. 1022.

37 See Duggan, *The Song of Roland: Formulaic style and poetic craft*, 152, 156.

38 Cf. Blancandrin's oath in the Oxford *Chanson*: 'Par ceste meie destre / e par la barbe ki al piz me ventelet' (47–8).

39 The version of the text contained in V4 describes the old heathen's beard in advance of his oath but there is no braiding here either: 'blança oit la barbe et lo vis cler' (28). A still more elaborate portrait of Blanscandiz occurs in the thirteenth-century Welsh translation of the *Chanson*, where the heathen's wisdom is emphasized: 'That pagan was the wisest of them, and a proof of his wisdom was evident in him in the grayness of his hair and his beard, and his gray tresses down to his belt over his back, and his gray beard over his breast down to his belt in front' (*Cân Rolant* III: 1–4).

40 Cf. V4: 'Çiraldo li barbé' (66). In C/V7 this reference has been lost: 'Galan e Babüer' (76).

41 For similar references to Charles, as made by Marsile, in the Oxford *Chanson* cf. 537–8, 550–1. Cf. also V4: 447, 462; C/V7: 842, 2853–5.

42 For more on the striking a-perspectivism of the *Chanson de Roland* (in comparison to the *Rolandslied*) see Müller, *'Episches' Erzählen*, 215–20.

43 https://digi.ub.uni-heidelberg.de/diglit/cpg112. Accessed 7 March 2021.

44 Lejeune and Stiennon, *La Légende de Roland dans l'art*, I, 111–38.

45 Stones, 'The *Codex Calixtinus* and the iconography of Charlemagne'.

46 Another, even earlier, manuscript copy of the *Rolandslied* (Strasbourg, Stadtbibl., no signature, destroyed 1870) is known to have contained pictures. Reproductions (of eighteenth-century copies of these) make it clear that these drawings too featured numerous figures with long, stranded beards; cf. Lejeune and Stiennon, *La Légende de Roland dans l'art*, II, plates 91 and 93.

47 Lejeune and Stiennon, *La Légende de Roland dans l'art*, I, 135; Bertemes, *Bild- und Textstruktur*, 42–9.

48 Kern, 'Bildprogramm und Text', 1972, 254–5; Henkel, *Lesen in Bild und Text*, 41.

49 Even in battle Turpin is consistently portrayed in ecclesiastical garb. He is bearded in scenes where he is sitting in council (fol. 15v), or administering the last sacrament (47r) and blessing his brothers in arms (53v). He is beardless (as his own death approaches?) when blessing Roland (85v) and when slain by the heathens (91v).

50 See also Kern, 'Bildprogramm und Text', 1972, 265; Bertemes, *Bild- und Textstruktur*, 65; Brähler-Körner, 'Von der Handschrift zum Sammelbild', 51–4.

51 The patriarchal-beard type also seems to have been a feature of the drawings contained in the lost Strasbourg codex.

52 The depiction of Genelun throughout the cycle varies very considerably; see Bertemes, *Bild- und Textstruktur*, 127, 201.

53 See the extensive materials collected by Lejeune and Stiennon, *La Légende de Roland dans l'art*. Of particular note is the mid-thirteenth-century manuscript of the *Chanson d'Aspremont* (British Library, Ms. Lansdowne 782), in which the beards of both Charles and the heathen emir are tinged blue (fols 22r, 28r, 29r).

54 The bushy-bearded figures in another illustrated *Fierabras* codex (British Library, Egerton 3028, c. 1325–50) are striking by virtue of the ruddy-brown colouring of most of the beards on display with only the odd case of fair (fol. 93r) or blue-black (117r) hair.

55 https://manuscripta.at/?ID=33325. Accessed 8 March 2021.

56 https://jbc.bj.uj.edu.pl/dlibra/doccontent?id=159362. Accessed 8 March 2021.

57 http://resolver.staatsbibliothek-berlin.de/SBB0001AE7F00000000. Accessed 8 March 2021.

58 Heidelberg, Cpg 112: fols 5v, 6r, 19r, 43v, 52r, 84r, 109v, 119r; Klagenfurt, Cod. GV 6/19: fols 34r, 58v, 59v, 60v, 70v, 74r; Krakow, Berol. mgo 109: fols 60r, 75v; Berlin, mgf 282: fols 34r (i), 57r, 57v, 64r (i).

59 See also Diemer and Diemer, 'Die Bilder der Berliner Veldeke-Handschrift', 944.

60 'des wnderot verre / die ammen vnd ouch den grisen' (4027–8).

61 Bastert, *Helden als Heilige*, 184–90.

62 The most faithful adoption of beard lines occurs in respect of the heathen nobleman with the striking epithet ('mit dem barte' 1158) and Genelun's oath ('so mir dirre min bart' 2139).

63 Ott, '*Pictura docet*', 198.

64 http://e-codices.unifr.ch./en/vad/0302. Accessed 8 March 2021.

65 Cf. Part I, fols 15v (Abraham), 21v (Isaac), 39r (Jacob), 65r (Moses), 81r (Balaam), 97v (Joshua), 105v (Gideon), 135v (Samuel), 172v (David).

66 Facsimile consulted: *Rudolf von Ems, Weltchronik. Der Stricker, Karl der Große. Faksimile der Handschrift Ms. germ. fol. 623 der Staatsbibliothek Preußischer Kulturbesitz Berlin*.

67 This is by no means a comprehensive account of German manuscript miniatures of Karl; the focus here is on the images found in codices of Der Stricker's *Karl*.

68 http://dfg-viewer.de/show/?tx_dlf[id]=http://mets.sub.uni-hamburg.de/kitodo/HANSh4255. Accessed 8 March 2021.

69 For more on this codex see Saurma-Jeltsch, *Spätformen mittelalterlicher Buchherstellung*, I, passim; II, 8–9.

70 Images from this codex are reproduced in Lejeune and Stiennon, *La Légende de Roland dans l'art*: I, 241; II, Plates 212–36.

71 Cf. *König Rother* (c. 1140–70), where the outstanding beard does not belong to the young king but to his stalwart counsellor Berchter; see Chapter 3.

72 Cf. *Roman de Renart* Ib: 3057, VII: 479, II: 885.

73 Kolb, 'Nobel und Vrevel', 335–46.

74 Cf. the depiction of Etzel's despair in the *Rabenschlacht*: 'Er rouft sich bi dem barte, / michel was sin ungemach' (1113,3–4).

75 Cf. the reference to King Peleus's long and bushy beard in Herbort's *Liet von Troye* (17927), which forms part of a broader description that is justified by the narrator because of the unusual circumstances: 'Er was doch niht als alt / Als in geeldet hete / Sorge vnd vngerete' (17928–30).

76 Heinrich himself is visited by St Wolfgang (215) and St Benedict (1738–9). Towards the end of his work Ebernand sets out how the whole process of Cunigunde's canonization was set in motion by Heinrich himself when he miraculously appears, in a dream, to a certain monk in Bamberg by the name of Reimbote (4138–9).

77 See Goetz, *Geschichtsschreibung und Geschichtsbewußtsein*, 164–6.

78 The anecdote in Frutolf's *Chronicon universale* (anno 1025, pp. 56–9) is repeated pretty much word for word in Ekkehard's *Chronica*, in MGH SS 6, p. 194.

79 *Annales Palidenses*: 'E contra rex affirmabat per barbam Ottonis – quod suum iurasse fuit – raptorem preiudicatum de illa sua bipenni sapere debere' / 'In reply the king declared by Otto's beard – which was how he used to swear – that the man she had judged to be a rapist should [now] taste his axe' (MGH SS 16, p. 63).

80 Both anecdotes had already featured in the same Latin chronicle as early as c. 1150; cf. the chronicle of imperial history by the so-called Saxon Annalist, in MGH SS 6, pp. 608, 676.

81 Neudeck, *Erzählen von Kaiser Otto*, 89–96.

82 At least one manuscript of the A version contains the more conventional formulation of 'Sam mir min part' / 'By this very beard of mine' (Munich, BSB, Cgm 55, fol. 46v).

83 For a more detailed discussion of this anecdote see Chapter 5.

84 'Hic namque ex barbis regum quos peremerat fecerat sibi pelles et mandauerat Arturo ut suam barbam diligenter excoriaret atque excoriatam sibi dirigeret et quemadmodum ipse ceteris praeerat regibus ita in honore eius eam ceteris barbis superponeret; sin autem prouocabat eum ad proelium et qui fortior superuenisset pelles et barbam deuicti tulisset. Inito itaque certamine, triumphauit Arturus et barbam alterius cepit et spolium, et postea nulli fortiori isto obuiauerat ut superius asserebat' (X, 97–104; translation: Neil Wright). In the mid-thirteenth century Latin versification of Geoffrey's text, the *Gesta Regum Britannie*, Arthur himself tells the tale of Ritho and his cloak of beards: 'Excoriare meam barbam michi iussit' / 'He commanded me to rip out my beard' (VIII, 271; translation: Neil Wright).

85 Livingston, 'Losing face'.

86 For a comparable example of this motif from the tradition of the *chansons de geste*, cf. the humiliating terms Karl imposes on the king of Denmark at the outset of *Ogier von Dänemark*: 'Auch solt er mir bringen / Alle jar in waren dingen / Uß sinem bart vier hare / Und vier pfennige offenbare / Zuo zinse von seinem haubte mede' (589–93).

87 Cf. the striking miniature of the bearded Arthur in one later twelfth-century manuscript: Paris, BnF, 8501A, fol. 108v. http://gallica.bnf.fr./ark:/12148/btv1b10542189p. Accessed 8 March 2021.

88 In Wace's rendering the episode is covered in just under thirty lines of verse (11565–92).

89 The influence of the *chansons de geste* at this time is illustrated by the *Roman de Thèbes* (c. 1150–65), an early 'roman d'antiquité', where the Greek king Adrastus leads a force of white-bearded veterans reminiscent of Charles and his Franks: 'Dez mile sont d'antive geste; / chescuns d'els ad blanche la teste,/ les barbes ont fors des ventailles' (4930–2). Adrastus himself repeatedly refers to the white beards of his men as an emblem of old age to be proud of, urging them to unlace their helmets and display their 'grantz barbes encrues' (4963) like a 'ruste barnage' (4964).

90 'don li mainz nez avoit cent anz; / les chiés orent chenuz et blans, / que vescu avoient lonc tans, / et les barbes jusq'as ceinturs' (1936–9).

91 This line is subject to some debate by textual critics; see Hartmann von Aue, *Erec*, ed. Scholz, pp. 689–90.

92 Cf. *Erec* 1941–53, 1954–78, 1979–2028.

93 Cf. also the description of Enite's father, Koralus: '[...] der was grâ, / sîn hâr von alter snêwîz. / des hete er dannoch guoten vlîz / daz ers nâch reinem site phlac. / vil wol gestraelet ez lac / über sîn ahsel ze tal' (*Erec* 275–80).

94 Cf. also the process of Yvain's rehabilitation and return to civilized society (following his period of wild madness), which involves a good shave (3134–7).

95 Cf. also the extended description of the hideous squire (with a forked and curled beard) who accosts Gawain (6987–97).

96 Translations of Wolfram's *Parzival* are taken from *Wolfram von Eschenbach: Parzival and Titurel*, transl. Cyril Edwards (2006).

97 See also Wyss, 'Der Schatten des Körpers des Königs': 'Sollen wir versuchsweise von King Arthur's two bodies sprechen? Des Artus' natürlicher Körper wäre, so gesehen, um so eher verdunkelt und verschattet, als es allein auf den anderen, den charismatischen, den unsterblichen, ankommt' (28).

98 http://daten.digitale-sammlungen.de/bsb00071690/image_1. Accessed 8 March 2021.

99 http://e-codices.ch/en/list/one/bbb/AA0091. Accessed 8 March 2021.

100 Cf. Cgm 19, fols 49r, 49v; Cod. AA 91, fols 61v, 62r, 63v.

101 *Parzival* 'm': Vienna, Österreichische Nationalbibl., Cod. 2914, c. 1440–3 (http://data.onb.ac.at/rep/1002754D); 'o': Dresden, Sächsische Landesbibl., Mscr. M 66, c. 1439–46 (http://digital.slub-dresden.de/werkansicht/dlf/12735); 'n': Heidelberg, UB, Cpg 339, c. 1443–6 (https://digi.ub.uni-heidelberg.de/diglit/cpg339i). All accessed 8 March 2021.

102 Cf. Vienna, Cod. 2914, fol. 425r; Dresden, M66, fols 105r, 226r, 452v.

103 See also Ohlendorf, *Das Fremde im Parzifal*, 196–7.

3
Beards and humanity: Wolfram's *Willehalm*

> 'dô mir êrste die granen sprungen,
> mich nam diu minne in ir gebot
> noch sêrer dan dehein mîn got.'
>
> Wolfram von Eschenbach, *Willehalm* 338,12–14[1]

Over and above the privileged image of bearded majesty, beards represent a very basic and common means of differentiating younger men from older men and of characterizing these older men. Indeed, medieval German literature, no different to the literature of, say, classical antiquity, features a whole host of greybeards and whitebeards, starting with the venerable Berchter in *König Rother* (c. 1140–70), whose characterization as a greybeard would not be out of place in a *chanson de geste*.[2] Berchter's beard is described at various points, and by various speakers including himself, as magnificent (2470), grey but not so grey that he cannot accompany his king on a dangerous mission (3377–8), long enough to reach his belt (3508) and bushy (4961).[3] In a gently mocking, almost affectionate, tone the author-narrator even measures the passing of many cold winters in terms of Berchter's beard: 'vil dicke deme alden / sin bart rinne began' / 'Many was the time the old man's [frozen] beard dripped [as it thawed]' (4893–4) – an image of striking originality (as far as I have been able to establish).

The outstanding thirteenth-century narrative treatment of beards and age comes with Wolfram von Eschenbach's *Willehalm* (c. 1210–20), one of several texts upon which the reputation of the Golden Age of Middle High German literature rests. Within around twenty to thirty years of the composition of the *Rolandslied*, secular narrative in the vernacular had developed to a remarkable extent in respect of both narrative technique and thematic range, as poets explored the ideals of courtly love and chivalry in the context of all sorts of human relationships and experiences. Beards had their part to play in this, especially in Wolfram's work, which set the standard in matters pogonographic for narrative poets for the next hundred years or more.

Wolfram von Eschenbach's *Willehalm*

Wolfram's *Willehalm* represents another German reworking of an Old French *chanson de geste* (*Aliscans* or the *Bataille d'Aliscans*, c. 1185), albeit an incomplete one: Wolfram most likely worked on – but never finished – his text at the court of Hermann of Thuringia (d. 1218), the leading patron of vernacular literature of his day, during the second decade of the thirteenth century.[4] The story revolves around two battles on the plain of Alischanz in southern France fought between a huge invading force of Saracens, led by Terramer (whose daughter Arabel, baptized as Giburc, is now married to the famous warrior Willehalm 'ehkurneis' / '*au court nez*' 11,25), and a number of Christian armies under the same Willehalm, Margrave of Provence and defender-in-chief of the realm of King Louis, son of Charles (Karl).[5] The first battle is a catastrophe and sees the whole of Willehalm's small troop of defenders wiped out, including his beloved nephew Vivianz. Full retribution for this is taken some time later in a second battle, in which the assembled Christian forces of Willehalm's kinsmen (together with the French army sent by Louis) triumph and most of the heathens are slaughtered. Seriously wounded, Terramer himself only just manages to escape with his life. The text breaks off in the aftermath of battle with Willehalm lamenting the loss of his 'right hand' Rennewart, the prodigiously strong Saracen youth rescued by Willehalm from Louis's kitchen, who is missing presumed dead.

Willehalm was evidently intended to be listened to (and read?) against the backdrop of the *Rolandslied*, the events and leading personages of which are referred to throughout as relatively recent historical background.[6] This is primarily achieved by means of the speeches and spoken thoughts of the figures themselves: Terramer, for example, is keenly aware that he is the nephew of Baligan, who was utterly vanquished by Karl (in the *Rolandslied*), and Willehalm is prone to comparing his own losses and sorrow with those endured by Karl.[7] As a result Wolfram's audience too is encouraged to think of the battles on Alischanz as a continuation of the religious war conducted by Karl against first Marsilje and then Baligan. However, this perceived historical continuity should not mask the striking differences between *Willehalm* and the *Rolandslied* in terms of their ethos. Whereas the earlier work is dominated by a simplistic and aggressive crusading ideology which glorifies the Christians and demonizes the heathens, Wolfram's work – as most scholars agree – seems to uphold a relatively enlightened attitude towards the non-Christian enemy.[8] The necessity of killing to win the battle is not questioned, nor is there any doubt about the fate of heathen knights who are killed: they are damned. But from the beginning Wolfram conveys a sense of sorrow or regret at the 'tragedy' of such an outcome (20,10–12). And just as the author-narrator judges it a great sin that so many of the heathens were butchered 'alsam ein vihe' / 'like cattle' (450,17) once the second and decisive battle has been won, so Willehalm, on the narrative level, demonstrates a considerable degree of compassion in allowing the heathen king Matribleiz to take proper care of the heathen slain (461,3–467,4).

This unprecedented thematic emphasis goes hand in hand with Wolfram's idiosyncratic method(s) of storytelling, the sheer weight of narrative detail the audience is expected to deal with and a narratorial style which delights in obscure metaphors, bawdy humour and intertextual reference.[9] Challenged and amused in equal measure, recipients are confronted with different perspectives – the voices of both Christian and heathen figures are heard throughout – which play on their sympathies and antipathies.[10] In short, Wolfram introduces an unparalleled degree of complexity and ambiguity into practically every facet of his narrative, rarely content, it would seem, to tell his story straightforwardly.[11]

This is exemplified by the strategies Wolfram employs in respect of the physical appearance of his characters. Critical analysis of *Parzival* in particular has shown how Wolfram eschews the conventions of rhetorical *descriptio* in favour of metaphorically dense and sometimes abstruse reference, often preferring to embed details in the narrative rather than offer a parade of set-piece descriptions.[12] The same tendencies are at work in *Willehalm*, although the heroic nature and basic content of the source material, the lengthy depictions of battle, are such that the parameters for portraying the figures, both Christian and heathen, are somewhat different. The space devoted to female characterization is highly curtailed in comparison to the Arthurian romance. Thus, when it comes to references to hair throughout the story, it is male hair that predominates. Two principles catch the eye in this context. First, however formulaic a number of these references are ('der brûne' / 'brown-haired' 15,1; 'der grîse man' / 'the grey-haired man' 263,1), they are used to denote both Christians and heathens,[13] thereby consolidating the notion of a fundamental physical compatibility between the two sides – a significant departure from the monstrous heathens depicted in the *Rolandslied*.[14] Secondly, inventive hair references help to characterize figures of primary importance, the Saracen kitchen lad Rennewart being just one example (see below). In Wolfram's narrative, hair is very far from being a mundane detail. Connoting in the first instance courtliness (versus uncourtliness), hair is often made part of the action by the author-narrator as a means of conveying *in nuce* the extremes of human experience.

When we study *Willehalm* it readily becomes apparent that details pertaining to beards and beardlessness occupy a privileged position within this thematic complex, accumulating meaning as the story unfolds and as the audience is invited to engage with a cast of characters made up principally of young(er) and old(er) men.[15] The first of over twenty beard references occurs just as the first battle is about to get underway. As the heathen forces land and spread out to cover 'berge und tal' / 'hills and valleys' (10,12), they are met by Willehalm's defending company, a mere 'hant vol' / 'handful' (13,9) by comparison. Having introduced several of the more eminent heathens – including Tibalt, Terramer's son-in-law, the man abandoned by Giburc – the author-narrator names a few of the Christian warriors (Witschart, Gerart, Berhtram), before singling out a certain Vivianz, 'der klâre' / 'the radiant' (13,21), with the lament 'ouwê, daz sîniu jungen jâr / âne mundes granhâr / mit tôde nâmen ende!' / 'Alas, that his tender years should have ended in death before he had time to grow a beard!' (13,25–7). By virtue of this prolepsis, even before we see Vivianz fight, we know that he is doomed to die, as indeed, we cannot help but think, are most if not all his brothers-in-arms. That this already is a cause for sorrow and regret on the part of the narrator is explained by Vivianz's youthfulness, and this youthfulness is encapsulated by his lack of a beard, the mark of manhood.[16]

The special status accorded to Vivianz by this highly emotional outburst by the narrator is subsequently seen to be justified by his close kinship with Willehalm,[17] his acts of heroism and his astounding bravery in death – in spite of his young age. The full sentimental force of beardlessness as a metonym for the promise of male youth is then exerted in the speech of Willehalm himself, for even as he tends to Vivianz in his dying moments he is overwhelmed by a sense of guilt for having allowed his nephew to take part in the battle: 'swaz dînes liehten antlützes was, / dar an gewuohs noch nie dehein gran: / war umbe hiez ich dich ein man?' / 'Not a single whisker had so far grown on any part of your handsome face. Why did I call you a man?' (67,14–16). Once again an image of Vivianz's physical appearance is summoned up for the audience in impassioned terms; once again beardlessness serves as an emblem for the terrible price exacted by heroism on young life, no matter how justified the cause. In the aftermath of the battle, as word spreads of what has happened, Ernalt (Willehalm's brother) sums up the calamity that has befallen his family, the number of slain and captured, in similar fashion: 'die vürsten alle wâren / almeistic von den jâren, / daz ir neheiner gran noch truoc' / 'Those noblemen were mostly all of such tender years that none had a beard yet' (124,19–21). For all of his superlative qualities the youthful Vivianz, it now becomes clear, was representative of the vanquished force of men as a whole.

The story subsequently turns to Willehalm's mission to secure military aid and the self-imposed hardship he suffers out of solidarity with Giburc, whom he has left behind with next to no garrison to defend Orange. Forced to wear heathen armour to make his escape, he presents a terrifying spectacle upon arriving at the royal court at Laon several days later, where he is welcomed and attended to by no one.[18] The ferocious impression he makes is only furthered when he removes helmet and coif: 'dô was sîn vel nâch râme var, / bart und hâr verworren gar' / 'His skin was grimy and his beard and hair all tangled' (127,29–30).[19] In the eyes of the audience, who know what Willehalm has gone through, his unkempt appearance (which is so out of keeping with the festive atmosphere at Laon) has a twofold significance. On the one hand, Willehalm's refusal to look after himself is tantamount to a gesture of good faith towards Giburc, an unspoken ascetic corollary of his oath to her (105,1–13) to sustain himself on bread and water alone until he returns with an army to save her. On the other hand, there is something heroically defiant about his flagrant disregard for courtly etiquette; here Willehalm embodies a grim reality which renders courtly convention and more civilized trappings quite superfluous.

This episode does little to assure us that Louis is a king in the mould of his father, Charles, who is celebrated in the *Rolandslied* and elsewhere. Even though he and his queen (Willehalm's sister) realize who this armed warrior must be and what he most likely wants, orders are issued to deny him entrance, and consequently Willehalm has no choice but to accept the hospitality of a noble-minded merchant. Louis too may have a beard, but it is referred to solely in the words of a furious Willehalm, whose expression of gratitude towards his host the next morning takes a terrifying turn: 'durh's küneges swarte ûf sînen bart / ditze swert sol durhverte gern: / des wil ich in vor den vürsten wern'/ 'I'll part the King's hair all the way down to his beard with this sword, and I'll do it in front of all the nobles' (138,6–8). This imagined act of violence, borrowed as it were from the battlefield, conjures up an image of Louis's bearded majesty only to desecrate it. Just as Willehalm was the one who installed Louis on his throne against the will of many of the foremost nobles in France,[20] so Willehalm exults for a moment in the prospect of killing the king in front of his own court. Ultimately, however, consideration of Giburc's plight leads him to exercise some self-restraint towards the person of the king,[21] and it is the queen, Willehalm's sister, who bears the brunt of his ire when she rebuffs him at court and he grabs her 'bî den zöpfen' / 'by her braids' (147,19) in order to chop her head off. The queen's life is saved by Irmschart, their mother, but it is only Willehalm's niece, Alize, who can properly pacify him and bring him to his senses, appearing as she does as a vision of decorous courtly beauty: 'diu junge, reine, süeze, klâr – / manege kurze scheiteln truoc ir hâr, / krisp unz in die swarten'/ 'The pure, sweet, beautiful young maiden wore her hair in short locks, curled tightly against her head' (154,9–11).[22]

References to Willehalm's beard thus form part of a narrative sequence in which moments of violent disorder (real or otherwise) and the return of order at the royal court involve the depiction of hair of all kinds, culminating in an alliance of gendered extremes, as embodied by Willehalm and Alize. The queen's subsequent change of heart – behind closed doors she is shown to mourn Vivianz deeply – leads to reconciliation with Willehalm. As a concession to social harmony Willehalm reluctantly agrees to wear the luxurious apparel offered to him by his sister. But he will as yet not wash; the symbolic quality of his begrimed face and rust-stained beard (175,11) must continue to remind everyone of his desperate cause, even at the banquet table (175,24–5). Only when Louis has agreed to contribute a French army and both he and the queen accompany Willehalm for part of the journey back to Orange is the latent aggression in Willehalm's unkempt appearance directed away from the royal court. In an extraordinary account (203,19–207,30) of the first battle, for the benefit of Louis and his queen, in which Willehalm both names and praises the eminent heathens he killed, an entirely characteristic point of comparison is used by him to convey the scale of his heroic effort in defeat: 'der heiden hât mîn hant erslagen / (ob ich die wârheit prüeven kan) / mêr, denn mîn houbet und die gran / der hâre hab mit sunder zal' / 'my hand slew more heathens, if I can judge properly, than I have individual hairs in my beard and on my head' (206,20–3).

Such rhetorical transformation of Willehalm's beard signals the end of its usefulness as a constant visual reproach to the French royal court. Another thematic closure is implemented when Willehalm finally reaches Orange – the heathens have temporarily lifted their own siege and returned to their camp by the sea – and is reunited with Giburc. The two embrace and for the first time since his departure he allows himself to kiss and be kissed, prompting the author-narrator to exclaim in mock lament: 'ouwê, daz ein sô rûher bart / sich immer solt erbieten dar!' / 'Alas, that he had such a rough beard to offer to her!' (229,24–5). This intervention offers an ironic perspective on the tender kiss between (married) lovers, spoiled for Giburc, the poet speculates, by Willehalm's bristly beard, which itself bears testimony to his utter devotion to her.

These same lines, moreover, represent a typically mischievous twist on Wolfram's part in a scene characterized by gender transgression. Giburc, who has staunchly defended the castle in Willehalm's absence and who even now is wearing armour 'manlîch, ninder als ein wîp' / 'like a man, in no way like a woman' (226,30), is confronted, most palpably, with true masculinity. With Willehalm's return, Giburc and the damsels who serve her are able to dress and behave like ladies again.[23] As Willehalm gazes at the armour worn by the damsels (231,22–3), the author-narrator gives his own bawdy blessing to the return of conventional gender roles by mentally undressing the group of armed women, comparing their pubic hair to a very specific piece of under-armour protection, the 'semftenier' / 'soft padding [for the loins]' (231,25). Although such hair growth – like the male beard – functions as a natural sign of sexual maturity, its exclusively sexual significance and consequently its taboo status mean that it can only be referred to 'humorously' as part of a provocative strategy of mentioning the unmentionable and exposing what is normally hidden from view.[24]

Giburc's relationship with Willehalm's family now comes to the fore, as she plays the role of courtly hostess and welcomes the most honourable men among the assembled Christian host, allowing herself to be guided throughout by Heimrich von Narbonne, Willehalm's father and head of the clan. Here too an important moment features another beard. No sooner has Heimrich taken his seat beside Giburc at the banquet table than she is overwhelmed by sorrow: 'daz süeze minneclîch geschaf, / ir antlütze begozzen wart, / Heimrîches blanker bart / mit zeheren ouch berêret' / 'The face of that sweet, lovely creature was wet with tears. Heimrich's white beard was sprinkled with tears too' (251,8–11). This extraordinary image of compassionate intimacy between 'father'[25] and daughter leads to a dialogue in which Giburc gives full expression both to her sense of guilt at having caused the conflict and to her grief for the fallen Vivianz (253,24–254,6) and so many others, both Christian and heathen. Having earlier been reunited with her beloved husband Willehalm, who returns to her as the bearded warrior, Giburc is now reassured by Heimrich the white-bearded[26] patriarch of her position within his family. This latter scene is all the more impactful for its portrayal of weeping. Just as Giburc's tears run down her face, as per literary convention,[27] so Heimrich's fall upon his beard: an outward, bodily manifestation of solidarity in the most distressing of circumstances. Wolfram's elliptical style even allows another interpretation of these lines, in which Heimrich's beard is 'bedewed' by Giburc's tears (and not his own).[28]

A review of the principal male figures in the story so far makes clear that they are based on a straightforward generational template: Vivianz (young, beardless) – Willehalm (mature, bearded) – Heimrich (old, white-bearded).[29] The depiction of a fourth figure, Rennewart, complicates this scheme. When Rennewart first comes to Willehalm's attention at the court of Laon, by virtue of his inordinate strength, he is described by the narrator as 'noch âne bart' / 'as yet without a beard' (191,30). Such incongruity is in keeping with other aspects of his appearance: noble yet engaged in lowly kitchen service, beautiful yet covered in filth. However, given the grievous personal loss Willehalm suffers with the death of the young (beardless) Vivianz, when Willehalm recruits Rennewart to fight by his side it is hard not to view Rennewart, for all of the other obvious differences, not least his status as a heathen, as a rough and ready replacement.

The next time we are invited to reflect upon Rennewart's appearance – at the banquet hosted by Giburc and Heimrich in Orange – something about him has changed: 'sît der von Munlêûn ûf die vart / schiet, im wuohs sîn junger bart' / 'His beard was only just beginning to grow since he had set off from Laon on this march' (270,29–30).[30] This remarkable development defies Rennewart's age, the narrator assures us. It is due instead to love: 'Alîzen kus het in gequelt' / 'Alize's kiss had caused it to sprout' (271,3). The miraculous power of the kiss between the two childhood sweethearts, when Rennewart leaves for Orange with Willehalm,[31] has been read by some as a courtly variant on a folkloric motif.[32] It certainly plays on the notion of beard growth and (male) sexual maturation. Rennewart's beard growth is also the sign of an experience denied to Vivianz (as lamented by Willehalm), which adds the motive of love service to his participation in the battle ahead. The hairs on Rennewart's chin, the narrator emphasizes, are so few in number that they could have been counted (271,4–5). Although he is no longer like Vivianz, he is still nothing like Willehalm. Rennewart stands in dynamic relation to the generational template; his position is not yet fixed: he has the beautiful skin of youth, no different to that of the young Parzival (271,15–21),[33] and yet he is bearded.

As the narrative progresses Wolfram finds other ways of first revealing and then reconstructing Rennewart's identity with reference to his first beard growth.[34] In a capricious move, within around 100 lines of mentioning Rennewart's whiskers for the first time, the narrator wishes them away again in order to persuade the audience of the facial similarity between Rennewart and Giburc: 'daz underschiet niht wan sîn gran. / mir waere noch liep, waeren die her dan: / man ersaehe den man wol vür daz wîp' / 'the only difference was his tender beard, and I should have been glad if that had not been there, for then one could easily have mistaken the man for the woman' (274,23–5). In one sense this passage illustrates an ideal of kinship which runs so deep that it calls into question the primacy of obvious gender markers.[35] In another, it represents the latest in a series of ever more obvious clues as to Rennewart's heathen family background, which has as yet not been spelled out for the audience.[36] Giburc herself remains in the dark about their close kinship, although she too is struck by his resemblance to members of her family (272,26–7).

The author-narrator's wish would seem to come true when shortly afterwards a cook plays a crude prank on Rennewart (asleep on a bench in the kitchen) by taking a brand to his precious whiskers and singeing them (286,8–9). Rennewart's egregious reaction – he roasts the unfortunate cook over his own fire (286,11–15) – is explained in the extensive lament that follows, for Rennewart himself understands his beard growth to be the result of Alize's love and kiss rather than his age or his demeaning kitchen duties (287,12–19). The attack on his beard constitutes an attack on Alize's love for him and it is this which provokes such brutal retribution. As word spreads of the indignity Rennewart has suffered, Giburc in particular shows compassion for 'sîne grene, die besancten' / 'his singed whiskers' (290,15). This in turn leads to a poignant conversation with Rennewart concerning his background and family, during which Giburc's heart tells her, even if he does not, that they must be closely related (291,2–3), estranged siblings in fact – something the attentive recipient is expected to have grasped already.[37]

For all Giburc's sympathy, nothing can be done about Rennewart's face.[38] He must bear this mark, a sign of the time he has spent in the kitchens of Orange. Indeed, no matter how magnificently he is equipped, when he joins Heimrich, Willehalm and others for a final meal (before battle), his burnt whiskers are the first of his attributes to be listed by the author-narrator.[39] It is a feature of Wolfram's characterization of Rennewart, then, that his beard accumulates significance, accruing different connotations (courtly love, and neglect and humiliation) as his story unfolds. This strategy recurs during the depiction of the battle itself, when the narrator interjects to draw our attention to the toll the fighting is taking on Rennewart after various heroic feats and decisive interventions (such as driving the cowardly French noblemen back into battle): 'ob sîn besenget junger bart / mit sweize iht waere behangen / und ob in sîne stangen / waere inder swertes slac geschehen? / jâ!' / 'Do you suppose that his singed young beard was covered at all with sweat and that sword blows had landed on his club anywhere? Yes, indeed' (423,16–20). Rennewart's exertions represent a coming of age with 'sweaty' being added to the established list of descriptors for his beard. Sweat, in this context, is conceived as a kind of 'heroic humour',[40] the sign of a true warrior, confirming Rennewart's status as the absolute antithesis to the cowardly French, dismissed earlier by Willehalm as 'hârslihtaere' / 'dandies' (322,21).

The fragmentary state of *Willehalm* makes it impossible to say whether Rennewart's beard continued to receive such close poetic attention after the second battle. What is evident is that a number of other beard references occur in this 'final' phase of the narrative (as we have it) in respect of figures on both sides of the conflict, not least the supreme heathen ruler and commander Terramer. Alerted to the approach of the Christian armies, Terramer exhorts his leading men to take revenge for those who lost their lives in the first battle, fighting for 'unser gote' / 'our gods' (338,2) and for ladies (338,3). This twofold motivation Terramer shows he understands only too well by recalling his own attitude as a younger man, more concerned as he was with courtly love than with religion: 'dô mir êrste die granen sprungen, / mich nam diu minne in ir gebot / noch sêrer dan dehein mîn got' / 'When my first whiskers appeared Love held me enthralled even more than any of my gods' (338,12–14). Fighting for both, he concludes, will not only bring glory but enable him to displace Louis and seize the (Roman) imperial crown, which is his by right (338,17–30). However outrageous, abhorrent even, these political claims must have seemed to Wolfram's audience, the insight we are afforded into Terramer's thinking and life experience reveals him as misguided but not a monster.[41] The image of his own first beard growth, connoting – as in the case of Rennewart (his son) – courtly love, presents him as a man first and foremost, a man who was not always concerned with fighting for false gods.

When the two sides finally meet and the battle intensifies, turning into a murderous press, the author-narrator focusses increasingly on named individuals and their slaying of other named individuals. The first figure to be privileged in this way is old Heimrich, whose war garb receives an unusually detailed description (406,6–407,7) before he is obliged to defend himself against a notable adversary: 'dô kêrte der künic Zernubilê / gein dem, der wîz sô den snê / ime strîte truoc den bart,/ mit der vintâlen niht bewart' / 'Then King Zernubile turned towards the man who was wearing in battle the beard white as snow, unprotected by a ventail' (408,1–4).

The beard-first reference to Heimrich at the start of this encounter places renewed emphasis on this outstanding feature of his. Heimrich's beard may be 'white as snow' but his strength is seemingly undiminished and he kills Zernubile in heroic fashion, driving his sword into his foe's helmet 'unz ûf die zene' / 'all the way to his teeth' (408,29). The fact that Heimrich's splendid beard is on display in the first place is rationalized by the narrator who shines a spotlight on the old-fashioned design of the veteran's helmet, which leaves the lower part of his face uncovered.[42] This singular portrayal of Heimrich as a redoubtable old-timer in the thick of battle reads like Wolfram's nod to the literary tradition of the *chansons de geste* and their celebration of Charles's long-bearded warriors.

On the heathen side several figures are denoted as old by the colour of their hair. Terramer himself is disrespectfully challenged by one Milon von Nevers in precisely this way: 'her an mich, alt grîser man!' / 'Come over here, you grey old man!' (413,15). Other such references can hardly be described as disparaging, whether in respect of King Oukin (421,18), who grieves at the sight of his son's riderless horse, or the valiant warrior-king Purrel, distinguished by the number of sons he has brought with him and by his beard: 'sîn bart was grâwer dan der tuft, / des alten künec Purrel' / 'Old King Purrel's beard was greyer than hoar frost' (425,12–13). Purrel's counter-attack to protect his wounded sons (427,23–4) is so devastating, in fact, that it attracts the attention of Rennewart. He in turn fails to kill Purrel ('der grîse künec alt' / 'the grey old King' 431,21) only because the latter's armour, helmet and shield are covered with the diamond-hard skins of dragons (425,25–426,30). The colour of Purrel's beard may seem inferior to Heimrich's unsullied and patriarchal white, yet this depiction of Purrel goes some way towards humanizing him. His grey hair and beard serve as a counterweight to his highly exotic armour,[43] reminding the audience that the Christians are fighting and killing men who – like themselves – are fathers, brothers and sons.

Translating beards

Some sense of Wolfram's achievement can be gained from an examination of his Old French source material. Irrespective of which extant version of the *Aliscans* is closest to the one drawn on by Wolfram (see below), the epic itself represents a reworking of older stories concerning heroes such as Vivien, Willame and Reneward, which were cobbled together in one of the earliest known *chansons de geste*, the *Chançun de Willame* (c. 1150–75).[44] Much of the action in this archaic text seems familiar, much quite different; and this also applies to the construction of certain figures and their beardedness. In the first part of the text (known as G1), Vivien's grief over his slain comrades reveals him to be older: 'dunc tort ses mains, tire sun chef et sa barbe' / 'then he wrings his hands, tears his hair and beard' (477).[45] Willame, on the other hand, is depicted as the aged patriarch, whose tears at the news of Vivien's likely death wet his 'blanche barbe' / 'white beard' (1010). In the lament which follows, Willame reveals himself to be 350(!) years old (1334–6). The role of beardless boy is played by Vivien's younger brother Gui, who in spite of his age ('N'out uncore .xv. anz, asez esteit petiz; / n'out point de barbe' / 'He was not yet fifteen and was quite small; he had no beard' 1441–2) proves himself as valiant a warrior as anyone. In heroic tales dominated by male figures there is always the potential for beard references to be used to indicate age as well as to accentuate the emotional impact of certain gestures. The fact that the *Aliscans* (c. 1185), across its various manuscripts, already handles the issue of beardedness somewhat differently to the *Chançun de Willame* is symptomatic of the productive variability at the heart of this tradition.

In the Franco-Italian version of the *Aliscans* ('M' or the *Bataille d'Aliscans*, preserved in a fourteenth-century copy: Venice, Codex Marcianus fr. VIII [= 252]), which many but by no means all scholars view as the version closest to the one used by Wolfram,[46] the most conspicuously bearded individuals – Aymeri, Guillelmes, Renoard, Deramé – are the same as in *Willehalm*. In each case, however, it soon becomes apparent that Wolfram creates the poetic space to develop the motif in accordance with his own thematic interests.

In the aftermath of the first battle Aymeri (Heimrich) is repeatedly invoked – by Guiburc, Guillelmes and his sister – as the white-bearded or grizzled patriarch of the Narbonese clan.[47] Wolfram translates these formulaic references into two intense moments of visualization: when Heimrich's beard is drenched by his own and Giburc's tears, and when Heimrich's beard is proudly displayed in battle.

The uncourtly appearance of Guillelmes (Willehalm) at the royal court is most definitely of interest here ('De canes ot la barbe entramaslee' / 'His hair and beard are a wild sight' 2950), and the French hero literally bristles with rage at the lack of support he receives (2964, 3263). The prickly kiss Willehalm offers to Giburc is only to be found in *Willehalm*.

Renoard (Rennewart) has the beard of a young man from the start ('Gregnon li pongent selon lo suen a[l]é'/ 'He had the whiskers of one his age' 3425) and, appalled at the prank played on him in the kitchen at

Orange (4372–4), takes grotesquely brutal retribution for the indignity (4405–6) he has suffered.[48] There is no notion of this first beard growth being both the tangible result and symbol of his love for Aaliz, the French king's daughter (whom he eventually marries).

The beardedness of the heathen ruler Deramé (Terramer) is thematized at an earlier stage in the story, when he swears 'a sa barbe' / 'by his beard' (4007) that he will drown Giborg in the ocean to punish her (4008–9), only for the narrator to mock him for doing so: 'Mes je cuit bien, sa barbe ert periuree' / 'But I am sure his beard will perjure itself' (4010). This invitation to the audience to take pleasure in the heathen's angry frustration plays on their antipathy towards Deramé as a vile foe, an unconscionable villain whose two-dimensional characterization is far removed from Wolfram's empathetic, if not quite sympathetic, presentation of Terramer.

Strictly speaking, the absence of compatible detail in the *Bataille d'Aliscans* does not completely rule out the possibility that other redactions of the Old French text did provide Wolfram with more ideas, not least perhaps the inference that Vivien (Vivianz) is a (beardless?) young man.[49] 'M' represents something of an abbreviated version of the work. Other *Aliscans* texts (such as version 'ars': Paris, Arsenal 6562, c. 1225) refer also to the beards of Guillaume's red-haired brother Hernault (3060), King Louis himself (3089) and a certain crippled monastery porter – 'La barbe avoit dusque au neu dou baudré, / Et s'ert si blance com estoit flors en pré' / 'Down to the knot upon his belt his beard / Flutters as white as the flowers on the field' (3577–8) – who hilariously tries to deny Renoart entry. Otherwise, no differently to the portrayal of Charles in later versions of the *Chanson de Roland*, recipients are presented with more of the same, that is, further references to Renoart's youthful beard growth, to white-bearded Aymeri (on the occasion of Renoart's baptism) and even to Desramé's perjured beard.[50] If anything, knowledge of the broader literary tradition of the *Aliscans* only sets Wolfram's originality in greater relief.

This impression is further strengthened by casting an eye over Wolfram's first major narrative, his Arthurian romance *Parzival*, a move which is particularly sound, since Wolfram explicitly identifies himself as the poet of *Parzival* at the outset of *Willehalm* (4,19–24) and goes on to allude to figures from the earlier work on numerous occasions.[51] Beardedness and beardlessness are significant motifs in *Parzival* too. In so far as it is possible to find a tangible explanation for this, it seems entirely feasible that this feature of Wolfram's work was prompted by a particular episode in Chrétien's *Perceval/Conte du Graal* where the male populace at the Proud Castle are described (to Gawain) in quite striking fashion (7566–73):

> There are easily as many as five hundred, some with beards, others not: a hundred without beard or moustache, another hundred with growing beards, and a hundred who shave and trim their beards every week. There are a hundred with hair whiter than lamb's wool, and a hundred who are turning grey.[52]

This approach to denoting men of varying ages, which goes into a surprising amount of detail, is placed in the mouth of the boatman ferrying Gawain across to the castle. Its resonance or its effectiveness is then compounded at the conclusion of the episode when the same principle is used by the author-narrator to portray the squires serving at the banquet table, some of whom are old enough to be completely white-headed or greying (8238), while others have neither 'beard nor moustache' ('barbe ne guernon' 8240).

In his *Parzival* Wolfram applies this technique to the broader cast of male characters, focussing on the beardlessness or beardedness of various (named) figures. First and foremost, beardlessness represents one of the signal features of Parzival himself – 'der junge süeze âne bart' / 'That young, gentle, beardless man' (174,23) –, his youthfulness being a point of emphasis throughout the first part of the story.[53] Beardlessness characterizes several other named figures, some of whom seem younger than others. No distinction is explicitly made, however, between clean-shaven knights and those who have yet to grow any beard hairs at all. Thus, Parzival's father, Gahmuret (63,28), the young hothead Segramors (286,23), Meljanz and two other (young?) kings (395,17–18) and many of the young knights and squires in the retinue of the 'Grey Knight' (446,30) are all simply referred to as 'âne bart'.[54]

Secondly, both Parzival and Gawan encounter older bearded knights who seem to epitomize the thematic weighting of their respective journeys.[55] The humble yet beautiful Kahenis (the 'Grey Knight') displays on Good Friday the appropriately penitent attitude towards God that Parzival himself so sorely lacks. His grey beard ('des part al grâ was gevar' 446,11), indicative of course of age and mortality, is matched by his grey garments made of coarse material, while his beautiful and radiant skin reflects his hope in the promise of salvation ('dâ bî sîn vel lieht unde clâr' 446,12). By contrast, the elderly knight who warns Gawan about Orgeluse cuts a very courtly figure. Distinguished by 'a broad beard, well braided and grey' ('mit einem barte breit / wol geflohten unde grâ' 513,24–5), this older man still has a (dubious?) taste for courtly fashion, reminiscent in fact of that of the heathen Blanscandiz in the *Rolandslied* (see Chapter 2). Unlike Kahenis, this knight fails in his attempt to give Gawan the benefit of his worldly wisdom, and is subsequently proved wrong about his lady, whom Gawan succeeds in rehabilitating.

Even more relevant for our reading of *Willehalm* is the fact that a number of the more poetic treatments of beards it contains are foreshadowed in *Parzival*: the two outstanding examples of this are Rennewart's beard growth as a result of Alize's kiss and love, and the author-narrator's playful 'de-bearding' of Rennewart to reveal his facial similarity to Giburc. Both of these ideas are present in *Parzival*, although they are not formulated in respect of the two protagonists Parzival or Gawan but rather with reference to other members of their families. Thus, when the hermit Trevrizent tells Parzival about his mother's family and explains why the Grail King Anfortas is being punished so terribly – he chose his own lady-love rather than obey the dictates of the Grail – he emphasizes Anfortas's youthfulness at the time, linking beard growth with the first experiences of all-powerful love: 'dô mîn bruoder gein den jâren / kom für der gransprunge zît, / mit selher jugent hât minne ir strît' / 'When my brother approached the years of downy beard growth – Love wages war with such youths' (478,8–10). Looking back at his own life Trevrizent then recalls how Parzival's father recognized him as his wife's brother (even though he had never seen him before) because he and Herzeloyde looked so very alike (497,22–9), those being the days, he concludes, when he was still 'âne bart' / 'beardless' (497,30).[56] The notion that the beard as a gender-specific feature is somehow secondary and that (beardless) brothers and their sisters look very alike, provided they are of sufficiently noble birth and suitably beautiful, is enacted later in the work in relation to Gawan's siblings (Beacurs and Itonje). Gramoflanz, Itonje's would-be lover, is able to identify her amid all the other ladies at Arthur's court – in spite of the fact that he has never seen her before – because he has already met her (young) brother Beacurs: 'im sagte, wer sîn friundin was, / ein brief den er ze velde las' / 'He was told which was his lady-love by a letter he had read out in the fields' (724,19–20). The possibility of such facial recognition on the basis of Gawan's bearded(?) features is never entertained by the author-narrator.[57]

Wolfram's two principal narrative works, for all their difference in terms of story material, share a poetic interest in beards. In respect of *Willehalm* more specifically, we can be fairly certain that Wolfram adds to what he found in his Old French source, enhancing the beard motif in order to exaggerate the effect of several scenes and to foreground certain themes, most notably the common humanity of Christians and heathens. No matter what literary benchmark we take, Wolfram is outstanding in terms of the quantity and poetic quality of his beard references. Eschewing formulaic beard gestures – as expressive of anger or sorrow, for example – he develops his own ways of making beardedness and beardlessness more meaningful, expressly imbuing each of these states with subjective value from the perspective of the author-narrator and in the words of the fictional figures themselves.

Tearful beards

Having emphasized Wolfram's originality, we must also recognize that he was not the only narrative poet of his day to do imaginative things with beards. From earlier on in the 'Blütezeit' there are several examples of thematically resonant beard references which underscore the humanity of certain figures at pivotal moments. The significance of this material lies less in the fact that some of it may well have inspired Wolfram, than in its status as corroborating evidence for the sizeable developments in vernacular narrative in this period. Poets were investing more in the characterization, if not exactly the inner lives, of their protagonists, and in respect of male figures this new interest had consequences for how and when poets chose to embed references to beards.

Hartmann von Aue's *Gregorius* (c. 1185), the quite extraordinary tale of a man who becomes pope even though he is born of incest and himself later unwittingly commits incest with his mother, is one such text. This miraculous reversal of Gregorius's fortunes follows seventeen years of the most extreme penance, during which he lives chained to a rock in the sea, exposed to all the elements, dressed only in a hair shirt and surviving (by God's grace) on minute quantities of rainwater. He has himself abandoned there by a malicious fisherman who tosses the key to Gregorius's chains into the waves, scornfully declaring that Gregorius will become a holy man before the key is ever seen again (3095–9). This is precisely what occurs, some seventeen years later, when the fisherman carves up a fish he wishes to serve to two elderly Roman envoys. At the sight of the key in the belly of the fish the fisherman pulls and tears at his hair in dismay (3308–12), this customary gesture of despair being rendered rather less conventional by the author-narrator's humorous willingness to help the foul man hurt himself.[58] This less than sympathetic view is not sustained in what follows. The fisherman's contrition is genuine. Utterly convinced that Gregorius must have died a long time ago, he finds the prospect of returning to the exile's rock overwhelming: 'nû sâhen im die grîsen / diu ougen über wallen, / die heizen zäher vallen / über sînen grâwen bart' / 'The grey-haired men saw his eyes fill up and the hot tears fall down over his grey beard' (3346–9). The transformation of the fisherman from avaricious host into sorrowful penitent constitutes another miracle. Within this picture of true remorse the fisherman's tear-soaked grey beard marks him out as an older sinner, a man who has been brought to see the error of his ways after many years of mean and uncharitable behaviour.[59]

The story of Gregorius's survival is made all the more arresting by the extended description of 'der lebende marteraere' / 'the living martyr' (3378) whom the envoys discover on the rock the next day.[60] As part of an elaborate rhetorical strategy the author-narrator conjures up the image of the perfect nobleman (3379–402) – dressed in the finest garb, with radiant eyes and golden hair as well as a 'wol geschornem barte' / 'neatly cropped beard' (3396) – only to banish the idea once more, because this is exactly what the envoys do not see before them. Instead they find a filthy emaciated wretch (3423–65), his dreadful condition epitomized by the condition of his hair: 'erwahsen von dem hâre, / verwalken zuo der swarte, / an houbet und an barte' / 'the hair of his head and beard overgrown, matted and sticking to his scalp' (3423–6). The drastic displacement of ideal courtly appearance by its antithesis is calculated to grab the audience's attention. Abhorrent in the eyes of civilized men, this disgusting Gregorius is beloved of God ('gotes trût' 3418) and pleasing to heaven. His wild hair and beard are not just reminders of his base humanity but, as the direct consequence of his extreme asceticism, they are conspicuous marks of sanctity.

Beards connote weeping again in a very different kind of text, the *Nibelungenlied* (c. 1191–c. 1204), the first full-blown heroic epic (in literary form) of the period. The *Nibelungenlied* tells the story of the murder of Siegfried and the merciless revenge undertaken many years later by his beloved spouse Kriemhild on her Burgundian kinsmen, whom she treacherously invites to the court of her second husband, Etzel (or Attila the Hun). The beards and tears in question feature towards the end of the work in the sequence of events concerning the death of Rüdiger von Bechelarn, lauded by the narrator as the 'vater maneger tugende' / 'the father of all knightly excellence' (version B: 2199,4), who finds himself inextricably caught between the two warring factions and chooses death as the only way out. Rüdiger's fate would appear to encapsulate the heroic ethos at its most dreadful and compelling.[61] One of the many ways in which this figure is privileged is by the reactions of others to his momentous decision to fight and then, inevitably, to his death. The warriors of Dietrich von Bern, the renowned hero in exile at Etzel's court, are visibly moved when their worst fears are confirmed: 'den Dieterîches recken sach man trehene gân / über berte unde über kinne. in was vil leide getân' / 'you could see the tears flowing down their beards and chins, for they had suffered a cruel loss' (B 2254,3–4). The solidarity of the grieving heroes as men, their shared sense of allegiance and identity, is highlighted by their collective beardedness.[62] By associating these warriors' beards with their tears the poet presents us with a moment of gendered weeping which in principle is quite compatible with the depiction elsewhere in the text of female tears running over breasts,[63] effectively countering the pejorative notion (which is also to be found in the *Nibelungenlied*) that weeping is essentially an effeminate response to hurt and loss.[64] Rüdiger will be mourned for piteously by his wife and daughter, as described in some detail in the *Klage* (2807–3223), the companion piece and sequel to the *Nibelungenlied* in almost all of the main manuscripts. But at this moment, in the midst of a conflict which has spiralled out of control, sorrow is a matter for heroes as men.[65]

Collective beardedness in battle is one thing, whether for glorification (see Chapter 2) or in order to convey the horrors of war.[66] Portrayal of a group of bearded warriors as they weep is quite another, and this scene of heroic sentimentality is peculiar to the *Nibelungenlied*. By contrast the image of the remorseful grey-bearded fisherman in Hartmann's *Gregorius* served as a template for representing male emotion in at least one other work of about 1200. In Konrad von Fussesbrunnen's *Die Kindheit Jesu*, Joseph's sorrow – when he, Mary and the infant Jesus Christ are taken captive by a merciless robber as they make their way to Egypt – is conveyed in almost exactly the same way. Here it is the robber who observes Joseph's distress:

> nû vermist er an im nie,
> ern saehe im diu ougen ie
> mit trehern uber wallen
> unt von den wangen vallen
> uber den bart her ze tal. (1695–9)
>
> Now every time he looked at him, he could not fail to notice his eyes overflowing with tears that poured down his cheeks and over his beard.

This is not the first danger faced by this family on their journey, and it is not the first time the author-narrator has shown Joseph to be anxious and fearful. However, the previous references are fleeting and matter-of-fact.[67]

The visualization of Joseph's weeping at this moment helps to emphasize the perilous nature of this predicament: the robber poses a greater threat by far than dragons or wolves, lions and bears. An even higher level of literary lachrymosity is reached when the subsequent course of Joseph's tears is described: '[...] ein zaher den andern sluoc, / swaz er gewandes ane truoc, / unz er daz allez vor begôz' / 'one tear followed hard upon another so that all the garments he was wearing were drenched' (1701–3). The cruel robber himself is so affected by this sight that he has a change of heart, something which the author-narrator clearly interprets as a miracle and tantamount to divine intervention. Having previously regarded Joseph with utter contempt ('wie wart er müedinc ie so alt?' / 'How could the poor beggar have lived for so long?' 1667), the robber now speaks of him with nothing short of reverence: 'ein altherre guoter, / wîz als ein snê' / 'a venerable old gentleman with hair as white as snow' (1762–3); and the Holy Family are saved.

The sentimental effect of the tearful beard lies in the notion that the outpouring of emotion involved is entirely involuntary. Narrative moments of this kind play on the sympathies of the audience; they are designed to move recipients in order to make a thematic or a didactic point stick. This is illustrated further by the earliest known version of the moral-exemplary tale *Die halbe Decke* (second half of the thirteenth century), in which a man who neglects his elderly father is only brought to his senses by the naive intervention of his own young son.[68] The turning point in the story comes when the little boy hands over part of a coarse woollen blanket to his grandfather, who, half-frozen to death, cannot contain himself any longer: 'er begunde vor vreude weinen, / diu ougen im uber wielen, / daz im die treher vielen / zu tal über den grawen bart' / 'He burst into tears of joy. His eyes were overflowing so that the tears fell down over his grey beard' (version A/ II: 144–7). In a neat variation on the motif (as established in Hartmann's *Gregorius*), this tearful beard is rendered all the more piteous for being the result of such great joy over so lowly an object. However affecting this encounter between grandfather and grandchild is meant to be,[69] the episode simultaneously invites the audience to work out for themselves what the narrative consequences are likely to be, given that the small child is shown observing his grandfather's reaction very closely (151–3). In fact the little boy runs off to ask his father for the rest of the blanket so that he can do the right thing by him too when the time comes, and this is what shocks the man into changing his ways. The story's didactic message has thus already been made quite comprehensible for recipients before it is articulated in the epilogue as a basic principle of humanity: 'ein ieglich mensche ere / sinen vater und sin muter!' / 'Every person should honour their father and their mother!' (272–3).

Against this background the portrayal of Heimrich's tearful beard in *Willehalm* (251,8–11) comes into sharper focus. As a patriarchal figure with a white ('blank[er]' 251,10) as opposed to a grey beard, he seems less weighed down by guilt and sin or the misery of old age. The sorrow he feels is not his alone to bear; rather he is participating in the grief of another (Giburc 251,6–7). Far from leading to any spectacular action, the consequences of this shared moment are internalized, constituting a renewal of the bond between 'father' and 'daughter'. Heimrich's tearful beard could thus be construed as an innovative poetic image for paternal comfort sought and found.

Boys and men

If tearful beards were used by poets to depict the predicaments of old(er) men in ways calculated to move an audience, details pertaining to beardlessness exercised their own emotional effects, functioning not just as a poignant reminder of the promise of life to come but also as the mark of a kind of prelapsarian innocence, in which gender difference is not yet paramount. This notion is exemplified by the very early and widespread romance narrative of *Floire et Blancheflur* (c. 1150) – of which two known German renderings survive (*Trierer Floyris*, in fragments dating to c. 1170; Konrad Fleck's *Flore und Blanscheflur*, c. 1200–20) – concerning the tribulations of the eponymous childhood sweethearts (one heathen, one Christian) who are separated against their will. The outstanding scene across all these versions is doubtless when Flore is discovered in bed with Blanscheflur (in the tower where the latter is being held captive) by virtue of the fact that no one can tell whether the slumbering Flore is a man or a woman 'wan er enhâte bart noch gran, / glîch einer jungen maget' / 'since he had neither beard nor whiskers, just like a young maiden' (*Flore und Blanscheflur* 6342–3).[70] To the audience Flore's beardlessness is the most obvious sign of his age; the lovers are still only fifteen (6970–1). It is also in keeping with the chaste love he shares with Blanscheflur before marriage, which can only happen once Flore has been baptized. There is no scope for sexuality – or beard growth – in a story which presents courtly love in terms of virtue pleasing to God.[71]

Wolfram may have not been the first German poet to thematize beardlessness per se.[72] But he did break new ground in terms of the depiction of beard growth, the transition from one phase of life to another and the pain and suffering which come with it. In doing so he modelled the literary potential of this device for narrative poets in the so-called post-classical period, several of whom emulated their illustrious predecessor in respect of beards and characterization. Post-Wolfram it became more common in German courtly narrative for the course of events to be marked by references to varying states of beardedness, whether in respect of different groups of boys and men, or as a means of further delineating the life of the central protagonist.

Beards of various kinds denote a range of figures in Rudolf von Ems's *Der guote Gêrhart* (c. 1220–5), including the main character, Gerhard, a man of unparalleled humility, who is obliged to explain to Emperor Otto 'the Red' (87) just how he has come to be known as Gerhard 'the Good'.[73] Directed by a heavenly voice to seek out this Gerhard (in Cologne) and learn the true meaning of goodness, the emperor surveys an assembly of the city's leading citizens and is immediately struck by the noble appearance of one hoary-headed individual,[74] handsome for his age, well dressed and well groomed: 'sîn hâr was hovelîche / gespaenet wol, sleht und reit. / wol gemachet und vil gemeit / was geschorn im der bart' / 'His hair was curled in courtly fashion, his locks [were] quite splendid' (790–3). This, the author-narrator confirms, was indeed 'der guote Gêrhart' (794), and such a flattering portrayal of Gerhard places him in a line of idealized elderly male figures, including Heimrich in *Willehalm* of course, although there is a difference. The nobility of Gerhard's appearance, including his fashionably trimmed beard, is not matched by his birth; he is merely a virtuous merchant. Accordingly, his extraordinary deeds are of rather a different kind to those of the soldierly white-bearded Heimrich.

As the teller of his own tale (taking up some 5,000 of the work's 7,000 lines), Gerhard soon turns out to have an eye for the beards of others, or rather Rudolf von Ems makes a point of including such details in the course of the story-within-the-story. The first of several incredible deeds of altruism sees Gerhard spend his entire fortune, accumulated on a trading expedition to far-flung lands, on securing the release of a company of Christian knights and ladies from heathen captivity, so moved is he by the plight of the male prisoners in particular, who are being kept in heavy chains. The description of the sight that meets his eyes is carefully structured. First he is shown twelve young knights – 'die êrsten grane truog ir bart, / die man nie dâ vor versneit' / 'The first whiskers of their beards were showing; these had never been cut before' (1544–5) – then twelve elderly ones – 'an houbte und an barte gar / was in daz hâr ergrîset' / 'The hair on their heads and that of their beards had gone grey' (1594–5).

Only then is he taken to see the ladies (who are not being ill-treated).[75] These contrasting beard references do not simply function as elements within a broader rhetorical scheme. They make clear that the compassion Gerhard feels for his fellow Christians is grounded above all in his respect for their humanity and his ability to empathize with them as men: just as the young have so much life ahead of them, so the old and venerable deserve a better end.[76] Both groups are suffering, and their suffering is reflected in different ways in their facial hair.

A similar strategy informs a second episode, where Gerhard prevents his beloved son from marrying the fairest of the captive ladies (a Norwegian princess) at the last possible moment, when her long-lost betrothed, a young king of England by the name of Willehalm(!), suddenly appears. An even lengthier description of Willehalm's wretched condition is involved, which once again privileges details pertaining to his (first) beard growth – 'ein dünner bart, der was niht lanc, / wan er dô êrst an im entspranc' / 'a thin beard, it was not long, for it had only just sprouted forth' (3721–2) – that has still never been cropped (3723–4). Gerhard's own son is never accorded any such portrayal, which should perhaps act as a reminder to us that although Gerhard is, seemingly, telling his story to the emperor, the rhetorical function of all the details within it is matter of communication between the poet and the text's recipients. Gerhard's beard-focussed narration is therefore only partly consistent with his characterization as a latter-day mercantile patriarch. His son remains nondescript to prevent the recipients of the work from feeling too much empathy for him. We are meant to sympathize with the English prince before being impressed by Gerhard's altruism.

Other poets deploy multiple beard references to accentuate the changes their protagonists undergo in the course of events set over many years. One good example of this may be found in *Mai und Beaflor* (c. 1250–1300), a courtly romance concerning the exemplary love between a (Christian) princess of Rome, Beaflor, and a Greek count, Mai. These two get married relatively early in the story but suffer greatly because of the machinations of Mai's wicked mother, as a result of which they are separated for eight years (when Mai mistakenly believes his wife is dead). In terms of Mai's beardedness, this period represents something of a turning point. Having played the role of the perfect young knight, celebrated as valiant and 'sunder part' / 'beardless' both on the tournament field (3347) and in advance of a Crusade-like battle (4333), Mai goes on to repel a Saracen invasion of Spain just like another 'Rennwart' (4684) or 'Gahmuret' (6344). In his subsequent misery and self-neglect, however, he becomes a stranger to himself by leading the life of a penitent and, in true ascetic fashion, growing a beard down over his chest (7851–2). This drastic change in Mai's appearance is not really thematized when the couple see each other again, except perhaps for comic effect when their eight-year-old son voices his mistrust of the 'bartoht' / 'bearded' (8827, 8842) stranger who has upset his mother so.[77] When, shortly afterwards, Mai becomes emperor in Rome he does have his beard shaved off (9601–2), not so much out of deference for Roman (as opposed to Greek) attitudes towards facial hair, but 'durch die frawen sein, / durch Beafloren, dy kayserin' / 'for the sake of his lady, for the sake of Beaflor, the empress' (9602–3). This beard removal, which returns Mai to the man Beaflor treasured the thought of some eight years earlier,[78] seems like a rather singular act of devotion which prioritizes the couple's relationship over any notion of bearded majesty (see Chapter 2). It is not inconceivable that here, right at the end of the work, the not particularly original poet of *Mai und Beaflor* finally opted to innovate by finding a way, more effective than poetic, of overturning Wolfram's association of love with beard growth.

More cogent perhaps, if somewhat fewer in number, are the beard references which occur in *Wilhalm von Wenden* (c. 1287–97) by one Ulrich von Etzenbach, another Wolfram enthusiast.[79] These serve to add to the characterization of the leading male protagonist, yet another Wilhalm (or Willehalm), albeit a heathen one, a young Slavonic count who abandons his virtuous wife, having sold off their infant twin sons, in order to pursue his goal of becoming a Christian by making the journey to Jerusalem. There this Wilhalm is baptized and fights for his new faith for many years, before he returns and, having been reunited with his whole family, brings Christianity to the Slavonic East. He arrives in Jerusalem, the perfect image of a young nobleman on the cusp of manhood: 'etswâ ûzdrungen im die gran, / doch niht ze dicke alumb den munt'/ 'His [first] beard hairs were sprouting if not very thickly around the mouth' (2890–1), and leaves 24 years later, having fought ceaselessly against the infidel, with a 'grâwen bart und blankez hâr' / 'grey beard and white hair' (5932). This staggering transformation is not, the author-narrator assures his listeners, the result of ageing, but the harsh price that such toil (over the years) exacts from young men in search of glory: 'ich hânz an rittern selbe gesehen. / also Wilhalm was beschehen' / 'I myself have seen this happen to knights. This is what had happened to Wilhalm' (5940–1). References to Wilhalm's beard seem calculated to elicit the sympathy of the work's recipients at significant moments in the narrative, and this emotional effect gathers momentum from pivotal scene to pivotal scene. Towards the end of the story the tears that pour from Wilhalm's eyes and soak his grey beard (6952–5) at the sight of his long-lost sons, erstwhile robbers in the forest, are not just a moving expression of the guilt he feels both as a father and as a husband, they indirectly lead Wilhalm's estranged wife to realize who he must be, which in turn paves the way for their reconciliation.

Christians (and heathens)

Poets such as Rudolf von Ems and Ulrich von Etzenbach go to some lengths to demonstrate the courtliness and nobility of the heathen figures in their stories. Nevertheless, details pertaining to beardlessness and beardedness tend to relate to Christians. In other words, it is above all the humanity of Christian protagonists which poets encourage their audiences to identify and sympathize with. There are one or two exceptions such as the beardless Flore or Wilhalm (of the Wends) with his first beard growth; but even these virtuous young heathen men are evidently Christians-in-the-making and are duly baptized in the course of their tales. Wolfram is evidently far more radical in his *Willehalm* when he thematizes the beards of heathens – whether in terms of courtly love (Terramer) or age and kinship (Purrel) – who remain heathens and have no interest in becoming Christian.

This crucial difference is set in even sharper relief by two works, composed independently of one another some forty to fifty years after *Willehalm*, which seek to complement Wolfram's fragmentary text by telling the stories of what happened before and after the battles on Alischanz.[80] Ulrich von dem Türlin's *Arabel* (c. 1260–70), a freely invented work, offers the prequel, dealing with the love affair between Willehalm and Arabel (she helps him to escape from the dungeons of her husband Tybald), her baptism (as Kyburg) and their marriage. Ulrich von Türheim's *Rennewart* (after 1254), which is based largely on *chanson de geste* source material, is the lengthy sequel, exploring Rennewart's subsequent life and adventures, as well as those of his son Malefer (born to Alyse who dies in childbirth), and Willehalm's experiences as monk and hermit. Within two or three decades (c. 1290–1300) all three works came to be compiled and transmitted as a Willehalm trilogy of sorts, a 'superwork' of great prestige.[81] In spite of their perceived unity – after all they share many of the same figures and both Ulrichs were extremely familiar with Wolfram's text – the three narratives in question are very different in their literary make-up, and this is reflected in their beard references.

As far as Ulrich von dem Türlin's *Arabel* is concerned, the narrative interest in courtly love (Willehalm and Arabel fall in love over a series of games of chess), courtly ceremony and festivity (not least the magnificent social event of Arabel's baptism) mean that on the whole greater emphasis is placed on female hair, whether as a matter of individual or collective beauty.[82] There are only three beard references in this work of some 10,000 lines. The first pertains to Willehalm who, following his capture in battle, spends eight years in heathen captivity. When Tybald has him brought before Arabel and four other heathen queens, who are all curious to see this famous Christian foe, they are quite struck by his appearance: 'langen bart und reidez hâr / nam man an dem helde war' / 'They gazed at the hero's long beard and curly locks' (83,30–1). This image of Willehalm is an incongruous one. His long beard betokens his hardship, while his lovely locks serve as a reminder that he is still handsome enough to attract rather than repel Arabel. Such a description may be rather inconsistent but its purpose is to fulfil two thematic requirements at the same time. As a beard reference it is a one-off, this being symptomatic of a most un-Wolfram-like short-term interest. In the subsequent course of the narrative this long beard of Willehalm's is never mentioned again, not even when Arabel tearfully kisses him on the cheek (130,8–9) shortly after he emerges from prison – a scene with a clear parallel in *Willehalm*, when a bristly Willehalm kisses Gyburg upon his return to Oransche (as 'lamented' by Wolfram's narrator).

The two other beard references in *Arabel* are also one-offs. However, these do relate in a meaningful way to Wolfram's text. Both occur in the latter part of the work, when the news breaks of Willehalm's escape and return to France. In the first instance, Heimerich, who has not really featured in the story before now, reacts by appealing to God, testifying to just how much he has suffered and aged in recent years: 'mîn hâr, mîn bart ist worden grîse, / sît daz ich Kylloys verlôs' / 'My hair, my beard has gone grey in the time since I lost Willehalm' (201,14–15). These lines represent more than just a nod to Wolfram's characterization of Heimrich; they pre-empt it by providing an explanation for his appearance, marking the first step along his way to becoming the white-bearded patriarch we know in *Willehalm*.[83] When Heimerich himself relays the news to the royal court, the expressions of joy on the part of queen and king are followed by that of a certain Fivianz, whose beauty and tender years the author-narrator is at pains to point out: 'dô sprach der klâre Fivianz, / des kintheit noch niht granen warf' / 'Then fair Fivianz spoke, whose young age had not yet caused any beard to grow' (211,10–11). Beardlessness is thus presented as the defining feature of Fivianz from the moment he first enters the story, effectively supplying an objective starting point for the subjective and emotional references to be found in *Willehalm*. Ulrich von dem Türlin, we may conclude, is quite capable of responding in kind to Wolfram's use of the beard motif, when it suits; that is, when it is a matter of introducing two figures – Christians and kinsmen of Willehalm – who will go on to play such an important role in Wolfram's famous story.

Ulrich von Türheim's *Rennewart*, a real blockbuster of a work, sets a very different tone, depicting in some 36,000 lines an almost endless series of invasions and battles, in both West and East, and over several generations (Rennewart's son Malefer comes to play a starring role, for example). Informed by a more primitive religiosity – certainly in comparison with Wolfram – and at times by burlesque comedy, Ulrich von Türheim's narrative also brings the lives of all the familiar characters to a close, taking particular interest in the attempts both Rennewart and Willehalm make to do penance and become monks. Based largely, if not always very closely, on several *chansons de geste* – the exact versions of which escape us today – the focus in *Rennewart* well and truly returns to male hair, most especially the grey or white hair of old(er) men and the tonsures of monks.[84] References to beards (there are fourteen in total) are concentrated in the opening and closing phases of the narrative.

The first part of *Rennewart* completes an alternative account of the second Alischanz battle (in accordance with another version of *Aliscans*),[85] before relating Rennewart's baptism, knighting and marriage with Alyse. Four references to beards in the first 4,500 lines draw attention to two old(er) men. Indeed, an implicit comparison is drawn between Terramer and Heimrich in two separate speeches, by Rennewart, no less, who suggests that it is high time for Heimrich to hang up his sword ('sin bart der ist von jaren wiz' / 'his beard is white with [all his] years' 2107), having already tried in vain to persuade his father, Terramer, to abandon his gods and embrace Christianity while he still can: 'vater, du bist an jaren alt, / von vil tagen din bart ist wiz' / 'Father, you are old in years. Your beard is white from [all your] many days' (346–7). After the battle is over and Heimrich returns to the royal court, he is shown affectionate respect by Alyse, who kisses him sweetly 'durch sinen bart vil grisen' / 'through his grey beard' (3921). Ulrich later refers to Heimrich 'beard-first', playing on his audience's knowledge of this stock character when describing the welcome given to Willehalm and Rennewart back at the French royal court: Rennewart is approached by 'ein man der was gris / an haupte und an dem barte' / 'a man with grey hair on his head and in his beard' (4512–13), whose identity the narrator then teasingly reveals: 'nu hoeret wer er waere: / ez was der lobebaere / von Naribon Heymrich' / 'Now hear who this was: it was that praiseworthy man, Heymrich of

Naribon' (4515–17). The form and ethos of such references are entirely in keeping with Wolfram and are most likely of Ulrich's own devising. For recipients well versed in *Willehalm*, details like this may even have served to demonstrate Ulrich's credentials as a Wolfram devotee who is up to the task of completing the work begun by his master.[86]

The final part of *Rennewart* depicts Willehalm's last deeds and sanctity, and owes much by way of content, if not always tone, to one version or another of the *Moniage Guillaume*.[87] By this time both Willehalm and Kyburg are old and grey-haired (33217–19) and fearful of death, so they retire to separate religious houses where they pray for each other's souls. Willehalm's retirement is eventful, to say the least, one gauge of this being the six references to his beard that occur in the next 3,000 lines.

Instructed by his abbot to protect the property of the monastery (the same house that Rennewart joined many years earlier) Willehalm encounters a band of thieves stealing wood. They insult and threaten him ('ez geriwet iuch alten baerting' / 'You will regret this, you old beardy!' 34007), and then he brutally kills four of them.

Following the news of Kyburg's death Willehalm is so distraught that he becomes a hermit in the wilderness, where he is kept alive miraculously by God. During this period his hair grows incredibly long and his grey beard turns white (34309–12).

Called to help King Louis, when Paris comes under attack from Terramer's son, the unsightly Willehalm makes himself presentable – a far cry from his expedition to the royal court in *Willehalm* – to meet the king: 'der hete daz har und den bart / wol gestraelt und getwagen' / 'He had combed and washed his hair and beard' (34721–3).

Willehalm puts the heathens to flight without even fighting, whereupon he is directed by God to build his own monastery (near Montpellier). Thwarted by the devil in his attempts to build a bridge nearby, he swears by his own beard – 'sam mir des Willehelmes bart' (35583) – to make the devil pay, which he duly does by tossing the fiend into the river.[88]

Obliged once more to defend this second monastery against robbers, he is forbidden from using violence unless they try to steal his undergarments. Thus, he does not retaliate when one robber grabs him by the beard and tells him to remove his habit (36026–7). But he bludgeons them all to death when they tell him to strip naked.

King Louis has Willehalm's sister buried at his monastery before bidding a tearful farewell. For his part Willehalm weeps so copiously that the tears pour down his beard and soak his habit (36238–40).

This portrayal of Willehalm clearly seeks to satisfy two complementary narrative interests: the comedy of incongruity surrounding the hero as monk (the so-called moniage motif),[89] and the demonstration of Willehalm's sanctity by virtue of his special relationship with God. Although this part of the story does feature (yet) another heathen invasion, Ulrich, in stark contrast to the longer version of the *Moniage Guillaume*, deals with this plot point in perfunctory fashion.[90] As a result the antagonism within Christian society between religious and non-religious looms larger here. Within this scheme Willehalm's beard connotes variously age, religiosity, vigorous manhood and compassion. Indeed, the trials and tribulations of Willehalm's beard mark out, not always very subtly, his transition from older hero to saint.

To beard or not to beard

The texts which make up the *Willehalm* trilogy provide a very mixed picture in terms of the poetic strategies they bring to bear on beards. The material reality of the manuscripts containing the trilogy, however, is such that the three texts were almost always designed to look the same.[91] The impression of coherence and unity is accentuated in several lavish codices of the fourteenth century by virtue of their miniatures.[92] Just as the artistic style(s) on display differ from codex to codex, so the scenes chosen for illustration and their distribution throughout the trilogy varies, although there is inevitably some overlapping. As far as beards are concerned, a review of the different cycles of miniatures soon makes clear that, for recipients of the trilogy, the literary uses of the beard motif in the narratives themselves were complemented visually by beards in the pictures, albeit in ways which change from manuscript to manuscript.[93]

The earliest of these prestige books – Vienna, ÖNB, Cod. 2670, dated 1320 – also happens to be the only one whose cycle of illustrations is complete.[94] Throughout the codex the predominant type for male figures (when not helmeted or wearing a coif), whether Christian or heathen, is that of idealized courtly youthfulness (beardless and with golden-yellow locks). Unsurprisingly, Heimrich is the most frequently occurring bearded figure, depicted from first (fol. 5v) to last (291r) as a (whitish) greybeard. As befits his status Karl is assigned a light-brown beard on his deathbed (6v), whilst Louis is uniformly portrayed as beardless, a continual reminder perhaps that he is Karl's son.[95] Terramer is beardless too until fol. 202r, whereafter he is given a light-brown beard (216r, 297v), that is, one which matches Karl's but which conveys nothing of the old age suggested by the text (implicitly in *Willehalm*, explicitly in *Rennewart*). Attention to textual detail in the matter of beards was evidently not always of primary concern here. Rennewart is depicted by means of the beardless courtly type throughout, even on fol. 113r where both a rubric and the instructions to the artist expressly draw attention to this figure's beardedness: 'Hie wirfet Rennbart [sic!] den choch in daz fewer daz er im den part het verprant' / 'Here Rennbart tosses the cook into the fire because he burned his beard'.[96] Another(?) hand rather clumsily adds a black beard to the face of Rennewart the monk on fol. 236r, and the same kind of 'correction' is undertaken some 55 miniatures later on fol. 336v (Figure 3.1), where the messy semblance of a brown beard is added to Willehalm as (beardless) monk.

Originally, in spite of all the narrative detail to the contrary in the first two parts of the trilogy, Willehalm is indeed portrayed as beardless (in identical fashion to so many of the other figures) until towards the end of *Rennewart* (and the codex). Here, on fol. 339r (Figure 3.2), his special

Figure 3.1 Willehalm becomes a monk (Ulrich von Türheim's *Rennewart*). Vienna, ÖNB, Cod. 2670, fol. 336v.

Figure 3.2 God provides Willehalm the hermit with food (Ulrich von Türheim's *Rennewart*). Vienna, ÖNB, Cod. 2670, fol. 339r.

status as saintly hermit is spectacularly rendered by incredibly long golden hair and a golden beard, attributes which mark him out as a figure of singular importance in the story as a whole, if only on this page. (In the final miniature (351r) the dead Willehalm is portrayed once more as a beardless monk.) Willehalm's transformation from greybeard to whitebeard in this episode, as emphasized by the text of *Rennewart* itself, appears to have been displaced in the accompanying miniature as part of a process of thematic reprioritization.

In two of the other luxury manuscripts in question (Kassel, Wolfenbüttel) the cycles of miniatures are incomplete. Nevertheless, the extant illuminations reveal a number of alternative strategies and approaches to the beard as an iconographic motif.

Of the 479(!) planned miniatures in Kassel, UB/LMB, 2° Ms. poet. et roman. 1 (dated 1334), only those for *Arabel* were executed and a significant portion of these remain unfinished.[97] This is regrettable, not least because the relationship between text and image here is a subtle one, revealing both a certain sensitivity towards narrative detail and an independence of thought.[98] Unlike in Vienna, Cod. 2670, the sequence of miniatures depicting Willehalm's imprisonment, for instance, sees him grow a beard: he enters Tybalt's prison tower beardless (fols 13r, 14r), grows a (tidy) beard in his cell (15r), and is shown to the queens and Tybalt in the garden with longer hair and a fuller beard (18v) before being returned to prison (19v (i)) a bearded man. Thereafter the artist keeps a close eye on Willehalm's beardedness quite independently of the text. In the two-part miniature on fol. 22r (Figure 3.3) a somewhat lesser-bearded Willehalm is allowed out of prison and offered splendid (heathen) garments (i); then he dines (ii), now dressed in these same garments and beardless, his courtly rehabilitation evidently imagined here as a process which involves shaving.

The next five miniatures, portraying his games of chess and religious discussions with Arabel (22v, 24r, 25r), his return to the tower (27r) and four different moments pertaining to his subsequent escape (28v),[99] all present Willehalm as the perfect vision of beardless male beauty. Only when he is shown being escorted to Arabel's ship (Figure 3.4), dressed 'in vrouwen kleyderen' / 'in ladies' garments', as the rubric puts it (29v), is there a change of strategy. Now beneath a fine hood Willehalm's face is

Figure 3.3 Willehalm is allowed out of prison and dressed in heathen clothes (Ulrich von dem Türlin's *Arabel*). Kassel, UB/LMB, 2° Ms. poet. et roman. 1, fol. 22r.

dotted with black stubble, as if some additional reaffirmation of the hero's masculinity were required; the figure is otherwise clearly identifiable as Willehalm from the sword he is clutching.

Wolfenbüttel, HAB, cod. 30. 12 Aug. 2° (c. 1360–70) contains full-page pictures for both *Arabel* (some fourteen in number) and much of *Willehalm* (a total of 27), inserted into the codex on separate leaves.[100] Although generally regarded as less technically accomplished as those found elsewhere in the transmission of the trilogy, here too there are manifest signs that considerable attention was paid by the artist to the bearding of certain figures both in response to and independently of the actual text. Thus the very first miniature (*Arabel*, fol. 5r), a stock scene in which Heimrich sends his seven sons out into the world to seek their own fortune, does not just present Heimrich as a greybeard already (anticipating his role to come) but carefully distinguishes between his younger and older sons, attributing beards (of differing colours) to the latter. The depiction of Willehalm, by contrast, evolves: he is captured in battle and taken to Tybalt in *Arabel* as a beardless knight (10r, 13r), but the later

Figure 3.4 Willehalm escapes in disguise with Arabel (Ulrich von dem Türlin's *Arabel*). Kassel, UB/LMB, 2° Ms. poet. et roman. 1, fol. 29v.

events of *Willehalm* see him blond-bearded (93r, 100v).[101] Moreover, for the first time in any of the manuscripts described here, Rennewart is clearly shown to have the beginnings of a beard (138v) by the time he undertakes the journey to Oransche. Main figures aside, the artist also uses beards to help underscore the difference between the two warring sides: in several of the pictures devoted to the first battle in *Willehalm* (80r, 90r, 97r, 100v), the heathens have dark hair and long dark beards, while the hair and (occasional) beards of the Christians are noticeably lighter and shorter.[102]

A fourth codex, Vienna, ÖNB, Cod. ser. nova 2643 (dated 1387) – an especially lavish production for King Wenceslaus (IV) of Bohemia (and German king from 1376) – represents something a little different in that, entirely by design, its numerous and luxuriantly decorated historiated initials (over 240 in total) illustrate *Rennewart* only.[103] Very many of the scenes depicted are packed with bearded characters, Christian and heathen, amounting to a veritable gallery of beards of all shapes and styles, culminating in the white patriarchal beard of the hermit Willehalm, who is depicted in a series of 22 'miniatures' towards the end of the codex (from 401r onwards). The text of *Rennewart* opens and closes with an image of Ulrich von Türheim at prayer (161r, 421r) within a large and elaborate capital 'H' (the first letter in lines 1 and 36509 respectively). In both instances the poet is presented as beardless, a detail which no doubt served to reinforce the idea that Ulrich himself is not the ultimate literary authority in the context of this material. This honour goes to none other than Wolfram, as repeatedly stated by Ulrich throughout his work,[104] and as visualized on fol. 313r in a historiated 'O' – the line as a whole reads 'O kunstericher Wolfram' / 'O ingenious Wolfram' (21711) – where a white-bearded master poet in exotic garb is pictured, writing implements in hand, at a lectern.[105]

Conclusion

It is easy to lose sight of Wolfram's masterclass in beard referencing in *Willehalm* amid so much other relevant material, both narrative and pictorial, which accrues to it in the course of transmission. Later poets who engaged with Wolfram's text more closely, such as the two Ulrichs, evidently recognized the significance of the beard motif, which they replicated, to varying degrees and in different ways, in their own stories. Ulrich von Türheim's reception of this aspect of male characterization (in *Rennewart*) is especially important, for he shows himself more than capable of emulating Wolfram's thematic preoccupation with compassionate humanity, whether in respect of Terramer, Heimrich or Willehalm. On the other hand, two episodes from Willehalm's life as a monk – his violent encounters with thieves and robbers – are shaped by a rough-and-ready comedy derived from the *Moniage Guillaume*, which momentarily allows recipients to enjoy the prospect of Willehalm being manhandled by his beard before due retribution is taken. Such slapstick comedy feels very far removed from Wolfram's own poetic approach to beards, which is distinguished by more imaginative strategies and by an insistence on human dignity, on empathy with young(er) and old(er) men. This thematic agenda seems all the more significant for its inclusion of male heathen figures who are not necessarily Christians-in-waiting, and in respect of whom beardedness is anything but a marker of otherness.

Notes

1 'When my first whiskers appeared Love held me enthralled even more than any of my gods.' All translations of this text are taken from *Wolfram von Eschenbach: Willehalm*, translated by Gibbs and Johnson (1984).
2 The depiction of Rother could not be more different, as not a word is lost on his beard growth. The only reference to this king's hair comes towards the end of the work, when, many years later, Berchter (who by this time has hair as white as snow) exhorts Rother to think of his soul and do penance for his sins: 'du grawist, herre min' (5121). In this coming-of-age narrative the beard function is thus assigned to vassal rather than to king.
3 Just like Blanscandiz in the *Rolandslied*, Berchter is referred to disparagingly as 'ienir alde mit deme barde' (4006).
4 Bastert, *Helden als Heilige*, 87–8.
5 The spelling of the characters' names is taken from the Penguin Classics translation by Gibbs and Johnson.
6 Kiening, *Reflexion – Narration*, 86–94; Ashcroft, 'dicke Karel wart genant', 42–3.
7 Cf. 108,12–15; 51,11–17; 455,6–17.
8 For balanced views of Wolfram's portrayal of the heathen 'other' see Kleppel, *Erzählen von Fremdem*, 45–235; McFarland, 'Giburc's dilemma'.
9 Bumke, *Wolfram von Eschenbach*, 215–32, 358–75.
10 Barthel, *Empathie, Mitleid, Sympathie*, 83–269.
11 As emphasized by Bulang and Kellner, 'Wolframs *Willehalm*'.
12 Ernst, 'Differentielle Leiblichkeit', 2002; Brüggen, 'Körperschönheit'.
13 Young men: 15,2; 46,1–2; 93,24. Old men: 145,14; 249,16; 266,3; 278,22; 421,18; 431,2.
14 Only one heathen army, men from the Ganges, is described as less than human, with skin like horn and barking like dogs (35,13–25). See Kleppel, *Erzählen von Fremdem*, 126–33.
15 See also Kugler, 'Alte Ritter, junge Ritter'; Kerth, 'Wolframs Greise', 2015, 68–75.
16 Greenfield, *Vivianz*, 183–5.
17 Vivianz is 'des marcgrâven swester sun' (23,1).
18 Chinca, 'Willehalm at Laon'; Bumke, 'Emotion und Körperzeichen', 2003.
19 This alarming sight is duly reported back to King Louis: 'ouch ist im ninder alsô glanz / sîn bart, sîn vel, noch sîn hâr, / daz man in dürfe nennen klâr' (128,20–2).
20 This is the subject of the *chanson de geste* entitled *Le coronemenz Looïs*. These events are explicitly alluded to in Wolfram's text when Willehalm later reproaches King Louis for his ingratitude (145,16–29).
21 Gall, *Erzählen von 'unmâze'*, 97–100.
22 Ernst, 'Differentielle Leiblichkeit', 2002, 203.

23 This return of order is marked by attention to (female) hair once more, both in Giburc's instructions to her ladies to make themselves attractive (to men) again (247,2–5) and her own stated intent to revert to her conventional role as the leading lady at Orange (248,3–8).
24 Wolfram engages in the same kind of bawdy humour in *Parzival*: Antikonie's maidservants (424,3–6) and Orgeluse (644,1), and in *Titurel*: Herzeloyde (85,4).
25 Cf. 'ir liebstem vater' (252,29); 'ir gedienter vater' (268,7). The thematic link between sorrow and kinship in Willehalm is explored by Koch, *Trauer und Identität*, 80–158.
26 This scene is full of passing references to Heimrich's advanced age and white hair: 264,23; 265,5; 265,17; 266,3.
27 Cf. 242,12–13 (Heimrich); 311,4–5 (Giburc).
28 In an earlier scene Giburc's tears pour over Willehalm's face while he is asleep, although there is no mention of any beard here (102,21–4).
29 The iconography of the ages of man, a widespread artistic theme throughout the Middle Ages, uses beards in analogous fashion; see Sears, *The Ages of Man*, 80–94 and figs 26–9 (images from an Austrian prayer book, c. 1200).
30 Rennewart's beard has already been the subject of detailed analysis; see Lofmark, *Rennewart*, 151–6.
31 The scene in which the sweethearts kiss makes no mention of Rennewart's beard growth (213,9–25).
32 Knapp, *Rennewart*, 141.
33 Lofmark, *Rennewart*, 144–9; Kiening, *Reflexion – Narration*, 98–9.
34 Rennewart's first beard hair is never actually described (before it is singed). Physical properties, such as softness, are left to the audience's imagination. In the Low German *chanson de geste* known as *Morant und Galie* (c. 1230–60) the term 'garze' / 'milk-haired' (2009, 2190) is used to denote another young man (with his first beard).
35 Schultz, 'Bodies that don't matter', 94; Urban, *Gleiches zu Gleichem*, 324–6.
36 Cf. 269,28–30.
37 Rennewart's earlier lament concerning his singed beard goes on to refer to Terramer's ten sons as his brothers (288,3–20).
38 When the cooks at Laon singe the hair on Rennewart's head (198,20–1), Willehalm makes good the damage with a haircut (199,2–5).
39 'dem was besenget sîn junger bart, / des harnasch was tiuwer unde klâr, / er selbe was starc und wol gevar' (311,16–18).
40 Term coined by Kern, 'Heiliges Leiden', 8.
41 Barthel, *Empathie, Mitleid, Sympathie*, 228–9; Kohnen, 'Motivierung', 62–72.
42 'Heimrîch was undern ougen blôz: / diu barbier ez niht umbeslôz, / sîn helm et hete ein nasebant' (408,5–7). Cf. also the commentary in Heinzle's edition 1069–70.
43 Kleppel, *Erzählen von Fremdem*, 118–21.
44 Bastert, *Helden als Heilige*, 186.
45 See also Greenfield, *Vivianz*, 73–6.
46 For a somewhat sceptical overview see Bumke, *Wolfram von Eschenbach*, 384–8.
47 Cf. 2158, 2482, 3030, 3695.
48 This action evidently belonged to the story of Renoard before *Aliscans*. It is present in part two (G2) of the *Chançun de Willame* (2684–8, 2879–80).
49 Cf. *Aliscans* 873, 885. G2 of the *Chançun de Willame* is also markedly different to G1 in this respect, when Willame laments Vivien's 'teindre meissele' / 'tender cheek' (2002).
50 Cf. 4100–2, 7922, 8329–35.
51 See Volfing, 'Narrative continuity?'
52 'Bien en i a plus de cinc cens, / Les uns barbez, les autres non: / Cent qui n'ont barbe ne guernon / Et cent autres qui barbes poignant / Et cent qui reent et rooignent / Lor barbes chascune semaine, / S'en i a cent plus blans que laine / Et cent qui vont mellant de caines' (7566–73).
53 Cf. 211,16; 227,28; 244,7–10; 307,7. See also Rostek, *Bedeutung von Jugend*, 257–64.
54 See also Schultz, *The Knowledge of Childhood*, 120–1.
55 See also Kerth, 'Wolframs Greise', 2015, 56–65.
56 The facial similarity between Anfortas and his sister Repanse de Schoye is emphasized, following the former's miraculous recovery to health and beauty (813,1–5). Detail pertaining to Anfortas's beard is elided at this point.
57 Gawan's beard is alluded to obliquely by Urjans, who steals his horse and then mocks him for reacting in a manner more befitting a child 'denn ein bartohter man' (525,7).

58 'ich hete im geholfen vür wâr, / und waere ich im gewesen bî' (3310–11).

59 The portrayal of the fisherman in the *Vie du pape saint Grégoire* (c. 1150) does not feature an equivalent beard reference. Arnold von Lübeck's Latin reworking of Hartmann's text, the *Gesta Gregorii Peccatoris* (c. 1210), retains it: 'Ad hec ille luminibus / ploratu humectantibus / barba stillante lacrimis / sic respondebat flebilis' / 'At this with eyes moist from weeping and his beard dripping with tears he dolefully replied' (IV, xix: 17–20).

60 Ernst, *Der 'Gregorius' Hartmanns von Aue*, 44–53.

61 Schulze, *Das Nibelungenlied*, 162–76.

62 Identity is often a key thematic aspect of scenes of sorrow and grief in medieval (German) literature; see Koch, *Trauer und Identität*, 68–78.

63 Cf. B 371,2–3; B 1225,3.

64 Cf. B 2012,2–3; B 2300,1–2.

65 The extended bouts of lamentation and mourning in the *Klage* do not include the tearful beard motif. The sole beard reference here is of a different order altogether and is used to draw attention to the blood-soaked features of one of Dietrich's own dead men, the (younger) warrior Wolfhart: 'dô sach er Wolfharte / mit roetelohtem barte / gevallen nider in daz bluot' (1669–71). See also Coxon, 'Heroes and their beards', 2018, 28–32.

66 Cf. Herbort von Fritzlar's *Liet von Troye*: 'Die nase lac disem vf den granen / Dem lac die swarte / Vf dem buch bi dem barte' (5848–50).

67 Cf. 1352; 1381; 1383; 1499–1502.

68 Six versions of this verse-couplet tale have survived. The beard reference in question is preserved in the text transmitted by the early 'Mären' manuscripts H and K.

69 In version I of *Die halbe Decke* the encounter is summarily dealt with in one line: 'ain tail ez bracht dem alten' (104).

70 By chance one of the fragments of the *Trierer Floyris* preserves this line too: 'her ne hatte bart no die grane' (232).

71 See also Gilbert, 'Boys will be ... what?', 1997, 41–2; Gaunt, *Gender and Genre*, 89–90; Urban, *Gleiches zu Gleichem*, 194–6, 244–6.

72 In Priester Wernher's *Maria* (dateable to 1172) God himself appears to Joseph and Mary in the form of 'ein knappe schone ân bart' (3697) who accompanies them on the way to Bethlehem.

73 In medieval historiography Otto II was commonly given this epithet. See Neudeck, *Erzählen von Kaiser Otto*, 279 n. 813, 288–92.

74 'sîn hâr was grâ reht als ein îs / an houbte und an barte gar' (769–70).

75 The ladies may be weeping but they are still beautiful (1643–53); the royal princess in their midst is the fairest of all and her hair is still utterly pristine (1686–7).

76 As reflected upon by Gerhard himself (1604–15).

77 The comedy of this scene is further suggested by the laughter the boy's words elicit from a bystander (8853).

78 'Der werde ist noch sunder bart. / von weibe nie geporn wart / So schoner man, so suziu fruht' (7662–4).

79 Ulrich von Etzenbach pays tribute to Wolfram halfway through the work by suggesting that Wolfram would have done a better job of honouring Ulrich's patrons (King Wenceslaus IV of Bohemia and his wife) than he himself could ever do (4709–15).

80 Kreft, *Perspektivenwechsel*.

81 Bastert, *Helden als Heilige*, 191–214.

82 Individual: 67,9–13; 70,10–13; 72,28–73,1; 78,29–79,6; 93,3; 320,28–9. Collective: 226,1–6; 292,19–20; 300,30–1; 310,22–5. Ulrich von dem Türlin also takes a leaf out of Wolfram's book with a jocular reference to Arabel's pubic hair (280,14–20).

83 The notion that this news will have a rejuvenating effect appears only to apply to Irmenschart, Heimerich's wife (201,28–31; 206,29–30).

84 By comparison references to female hair are few and far between (there are seven in total), and details pertaining to the beautiful hair of courtly ladies are conspicuous by their absence. The closest the author-narrator comes to delivering such detail is when he affirms that none of the ladies gathered at Malefer's wedding has grey hair (32196). Having said that, Ulrich von Türheim does not fail to include bawdy reference to pubic hair either, whether for titillating (4222–4; 7342–4) or grotesquely humorous (pudenda of giantess: 30871–3) effect.

85 Ulrich von Türheim's sources are discussed in detail by Hennings, *Französische Heldenepik*, 264–501.

86 As per Ulrich's 'mission statement' which concludes his prologue (156–68).

87 Hennings, *Französische Heldenepik*, 421–87; Bastert, *Helden als Heilige*, 304–7.

88 In *Rennewart* Willehalm grabs the devil 'bi dem hare' (35587). In the later prose rendition of this text, the so-called *Buch vom Heiligen Wilhelm* (c. 1450–70), the devil is seized 'by dem bartt' (244,19).

89 See Hennings, *Französische Heldenepik*, 517–25.

90 The longer version of the *Moniage Guillaume* also features numerous references to the beards of the leading heathens, not least in the form of their oaths (2948, 3104, 3526, 3537, 4013, 4303, 4949, 5014).

91 For an overview see the essay by Diemer and Diemer in the *Willehalm* edition by Heinzle, 1093–1100.

92 Curschmann, 'Wort – Schrift – Bild', 437.

93 The so-called 'Große Bilderhandschrift' (c. 1270), known fragments of which preserve *Willehalm* only (Munich, BSB, Cgm 193/III; Nuremberg, Germ. Nationalmuseum, Graph. Slg, Kapsel 1607, Hz 1104–5), has been comprehensively analysed in Manuwald, *Medialer Dialog*. In the Munich fragments Heimrich (fols Av, 2r), a Jewish figure (1v) and Terramer (4v) are bearded. http://mdz-nbn-resolving.de/urn:nbn:de:bvb:12-bsb00012911-3. Accessed 10 March 2021.

94 See the two-volume facsimile edition by Knapp, *Willehalm: Codex Vindobonensis 2670 der Österreichischen Nationalbibliothek*.

95 Fols 40v, 46v, 56r, 88r, 92r, 93r, 96r, 168v, 200r.

96 The same line is repeated (in black ink) as an instruction to the artist: 'Hie wirfet Rennbart den choch in daz fewer daz er verprint zetot daz er in het part vnd haut verprant' (fol. 113r).

97 https://orka.bibliothek.uni-kassel.de/viewer/image/1300457892891/1/. Accessed 9 March 2021.

98 The portrayal of Heimrich is a case in point: whereas he is at first beardless (fol. 2v), no different to his beardless sons (5r, 5v), he is presented as older, by virtue of a cropped beard, on fol. 6v.

99 The miniature on fol. 28v is actually made up of four mini-scenes surrounding Willehalm's escape, including Arabel's kiss; he is depicted as beardless in all four.

100 The Wolfenbüttel *Willehalm* miniatures are reproduced and discussed in Heinzle's edition: 1100–11.

101 Cf. also fols 106r, 122r, 132r, 135r, 138v.

102 Long beards are a characteristic attribute of heathens in the *Arabel* miniatures too, whether in battle, fighting beardless Christians (fol. 10r), or at court (13r). Black-and-white images of these miniatures are reproduced in Milde, *Mittelalterliche Handschriften*, 146–9.

103 Digital reproduction of black-and-white microfilm: http://data.onb.ac.at/rep/1000636A. Accessed 10 March 2021.

104 Cf. 156–68, 4534–46, 21711–25.

105 See Wachinger, 'Wolfram von Eschenbach am Schreibpult', 1992.

4
Beards, teaching and learning: 'Sangspruchdichtung'

> Her Bart, ir zemt den mannen wol
> und niendert baz, daz nemt vür vol.
>
> Frauenlob ('Langer Ton') V,28: 13–14[1]

The literary beards discussed so far occur as thematically resonant narrative detail in stories of varying scale and epic dimension. They contribute to the characterization of certain figures who, not infrequently at crucial moments in the action, embody – in their person, speech or deeds – particular thematic interests. Generally speaking, the poets of these works aim to capture the attention of their listeners and readers by means of such details without necessarily spelling out all their meaning. Aside from the headline themes of majesty and humanity, for example, such beards may have been accorded moral significance. They may even reflect, more or less tacitly, societal norms in respect of beardedness per se: grown men should be capable of growing a beard ('bartoht'); long beards are visual and palpable proof of (long) years spent in captivity or social isolation, in exile or on pilgrimage.

There is another poetic approach, however, one which prioritizes teaching and learning. Literary beards governed by this didactic interest are used, for the most part quite explicitly, to illustrate moral lessons, and they are subject to more pronounced 'authorial' commentary within prescriptive discussions of good and bad behaviour. On occasion beardedness itself is the issue up for debate. When and for whom are beards (in)appropriate? How should bearded men behave? Notwithstanding the basic observation that, as a literary mode or method, didacticism can be found to operate in any genre,[2] overtly didactic literature certainly came to prominence in the course of the thirteenth century, and, if anything, the appetite for it grew throughout the later Middle Ages.[3] This chapter is principally concerned with works that aimed to satisfy that demand. As we shall see, in a series of explicitly didactic contexts beards of various kinds (including those of kings) serve as points of reference within ethical debates about wisdom, morality and society, with some being conducted with more urgency – and less humour – than others.

'Sangspruchdichtung'

As far as we can tell, the tradition of 'Sangspruchdichtung', or the didactic lyric, began in the last decades of the twelfth century and culminated in the early fourteenth century with the songs of Heinrich von Meissen (Frauenlob).[4] Lyrics of this kind dealt with a wide range of subject matter – from religious themes to ideals of courtly behaviour, from gnomic pronouncements to panegyric – and they are characterized further by the self-presentation of singers as impoverished travellers and moralists, teachers and proud masters of song.[5] References to beards occur in all phases of this tradition, as one poet after another tried their hand at accentuating the difference between the wise and the foolish, between men and boys.

This thematic complex is central to the work of the singer known as 'Herger' (c. 1200, if not before) whose thirty or so strophes – read by critics in groups of five (or pentads) – are preserved in the earliest manuscripts as part of a larger corpus of material attributed to a certain Spervogel (c. 1200). Herger's pentads represent loose groupings of varying degrees of internal consistency. Pentad II (MF 26,13–27,12), for example, evokes several different scenarios of the hardship associated with forfeiting one's position at court or having no fixed place at all, of being obliged to travel in old age, of being a guest rather than a host (with a roof over one's head). What is striking from our point of view is the way the singer refers to himself over several consecutive strophes in order to lend weight to his observations.[6] In the opening strophe (MF 26,13) this is achieved most emphatically when the singer denies the veracity of rumours concerning the end of the friendship between two named (and otherwise unknown) individuals ('Kerlinc' and 'Gebehart' 26,15): 'sie liegent, sem mir mîn bart' / 'They lie, [I swear] by my beard!' (26,16). By defining himself as a mature man, one whose word is good and legally binding, the singer lays claim to authority based on his gender. By inference this oath – which neatly dissects the strophe in two – also upholds the veracity of the singer's following observation and the grounds for his difference of opinion: no matter how angrily two brothers may argue with one another at court, they will always leave a path for reconciliation open (26,17–19).

The bearded singer comes further into view in the first line of the next strophe when he admits 'Mich müet daz alter sêre' / 'I am afflicted by old age' (26,20), backing this up by naming himself in the third person: 'wan ez Hergêre / alle sîne kraft benam' / 'for it [old age] has stripped Herger of all his strength' (26,21–2). It is precisely as an older man (with experience of the world) that the singer then turns to advise the young – 'ez sol der gransprunge man / Bedenken sich enzîte' / 'The man whose beard has just started to spring forth should take stock already' (26,23–4) – to ensure they have somewhere else to go should they encounter trouble at court (26,25–6). This recommendation to those on the cusp of manhood is seamlessly developed in MF 26,27, where the wealthy man's life of ease is contrasted with the hardship endured by the poor traveller, before the singer uses himself as a negative example by expressing his deep regret at not having been more prudent as a younger man: 'daz ich ze bûwe niht engreif, / Dô mir begonde entspringen / von alrêst mîn bart, / des muoz ich nû mit arbeiten ringen' / 'Because I chose not to build [a house] when my beard first started to spring forth, I now lead a life of hardship' (26,30–3). The two remaining strophes (26,33; 27,6) adopt alternative strategies to develop this same theme, ending with an appropriate moral lesson: whoever wishes to be a 'wirt' (host, householder) in their old age should avoid laziness in their youth (27,11–12).

The emphasis on first beard growth in MF 26,20 and 26,27 is suggestive of young adulthood (rather than childhood), of coming of age, decision-making and living with the consequences of one's own actions. A sprouting beard may thus represent manhood but it hardly guarantees the wisdom required to negotiate an unpredictable and at times hostile world. Herger's song is not just predicated on this idea, it thematizes it explicitly by virtue of the singer's (alleged) personal experience and thus his ability to put himself in the position of those young men he is addressing. This is the only pentad of Herger's with beard references. But this local strategy is entirely consistent with a broader tendency in these strophes to construct the social world at large almost exclusively in terms of relationships between men: brothers (26,17–19), host and guest (27,6–10), neighbours (29,20–6).[7] The beardedness of the older singer in the second pentad thus embodies a wider world-view, as well as complementing the first pentad, where the singer presents himself as an impoverished father with precious little to bequeath his sons: 'Ich sage iu, lieben süne mîn' / 'I tell you, dear sons of mine' (25,13).[8]

The sole beard reference in the lyrics of Spervogel also affirms the value of male experience. Strophe 21,29 depicts courtly society in a state of disorder – those who are fortunate rather than skilled prosper, the brave trail behind the cowardly (21,29–30) – only to sing the praises of certain courtly virtues (21,32–4), the social remedy, as it were. At the heart of these reflections lies an antithesis, albeit one phrased in Spervogel's pithy, aphoristic style, between foolish and exemplary lordship: 'erst tump, swer guot vor êren spart. / zuht diu wellet grâwen bart' / 'Any man who values money more than honour is foolish. Courtly discipline holds the grey beard in high regard' (21,31–2).[9] A well-functioning court appreciates the older man, the experienced singer who can help others to wisdom. Spervogel may well be inviting his audience to view him in this same light, but it is left to his listeners to make this inference.[10] Whereas Herger draws attention to himself in person, Spervogel adopts a more abstract approach by formulating a general principle of courtly ethics which depends upon the self-evident metonym of grey beard for wise man.

Several decades later another 'Sangspruch' singer, Süßkind von Trimberg (active most probably in the first half of the thirteenth century), plays on grey-beardedness, this time as part of an amusing threat to reject court life ('Ton' V,2). The refusal of lords to reward him appropriately leaves him no choice, he laments, but to forfeit his role in society: 'des ich ir hof wil fliehen / und wil mir einen langen bart / lân wachsen grîser hâre' / 'So I mean to abandon their courts and grow myself a long beard of grey hair' (4–6). The initial provocation lies in the singer's determination to lay claim to the status of greybeard, not for the benefit of others (as the archetypal wise man) but as befitting his new role as an exile from court. The radical nature of the singer's decision is fully revealed when he appears to embrace the notion of exclusion from Christian society per se: 'ich wil in alter juden leben / mich hinnân fürwert ziehen' / 'I mean to live like the Jews of old and move on from this place' (7–8). Süßkind's likely social status as a Jew is not an issue for discussion here.[11] We should note rather that the singer seems more interested in concealing his identity by various means – beard (5), long coat (9), hat (10) – than revealing it. Not that this self-imposed banishment, this exodus from exploitative conditions at court, is marked by a sense of shame. Most provocatively of all, the singer appropriates the cardinal Christian virtue of humility in his show of defiance: 'dêmüeteclich sol sîn mîn ganc, / und selten mê ich singe in hovelîchen sanc' / 'I shall tread [my path] humbly and I shall seldom sing courtly song for them again' (11–12).

In the 'Große Heidelberger ("Manessische") Liederhandschrift' (Heidelberg, UB, Cpg 848, ('Grundstock') c. 1300),[12] Süßkind's Jewish identity is presented as fact, although this knowledge may itself be derived from a reading of V,2: (rubric) 'Süsskint der Jude von Trimperg' (fol. 355r). In the corresponding miniature (by the so-called 'Nachtragsmaler I') the singer is marked out as a Jew by the characteristic pointed hat. His beard too, which is reddish-brown and not grey, identifies him ethnically within a scene which bears little correspondence to that suggested by strophe V,2.[13] In the picture Süßkind appears to be engaged in a disputation of some kind involving two beardless courtiers(?) and a figure of ecclesiastical authority (bishop-cum-abbot). The latter has a cropped beard,[14] a sign of status which is at the same time markedly different to Süßkind's thick and curly beard growth. None of the other miniatures generally attributed to 'Nachtragsmaler I' feature this kind of beard, although this artist's sense of 'ethnic diversity' is further evinced by the figure of the Mongolian warrior on fol. 226v with his long black beard and black tresses.[15]

Elsewhere in the 'Sangspruchdichtung' of the thirteenth century, singers make a point of mentioning beards when discussing the moral character of others. The pre-eminent rhetorical device in this context is 'apostrophe', where poets address the person or figure type in question directly. Reinmar von Zweter (active c. 1225–50) was something of an apostrophe specialist.[16] A prime instance of this occurs in the first of a series of strophes (101–5) (in von Zweter's 'Ehren-Ton' (II)), concerning the appropriate roles of men and women within marriage.[17] The 'Aufgesang' (lines 1–6) of strophe 101 presents the subservience of husbands to wives – of an Adam to his Eve (1–3) – as worthy of disgust. In the 'Abgesang' the singer speaks to one such Adam directly: 'Wie tuot ir sô, her Adam, mit dem barte? / ir volget iuwer Êven al ze harte!' / 'Why do you behave like this, Sir Adam, bearded as you are? You follow your Eve all too slavishly!' (7–8). Recrimination turns to encouragement, as the singer urges this (and every) Adam to 'man up!' ('ir mannet!' 9), uphold the honour of their sex (10), and ensure that their Eve does woman's work at home (11–12). The quasi-titular expression of 'her Adam[,] mit dem barte' exercises two functions. On the one hand, it evokes in condensed form all the norms and values associated with masculinity. On the other hand, the respect the singer shows to this 'Adam' – the Everyman of hen-pecked husbands – is evidently unwarranted and thus heavily ironic. The Adams targeted by Reinmar von Zweter undermine the received wisdom of male superiority: as bearded men they should know better.

Deficient masculinity of another kind is lampooned by Leutold von Seven (c. 1250), who identifies certain men as being adult and mature in body and years ('manzîtic' VIII,2: 1) yet childish in character, spirit and intellect. The singer addresses this type of man directly, demanding at first that he rid himself of the inner child that makes him unworthy to bear arms and prevents him from behaving as he should at court (4–6). Ridicule soon follows: 'bartloser muot, nu birc daz kinne! / ez spottet dîn, sam tuos du sîn: / dîn bloeze ist sîner riuhe ein vil unwerder schîn' / 'Beardless character, now hide your chin! It makes a mockery of you, as you do it: your hairlessness is an unworthy reflection of its hairiness' (7–9). Inner beardlessness contradicts and renders laughable the beard that may be seen on the man's chin. In the case of immature men, we can only conclude, the beard stands bereft of its dignity. Such mockery culminates in a third and somewhat obscure apostrophe: 'hie bart: hêr künec von kriechen, wâ nu sinne?' / 'Here is [your] beard, Lord King of Greece, so where are your senses?' (10). This punchline would seem to derive its full effect from certain negative stereotypes rather than any actual historical personage (as critics used to suppose):[18] weak and foolish rulers of Constantinople, beardedness of Greeks in the East as opposed to 'Romans' in the West. When beards are no guarantee of wisdom, there can be only scorn.

The very idea of challenging a king with direct reference to his beard was evidently an appealing one. We find something similar in another 'Sangspruch' strophe (probably from c. 1300, of uncertain authorship), which belongs to a larger group thematizing notable events and figures from the Old Testament (*Der Junge Meißner, (B) I,1–9). Strophes I,4–6 concern King David and his fall from grace, with I,5 giving an account of David's 'seduction' of Bathsheba (1–12) and his betrayal of her husband, Uriah, to his death (13–14). This train of thought culminates in an apostrophe, the singer being sufficiently outraged by the fate of Uriah to speak to King David himself: 'hei, kuonig, din bart / solte iz bewart / han an deme edelin rittir zart!' / 'Hey, King, your beard should have prevented this [fate] from befalling that noble and gentle knight!' (15–17). The righteousness which is the hallmark of David's ideal kingship before he succumbs to his desire for Bathsheba is condensed symbolically in the physical attribute of his beard, which also serves as a reminder of his sexual maturity. The singer's insolent or overfamiliar apostrophe is justified by his moral imperative: this episode from King David's life should be understood as a warning to all adulterers: 'ebrecher, seht diz bispel an: die helle ist uch gevere!' / 'Adulterers, pay attention to this example: hell is waiting for you!' (18).

Some of the most polemical strophes of 'Sangspruchdichtung' make do with third-person reference, as if to address their targets directly by means of apostrophe would be to pay them too much respect. Moral criticism and witty insult are thereby phrased in such a way as to create or strengthen the sense of group identity shared between singer and audience at the expense of an excluded and derided third party. Beards serve as an obvious point of personal attack in this context, and this tactic is executed no more brutally than by Rumelant von Sachsen (active c. 1250–1300) when belittling another singer (Der Marner). The strophe in question (IV,7) takes the form of a disparaging mock riddle, in the course of which Rumelant ridicules Marner for being senile in his old age, declaring this condition to be nothing short of miraculous (3–4).[19] Inverting the trope of the 'puer senex', the singer focusses on one aspect of his rival's appearance: 'daz wunderkint / treit grâer varwen stopfel hâr ûf kindes kinne' / 'The miracle child sports bristles grey in colour on its child's chin' (8–9). The undignified attribute of bristles appears even more unsightly in a young face, such incongruity banishing any conventional image the audience might have entertained previously of Marner as a wise old man.

Another derogatory connotation is explored by Der Meißner (active c. 1250–1300) when taking to task an unnamed patron (or friend?) for not rewarding him as promised (XVI,6): 'Bezzert her mir nicht, ich werfe im einen stein in sinen garten / Unde eine kletten in den bart' / 'If he does not make this up to me I shall throw a stone into his garden and some burrs at his beard' (7–8). The ruining of first his patron's garden and then his beard seems a little puerile, although the joke may partly have been to align two very different sites of cultivation or grooming. By threatening to treat the other's beard as if it were a suitable receptacle or carrier of burr suggests that, far from being elegant, the hair on the face of this individual is akin to animal fur or a woolly garment.[20] In this instance, then, the audience is being invited to consider the material reality of beardedness before its social or moral significance – and laugh at it.

'Her Bart' / 'Sir Beard'

As the archetypal sign of manliness the beard receives its most original treatment by a 'Sangspruchdichter' in the work of Heinrich von Meissen (d. 1318), otherwise known as Frauenlob, whose sophisticated lyric poetry brings this tradition to a close.[21] Of principal interest here are three strophes in Frauenlob's 'Langer Ton' (V), crammed into the margins of fols 104r and 104v of the 'Jenaer Liederhandschrift' (c. 1330).[22] These deal with the familiar themes of wisdom and maturity as part of the broader didactic concern of the 'Langer Ton' with right and proper conduct at court and in society at large.[23] The tone adopted by the singer throughout

(V,27, V,28 and V,29) is one of witty recrimination as opposed to the disparaging ridicule employed by, say, Leutold von Seven.

Strophe V,27 opens by addressing an Everyman ('Man'), confronting him with his own shameful behaviour:

> Man, wiltu kindes witze unz an din ende tragen,
> so mac wol klagen
> daz alter dinen jaren
> unt die jar den haren.
> swa gürtel zwischen berten liget, die dannoch gebaren,
> alsam ir blöze sin noch blanc, daz zimt nicht guten sinnen. (1–6)

> Man, if you mean to think like a child until the end of your days, age might well bemoan your years and years [bemoan] your hair. When beards reach as far as men's belts, yet those men behave as if their faces were hairless and white: that is unbecoming of a sound mind.

The essential problem under discussion, as stated in the very first line, is the shameful tendency of some men to fail to grow up, or rather to continue to think, and view the world, like a child ('kindes witze') throughout their adult lives. This is a truly lamentable situation, the singer avows, not by engaging in mock lament himself but by attributing a sense of outrage to such a man's (mature) age itself (3), his very own years decrying his hair (4) as a false witness. In the next two long lines the point of reference is narrowed down to beards and the singer draws a more dispassionate conclusion: when bearded men behave as if they were beardless, this is hardly consistent with any pretension to wisdom.

These lines, it turns out, represent a preamble of sorts. The singer now changes tack by means of an overtly poetic device – the personification of beardedness – which comes to dominate the rest of this strophe:

> Her Bart, ir waret doch ein manlich zeichen ie.
> welt ir iuch hie
> beschönen mit den kinden,
> daz ir iuch lat vinden
> bi kindes site? Her Bart, des muz manlich vreude iu swinden.
> welt [ir] in beidenthalben sin, her Bart, so muz ouch trinnen
>
> Ein strafen von mir uf iuch, her Bart:
> daz ment, sam ochsen tut ein gart.
> wes sit ir zart

des mannes art,
[...] wan daz ir sine wort bewart
vor aller missewende vart?
her Bart, des leret iuwer man   manliche wirde minnen! (7–19)

> Sir Beard, you have always been a sign of manliness. Do you mean to excuse yourself as children do, now that you have been found to conduct yourself childishly? If so, Sir Beard, your manly joy will [soon] vanish. If you mean to have it both ways, Sir Beard, then I will have no choice either // but to castigate you, Sir Beard: that will drive [you] on, just as a switch does oxen. Why should the male sex regard you with such affection [...] if not because you prevent their word from being debased and misused? For that reason, Sir Beard, teach your men to love manly dignity!

The repeated apostrophe and naming of Sir Beard (7, 11, 12, 13, 19) lend a real shape to the greater part of this strophe, drawing these lines together as a single speech.[24] In contrast to the familiar 'du' which the singer uses in respect of 'Man' at the outset, greater respect is ostensibly shown to Sir Beard ('ir'), making it immediately clear that this fictional entity is a proper adversary for the singer, worthy of his attention and, should it prove necessary, his rebuke ('strafen' 13). Reminding Sir Beard of his own significance as a sign of masculinity ('ein manlich zeichen' 7), the singer subsequently puts the personification on the spot with two questions, tantamount to expressions of incredulity, first in respect of Sir Beard's apparent (and childish) refusal to accept responsibility for immature behaviour (8–11), and secondly in so far as Sir Beard no longer stands as guarantor for the strength of men's words (15–18) – an oblique reference perhaps to the traditional practice of swearing by one's beard. Line 19 brings the strophe and the singer's first address to Sir Beard to an end. What is at stake here is more than just manly joy ('manlich vreude' 11), it is male dignity ('manliche wirde' 19), something which men themselves need to learn to hold in high regard once more.[25]

Strophe V,28 offers a variation on the thematic content of V,27, reprising the incongruity of beardedness and 'kindes witze' (1–2) before addressing 'Her Bart' again. What changes is that the modes of speech adopted by the singer are more clearly defined.

Accusation: 'her Bart, des sit geschuldet' / 'Sir Beard, you stand accused' (3). The singer charges Sir Beard with deferring to children these days rather than men (4–5). This is an inexplicable decision, since it is to Sir Beard's own detriment (5–6).

Encouragement: 'her Bart, her Bart' (8). There is no finer place for Sir Beard to be than by a man's mouth (9–11). How can such a 'banner of wisdom' / 'kluger witze ein van' (12) be so stupid as to think otherwise?

Instruction: 'Her Bart, ir zemt den mannen wol / und niendert baz, daz nemt vür vol' / 'Sir Beard, you are fit and becoming for men and no one else. You should accept this for a fact' (13–14). The beard that so dignifies men simply looks foolish on boys (17–18); beards should in fact mark the end of childhood (19).

As in V,27, for much of this strophe 'Her Bart' is kept present by means of multiple namings (3, 6, 8, 13) as well as by the use of second-person pronouns and verbal forms. By the end of the singer's reflections, however, Sir Beard no longer plays an explicit role. The didactic conclusion to the strophe as a whole is thus presented as a statement for the benefit of one and all, leaving behind the overtly fictional construct of the singer's discussion with beardedness personified.

Sir Beard does not make another appearance.[26] By virtue of its opening imagery – 'Bi barte kindes mut, bi starkem libe ein zage' / 'To have a beard and be childish is like being strong in body and cowardly' (1) – a coherent thematic link is established between strophe V,29 (1–6) and what has come before, if only for the singer to develop a new line of argument from line 7 onwards. Unseemly conduct is no longer just a matter of male (im)maturity, it is illustrated further with reference to gendered difference: 'Ez zimt auch nicht in wibes herzen mannes mut, / daz selbe entut, / swa mannes mut sich wibet' / 'Manliness has no place either in a woman's heart; nor, for the same reason, will it do for a man to become effeminate' (8–10). These conditions too rob a man of his dignity ('wirde' 10). What really preoccupies the singer, it is eventually revealed, is the moral character of young men, for this remains a mystery to him: 'ich meine dich, junges mannes mut, kein spürn dich mac erkriegen' / 'I mean you, mind of a young man; there are no tracks by which to catch you' (19). Thus, one final apostrophe rounds off this mini-cluster of strophes concerning masculinity, which started by addressing 'Man' (V,27: 1). Within this scheme the personification 'Sir Beard' is unequivocally associated with 'Man' in spite of all the problems that arise from men's childish behaviour, as perceived only too clearly by the singer. That the same commentator professes to be at a loss to fathom young(er) men is rather surprising, although it helps to make Frauenlob's final point: there are no easy signs to read when it comes to those who are no longer boys and not yet men.[27]

In the context of Frauenlob's 'Her Bart' strophes (V,27 and V,28), it is worth taking stock of another strophe – in another 'Ton' by Frauenlob – which is also preserved in the 'Jenaer Liederhandschrift' (fol. 110r). ('Grüner Ton') VII,42 is a piece of humorous invective which ridicules an unnamed singer, or just possibly a singer type, with pretensions to mastery, by ironically praising him to the hilt: 'Wa bistu gewest zu schule, / daz du so hohe bist gelart?' / 'Where did you go to school to have become so very learned?' (1–2). Such learning, it is observed, is all the more impressive – or unbelievable – in view of this person's tender years: 'man sprichet dich also kindes, / daz in der niuwe si din bart' / 'You are said to be so young, your beard is newly grown' (3–4). Such mockery of fledgling masculinity represents another variation on the theme of beards and wisdom. If, as some scholars suggest, this strophe was not actually composed by the erudite Frauenlob but aimed at him, it may have seemed particularly apposite to deride him in this way.[28] On the other hand, this strophe may provide us with evidence of Frauenlob's ability to refer to beards in different registers, both high and low.[29] Either way, yet another hand is behind the version of this same strophe in a later manuscript (Munich, BSB, Cgm 4997, c. 1460), in which beardedness and wisdom are configured somewhat differently again: 'Man seit von dinr wysheyde / Wie dir jn jugent wehst der bart' / 'You are said to be so wise that you've even grown a beard in your youth' ((t) 3–4). The fundamental connotations of beards did not have to change for those involved in the transmission of 'Sangspruchdichtung' occasionally to leave their mark too.

Teaching and learning

Alongside 'Sangspruchdichtung', the thirteenth century witnessed the development of several other forms of (primarily) didactic literature and the composition of several major works which aimed to instruct lay audiences in larger systems of knowledge. The first of these – Thomasin von Zerklaere's *Der Welsche Gast* (c. 1215/16) – is a moral compendium for courtly society, arranged in ten Books and amounting to just under 15,000 lines of verse.[30] Issues such as the nature of true nobility are explored, as well as the value of learning from others and the merits of fictional role models for the young. The earliest extant manuscript – Heidelberg, UB, Cpg 389, c. 1256 – contains over 100 illustrations in the margins.[31] This cycle, which is subject to some variation, is a striking feature of the transmission of the work across numerous codices, and in all likelihood it was part of Thomasin's original concept. The didactic content of *Der Welsche Gast* was thus conveyed to many recipients by a combination of text and image.[32]

Two unambiguous beard references occur in the text of *Der Welsche Gast*. The first is to be found in Book I, where the moral precepts are aimed at younger noblemen and noblewomen, in the midst of instruction regarding (courtly) love: Thomasin's very own 'Minnelehre'.[33] Love's nature is such, the poet reflects, that it makes the wise wiser and the foolish more foolish (1180–1). Like fire, which is useful but destroys everything if it gets out of control (1189–94), love that overwhelms causes havoc, blinding the wise man and bringing ruin to his soul and body, honour and property (1197–8). Thomasin's conclusion: 'swer zem viwer nâht ze hart / der besengt dick sînen bart' / 'He who gets too close to fire will often singe his beard' (1199–1200). Initially at least, the Everyman attribute of beardedness serves up a witty variation on the common proverbial wisdom that (young) children, if left to their own devices near a fire, will inevitably get burned – an adage used by other medieval German poets to sum up the dangers of love.[34] Here it is the sexually mature who run the greatest risk, those who might otherwise appear old enough to know better. At the same time the very pithiness of this formulation renders it amusing. Far from undermining the dire warnings that precede it, this effect may be understood rhetorically as a way of keeping younger (and beardless?) recipients entertained and engaged and therefore more receptive to the instructions to come as regards appropriate and inappropriate behaviour within love relationships.

The second beard reference appears in Book IV, representing a curious detail in the perennial discussion of why some people are faced with more hardship in this life than others. At the heart of Thomasin's explanation lies the notion of God as physician.[35] The life we are allotted is the medical treatment, whether harsh or benign, that God rightly judges to be best for our sickness, or rather the state of our souls (5077–80). To illustrate this point Thomasin lists several treatments, paying special attention to the more painful ones:

> Ein arzât der wol erzen kan,
> der erzent dicke einn siechen man
> mit durst, mit hunger und mit prant.
> er bint in ûf zuo einer want,
> er snîdet und stichet in vil hart.
> eim andern rouft er sînen bart
> und sîn hâr, wan er wil
> daz er niht enslâf ze vil. (5089–96)

A doctor who is good at treating others often treats a sick man by making him thirsty, making him hungry and burning him. One man he ties up to a wall; he cuts into him and stabs him deeply. Another man he plucks by the beard and pulls his hair, because he does not want him to sleep too much.

The enumeration of treatments that are more like horrible tortures takes a somewhat surprising turn when hair- and beard-pulling are cited. For a moment they seem oddly trivial by comparison before it becomes clear that they constitute a rough-and-ready method of sleep deprivation. Once again one wonders whether a humorous element is being brought into play here. As we shall see in Chapter 5 ('Laughter and beards') plucking by the beard is a widespread comedic motif, a straightforward but highly effective mechanism for stripping male figures of their authority. Laughter and recognition can of course work together. In this passage of *Der Welsche Gast* any amusement which this unexpected evocation of painful indignity may give rise to is not necessarily detrimental to Thomasin's purpose: to persuade his audience that all the trials and tribulations of this life are to be accepted, if not necessarily welcomed, as what God, the wisest physician of all, prescribes (5105–6).

Of the two scenarios involving beards in Thomasin's text it is the medical one which is assigned a miniature in the cycle of illustrations as preserved in Heidelberg, Cpg 389 (fol. 80r; Figure 4.1).[36] The picture seems designed to hold much of the latent comedy of beard-pulling in check, while retaining the example of sleep deprivation, alongside that

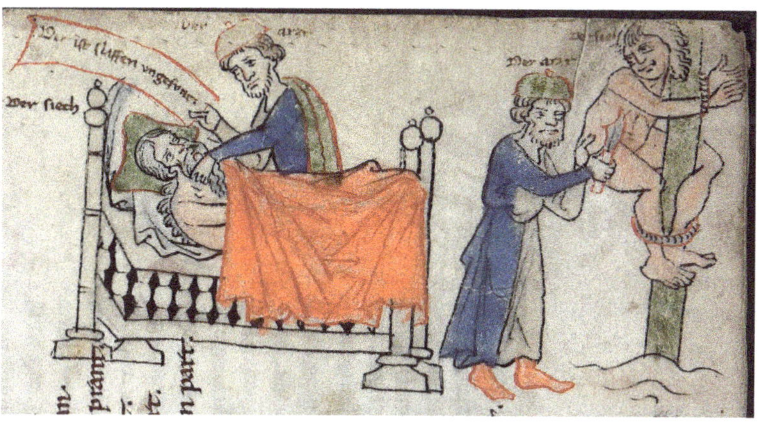

Figure 4.1 Medical treatments (Thomasin von Zerklaere's *Der Welsche Gast*). Heidelberg, UB, Cpg 389, fol. 80r. Public domain.

of surgery, as a noteworthy medical treatment.[37] First, the speech scroll in the physician's right hand reiterates the medical rationale behind his surprising intervention: 'Dir ist slaffen ungesunt' / 'Sleeping is bad for your health'. Secondly, the bedridden patient ('Der siech' / 'The sick man') is presented as an old man by virtue of his long grey locks and patriarchal beard, and his neat centre parting – as opposed to baldness – renders him even more dignified. By contrast the beard of the 'arzt' is short and magisterial; just like his bonnet or beret it serves as a marker of authority and expertise.[38] The physician is the same in both mini-scenes; the patient under the knife, however, is markedly younger and beardless. This variation generates an additional level of moral significance, reminding us that we are liable to be 'treated' for our 'illnesses' whether we are old or young. Such a reading could lead us to view sleep as a metaphor for death, with the hardships that beset the old, or pull at their beards, as the spur to reflect and repent before it is too late.

At least ten instances of this miniature, identified by scholars as motif nr 84 ('Unterschiedliche ärztliche Behandlung'), exist across all the numerous illustrated manuscripts of *Der Welsche Gast*.[39] The basic two-scene structure is retained in almost every case, but the beard semantics vary and for the most part are considerably diminished.[40] As Ernst Hellgardt has observed, later copyists evidently struggled at times to make sense of the images they were reproducing.[41] In one of the copies of the work closest to that of Cpg 389 (= 'A') – Dresden, LB, Mscr. M 67, c. 1450–70 (= 'D') – a youthful physician prevents an equally youthful and beardless patient from sleeping by sticking a finger in his mouth, while the sick man undergoing surgery is distinctly older and bearded (fol. 40v).[42] It might just be that the more drastic procedure was felt to be a better representation of the emergency treatment required in old age. Whatever the thinking (if any) behind this change, image and text at this point are no longer squarely aligned.[43]

One question we cannot really answer in respect of the content of the miniatures in Cpg 389 is the extent of Thomasin's input – or did responsibility for the finer details lie primarily with the artist(s)? In two pictures at least grey-bearded figures are drawn straight from the standard repertoire. The bearded boatmen on fols 49v (ii) and 173v are based on a widespread iconographic type – the ship's pilot – which is also to be found in some of the earliest illustrated manuscripts of German vernacular epic.[44] In the end it seems more productive to consider the (putative) impact of certain images on recipients as part of their process of learning. There is a definite tendency for half-naked destitute figures to be characterized further as old grey-haired or balding men with long grey beards.[45] On fol. 59r, for example, a vain lord is pictured ignoring the pleas of a beggar: 'Herre gebet mir einen phennich!' / 'Lord, please give me a penny!' (speech scroll). The misery of poverty is exaggerated by being associated with the wretchedness of old age, thus eliciting even more sympathy for 'Der arme' / 'The poor man' and feeding moral outrage at the lord's decision to reward flattery instead. By contrast, on fol. 100v, where social disorder is exemplified by a young man elbowing an old man out of the way at court ('La mich vor alter tor' / 'Let me go first, you old fool!' (speech scroll)), beardedness betokens age and wisdom. This figure has something to offer and is foolishly ignored; he is hardly in need of charity and thus he is not pictured in a way calculated to move us. Instead, he is lent quasi-authorial status by virtue of his commentary: 'Also stet dev werld nv' / 'This is the way of the world now' (speech scroll).

The magisterial type of bearded figure, which is used for the physician on fol. 80r, first appears on fol. 10r in the context of Thomasin's discussion in Book I of how best the young learn.

The miniature portrays a bearded master acting on behalf of the personification of 'Zuht' / 'Courtly discipline' (a beautiful courtly lady), lending his authority to her demand ('Gebar reht vnd wol' / 'Act fairly and well') by issuing an instruction of his own to the child (or beardless boy) before him: 'Tuo swaz zuht gebivtet' / 'Do what courtly discipline demands'. The child is suitably obedient – 'Vil gern maister' / 'Most gladly, master' – and respectful, urged on as he is by the personification of 'Vorht' / 'Fear' (another lady): 'Merch iz wol wil du genesen' / 'Remember this, if you want to do well'.

The lines to which this picture refers (591–5) focus exclusively on the correct attitude of the child, who should learn 'mit vorhten' / 'fearfully', the poet maintains, as fear helps with listening and understanding (593–5). The figures of master (who wields a switch) and 'Zuht', who together constitute the other side of the learning process, are thus introduced by the miniaturist in order to make clear perhaps how fear is to be instilled. This 'maister' is the first bearded figure to appear in the cycle of Cpg 389, and there is a paradigmatic quality to this image. A variation on this same figure type features in the very next miniature as well (fol. 10v), illustrating another pedagogic principle: a child should always behave as if 'ein biderbe man' / 'an upstanding man' (643) were present.[46] Something of the fear factor is conveyed by this picture too (and its speech scrolls) when the young squire is seen to enquire: 'Sit ir da maister' / 'Master, are you there?', to which the wise man replies: 'Ich siehe [u]ch wol' / 'I can see you alright'. Teaching and learning and male authority would thus seem to be irrevocably interlinked within Thomasin's text.[47]

Exemplary beards

The somewhat random nature of the relevant passages in *Der Welsche Gast* is indicative of the eclecticism of extended didactic works. The more beard-related material such a text contains, the more obvious its eclecticism becomes. This is demonstrated by the copious poem (of some 25,000 verses) composed by Hugo von Trimberg (d. 1313), which, from about the middle of the fourteenth century, came to be known as *Der Renner*.[48] Structured loosely around the seven deadly sins – in six(!) *distinctiones* – *Der Renner* is made up of a colourful blend of allegory, moralizing commentary and accomplished storytelling.[49] All of this was intended for the benefit of society at large, for sinners everywhere, in whose number Hugo seems to have counted himself. Indeed, this slightly shambolic work is held together by the voice of the author-narrator, who is highly conscious of his own age, whether in terms of bodily ailments (ringing ears, watery eyes), fading memory (less than half as good as it used to be) or simply his many years (77).[50]

Hugo's pedagogical insistence on the transience of this life explains why a significant number of hair and beard references relate, in one way or another, to age and mortality. The beards in question are never white and resplendent like those worn by dignified wise old men. Instead they are grey, like the beard of the man who has spent too many (soulless) years at court, no different to a guard dog, in pursuit of worldly gain (729–30). If it were not for the forbearance of God since the birth of Christ, the author reminds his audience, there would be no greybeards alive today ('Wer hêt nu grâ hâr oder bart?' 3394). Sinfulness is even more foolish in the old, who should know better and have the benefit of experience. Thus, there can be no more shameful example of avarice than the case of an old man – 'Der het grâ houbet und grâwen bart' / 'He had a head of grey hair and a grey beard' (8802) – who is exposed in an instant for hoping (with no good reason) to make personal profit in a court of law, so that he ends up looking like a thief (8807).

These references are taken from *distinctiones* I (Pride) and II (Avarice). The final part of this work (18001–24611), which follows *distinctio* VI (Sloth), contains urgent reflections on repentance before death, and here (grey) beards and old age are linked five more times.[51] The figure of the elderly 'guard dog' at court returns; his beard, we now learn, turns grey from anxiety ('sorge' 18112). Sin, exasperation and old age are also summed up by greying beards as part of yet another iteration of the dismal consequences, both personal and social, of pride: 'Hôchfart wider hôchfart / Machet manigen liuten grâwen bart' / 'Pride against pride turns the beards of many folk grey' (21317–18).[52] More innovative perhaps is the way Hugo emphasizes the physical wretchedness of the old, when he utters a lament from the point of view of one such man, reflecting on his own horrendous appearance: 'Nu sitze ich als ein schembart / Trûric als ein flühtic hûwe, / Mir selber und andern liuten ein grûwe' / 'Now here I sit with a face like a [hideous] bearded mask, as melancholy as a timorous night owl, horrible to behold for myself and for others' (18136–8). Such self-alienation, the perception of one's own beardedness as not really being a part of oneself, is so exaggerated that it could easily be regarded as ridiculous; and this impression is strengthened by the old man's likening of his eyebrows, which were once like 'slender brown wreaths' ('brûniu krenzelîn' 18140), to a 'hairy forest' ('rûher walt' 18142). If laughter is one of the intended recipient responses to this grotesque vision of bodily ugliness – as opposed to the sublimity of the human soul –, it involves recognizing that this fate awaits everyone, as expressly stipulated by the author towards the end of the work: 'Swie sêre wir nu dem lîbe zarten, / Doch werde wir gelîch den schemebarten' / 'No matter how much we indulge our bodies, we will still end up [with faces] like [hideous] bearded masks' (23189–90). The signs of old age are enumerated one last time in one of Hugo's final moral-exemplary tales: here Death himself reproves a man for failing to recognize the many 'messengers' he sent ahead to warn him of his arrival, such as the hoarseness in the man's voice and the grey hairs in his beard (23759–60).

Not all the beards in *Der Renner* are thematized like this. Almost as many other kinds of reference are featured throughout, giving a truly mixed picture.

Fictional monologue (*dist.* I, Pride): a vain young woman finds fault with prospective suitors for any number of reasons (322–86), including aspects of their appearance. From her point of view an old 'bearded' ('bartoht' 323) man is as undesirable as an ugly young one (324) or someone who is too thin or fat or bald ('kal' 326). In the end it is the curly-locked (383) gallant who meets with her approval, yet he remains out of reach because of the spying eyes of others (at court?). Lesson: maidens like this entertain such thoughts to their own detriment (387–8).[53]

Biblical 'exemplum' (*dist.* I): Hugo is accosted by a group of drunken peasants who demand that he discuss social order and injustice with them (1315–2285). Among other things he demonstrates that ingratitude has always existed by alluding to a notorious – and suitably scurrilous – historical incident from the time of King David (II Samuel 10: 4). Who can forget how another king (Hanun) violated the messengers David sent to him in good faith: 'Wenne er die berte in abe schar / Und hiez ir kleider in unden gar / Abe snîden biz an ir scham'/ 'For he shaved off their beards and had their lower garments cut off to reveal their genitals' (2087–9)?

Idiomatic expression (*dist.* I): Hugo tells the fable of the ass who was devoured by his fellow pilgrims (wolf and fox) on their way to Rome (3455–575), using it to introduce the subject of immorality in monasteries. Envy and unruliness are serious problems; monks who cause trouble in their communities are in cahoots with the devil: 'Swer in conventen machet part, / Dem machet der tiufel sînen bart' / 'Whoever stirs up conflict in their monastery has his beard groomed by the devil himself' (3597–8).

Speaking name (*dist.* II, Avarice): a satirical depiction of the Curia (9019–130), which would not be out of place in the strophes of a 'Sangspruchdichter', features a list of named officers who control access to the papal court, officers such as 'Nimmervol' / 'Never-sated' (9070) and 'Lêrenbiutel'/ 'Empty-the-purse' (9075).[54] This company of villains includes one 'Jüdenbart' / 'Jew's Beard' (9074), a detail which adds insult to injury by using the benchmark of Jewishness to encapsulate the hold Avarice has over Rome.

'Schwank' motif (*dist.* IV, Lust): goats and cuckolds have beards; lovers have none. In this comic tale (12185–244) a furious husband refuses at first to believe his wife when she claims that it was their goat he saw escaping from the bedchamber: '"Er hete weder langen bart noch horn", / Sprach er, "der durch daz venster fuor!"' / '"He didn't have a long beard or horns," he said, "the one who jumped out of the window!"' (12212–13). Typically, the adulterous woman is still crafty enough to persuade him not to trust the evidence of his own eyes. Lesson: whoever believes what women say will soon be persuaded that a raven is a swan (12254–6).

Pseudo-biblical 'exemplum' (*dist.* IV): Hugo substantiates his disapproval of lascivious dancing with reference to those Israelites who feasted and danced around the golden calf in Moses's absence (12415–40). In accordance with medieval exegetical tradition (if not exactly the text of Exodus 32 – see below) the many thousands of idolaters were identified when Moses scattered the ashes of the destroyed idol on the water: 'Swelch man des tranc, dem wart sîn bart / Goltvar'/ 'All the [guilty] men who drank of it, their beards turned the colour of gold' (12432–3).

Circumlocution (miscellaneous reflections post-*dist.* VI, Sloth): two very different kinds of people live in forests: robbers and hermits (22765–82). But who – other than God, it seems fair to surmise – can truly tell the wicked from the good? Just as the souls of some murderers are saved, so not every man 'Der manic jâr nie geschar den bart' / 'Who has not shaved his beard for many a year' (22778) escapes damnation. Appearances are deceptive and long beards are not always proof of piety.[55]

These passages give us a sense of the range of uses literary beards could have for a didactic poet by the end of the thirteenth century, especially one with Hugo's magpie-like eye for detail. If we also take the grey-beard references into consideration two further poetic principles stand out. First, notwithstanding all the extensive moral commentary in his 'own' voice, Hugo imaginatively presents the thoughts and perspectives of others through free-standing monologues or as a feature of his various instructive short narratives – and these are as likely to feature beard references as any other part of his work.[56] Secondly, the thematic contexts in which such references appear are overwhelmingly negative, this being a function of Hugo's unwavering focus on sinful behaviour and human deficiencies of all kinds. That he is able to sustain this as well as he does comes down to his commitment to *delectatio* as well as to *utilitas*, although quite patently the comedic sequences too serve to depreciate bodily matters in favour of spiritual concerns, or vices in favour of virtues. It is worth underlining that this comedy is not always openly hostile; it can be self-deprecating too.

Golden beards

Hugo von Trimberg's eclectic choice of material should not mask the fact that some sources were more authoritative than others. Biblical stories were of prime significance, and if we cast our net a little wider it becomes apparent that Hugo was not one to let a good biblical hair reference go to waste: whether Samson (seven locks as source of strength, instrument of vengeful Old Testament God (6864–74)), the prophet Elisha (mocked for his baldness, wicked children punished forthwith (14841–7)) or King David's astonishingly handsome son Absalom (hair like gold, headstrong vanity meets a bad end (15765–89)).[57] As far as the two examples of biblical beards in *Der Renner* are concerned, whereas the first (Hanun and David's envoys) exemplifies an ill-judged demonstration of defiance, the second (false believers revealed) represents a memorable instance in which God chose to work through the beards of men. From the mid-thirteenth century onwards knowledge of the Israelites' (apocryphal) golden beards was fairly widespread in medieval German literature. Comparing several other renderings of this story will not only allow us to follow the literary trajectory of one particular beard reference but will also help put Hugo's practice into perspective.

The story itself is only partly found in the Bible (Vulgate), where Moses makes the Israelites drink from the stream into which he has cast the powder of the destroyed golden calf (Exodus 32: 20), only to put a large number of them to the sword with the help of the Levites (Exodus 32: 26–8). One question that evidently troubled the earliest scriptural authorities was how the guilty were recognized as such, to which various ingenious answers were offered over the centuries.[58] In the (twelfth-century) *Glossa ordinaria,* medieval exegesis even defers to rabbinical learning on precisely this point, citing the Jewish explanation ('Tradunt hebrei' / 'Jewish tradition has it') that having drunk the contaminated water, those guilty of idolatry were seen to have 'golden dust in their beards' ('in barbis pulverem auri').[59] Decisively, perhaps, Peter Comestor includes this detail in his highly influential *Historia scholastica* (completed by 1173): here the miraculous nature of the events is underlined as God reveals the true 'authors of the crime' ('sceleris auctores') by virtue of what happens to their beards.[60]

Comestor's *Historia scholastica* provided the impetus for this episode to be included in a number of German chronicles of universal history, for which the events described in the Old Testament (from the moment of Creation) were naturally of the utmost importance.[61] The time of Moses, audiences were repeatedly informed, was one in which God performed countless miracles for his 'chosen people', many of whom did not deserve to see the Promised Land. In such history on the grand scale, the incident of the golden calf (and the golden beards) generally served as an archetypal example of the Israelites' lack of faith. However, the story varied in the telling from chronicle to chronicle.

1. Rudolf von Ems's *Weltchronik* (c. 1240; incomplete; over 33,000 lines): counter-intuitively perhaps, Rudolf goes some way towards

rationalizing the extraordinary events (12042–219). Catching sight of the golden calf for the first time, Moses smashes the tablets in anger, whereupon the author-narrator normalizes this outburst: 'als noch die lute in zornne tuont' / 'just as even today people do such things in anger' (12171). The subsequent action – Moses's destruction of the idol, the scattering of the ashes on the water, the people's drinking of the water and the transformation of their beards ('nah golde golt var der bart' / 'their beards [turned] the golden colour of gold' 12183) – is narrated without deviation and explained forthwith: 'alse Got alsus gescheit / die ubln von den rehten dan' / 'This then was how God separated the wicked from the righteous' (12187–8). The truth is plain for all to see and there are no false protestations of innocence before Moses takes just and bloody revenge.

2. *Christherre-Chronik* (c. 1244–87; incomplete; over 24,000 lines): there is far more controversy among the Israelites in this account (17375–614). Moses's destruction of the golden calf is followed by recriminations between the people and Aaron. Moses ('Der wise degin' / 'The wise hero' 17578) silences everyone by scattering the ash on the water and obliging them to drink from it. The situation thus becomes one of an ordeal, or trial by 'polluted water', by means of which God allows the truth to emerge, a process summed up by the enthusiastic author-narrator as 'Ein wunderlichez wundir' / 'a miraculous miracle' (17584). The resulting manifestation of guilt is described twice over. It makes no difference how clandestine their idolatry has been, the beards of the guilty are still coloured gold by the ash (17588–90); nor does it matter how old or how young(!) these men are: 'Den wart der bart gestalt / Als golt'/ 'Their beards were made gold-like' (17592–3). This divine intervention is so extraordinary, a single mention does not do it justice.
3. *Weltchronik* of Jans ('Enikel') von Wien (early 1270s; first complete text of its kind; over 27,000 lines): in typically idiosyncratic fashion Jans follows an alternative source for this episode (8731–993), resulting in a version which manages to be both obscure and lurid.[62] Aaron plays a different role altogether: he is the one who instigates the fashioning of idols ('zwei kalp rôt' / 'two calves of red [gold]' 8777) and who urges the mob to kill Ur (Hur), the only person who objects, with their spittle (8807–12).[63] The combination of this killing and the Israelites' idolatry causes Moses to smash the tablets in anger, before an angel comes down from heaven to help him

distinguish the wicked from the good (8949–51). Promising Moses the sight of a 'seltsaenen list' / 'marvellous ruse' (8972), the angel instructs Moses to get everyone to drink from 'daz wasser rein' / 'the clean water' (8973), unpolluted by the ashes, we must surmise. The results, Jans confirms, are truly marvellous ('seltsaeniu dinc' 8978); the beards on the faces of the idolatrous now stand 'fiuwerrôt' / 'fiery red' (8981). The wrathful angel reiterates the link between the transformation of the worshippers' beards and their idol ('daz rôte kelbelîn' / 'the little red calf' 8986) even as he curses and condemns them to death (8985–90).[64] Livelier and trashier, this rendering of the episode also draws wholeheartedly on the stigma of red hair to malign the faithless Jews still further (see Chapter 5). The red beards of the guilty are conspicuous in the corresponding miniatures in at least two of the work's illustrated codices.[65] The dominant sentiment, as articulated by the avenging angel, no less, is unmistakeably one of Schadenfreude.

Poets working within other vernacular literary traditions made use of this episode in different ways. The most poetically condensed rendering is to be found in Frauenlob's *Kreuzleich*, a mesmerizing lyrical exploration (in 22 strophes of unequal length) of the Holy Trinity and the Crucifixion. During one of the song's 'movements' the poet calls upon several figures from the Old Testament to bear witness to God's power (II,7–9). Miraculous visitations and divine appearances represent the narrower theme of strophe II,8, in which Isaiah (1), Ezekiel (5) and St John the Divine (6–8) are all appealed to directly.[66] Moses belongs to this group too, although reference to his encounter with God on Mount Sinai (2) is followed by an account *in nuce* of what he did next (on returning to his people):

> welch sünders verge   rach mit kerge,   kalbes scherge,
> bartes erge,
> der mit golde was betroffen,   offen   wandel meinte? (II,8: 3–4)

> Which leader of sinners took fierce revenge – butcher of the calf – on the beard's vice, [the beard] which, dripping with gold, conveyed the intention to do ill?

By means of Frauenlob's elusive phrasing, a thought-provoking combination of the abstract and the concrete-material, these lines offer a summary of sorts, rather than an explanation of the events surrounding the Israelites' idolatry.[67] They can only fully make sense to those with the requisite knowledge of both canonical (golden calf) and apocryphal (golden beards) detail. Both are presented as objects of Moses's ire; both connote vice and venality. But the relationship between them – the mechanics, as it were, of the miracle (ashes, water, drinking) – are elided. Attention shifts from Moses as guide, 'butcher' and punisher to that which reveals the true nature of the wicked, and the metonym of 'bartes erge' / 'the beard's vice' (3) seems entirely in keeping with Frauenlob's personification of the beard ('Her Bart') elsewhere in his oeuvre. In the context of the whole strophe lines 3–4 read a little like a digression; the miracle they allude to hardly fits the bill of visual manifestations of divinity. What they reference instead is an instance of God's merciless vengeance (through Moses) on those who only worship what they see, who even fashion their own idol, unable to accept that a true vision of divinity, as exemplified for us by the experience of great prophets (Isaiah, Ezekiel) and Moses the patriarch, is a blessing beyond measure which can only come from God and cannot be demanded.

Elsewhere, greater store is set by comprehensibility. The very definition of this approach is adopted by the poet of the *Großer Seelentrost* (c. 1300–50), a Low German prose collection of over two hundred 'exempla' pertaining to the Ten Commandments.[68] The biblical story of the golden calf occupies a privileged position here, since it serves as the first exemplary tale for the First Commandment: 'Non adorabis deos alienos' / 'You shall not worship other gods' (5,3). Its didactic significance could not be clearer, there being no more obvious proof (according to the poet) of just how much God hates this sin: 'dat heft he wol bewiset an deme yodeschen volke' / 'this he demonstrated in respect of the Jewish people' (5,8). The following account, which is probably derived from medieval Dutch historiographical tradition (Jacob van Maerlant),[69] contains only one surprise. Less gold was evidently deemed more when it came to identifying the guilty: 'Alle, de dar schuldich weren, de den affgod hadden angebedet, den hengk yo eyn gulden drope to dem barde' / 'All those who were guilty, those who had worshipped the idol, they had a drop of gold hanging from their beards' (6,7–9).[70] If anything, this unexpectedly subtle detail makes the divine intervention more distinctive, forestalling any notion that the gold in the Israelites' beards is a natural consequence of drinking water containing (golden) 'puluere' / 'powder' (6,6). The slightness of the incriminating sign also sets the magnitude of the resulting punishment into sharper relief: 'De let he alle doden, der weren drevndetwintich dusent' / 'He had all of them killed; there were twenty-three thousand of them' (6,9).

There can be little doubt that for some, if by no means all, poets and their target audiences this story provided a memorable historical precedent for prejudicial notions concerning the faithlessness and avarice of Jews. This is most blatantly the case in one late medieval tale of disputation and conversion – *Streitgespräch zwischen Christ und Jude* (c. 1400) – where a Christian Everyman repeatedly mocks a Jew before the latter sees the error of his ways.[71] When the Jew proudly asserts, for instance, just how special the relationship was between God and the Israelites ((w^{18}) 87–96), he invites only scorn for his people's history of faithlessness and idolatry: 'ir betten an ein gulden kalp / in der vinsternisse vf der fart: / dar vmb heistu "guldin bart"' / 'Your people prayed to a golden calf in the darkness as they journeyed: that's why you're called "Golden Beard"' (104–6).[72] Golden beards are no longer confined to the past. They represent a stigma which can be held against Jews in the present too, one which lends itself to ridicule by reducing a people, a person, to a single body part or facial feature. Knowledge of the causal relationship between the calf and the golden-bearded Israelites was hardly required to appreciate this 'joke'.

Bearing all of this other material in mind, it becomes readily apparent that Hugo puts the golden calf/golden beards 'exemplum' (12415–40) to unusual use. Yes, he too promotes antipathy towards the idolatrous Israelites, repeatedly gloating over what lies in store for them (12417–18, 12430). But his real interest lies elsewhere, in the sinful temptations associated with dancing. Men who loiter at dances, he concludes, behave as sinfully as the 'Jews' who danced around the golden calf: both behaviours represent an offence against Christianity (12436–40). The golden beards of the Israelites thus represent an eye-catching motif whose principal function is to grab and hold the attention of the audience. Hugo's skill as a didactic poet, one might argue, lies less in his choice of material than what he does with it, in this case retelling an extraordinary episode of grand historical significance in order to make a point about the moral challenges of everyday life.

Running with *Der Renner*

The enormous popularity of *Der Renner* throughout the fourteenth and fifteenth centuries is reflected in the large number of extant manuscripts (over fifty without taking fragments into account). The text itself survives in several redactions which are based ultimately on two authorial versions: 'B' (Hugo's first draft, completed c. 1300) and 'A' (a more polished text which Hugo worked on until his death in 1313).[73] Almost all the beard references discussed so far are found in both 'Hugo' versions as we know them today. However, several codices include variations which change the beards profile of *Der Renner* to a greater or lesser extent. The text accrues beard references, for example, in the earliest surviving copy of 'A' (Erlangen, UB, Ms. B 4, dated 1347), where one of the grey-beard images from the final part of the work – 'Hôchfart wider hôchfart / Machet manigen liuten grâwen bart' / 'Pride against pride turns the beards of many folk grey' (21317–18) – is repeated and added to an earlier anaphoric sequence concerning 'Hôchfart' (467–96) in the very first *distinctio* (here fol. 8v).[74] Elsewhere in this copy (63v), as part of the biting satire concerning the Curia, the speaking name of 'Jüdenbart' (9074) seems to have inspired the adaptation of the name immediately preceding it: thus 'Krazhart' / 'Scratch-hard' (9074) becomes 'kratzpart'/ 'Scratch-beard' or 'Beard-scratcher', an even more vivid metaphor for pecuniary fleecing.

By the same token beard references were also done away with. In the family of manuscripts containing version 'B' the vain maiden's objection to beardedness, as found in version 'A' – 'Einer ist bartoht' / 'One is bearded' (323) –, is elided in favour of a moral failing ('Der eine ist hoffertig' / 'One is vain' (F1, fol. 9r)) or an actual physical impairment ('Ainer ist pukloht' / 'One is hunchbacked' (Le1, 9r)). Other redactions of *Der Renner* entailed swingeing cuts. By around 1400 a shorter version of the work (in the 'B' tradition) had established itself – referred to as 'Bz' by scholars – complete with a cycle of over 80 illustrations.[75] It is shortened by some 11,000 lines, and just over half of Hugo's beard references are lost, including those pertaining to Avarice (8802, 9074), the golden beards of the idolatrous Israelites (12432–3) and the likening of old men's faces to hideous (bearded) masks (18138, 23190). The text is scaled back even further in a sub-group of 'Bz' codices ('Bz10'), where *Der Renner* now amounts to 5,300 lines of largely narrative content, constituting just another late medieval collection of fables and 'exempla', with relatively little of Hugo's original didactic programme left intact.[76] Of the four beard references which survive the cut, two pertain to fables (dog maltreated at court, ageing courtier (730); wolf, fox and ass as pilgrims, monastic misdeeds (3598)), and two occur as details within short narratives ('goat as lover' (12212), grey beard as portent of death (23760)).

What goes missing in the way of beards in terms of literary material in both 'Bz' redactions is amply compensated for by the many miniatures across the various manuscripts which feature bearded characters. For the most part, however, the beard motif functions independently in these illustrations, used by artists in traditional fashion to reaffirm the status and significance of certain figure types such as kings (including Alexander the Great!) and the wise. The earliest extant 'Bz' codex (Leiden, University Library, VGG F4, dated 1402) comes close to offering a celebration of male beardedness, its relatively lavish pictures exhibiting numerous intricately drawn beards, almost all of which are golden-yellow in colour.[77] Hugo himself may be portrayed as beardless, if unshaven, in dialogue with ugly peasants (fol. 25r), but a stylish norm is established at the very outset (1v) with the pointed beard of the 'Renner', the rider figure who personifies the work as a whole.[78] An array of pointed, forked and full beards follows. The beards of the nobility and the wealthy tend to be highly groomed. The dialogue between courtier and monk on fol. 249, for example, simultaneously represents an encounter between two beards, where worldly fashion comes face to face with a more honest, more vigorous beard growth.[79] One particularly refined chin-beard, preened to the point of being almost horizontal, forms the focal point of the picture on fol. 251v, framed as it is by a drawn bow and arrow right in the centre of the scene (see the front cover of this book). The beards of plainer folk are full yet unelaborate, as in the miniature for the 'goat as lover' tale

Figure 4.2 A husband returns home unexpectedly (Hugo von Trimberg's *Renner*). Leiden, University Library, VGG F4, fol. 138v. CC BY licence.

(138v), where the bearded husband is shown waiting at his own door (Figure 4.2).[80] In this particular instance the beard motif also stands in meaningful relation to the literary passage it illustrates, since the comedic effect of (Hugo's) text – the husband's futile insistence that his wife was cheating on him – is rendered visually by the affinity between husband and goat. Both are bearded, outside the house and unattractive to the wife, who is embracing her beardless young lover inside.

The most systematic and well-conceived redaction of Hugo von Trimberg's *Renner* is the copy of the text (in the 'A'-version tradition) which a certain Johannes Vorster made for himself in the early fifteenth century (Heidelberg, UB, Cpg 471, c. 1425–31).[81] Rearranging a total of 11,000 of Hugo's lines of verse, Vorster constructed a more orderly sequence of chapters (*distinctiones*) on the seven deadly sins (fols 12v–56r), prefacing them with sections on Youth (1r–6r) and Old Age (6r–12v), and ending with a chapter on God's benevolent omnipotence (56v–65v). Points of special significance in the main body of the 'new' text are highlighted by numerous Latin quotations (from the Vulgate) in the margins. Eight beard references are retained by Vorster; four of these – all from the final part of Hugo's work – are brought forward and recycled as part of the newly devised *distinctio* on Old Age, where Vorster has collected Hugo's principal comments on ageing and grey hair. Thus, one of Hugo's references to bearded masks, an image of the physical deterioration that is an inevitable part of growing old ('Wie ser wir nv dem leib zarten / Doch werd wir gleich den Schemparten' 7ra: 30–1 = (Hugo) 23189–90), now follows hard upon the scornful description of old fools as 'kint von sibenczig Jaren / Mit tieffen rvnczzelen vnd grawen haren' / 'children of seventy years with deep wrinkles and grey hair' (7ra: 25–6 = 21087–8). Rearrangements like these result in a tidier text, which arguably packs a more powerful punch in relation to Hugo's scattered observations concerning sin and age.[82]

The subdivision of Vorster's text is highlighted by a series of miniatures, commissioned and designed (by Vorster?) specifically for this work, depicting first beardless Youth (fol. 1r), then bearded Old Age (6r), before illustrating each of the seven deadly sins.[83] As the prefatory images of the first two distinctions make clear, foolish behaviour is not restricted to the young, nor is wisdom necessarily an attribute of the old. Similarly, several of the pictures that follow make a point of featuring both bearded and beardless men. The first of the three mini-scenes representing Lust (27r), for instance, shows a bearded old man buying the affections of a young woman, while the two other scenarios show how younger men are ensnared by this sin too. A more nuanced understanding of human wrongdoing is thereby displayed, as relevant for the bearded recipient as it is for the beardless.

The shift of emphasis from Youth to Old Age which Vorster's second *distinctio* entails is marked on another textual level by a distinctive aspect of his scribal practice, namely the numerous sketched heads which sprout from certain initials, such as 'W', 'V' and 'M'. At times these function as drolleries, but more often than not they also draw attention to a particular sentiment or moral observation, or help to define paragraphing on the page.[84] Bearded heads of this kind first appear in chapter 2 (starting on fol. 6va: 37), with several quite conspicuously illustrating the content of the lines to which they are attached: 'Man vindt mangen hofwart / Dem Sorg macht groen part' (9va: 17–18 = 18111–2); 'Weilend waz ich den lewten zart / Nu siczz ich Als ein schempart' (9va: 41–2 = 18135–6; Figure 4.3). There are some 24 bearded heads in total throughout the work, seven of which occur in 'Old Age'.[85] In the following chapters, where old age is less prominent as a theme, identifiable prompts to feature a bearded head (as opposed to a tonsured or an 'ugly' one) come in lines concerning wisdom or authorities of various kinds, not least God himself: 'Wer vnsern herren vor awgen het' / 'Whoever keeps sight of our Lord' (26va: 43 = 13363); 'Vor gotes awgen' / 'Before the eyes of God' (56ra: 1 = 6015). While not without parallel in the transmission of Hugo's *Renner* – one of the main 'B'-version codices (Frankfurt am Main, UB, Ms. Carm. 3, early 1400s) has at least four initials like this[86] – the many miniature sketched heads in Vorster's lavish copy represent a sustained and not infrequently humorous attempt to bring the knowledge on the page to life.

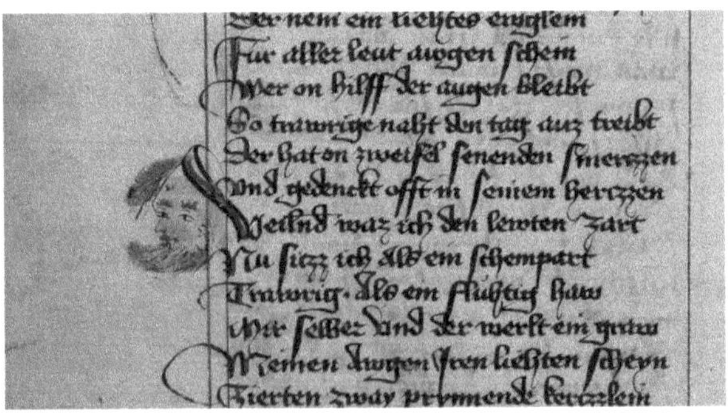

Figure 4.3 'Weilend waz ich den lewten zart' / 'I used to be regarded fondly by others' (Johannes Vorster's *Renner*). Heidelberg, UB, Cpg 471, fol. 9va. Public domain.

Social critique

The moral-didactic significance of beards was as readily comprehensible to listeners and readers of vernacular literature in the thirteenth as in the fifteenth century. In the real world, however, especially higher up in medieval society, the status of beards fluctuated somewhat, beards like other aspects of male appearance being subject to the dictates of fashion.[87] Miniatures in manuscripts such as the Leiden *Renner* codex provide far more eloquent testimony to this than any poetic work, although just occasionally changes in practices of grooming and shaving do make themselves felt in texts, especially those where the poet is casting a critical view over the mores of his society.

The fashion for beards at German courts around 1330, even among younger men, probably lies behind a pogonographic poem by the self-dubbed 'König vom Odenwald' (a travelling singer), entitled simply 'Von den berten' / 'Concerning beards' by one scribe (Gotha, FB der Uni. Erfurt, Cod. Chart. A 216, c. 1342–5, fol. 94r) and 'Von den langen berten der lute, / Die sie von zehen sachen tragen hute' / 'Concerning the long beards of people and the ten reasons they wear them these days' by another (UB der LMU Munich, Cim. 4 (Cod. ms. 731), c. 1345–54, fol. 198r). Unusual as this text may be in the broader context of medieval German literature, in various respects it is quite compatible with other poems commonly attributed to the König vom Odenwald. These reveal a general preoccupation with 'realia', such as the usefulness of the pig (*Gedicht vom Schwein*),[88] and a love of lists and enumeration, including the twenty reasons why people go to the baths (*Vom Baden*).[89] Social criticism (*Vom Verfall der guten Sitten*) and satire (*Vom Hausrat*) have a role to play in this repertoire too.

The poet begins *Von Bärten* by promising his listeners something curious (1–2), there being 'nowt so queer as folk' ('Als manig haubt als manig sin!' 4). This initial observation is followed by the poet's account of a dream he claims to have had, which frames the main body of the poem: 'Mich duht in einem traume, / Wie unter einem baume / Ein schone frauwe mir widergienck' / 'I had a dream in which I saw a beautiful lady coming towards me beneath a tree' (5–7). Somewhat surprisingly, this mysterious lady, who of course knows the poet by name ('Saga, kunig, war stet din ger?' / 'Tell [me], King, where do you wish to go?' 11), turns out not to be a personification although she behaves very like one. In fact the poet never asks who she is; instead he agrees to her unusual request – 'Du solt mich unterwise, / Die die langen berte tragen' / 'Please tell me about those [men] who sport long beards' (20–1). Her own speculative attempts to answer this troubling question (25–6) are rejected out of hand by the poet who, as a man of the world perhaps, simply knows better: 'ich weiz einen andern sin' / 'I know different!' (28).

The ten explanations that follow are assigned their own rubrics in the Munich manuscript, from 'Worumbe der erste treit den bart' / 'Why the first [man] is bearded' (fol. 198va) to 'Wovon der zehende trage bart' / 'Why the tenth might be bearded' (199rb), with Roman numerals also penned in red ink in the margins (Figure 4.4). Most of these reasons cast the respective beard-wearers in a less than flattering light. In respect of the first three men, long beards are the result of procrastination, irrefutable evidence of their inability to do what they declared they would before shaving again, whether taking revenge (32–9), settling a debt (43–8) or going on a pilgrimage (52–7). There is a sense here that these beards now mean more to their wearers than any proper course of honourable action. The fourth grows his beard to prove his 'manheit' /

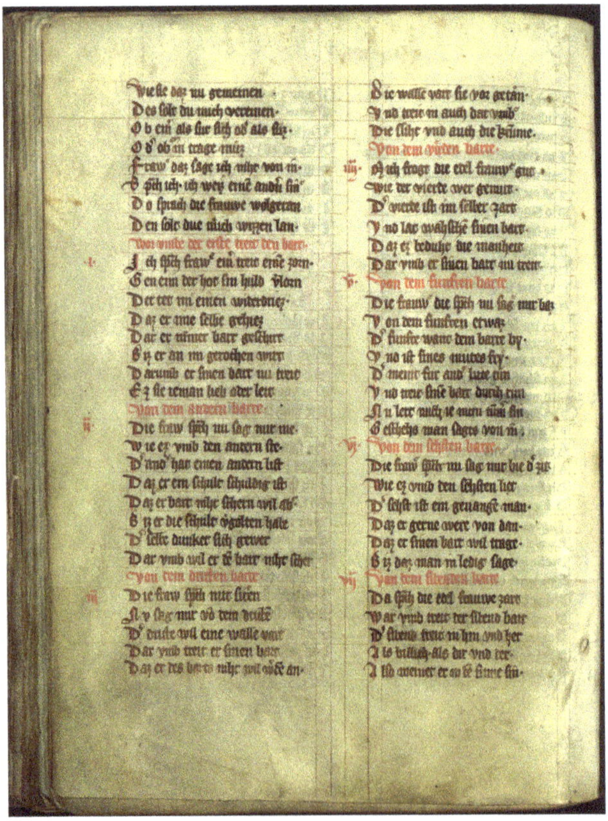

Figure 4.4 Reasons to be bearded (i)–(vii) (König vom Odenwald's *Von den Bärten*). UB der LMU Munich, Cim. 4 (Cod. ms. 731), fol. 198v.

'manhood' (63) to himself, whereas the fifth wants to show off ('durch run' 71) in front of others. For the sixth his beard is most befitting of his status as a captive; the seventh, by contrast, only grows his because others are growing theirs. The eighth will not shave until he has had his way with a certain woman, and equally ludicrously the ninth grows his beard to prove himself a loyal servitor to his beloved. The tenth – a monk – is obliged by his order to be bearded (116), which represents perhaps the only reasonable justification, unless we are meant to understand that the beard growth of this man of God is as far as his *imitatio Christi* goes (117–18).

By listing various spurious reasons for having a long beard, the poet is challenging his audience to reflect on why anyone would want to look like one of these men, anyone who is not a prisoner or a monk, that is. By the end of the dream-vision the criticism of long beards becomes quite overt. The lady, who seemed happy enough with the poet's explanations before taking her leave, calls back with an observation of her own: 'da liez ichs gut sin, / Daz in der bart niht in den win / Hieng, wan er trunke' / 'That would be all well and good as long as the beard of such a man did not hang into his wine while he was drinking' (131–3). Her reasoning: beard hair is far less palatable (in wine) than medicinal herbs like sage and hyssop (135–8). The courtly lady is the one, then, who explicitly mocks long beards – and their unappealing material-bodily reality – as incompatible with civilized table manners. For his part the poet refuses to repeat this criticism to the long-bearded, suggesting that the lady should do so herself. The only thing left for him to say is that he at least has no intention of besmirching himself with wine in this way (141–2). The König vom Odenwald thus ends this poem by confirming what recipients must have suspected all along: that he is not part of the long-bearded crowd.[90]

Another fourteenth-century poet, Heinrich der Teichner (c. 1310–c. 1375), adopts a far sharper tone when discussing the fashion for longer beards, which he does in some detail in three of his rhymed poems or 'Reden'. Although this represents just a drop in the ocean of his enormous body of work, which encompasses almost 800 of these shorter texts on a range of ethical, moral and religious themes, his interest in male hair and beards cannot be denied.[91] For Teichner, modern trends of fashion are symptomatic of a world that is dangerously out of kilter, of a courtly society that has become inexcusably vain and frivolous or 'reinish' / 'Rhinish' (nr 191: 71).[92] While women too play their part in this, Teichner is especially contemptuous of dandies who grow their hair, choosing to take after their mothers rather than their fathers (191: 17–28). The situation has become so dire, he complains, that the proverbial wisdom concerning the fickleness of women – 'langez har und churtzen müt' / 'long in hair and short on resolve' (191: 32) – is more applicable these days to men (191: 34–6).[93]

Where long beards are Teichner's target the insult of effeminacy is dropped in favour of other charges. In poem nr 193 Teichner makes it very clear when and for whom long beards used to be appropriate: penitents and monks. Now, in a society that has lost its way, it is monks who shave while knights and their squires disfigure themselves by allowing their hair and beards to grow wild (4–21). The sheer folly of this new custom is revealed by the fact that such would-be courtly lovers now lose out to monks and priests who appear as elegant 'als dw layen weilent waren' / 'as (noble) laymen once did' (26).[94] To consolidate his argument Teichner cites the case of a disappointed – shock-haired – courtier who once sought him out specifically to get him to compose a poem on this very subject (32). The poet readily admits to being baffled by young men who think themselves attractive yet look more like grief-stricken mourners (44).[95] He even takes the radical step of imagining things from a female point of view: 'wär ich ein weib, / wa ich saech eins mans leib / der sich waidenleich schaer, / daz mir der vil lieber wär' / 'If I were a woman, if I saw a man who had had his beard elegantly shaved, he would be much more to my liking' (53–6). The poem concludes, however, on a decidedly masculine note. Men who grow their beards to intimidate other men are foolish (too), for in itself hair proves nothing: 'nu hilft den pern nicht sein raüch; / in pringt ein plozzer man in swär' / 'The bear's hairiness does not prevent it from being vanquished by a hairless man' (60–1).

The significance of beards for men and between men is developed in text nr 612. In classic Teichner style, the poem is presented as the response to a question: 'Ayner pat, ich scholt im sagen, / langs har und part tragen, / warumb das erfunden sey' / 'A man [once] asked me to explain to him why wearing long hair and a beard first started' (1–3). The poet begins his answer by refuting two regrettably common misconceptions:

Some knights these days take the example of Samson, believing that growing their hair and beards excessively will make them stronger (5–11). They are proved wrong by everyday experience and by historical precedent: bearded Hungarians were always routed by Germans until they started to shave (17–36).[96] Others claim that their beards make them more attractive to ladies, but this notion is quite inane as they end up with faces that are about as pleasing to the touch as hedgehogs (41) and look more like grieving mourners than joyful lovers (42–6); the only thing a long beard is good for is as a means of concealing one's identity (47–57).

A third justification of beardedness comes in the form of a dialogue proper, as Teichner recalls one particular (fictitious) encounter with a fellow who explains why he has not cut his beard in over three years: 'ich chlag den todt / der getrewen herschaft' / 'I mourn the death of honest lords' (68–9). Sympathetic as the poet is with this social criticism, he still advises the other to get rid of his beard, for he will be growing it until the Day of Judgement before the (righteous) rulers of old return; it is either that or become a monk, since beards like this are 'ein geistleich ding' / 'a religious thing' (104). In support of this, his final point, Teichner purports to cite the words of another figure: a (bearded) monk ('ein pärting' 105) who confesses himself distressed by the sight of so many other men who look like him yet do not observe the canonical hours by leading a life of prayer (106–11).

In his poems Teichner thus repeatedly reminds his audience of traditional social norms concerning male appearance and beardedness, against which the modern fashion for long beards is measured and found wanting. The satirical effect of his observations is twofold. First, the pretensions of the lay nobility who follow this trend are demolished in terms of their status both as courtly lovers and as fighting men. Secondly, Teichner uses the beard debate to voice broader social criticism, finding vanity and folly rife wherever he looks. This perspective is articulated most vociferously in poem nr 726, in which Teichner takes the peasantry to task for 'reinischait' and sinful attempts to look and dress like noblemen: 'die hochfart geet von dem tewfel her' / 'This pride comes straight from the devil' (10). The poet exercises extreme prejudice throughout, mocking peasants at one and the same time for their effeminate tresses and their long beards (30–4). The consequences of this development are dire, since now it has become impossible to tell a nobleman from a lowly peasant's servant (52–7). The gravity of the situation gives the poet licence to be derisive and ever more aggressive. Not only does he debase the hate figure of the uppity peasant by portraying him with enough breadcrumbs in his beard to feed a hen (71), he engages in violent fantasies about de-bearding rustics (73–90). For any red-bearded villains among them, he threatens, he would not even bother with a knife: 'ich wolt ims mit den henden aus rauffen' / 'I would tear his beard out with my [bare] hands' (82). Evidently, when it came to criticising this social estate reasoned argument was no longer required.

One point of reference is arguably missing throughout Teichner's discussion of beards, as expert as it is remonstrative, and that is himself. Listeners and readers are left none the wiser in respect of Teichner's own beardedness and must imagine it for themselves. The author portrait contained in a later manuscript, dated 1472 (Berlin, SBPK, Mgf 564, fol. 7v), is striking in this context.[97] Quite unlike the famous images of such vernacular literary authorities as Wolfram (Vienna, ÖNB, Cod. ser. nova 2643, fol. 313r) and Frauenlob ('Manesse' manuscript, fols 381r ('Nachtragsmaler I'), 399r ('Nachtragsmaler II')), the master poet Teichner is pictured as beardless and dressed in clerical-cum-academic garb. Remarkably, such beardlessness in no way diminishes Teichner's status, as indicated by the inscription encircling the medallion-shaped picture which spells out this didactic poet's all-encompassing remit.[98] By coincidence, later in the same codex a humorous poem, spuriously attributed to Teichner,[99] which takes as its central theme the 'miraculous' properties of wine (*Zwölf Kräfte des Weins*, fols 117v–120r), plays on its author-narrator's youthful beardlessness. His fourth cup of wine, the poet enthuses, imbued him with such wisdom 'von jüngeling on part / wart solich witz nie gehort' / 'No one had ever heard beardless youth speak so shrewdly' (32–3), entirely eclipsing the efforts of 'Frawenlob', 'Eschenpach' and 'maister Gottifried [von Strassburg]' (35–7). But this younger, beardless man is obviously drunk and deluded: he is no more wise than he is related to the king of England (91). The author portrait on fol. 7v is far less conventional, constituting a representation of learning and wisdom that really does look beyond beardedness.

Conclusion

Throughout the German Middle Ages most didactic poetry was composed for the benefit of men and women alike by male poets who invariably discussed morality and codes of conduct in gender-specific terms.[100] This does not mean that male and female bodies were represented or constructed in this literature to the same degree: the human condition in general was discussed from a fundamentally androcentric point of view.[101] Beard references from across the whole spectrum of didactic literature are evidence of this, as is the fact that in the texts investigated here no female physical feature, not even female hair, comes close to being thematized in an equivalent way.[102] There is no ready-made literary or iconographic motif for female wisdom.[103] Moreover, female features betokening physical maturity seem to have been evaluated primarily in sexual terms and thus they were subject to social and linguistic taboos and kept concealed. Bawdy, transgressive references to female pubic hair are another matter (see Chapter 5). The perceived relevance of beards was symptomatic of patriarchal society's tendency to privilege male perspectives and male experience.

Nevertheless, the semiotics of beards were as comprehensible to women as to men, and it appears likely that female listeners were as entertained as male listeners by didactic poets who came up with beard-related images or told exemplary stories of beardedness to instruct and educate others. Poets like the König vom Odenwald and Heinrich der Teichner even explicitly invoke female attitudes towards beards in the process. If there is one ideal – norm, even – that Frauenlob's 'Her Bart' strophes make quite clear, it is that the beard was supposed to bestow dignity upon its wearer. Age and experience were held to be visually manifest in men's faces. Depending on their didactic agenda poets construed this emblematic quality of beards in terms either of wisdom or of mortality.

Notes

1 'Sir Beard, you are fit and becoming for men and no one else. You should accept this for a fact.' All translations in this chapter are my own.
2 See Huber, 'Lehrdichtung'; Lähnemann and Linden (eds), *Dichtung und Didaxe*.
3 Brüggen, 'Fiktionalität und Didaxe'.
4 Bein, *Deutschsprachige Lyrik des Mittelalters*, 200–27.
5 Tervooren, *Sangspruchdichtung*, 20–44, 48–59.
6 Brem, '"Herger"/Spervogel', 10–26.
7 By contrast marital relationships are only thematized once: 29,27–33.
8 Lauer, *Ästhetik der Identität*, 144–54.
9 Ludwig, 'Die Priameln Spervogels', 1963, 298–301.
10 Brem, '"Herger"/Spervogel', 27–33.
11 Bauschke, 'Ein jüdischer Autor', 62–6; Przybilski, *Kulturtransfer*, 267–78.
12 https://digi.ub.uni-heidelberg.de/diglit/cpg848/0705. Accessed 9 March 2021.
13 See also Gerhardt, *Süsskind von Trimberg*, 25–38.
14 This figure is closely copied from an earlier 'Grundstock' miniature (fol. 205r).
15 The other bearded figures in the miniatures of 'Nachtragsmaler I' are given much shorter, cropped or jawline beard growth; cf. fols 10r (King Wenzel of Bohemia; one musician), 190v (Johann von Ringenberg), 281v (Meister Heinrich Teschler), 292v (Der Schulmeister von Eßlingen), 381r (Frauenlob – beard possibly added by another hand).
16 See also *Die Gedichte Reinmars von Zweter*, ed. Roethe, 264–6.
17 This is a significant theme in the work of several 'Sangspruchdichter'; see Moshövel, *Effemination*, 69–81.
18 Wachinger, *Sängerkrieg*, 129.
19 IV,7 is the last in a sequence of polemical strophes (IV,4–7) aimed at Der Marner. See Wachinger, *Sängerkrieg*, 164–70; Haustein, *Marner-Studien*, 43–6.
20 A bawdy variant of this image is found in the *Innsbrucker Osterspiel*: 'ich ribe er [ir] kletten in den bart' (688).
21 Lauer, 'Sangspruchdichtung'.
22 https://collections.thulb.uni-jena.de/receive/HisBest_cbu_00008190. Accessed 10 March 2021.

23 Wenzel, *Meisterschaft*, 125–87.
24 See also Wenzel, *Meisterschaft*, 171–2.
25 Moshövel, *Effemination*, 60–9, 93–4.
26 Another strophe in the 'Langer Ton' (V,33) is addressed to the comparable personification 'Her Hof' / 'Sir Court'.
27 Huber, *Wort sint der dinge zeichen*, 156–7.
28 Wachinger, *Sängerkrieg*, 278–9.
29 In two of his anti-clerical songs Frauenlob refers satirically to bishops' beards when criticizing the Church: 'blate unde bart, / die sint nu gar enwicht' (VIII,14: 6–7); 'swie krum ein stab, ein bart und griser stimme, / Man sol sie doch nicht fürsten heizen' (XI,6: 6–7).
30 Schanze, *Tugendlehre und Wissensvermittlung*.
31 https://digi.ub.uni-heidelberg.de/diglit/cpg389. Accessed 10 March 2021. Vetter, 'Die Handschrift und ihre Bilder'.
32 Schneider, 'Textstruktur und Illustrationsprinzipien', 2017.
33 Ruff, *Der Wälsche Gast*, 37–47.
34 Cf. Freidank, *Bescheidenheit* 106,8–11, and the lesser-known moral-exemplary tale *Das gebratene Ei*.
35 Fichtner, 'Christus als Arzt'.
36 For another reading of this miniature see Wenzel, *Spiegelungen*, 31–3.
37 Vetter, 'Die Handschrift und ihre Bilder', 167.
38 The figure of the physician in the miniature is a very human one; there is no pictorial trace here of the text's insistence on God as physician.
39 All the material is accessible via the *Welscher Gast* digital project webpages: http://wgd.materiale-textkulturen.de/illustrationen/motive.php. Accessed 11 March 2021.
40 The physician treating the bedridden man is bearded in only one other manuscript: New York, Pierpont Morgan Library, MS G.54, c. 1380, fol. 29v. In this picture both patients are bearded also.
41 Hellgardt, 'Probleme der Bilderkennung', 134.
42 https://digital.slub-dresden.de/werkansicht/dlf/14347. Accessed 11 March 2021.
43 In the corresponding miniature in six other manuscripts (U, W, a, Erl, H, b) both sick men as well as the physician are beardless, thus marking a complete departure from the beard semantics of the picture in Cpg 389.
44 Cf. Heidelberg, UB, Cpg 112, c. 1200, fol. 100r (Pfaffe Konrad's *Rolandslied*); Berlin, Staatsbibl., Mgf 282, c. 1220–30, fol. 4r (Heinrich von Veldeke's *Eneasroman*).
45 Cf. also fols 28r and 59v.
46 The red ink colouring the cheeks of this 'wise man' gives this figure a surprisingly youthful look; in the corresponding miniature in several other manuscripts the figure is bearded; see also Schanze, *Tugendlehre und Wissensvermittlung*, 109–11.
47 The authority of lordship is conveyed by a cropped beard in several other miniatures: fols 28r, 33v, 49v (i).
48 Cuadra, *Allegorische Denkformen*, 3–4.
49 Schwarzbach-Dobson, *Exemplarisches Erzählen*, 125–31.
50 Cf. 1–14, 9318–34, 10493–5.
51 For an insightful structural overview see Weigand, *Der 'Renner'*, 365–74.
52 The consequences of 'Hôchfart wider hôchfart' are five (21315–24). This anaphoric passage complements an earlier list of examples of Pride in *dist.* I (467–96).
53 This anti-feminist section (309–462) of Hugo's work also circulated as a free-standing short text: Munich, BSB, Cgm 714, c. 1450–75, fols 28v–32v (under the rubric 'Die Spehen mayd' / 'Sharp-eyed maidens').
54 See also Cuadra, *Allegorische Denkformen*, 229–33.
55 For more on this age-old topos see Chapter 1.
56 This aspect of Hugo's work has been termed 'polyvocality' by Murray, 'Quotation, form, and didacticism', 271.
57 Cf. Judges 16: 13–30; II Kings 2: 23–4; II Samuel 14: 25–6.
58 One Church Father in the Eastern Orthodox tradition, Ephrem the Syrian (c. 306–73), took inspiration from a later book in the Pentateuch (Numbers 5:17–27), which sets out the ordeal suspected adulteresses were obliged to undergo ('bitter water') and the manifestation of guilt in certain physical symptoms. This law, Ephrem claims, was derived from Moses's treatment of those responsible for the golden calf by forcing them 'to drink of the water of ordeal, that the

mark of adulteresses might appear in it' (*Three Homilies* I,6). This analogy represents the polar opposite of the androcentric idea of 'guilt by golden beard'.

59 This belongs to the commentary on Exodus 32: 20, 'Et dedit ex eo potum filiis Israel' (PL 113: 287).

60 The relevant passage is found in chapter 73 of Comestor's 'Liber Exodi', entitled *De vitulo conflatili* / 'The molten calf' (PL 198: 1189–90). For the popularity of Comestor's work see Sherwood-Smith, *Studies in the Reception*, 1–34.

61 Dunphy, *Old Testament material*, 52–66.

62 See also the note in Philipp Strauch's edition of the text: p. 167 n. 2. For the scurrilous tendencies within this chronicle see Mierke, *Riskante Ordnungen*, 204–13.

63 Jans names a (Bohemian) priest called 'Vriderîch' (8815) as his source for this bizarre incident. In both Rudolf's *Weltchronik* (12060–2) and the *Christherre-Chronik* (17409) the killing of Ur (who is married to Moses's sister) is mentioned only in passing and not specified. See also Dunphy, *Old Testament material*, 194–8.

64 There is no mention in this version of the guilty being put to the sword (in their thousands); their deaths are conveyed solely by the words of the angel.

65 Munich, BSB, Cgm 199 (fragm.), early fourteenth century, fol. 4r. http://mdz-nbn-resolving.de/urn:nbn:de:bvb:12-bsb00096309-6. Accessed 11 March 2021. Munich BSB, Cgm 11, c. 1340, fol. 49r. http://mdz-nbn-resolving.de/urn:nbn:de:bvb:12-bsb00093674-2. Accessed 11 March 2021.

66 Cf. Isaiah 6: 1–6; Ezekiel 44: 1–4; Revelation 7: 3–8, 14: 1.

67 See also the commentary by the text's editors (II, 671).

68 Schwarzbach-Dobson, *Exemplarisches Erzählen*, 159–60, 163–7.

69 Jacob van Maerlant in turn drew heavily on Peter Comestor for his *Rijmbijbel* (c. 1270). See also Sherwood-Smith, *Studies in the Reception*, 133–45.

70 Jacob van Maerlant, *Rijmbijbel*: 'Dat hem tgoud hinc an den baert' / 'so that gold was hanging in their beards' (5073).

71 See also Niesner, 'Christliche Laien im Glaubensdisput', 2007, 13–15.

72 In another manuscript the nickname of 'golden-beard' is given to Jewish men in general ('davan heist yr noch' (k^6) 102). The sense of the passage is largely lost in codex b^{11}, where the far plainer insult of 'judenbart' / 'Jew's beard' (106) is used.

73 Weigand, *Der 'Renner'*, 163–4.

74 https://nbn-resolving.org/urn:nbn:de:bvb:29-bv040779348-7. Accessed 13 April 2021.

75 Weigand, *Der 'Renner'*, 189–205.

76 Weigand, *Der 'Renner'*, 198–9.

77 http://hdl.handle.net/1887.1/item:1520176. Accessed 11 March 2021.

78 See also Müller, 'Die Titelbilder', 1966.

79 The miniature illustrates an 'exemplum' concerning the wealthy man who enters a monastery and refuses to return to his former life when called upon to do so (23843–75).

80 The corresponding miniature in Vienna, ÖNB, Cod. Nr. 3086, dated 1426, fol. 81v, uses beards in the same way. Innsbruck, UB, Cod. Nr. 900, dated 1411–13, fol. 99v, features a bearded husband and a goat but no (beardless) lover.

81 As discussed in the edition of Vorster's work by Lähnemann, 3–191. https://digi.ub.uni-heidelberg.de/diglit/cpg471. Accessed 11 March 2021.

82 Cf. fols 9va: 17–8 (= 18112–13); 9va: 42 (= 18136); 11vb: 40 (= 23760); 20ra: 33 (= 9074); 29vb: 31 (= 12212); 32rb: 46 (= 323); 37ra: 17 (= 3394).

83 *Der 'Renner' des Johannes Vorster*, ed. Lähnemann, 130–48.

84 *Der 'Renner' des Johannes Vorster*, ed. Lähnemann, 71–2.

85 Fols 6va: 37, 7ra: 23, 9rb: 29, 9va: 17, 9va: 41, 12ra: 40, 12rb: 7.

86 Fols 7v, 15r, 32v, 60v. http://nbn-resolving.de/urn:nbn:de:hebis:30:2-11711. Accessed 11 March 2021.

87 For an overview see Chapter 1.

88 The straps on which barbers wipe their razors are just one of many practical items made from pigskin (*Gedicht vom Schwein* 67–70).

89 Shaving is listed as the ninth reason people go to the baths (*Vom Baden* 23–4).

90 In another poem the König vom Odenwald sends himself up as an impoverished householder who, far removed from life at court, grows a beard and goes grey from anxiety: 'Mir wehset der bart und grawet das hor' (*Vom Hausrat* 10).

91 For a general overview see Lämmert, *Reimsprecherkunst*.

92 Frivolous 'Rhinish' fashion is attested as a satirical motif as far back as thirteenth-century 'Sangspruchdichtung'; cf. Bruder Wernher III,50: 1–3; Der Marner III,2: 1–5.

93 Cf. Hugo von Trimberg, *Der Renner*, 309–10.

94 Cf. also nr 543, where a lady has an affair with a monk behind her would-be lover's back. This long-haired courtier grows his beard (10–11) while on a hazardous expedition undertaken for her sake.

95 For beard growth and mourning cf. also 551: 72–83. In this text Teichner also describes how some dishonest men grow beards in order to give the impression of having undergone much hardship in the name of their beloved.

96 Cf. also the references to Hungarian warriors in Ottokar von Gaal's *Steirische Reimchronik*: 'die mit den langen berten' (16236); 'mit iren langen berten' (26386).

97 http://resolver.staatsbibliothek-berlin.de/SBB00015AE100000000. Accessed 12 March 2021.

98 'Hie heb ich an zv tichten vnd wil geistlich vnd weltlich sachen vsriehten' (fol. 7v).

99 This text (in this codex) features Teichner's characteristic final signature line: 'also sprach der Teichnär' (142).

100 See also Weichselbaumer, *Der konstruierte Mann*, 7–26.

101 Weichselbaumer, *Der konstruierte Mann*, 259–65.

102 Thomasin von Zerklaere does not mention female hair at all in *Der Welsche Gast*; and in *Der Renner* Hugo only does so twice, within the same section, on female frivolity and vanity (309–10, 397–404).

103 This is confirmed by the 'Manesse' miniatures (Heidelberg, UB, Cpg 848, fols 213r, 217v), which preface the complementary didactic poems *Der Winsbeke* (grey-haired bearded father, beardless son) and *Die Winsbekin* (mother and daughter in dialogue). The principal visual differences between mother and daughter relate to marital status (hair covered, hair uncovered) and posture (seated, standing). Otherwise they are based on the same model of courtly female beauty. For a 'gendered' reading of these texts see Rasmussen, 'Fathers to think back through'.

5
Laughter and beards: Wittenwiler's *Ring*

> Er nam den einen pei dem part
> Und rauft in, daz er schreient wart.
>
> Heinrich Wittenwiler, *Ring* 5825–6[1]

Much of what we have observed so far indicates that the beard was the ideal symbol for patriarchal values and hierarchical social relations. For the very same reason, beard references also worked extremely effectively in literary contexts governed by structural principles such as incongruity and inversion (the 'topsy-turvy' world), where established cultural norms and power relations were turned on their head in order to amuse and elicit laughter. The comedic effects in question vary quite considerably, encompassing both gentle irony and, in the later Middle Ages especially, the drastically bawdy. However, one element remains fairly constant: the entertainment value of beard-specific abuse, whether verbal or physical, when men in positions of authority of one kind or another are flagrantly denied the respect normally afforded to them. This might help to explain the enduring popularity (from the twelfth to the sixteenth centuries, in both Latin and the vernacular) of the 'fable' of the philosopher who spat in a king's beard because, in a magnificent dining hall full of splendid furniture, it was the foulest and thus most suitable place he could see.[2]

The analysis of literary comedy as a historical phenomenon is of course fraught with difficulty. There is no doubt that it existed but the interpretation of any specific instance almost invariably involves conjecture and uncertainty.[3] This may be offset, to a degree, by taking into account the broader literary context and the cumulative weight of evidence gathered from numerous sources. There is a lot of material to consider. From the mid-thirteenth century onwards various literary forms in German emerged which quite blatantly sought to provoke laughter, just as more established literary traditions lent themselves to parody. One key aspect of literary comedy, medieval or otherwise, relates to recipient sympathy, where it is directed, and when it is dampened.[4] Like many other types of aggressive behaviour, beard-pulling and beard-related insults are perceived as either hilarious or despicable depending on whether the (bearded) person in question represents a figure of negative or positive identification, and whether such abusive treatment is viewed as merited or undeserved. A final caveat concerns the range of purposes to which medieval literary comedy was applied, especially in relation to its didactic quality. However tempting it may be for the modern reader to view inversion as subversion, and transgression as undermining of the status quo, it is quite conceivable that in practice the effect was often the opposite.[5] The pleasure or relief afforded to a group of recipients by the temporary suspension of traditional values could only have ensued if all were agreed on their validity in the first place.

Heinrich Wittenwiler's *Ring*

Few medieval German texts, if any, combine didactic intent and comedy to such controversial effect as Heinrich Wittenwiler's masterful story of a peasant wedding, entitled *Der Ring* (c. 1408–10). Based on a fourteenth-century short comic tale, *Die Bauernhochzeit*, Wittenwiler's *Ring* expands the burlesque action over the course of approximately 10,000 lines to include slapstick scenes of rustic wooing as well as a fantastical world war of sorts. At the same time, the bawdy narrative, which shirks from very little sexual or scatological detail, frames an extensive series of instructive debates on issues ranging from marriage to table manners, from personal hygiene to warfare. The juxtaposition of so much learning and doctrine next to so much absurd narrative action is singular, as is the extent to which Wittenwiler draws on a host of literary forms and traditions, both Latin and vernacular.[6] The fact that the *Ring* itself appears to have been largely unknown in the fifteenth century, outside its primary audience of pre-eminent citizens in Constance, merely adds to the extraordinary impression which this work makes.[7]

The Janus-like character of the *Ring* becomes clear to recipients in the prologue (1–54).[8] The opening dedication to the Holy Trinity, the Virgin Mary and the heavenly host (1–4) is followed by an explanation of the work's title, scope ('Der welte lauff' / 'the course of the world' 11) and essential didactic purpose ('Was man tuon und lassen schol' / 'what one should and should not do' 12). Having set out the (tripartite) structure of the narrative in terms of its principal topics (tourneying, housekeeping and self-care, war), the poet concedes that no one has the stamina to listen for long to 'serious matters without some amusement' (34). For this reason, he announces, he has mixed his instruction with 'der gpauren gschrai' / 'the raucous antics of peasants' (36) and these two dimensions are even colour-coordinated in the manuscript book: 'Die rot die ist dem ernst gemain, / Die grüen ertzaigt uns törpelleben' / 'Red is the mark of what is serious; green indicates to us foolish behaviour' (40–1).[9] The red and green lines which run down through the first letters of every line throughout the following story (55–9695) are thus a very visual reminder of Wittenwiler's twofold poetic purpose: to provide comprehensive instruction in virtuous and socially responsible conduct and to offer an extensive narrative portrayal, in gleefully lurid detail, of what bad and foolish behaviour looks like. Within this scheme the figure of the peasant, the poet hastens to point out, has general significance: 'Er ist ein gpaur in meinem muot, / Der unrecht lept und läppisch tuot' / 'To my mind anyone is a peasant who lives wrongly and behaves like an idiot' (43–4). By means of this disqualification Wittenwiler effectively issues himself with a licence to be as demeaning as he likes when it comes to the boorish peasants in his story. The prologue ends on a note of joyful anticipation, which seems almost harmless (53–4); but in actual fact much of the comedy is highly aggressive and disparaging.

References to beards (and hair) feature throughout the *Ring* in lines and passages which are marked red as well as in those marked green. Several of these references take the form of a proverbial wisdom; the majority occur within comic scenes involving the coarse and crude antics of the peasants. Notwithstanding Wittenwiler's moral-didactic imperative, the text betrays a fascination with bodies and body parts, with a predilection for the sexual and the scatological, a drastic corporeality which anticipates some of the most 'obscene' comedic literature of the later fifteenth century.[10] Beards evidently form part of the comic anatomy of Wittenwiler's peasants. This is illustrated at the outset by the pen-and-ink drawing situated beneath the prologue on the first page of the work's sole manuscript (Munich, BSB, Cgm 9300, c. 1410–20, fol. 1v), which portrays the peasant couple at the heart of the story: Bertschi Triefnas ('Snot-nose') and Mätzli Rüerenzumph ('Rub-the-prick') (see Figure 5.1). The unkempt hair and beard growth of the corpulent Bertschi are suggestive of a base existence dominated by bodily urges and blind lust rather than by morality and reason, as further evinced by his unconcealed groping of the hideous Mätzli.[11] This vision of Mätzli's ugliness, including her pendulous goitre, is derived from the

Figure 5.1 Bertschi Triefnas and Mätzli Rüerenzumph embrace (Heinrich Wittenwiler's *Ring*). Munich, BSB, Cgm 9300, fol. 1v.

relatively lengthy portrayal of her in the text (76–96), in a passage marked red which serves as an inverted model of rhetorical *descriptio*.[12] By contrast, Bertschi's body is never described in such detail. More to the point, his beard is mentioned only when the comic action dictates it, in scenes of brutal mishap and violence.

This strategy is epitomized – in Part I of the *Ring* (55–2622) – by the predominantly green narrative sequence concerning Bertschi's attempt to impress the women of his village (Lappenhausen) by engaging in a series of 'chivalric' pursuits together with a number of other ill-equipped yokels. They are joined in this travesty of courtly culture by a certain Sir Neithart, sworn enemy of all peasants (158–60), a figure Wittenwiler borrows from broader literary tradition in order to bring Bertschi and company to grief.[13] Hopelessly outmatched by Neithart, Bertschi has himself tied so securely to his steed that he cannot fall to safety when knocked off his saddle. Hanging down, his head receives a pounding from the hooves of his own horse, prompting the author-narrator to issue the ironic understatement: 'Ob ich es rechte brüefe, / Ze hart im an der selben vart / Gestrigelt ward sein har und bart' / 'As far as I can tell, his hair and beard were given too vigorous a grooming during this same ride' (609–11). The pain and humiliation suffered by Bertschi and others during this episode (and several others like it) were evidently intended to be entertaining. In this particular instance the aggressive comedic effect is compounded by the deliberate confusion of rider and horse, as the notion of combing a horse's coat is (mis)applied to Bertschi's hair and beard.

The peasants' aspiration to impress as knights is lampooned further by their speech: when not giving crude expression to their emotions, they speak only to ridicule and threaten one other. When Neithart eventually orchestrates a team tournament for those who are still capable, the yokels on both sides immediately start to argue among themselves about whom they should capture first and why. The anti-social crime of cleaning a stable on a Sunday is enough for a certain Eisengrein to be singled out by one team: 'Dar umb man schol in vassen / Pai dem har und pei dem part' / 'That's why we should grab him by the hair and beard!' (981–2). Such primitive settling of rustic scores flatly contradicts the loftier aims of tourneying as previously explained – in a passage marked red (898–913) – by Neithart. The threat to pull Eisengrein's hair and beard, which comes to nothing, also stands in comic contrast to the actual bludgeoning dished out by Neithart. He is only pretending to be using a club of straw like the others, and so the event is soon brought to a bone-crunching conclusion.

The narrative focus of Part I turns to Bertschi's ham-fisted attempts to win the affections of a fiercely resistant Mätzli. In the course of this bawdy action, most of which is marked green, Wittenwiler has no qualms about showcasing Mätzli's physical maturity – that hair growth which corresponds to Bertschi's beard, as it were. Locked away in a shed by her father, she pays attention to her pudenda ('ier vil praunen mutzen' / 'her dark brown muff' 1566), beating it in fury before starting to masturbate (1588–1604).[14] This change of heart is anticipated by the narrator with proverbial reference, in two lines marked red, to the hair on her head: 'Do hiet Mätzel langes har / Und churtzen muot: ja, daz ist war!'/ 'So Mätzel's hair was indeed long and her resolve short: yes, that's true!' (1584–5). If the latter utterance represents entirely respectable didactic content, as shared with, say, Hugo von Trimberg,[15] the reference to Mätzli's pubic hair in an explicitly sexual context speaks to Wittenwiler's penchant for ignoring literary taboos.

The one beard reference to feature in this narrative phase also takes the form of a quasi-proverbial expression, attributed this time to a priest as part of an elaborate fiction concocted by the unscrupulous village doctor (Chrippenchra) on behalf of Mätzli – she finds herself pregnant (by Chrippenchra himself) and in dire need of a husband.

Bertschi is sent a letter which purports to relate a dream-vision in which two female figures (Venus and the Virgin Mary) appear to Mätzli and give her conflicting advice regarding Bertschi (pleasure vs marriage). These figures are identified for her, so the fictitious account goes, by her priest, who expounds their various allegorical attributes,[16] including Venus's blindness (as opposed to the 'four eyes' of Mary): 'Daz weteut, sam ich es vind, / Daz oft ein schönes mensch von art / Minnet einen grausen part' / 'In my opinion this means that a beautiful person of high birth often falls in love with an ugly beard' (2430–2).

All such details are wasted on the illiterate Bertschi, who requires the local notary (Nabelreiber) to sum the letter up for him. But the lack of narrative consequence does not seem to matter when it comes to the validity of the letter's content (upholding Christian marriage as a vehicle for sexuality), nor is it an issue that the letter represents a fiction within a fiction: the whole of this passage (2261–554) is marked red.[17] As far as the beard saying (2431–2) is concerned, there is no real need to doubt its perceived validity as an abstract truism.[18] The connotation of beardedness with ugliness was a commonplace of the discourse of courtly love (see below). It is the narrative context which casts the priest's (alleged) words of wisdom in an ironic light, for they could hardly be less appropriate. Mätzli – who herself is the exact opposite of a 'beautiful person of high birth' (2431) – is anything but blinded by love for Bertschi.

Part II of *Der Ring* (2623–6457) is dominated by didactic content which initially takes the form of an extensive debate among Bertschi's kin about the institution of marriage (2668–3525). When the voices of younger members of Bertschi's family are eventually eclipsed by those of their elders, the theme of wisdom itself is foregrounded by means of several beard references. The first major contribution by a certain grey-haired (3069) old man by the name of Colman begins auspiciously enough: the wisdom of old men may be proverbial, he concedes – 'Daz sprüchwart ist mir oft gesait: / Alter part hat weisshait' / 'I have often heard the saying: an old beard has wisdom' (3071–2) – but experience has taught him that the young (3074) and even women are not without cleverness (3076). In fact, this statement presages the course of the following discussion, in which the matriarchal Berchta Laichdenman ('Deceive-the-man') scornfully rebuffs Colman's rather cynical arguments.[19] If it is shameful for a 77-year-old 'greisen *partt*' / 'greybeard' (3211) to still require schooling, she mocks, the inability or reluctance to learn is even worse.[20] Colman subsequently changes strategy by launching a vituperative personal attack on Mätzli, whereupon the author-narrator reduces him (sarcastically?) to a single feature: 'Dennocht ruort sich alter part / Hin wider umb ein ander vart' / 'The old beard stirred himself once more to engage in another round' (3419–20). Colman may have a beard, he may even be wise (in comparison to many of the other peasants), but this does not translate into success in the debate. In a display of considerable rhetorical skill and wit Laichdenman turns every one of Mätzli's (many) deficiencies into a welcome attribute, and so Bertschi's marriage proposal is approved.

In the discussions held by Mätzli's family (3631–817) there is less controversy and the antagonism between the sexes is less belligerent. On the other hand, the incongruity between the boorish nature of the speakers as revealed by their ridiculous names and the wise and noble sentiments they express is all the more marked. Thus, the ideal physical attributes of a (sexually mature) husband are comprehensively enumerated by one Ochsenkropf ('Ox-goitre') who explains that such a man's hair and beard should be 'on the curly side' ('Ein wenich straublocht an irm schein' 3658) and not too black or too red but brownish (3659–60). The physiognomic aspect of such features is left unspoken.[21] Nevertheless, Ochsenkropf's respectful description of the ideal beard bears about as much relation to Mätzli's kinsmen's subsequent treatment of Bertschi as rules of good diet and dining do to the actual conduct of the peasants at the wedding feast. Indeed, Wittenwiler misses no opportunity to exaggerate the gross discrepancy between theory and rustic practice. Once Bertschi has been examined in various matters (faith, hygiene, diet, ethics and the principles of good housekeeping), once he has received Mätzli's consent, he is brutally welcomed into the family. In a passage marked green he is subjected to a ritual buffeting in which the hair is torn from his head and beard (5288–90), leaving him quite 'glatzocht' / 'bald' (5292).

Bertschi's baldness turns out to be short-lived, representing a moment of comic hyperbole. Later, while hosting the wedding celebrations, he falls victim again to the same kind of violence when he becomes involved in a brawl with those serving at the banquet table and doing a bad job of it (5816–22). By chastising one of them in customary fashion – 'Er nam den einen pei dem part / Und rauft in, daz er schreient wart' / 'He grabbed one of them by the beard and tore away at it, making him scream' (5825–6) – Bertschi merely prompts retribution in kind at the hands of three others (5827–9). This time beard-pulling serves as a prelude for rather more demeaning abuse, as the men pull down the groom's breeches and give him what can only be described as an impromptu enema (5830–1). The spectacle of the groom being stripped of his position of authority in such primitive fashion is enjoyed tremendously by the boorish guests

(5837–8), while a lesson in saving face is provided by Bertschi when he reminds others, somewhat stiffly, of the received wisdom: 'Drei sein alweg eines herren' / 'Three will always have mastery over one' (5842).[22]

No matter how base the action gets during the feast (5541–6186), this entire narrative sequence is marked red. While some critics are convinced that Wittenwiler's colour scheme subverts any straightforward didacticism,[23] it seems likely that in this episode at least the peasants' crude antics paint an uncensored picture of what not to do and how not to behave, offering an extended lesson *ex negativo* in gluttony and related vices.[24] The poet certainly employs all sorts of devices to keep his recipients amused, including repeatedly comparing the guests to animals.[25] The manner in which they compete with one another over a dish of cabbage and bacon is likened to a kind of banquet-table warfare, with hands and spoons clashing 'sam die sper' / 'like lances' (5738). When the peasant named Twerg ('Dwarf') stuffs his portion into his mouth so greedily 'daz im sein part / Mit enander smaltzich wart!' / 'that his beard was altogether drenched in grease' (5743–4), this detail does more than just epitomize vulgar self-indulgence. It travesties the image of the bearded hero on the battlefield – the figure of Rennewart in the second battle on Alischanz springs to mind – whose beard is soaked with sweat or blood.

The feasting becomes increasingly grotesque and orgiastic as foodstuffs and bodily fluids intermingle, and as inordinate quantities of food and drink are poured into gaping mouths.[26] Many of these details would seem to conform to Bakhtin's famous vision of the carnivalesque.[27] One essential difference, however, lies in the antagonism and aggression which are present throughout. The joys and pleasures experienced by the wedding guests are hardly those with which the text's recipients would have wanted to associate themselves, whether these be throwing snot in Bertschi's face (5961–5) or quaffing from a communal bucket (6010–5). Ingestion gives way to digestion as surely as drinking leads to pissing. Nor would the scene be complete without vomiting, which duly occurs when a certain Graf Purkhart is assailed by the fart stench made by a nearby (female) table companion: 'Die speis die schluog im zuo dem maul; / Des muost er speiben ze der vart / Auf den tisch durch seinen part' / 'The food rose back up into his mouth; he had no choice but to puke through his beard and onto the table' (6158–60). The befouled beard represents the very antithesis of personal dignity. If in theory the beard betokens wisdom, then there can be no more telling display of the folly of gluttony than this. As a 'signature event of extreme disgust'[28] such vomiting confirms and hilariously exaggerates the revolting behaviour of these peasants.

Part III (6458–9696) deals with the outbreak of hostilities among the drunken peasantry as they dance, which develops into a bizarre war. The cause is relatively innocuous: Gredel, a maiden from a nearby village (Nissingen), is dishonoured when Eisengrein (from Bertschi's own village of Lappenhausen) furtively scratches her palm (6449–55). Yet the conflict itself soon spirals out of control, as sexually aggressive insults and threats are traded between Gredel's uncle and Eisengrein before kinsmen of the two respective families assault each other.[29] Tired of fighting with their fists, the men resort to spears and swords to wound and kill each other. A temporary lull in the conflict sees both villages call for reinforcements. Eventually, after extensive debates on each side concerning warfare, the peasants engage in a battle, which is no less ludicrous than savage, involving witches, dwarves, fabled Germanic heroes, giants and an army of Swiss mercenaries.

The very first phase of fighting within this scheme takes the form of 'rauffen' / 'hair yanking' (6475–96), where one act of manhandling automatically provokes another in retaliation.[30] The aggressive comedy at work here depends on the utter dehumanization of the peasants (in the eyes of the recipients) as well as on the moral-didactic significance of their actions, constituting a warning against the dangers of intemperance and anger. The expert hair-yanking technique of a certain Lappenhausener (named appropriately enough Fesafögili or 'Pluck-the-birdie') receives the narrator's ironic praise ('es was ein wunder' / 'It was wondrous to behold' 6483), before he himself is attacked with exaggerated brutality by one Dietreich: 'Er nam in pei seim langen part / Und zucht in so, daz an der vart / Der kumpagg viel zer erden' / 'He grabbed him by his long beard and gave it such a yank that the very next moment his jawbone fell to the ground' (6488–90).[31] By the time they are finished, the narrator observes, the brawling yokels have no locks left 'In dem haubt noch in dem part' / 'on their heads or in their beards' (6494). This comparatively harmless conclusion – marked green – returns to the comedic notion of baldness at the hands of others. This time, however, such 'decalvation' is of (logical) narrative consequence, for it is only when the peasants have no hair left that they start punching one another.

As the action unfolds Wittenwiler finds other ways to ridicule the peasant world he depicts with reference to their beards. His practice of according peasants ludicrous speaking names is taken to extreme lengths when the men of Lappenhausen gather for their own council of war (7149–557).[32] Among such 'herren' / 'gentlemen' (7150) as Künchelstil ('Distaff-handle'), Ochsenchäs ('Ox-cheese') and Fleugenschäss ('Fly-shit') there appears a certain Futzenpart ('Quim-beard'), who is named not just once but twice in the space of about a hundred lines (7158, 7264). Apart from the vulgar delight this name offers as yet another means of mentioning the unmentionable, its compound formation combines both the straightforwardly explicit ('Futzen-') and the euphemistic ('-part').[33] One of the bawdier moments in the narrative before this, Hüdellein's mishap at the wedding dance, dwells on the notice taken by all and sundry of her (hitherto unrecognized) sexual maturity: 'Seu schreuwen all: "Sei wil ein man: / Sei hat ein maul und har dar an"' / 'They all shouted out: "She wants a man: she has a mouth with hair hanging from it"' (6412–13).[34] In one respect, the phrase 'Futzenpart' develops this idea by alluding to female pubic hair in terms of male facial hair. In another, as a preposterous name for a male figure this 'type' of beard can only be demeaning, summoning up, in the crudest possible way, an image of the female body, when beardedness in men so often connotes masculinity. As with other absurd names in the *Ring*, the normality of 'Futzenpart' as a name in Lappenhausen serves to alienate the peasants still further from the recipients of Wittenwiler's text.[35]

Once the respective councils of war are concluded and battle is eventually joined, the depiction of the ensuing struggle, which is predominantly marked green, is both horrific and ludicrous, a parody no doubt of the bombastic excesses of the late medieval heroic epic. Another comedic effect lies in the appearance of certain proverbial wisdoms – marked red – which relate to the absurd action in various ways. One is placed in the mouth of the giant Ecke, for example, when he mocks Dietrich – in a comic reprise of the grave encounter between the two in the *Eckenlied* – for drawing his sword to little purpose, having failed to notice that the hero has actually sliced him in half: 'Narren messer, hüerren prüst / Sicht man bleken oft umb süst' / 'The knives of fools, the breasts of whores are often displayed to no avail' (9040–1). The final beard reference in the *Ring* occurs as part of another proverbial wisdom of this kind. This time it is uttered directly by the author-narrator in response to the horrendous fate of the newly made knights of Lappenhausen, who suffocate in their suits of armour in the terrible heat: 'Das geschach nicht ane sach; / Won der weis vil ofte sprach: / "Alter part der hat die witz, / Nüwer palg der hat die hitz"' / 'This did not occur for no reason, for as the wise man has said so often, "The old beard has the wits; the young hide has the heat"' (9186–9). A conventional comparison between the wisdom of old age and the heated behaviour of the young (as governed by their emotions and desires) is deliberately misused to pour scorn on the peasants and their pretensions of knighthood. By this stage in the narrative such cruel humour hardly requires further justification.

Nevertheless, there is clearly an element of poetic justice at work here. This very specific and, in literary terms at least, unusual form of death marks a fitting end for the hot-headed youngsters of Lappenhausen who so recklessly ignored all the warnings and words of caution of their elders in council, having no understanding of the dangers of battle and the suffering war entails.

The grotesque triteness of the narrator's commentary at this juncture does not actually undermine the fundamental association of the beards of old(er) men and wisdom as first articulated by Bertschi's kinsman Colman in the marriage debate ('Alter part hat weisshait' 3072). However, this proverbial content does stand in marked contrast to those sequences of action in which bearded peasants crudely assault one another or gorge themselves. In a text which takes such obvious pleasure in sexual and scatological references, in comically distorted representations of both the male and the female body, beards play their own part in illustrating moral turpitude for the amusement of recipients who are expected to know better.

Rustics

Wittenwiler's source, the comic tale known as *Die Bauernhochzeit*, is thought by most to be a (later?) fourteenth-century text, although its earliest known manuscript (Karlsruhe, Badische Landesbibl., Cod. Donaueschingen 104) is dateable to around 1433.[36] Transmitted in two versions – *Metzen hochzit* (680 lines) and *Meier Betz* (417 lines) – this 'Schwankmäre' covers the eventful rustic wedding of Bärschi (or Betz) and Metz. After Metz has given her consent in front of both families, a host of hilariously named peasants gathers to feast before bride and groom retire to consummate the marriage; a visit to church the next morning is followed by more feasting, then music and dancing, only for a violent brawl to erupt when the mirror of a certain peasant maid is accidentally broken.[37] *Meier Betz* tells pretty much the same story as *Metzen hochzit*, although it offers some variation in terms of the speaking names of the yokels. In both versions the peasants are portrayed as ridiculous boors, with *Meier Betz* going further to lampoon the bridegroom, especially in the wedding-night scene. In *Metzen hochzit* the couple fight and wrestle with one another until the bride ends up on her back and is robbed of her virginity. In *Meier Betz* Betz declares that he requires some light to perform his duty, an explanation which fails to impress Metz, who retorts that her father's manservant never needed any. Drunk as he is, Betz the 'fool' / 'der narr' (101) passes out and sleeps until morning.

It is quite clear that Wittenwiler is indebted to *Die Bauernhochzeit* – most likely in the form of the longer *Metzen hochzit* – for the basic plot of much of his *Ring* as well as for numerous minor details, whether this be names ('Ochsenkroppf' 93, 'Trieffnaß' 102, 'Kolman' 312), wedding gifts, or specific instances of wise and foolish behaviour at the banquet table. But reading the comic tale at the heart of Wittenwiler's experimental work also helps us to appreciate the scale of his retelling of this story.[38] Quite apart from the entirely new programme of extensive moral-didactic instruction, Wittenwiler expands the core narrative enormously (Part I) and in so doing pushes the limits of the comedy inherent in rustic scenarios of wooing and wedding to breaking point. The gluttony portrayed in *Die Bauernhochzeit* is massively amplified in the *Ring* (Part II), just as its relatively restrained bawdry is displaced by many more details of an explicitly sexual and scatological nature. This process of radicalization takes other forms too. Wittenwiler's recontextualization of the wedding night, which now takes place during a lull in hostilities between the villagers of Lappenhausen and Nissingen, enables the author-narrator to make a provocative comparison between the (hilarious) conjugal union of Bertschi and Mätzli (6979–7087, marked red) and the night as experienced by certain Nissinger wenches who are raped (7088–92, marked green): 'Hiet die praut nür einen man, / Kützeldarm ier vier gewan' / 'If the bride only had one husband, / Tickle-gut had four to herself' (7088–9).[39] This shocking passage should serve as a pertinent reminder that the *Ring*, to an even greater extent than *Die Bauernhochzeit*, depends on its recipients' utter sense of detachment from the rustic figures in the story.

In terms of beards *Die Bauernhochzeit* features one (very familiar) reference only, albeit one which appears in both *Metzen hochzit* and *Meier Betz*. It occurs in the context of the wedding feast, part of a relatively extended description of boorish behaviour and gluttony, when the yokels are devouring turnips and bacon: 'do baiß vil manig qualle / in den speck, daz im sin bart / mit ainander smaltzig wart' / 'Many of the oafs took such great bites of bacon that their beards were coated in grease' (*Metzen hochzit* 176–8). The satisfaction of bodily appetite is the peasants' sole concern, and their lack of self-control, their enslavement to their own bodies, is further illustrated when they subsequently burst out laughing, splattering the food from stuffed cheeks all over their legs (182–5).[40] Wittenwiler evidently adopts the detail of grease-drenched beards from his source, while changing it somewhat to refer to one figure in particular,

Twerg, as the parodic culmination of a battle of spoons. The laughter and spewing which follow in *Die Bauernhochzeit* is elided in the *Ring*, where Wittenwiler finds more drastic ways to produce his own comedy of disgust, including of course Graf Purkhart's involuntary reaction of vomiting over his own beard. In this way the equivalent episode in Wittenwiler's more expansive work, inspired as it is by *Die Bauernhochzeit*, focusses on the beards of individual gluttons as opposed to a bearded gluttonous collective.

Otherwise, the speaking name of 'Futzenpart' / 'Quim-beard' in the *Ring* would seem to be a slightly more 'ingenious' variation of the mock peasant name of 'Rochloch' / 'Hairy-hole' in *Metzen hochzit* (121).[41] And Bertschi's buffeting at the hands of Metzli's kinsmen, who brutally yank at his hair and beard, evidently reprises the groom's rite of passage in the shorter comic tale, which follows their visit to church first thing on the second day: 'Die törpel namen Bärschen her / und zugent in umb bi dem har / und roftent in zwar' / 'The yokels grabbed hold of Bärschi and dragged him around by his hair and pulled away at it for sure' (*Metzen hochzit* 322–4). The indignity of this primitive custom ('sit' 327) is exaggerated by Wittenwiler, who also has Bertschi manhandled by his beard. Both the repeated depiction of such rustic violence in the *Ring* and the author-narrator's unparalleled attention to the technique of 'raufen' (in the first phase of fighting following the dance) suggest that Wittenwiler found this behaviour to be significant in broader terms, not just as an uncultured ritual associated with marriage but as something quintessentially foolish.

The exaggerated boorishness of the peasantry as depicted in *Die Bauernhochzeit* and the *Ring* aligns both of these works to a popular literary tradition which ultimately extends back to the first half of the thirteenth century and the highly innovative songs of Neidhart (c. 1220–40/45). Neidhart it was who was the first to realize the comic potential of the foolish peasant – from a courtly aristocratic point of view – in conjunction with the theme of love, creating for himself the lyric persona of 'Der von Riuwental' as the darling of village wenches (in his 'Sommerlieder') and the bitter rival of vain (and violent) yokels or 'dörper' (in his 'Winterlieder').[42] Beard references play almost no role in this large body of material.[43] However, what Neidhart's 'Winterlieder' do provide is a blueprint for comic rustic violence, such as when one unwelcome boorish suitor is threatened with being dragged through the dance 'bî sîm reiden hâre' / 'by his curly locks' (WL 6: V,8).[44] The absurd pretensions of the peasants are frequently revealed by the care they lavish upon their hair, the way they grow it long and, occasionally, the inappropriately fine bonnets they wear, all of which emphasizes their folly and the poetic justice of any harm they suffer to their heads.[45] Wittenwiler dispenses with all such detail, taking it as read perhaps in his narrative concentration on the yanking and tearing of hair and beards.

The influence which Neidhart's vision came to exert on vernacular literature is demonstrated as early as the second half of the thirteenth century by Wernher der Gärtner's *Helmbrecht*, a tale concerning the terrible comeuppance meted out to a criminal young peasant with ideas above his station, as symbolized by his inordinately long locks (9–14) and preposterously embellished bonnet (32–103).[46] The violence directed at hair in this text, as befitting its unflinching moral agenda, is ferocious and points forward to Wittenwiler's *Ring*. On the one hand, young Helmbrecht's persecution of the peasantry at large – in his new-found role of robber-knight – involves tormenting them in various ways, as he himself gleefully reveals in dialogue with his father: 'enem ziuhe ich den loc / mit der zangen ûz dem barte, / dem andern rîz ich die swarte' / 'from the beard of one [peasant] I rip out locks of hair with tongs; from another I tear [the hair out of] his scalp' (1246–8). The very fact that Helmbrecht, a figure of negative identification, takes such delight in this kind of behaviour is likely to have nullified – in this particular narrative context – the comic potential of a peasant's beard being subjected to such abhorrent 'grooming'. By contrast, no such restrictions seem to be in place when it comes to Helmbrecht's own suffering in his final moments. Before stringing him up, several of his former victims (peasants and family men) first pay attention to the emblems of his pride and tear away at his glorious locks and bonnet, only for the author-narrator to report: 'ir gesâht nie swarte / ûf houbet alsô kalwe' / 'you never saw such a bald scalp on any head' (1896–7). Helmbrecht has brought this fate upon himself, and thus the audience is expected to relish his misfortune.[47] Helmbrecht's decalvation, prepared for throughout the story, represents the highlight in a brutal comedy of retribution.

The evolution of the Neidhart tradition sees 'Neidhart' himself become a literary figure in a number of early plays (c. 1350 onwards). Here he is cast as the arch-enemy of vain peasants who infamously spoil his discovery of the first violet in spring by defecating on it.[48] (Indeed, one cannot help but think that Wittenwiler is playing on this background when he pits his own 'Her Neithart' / 'Sir Neithart' against Bertschi and his companions in Part I of the *Ring*.) The extent to which rustic beardedness was enacted – with false beards? – must remain unclear, although it is not *that* far-fetched to suggest that spontaneous, unscripted bouts of hair- and beard-pulling between or during scenes would have lent themselves quite naturally to late medieval comedic performance (as we understand it today).[49] Faint reflections of this lost dimension may be discerned in the text of the so-called *Großes Neidhartspiel* (c. 1490), the longest secular drama in German (2624 lines), where two of Neithart's antagonists are named as 'Reupart' / 'Rue-beard' (1866) and 'Regenpart' / 'Rain-beard' (908). Isolated beard references in speeches can also be construed as implied stage directions. During the first of several dances in this play village maids discuss their choice of partner, drawing the audience's attention to the 'gelben har' / 'flaxen hair' (317) of one peasant, or, more dubiously, the 'rotten part' / 'red beard' (331) of another.[50] Towards the end of the play, when Regenpart exhorts his fellow yokels to prepare themselves for (yet another) dance – 'Wir wellen klaider vnd har / Dar zu sprintzen und sprantzen' / 'Let's gaily dress and adorn ourselves, our clothing and our hair, for the occasion' (1967–8) –, the players were at least presented with the opportunity of making fools of themselves by putting ribbons in their beards.

A sense of theatricality also permeates the verse narrative *Neithart Fuchs* (first printed c. 1491–7), which combines a number of Neidhart's original songs with all the episodes of provocation and retaliation previously known from the plays and more besides.[51] The beard Neithart wears to disguise himself as a sickly pilgrim is mentioned only in the direct speech of the singer's chief antagonist Engelmar, no different to an implied stage direction: 'er sach alß krankleich in den part, / alß sam er wer von einer siecher art' / 'He feebly looked [down] into his own beard just as if he had some sickness' (1637–8). And here too another peasant simply goes by the name of 'der Part' (3560), as if this were enough to maintain the supposition of the boorish peasants as bearded. Where *Neithart Fuchs* differs, however, is that it features additional commentary as supplied by a narrator. It is the author-narrator who illustrates the pseudo-gallantry of one spectacularly vain peasant by informing us of his habit of (only) shaving on feast days in order to please a certain wench (2353–5). More tellingly perhaps, it is the author-narrator who makes light of the misfortunes and injury suffered by the yokels with reference to their beards. In the prank of the 'foul ointment', Neithart's success in applying it to the peasants is gleefully welcomed by the narrator: 'nun was er kluog vnd so gelört, / das ers den pauren bracht in part' / 'Now he was so clever and smart that he rubbed it into the peasants' own beards!' (1655–6). Similarly, when the rustics are fighting furiously among themselves yet again, the narrator pokes fun at two in particular by trivializing the brutal beating they endure: 'Eczelman vnd Otterhan, den schar man vngeneczt den part' / 'Eczelman and Otterhan were given a dry shave, so they were!' (3761). Given that this violence is now being presented at one remove, in the form of narrative as opposed to the intoxicating immediacy of comedic performance, such commentary serves as compensation, offering an additional reason for the text's listeners to laugh.

It is worth reminding ourselves at this stage that comedy at the expense of (bearded) peasant figures was not always so violent (see also the next section) and that Wittenwiler's text is, quite possibly, nastier than most. Elsewhere, most notably in vernacular versions of the *Dialogus Salomonis et Marcolfi*, derisive comparison of the peasant-cum-trickster Markolf's beard with that of a goat, part of an extended *descriptio* of grotesque ugliness, is harmless by comparison.[52] As Hans Rudolf Velten has observed, the comedic point of Markolf's hideous appearance lies to some extent in the implied comparison with his principal interlocutor, King Solomon, whom he outwits at every turn.[53] This effect is exaggerated in Marcus Ayrer's prose version of 1487 (*Frag vnd antwort Salomonis vnd marcolfy*) where Markolf's physical attributes are rendered even more disgusting; thus here the peasant-cum-trickster is given 'Ein stinckenden part als ein pock' / 'a stinking beard like a billy goat' (12–13). The same principle is extended to Markolf's repulsively ugly wife (Policana), and she too now has 'ein part wy ein pock' / 'a beard like a billy goat' (22) to go with her other bestial features. Within this particular scheme of comedic dehumanization, then, peasant beards do not need to be torn out to be amusing. It is enough that they no longer differentiate men from women.

Pubic beards

In one quite specific respect, Wittenwiler seems to have anticipated another strain of comedy within vernacular literature as it developed in the course of the fifteenth century. His profane nomenclature of 'Futzenpart' / 'Quim-beard' (7158, 7264) offers us a relatively early glimpse of the crude humour which was to become so characteristic of certain literary forms in the second half of the fifteenth century.[54] As far as we can tell, such 'obscenity' was intended to be enjoyed by mixed audiences, and it was evidently held to be socially acceptable in particular cultural and literary contexts.[55] If John Friedman is correct and the removal of female body hair in this period was associated with higher social status,[56] then the entertainment afforded by references to women's pubic beards may also have served to reinforce certain social prejudices and stereotypes.

The festive, ludic quality of this kind of material is most tangible in Shrovetide plays, associated in this period above all with the city of Nuremberg, which were performed seasonally but were also written up and collected in large numbers for the enjoyment of readers.[57] A repertoire of plot types (mock court case, spurious medical diagnosis, and wooings and weddings) and stock figures (insatiable young women, fools of all kinds, peasants) soon established itself, with considerable emphasis being placed on vulgar euphemisms and metaphors of varying degrees of inventiveness.[58] As far as beards are concerned, many of the poets and wordsmiths who specialized in this area of entertainment stuck to the tried and tested. Audiences knew what they found funny and never tired of hearing it.[59]

Evidently, the idea of beardedness could always be relied upon to raise a laugh when used to allude to female genitalia and sexual maturity.[60] As in Wittenwiler's *Ring* this can take the form of 'obscenely' absurd and demeaning names for foolish male figures. Thus, almost inevitably, the cast of 17 peasants of (K45) *Bauernprahlereien*, as named aloud for the audience in the play's opening speech, includes one 'Votzpart' / 'Quim-beard' (342,12). Six of the ten jurymen named in (K40) *Das Hofgericht vom Ehebruch* share speaking names with *Bauernprahlereien*, with the slightly less explicit 'Götz Mauzenpart' / 'Götz Muff-beard' (306,22) representing a notable variation (for a more discerning audience?).[61] The joke of female pubic beards is developed most fully in (K25) *Frag und Antwort*, a mock debate concerning various aspects of sexual intercourse. The third speaker professes to be baffled by the question of why women grow beards 'down below' but not on their faces, which remain hairless even as they get older (225,3–10). The spurious answer: such beard growth occurs out of fear of attack from 'pruchwurmen' / 'breech-worms' (225,15), either that or out of (the heat of) great desire (225,19), a typically lewd distortion of contemporary humoral medical science.

Male anatomy too is transformed in the looking glass of Shrovetide plays, the penis becoming (among many other hilarious objects) 'ein wurst mit eim part' / 'a sausage with a beard': this is what one unhappy wife wants above all else, according to the herald of (K19) *Eheliche Verdächtigungen* (160,19). Another dissatisfied wife complains in court ((K42) *Das Chorgericht*) that her idiotic husband has no idea what she means when she tells him: 'Ich hab mir nie so gnuog geeßen, / Ich het danocht ain partte wurst geßen'/ 'I've never eaten myself so full that I couldn't still manage a bearded sausage' (324,24–5). And one of the troop of fools appearing in (K116) *Die Narren* invites the audience's derision when he reveals his failure to satisfy a young woman's 'night hunger' with the obvious delicacy at his disposal (1010,29–35). There can be no doubt that as a 'bearded' foodstuff male genitals were made to appear quite ridiculous.[62] But they are still presented as desirable from a mock-female perspective, which renders these female figures just as foolish as, if not more so than, the men over whom they presume to assert themselves. The ultimate target of this joke too, it would seem, is female sexuality, likened here to a base and insatiable appetite.[63]

Further comparison of these various pubic beards suggests that there were some gender-specific differences in their usage. As a crude euphemism the image of the bearded sausage is as likely to feature in the speeches of mock-female as male figures. However incongruous the juxtaposition of the two metaphorical elements,[64] the significance of male beardedness per se as sign of sexual maturity means that this type of bawdy beard has a certain (comedic) logic to it and thus represents a more familiar absurdity. References to female pubic beards exercise the opposite effect by virtue of their appropriation of an attribute of male physiology. This process of defamiliarization is supported by strategies of distancing: such beards feature either as ludicrous 'real' names for foolish male figures (as uttered by other male figures), or as a point of bawdy reference in a mock debate among men. They are kept offstage, as it were, and not brought to bear on actual female figures, no matter that these roles too were played by men.[65]

To a certain extent pubic beards make a poetic virtue of sexual profanity, which in turn is rendered all the more normal in these plays by the seasonal licence of Shrovetide. But it would be misleading not to point out that such jokes also led a life outside 'Fastnachtspiele' in short texts (both in rhyming couplets and in prose) that were transmitted in collective manuscripts from the second half of the fifteenth century onwards. One such collection, known as Codex Weimar Q 565 (c. 1450–1500), reveals an extraordinary appetite for bawdry, including a choice selection of pubic beards.

Dialogue (*Gespräche dreier Frauen*, nr 6, fol. 16r): three spinning-maids take it in turns to ponder a mysterious feature of their own genitalia. The first wonders how her 'votz' / 'quim' (4), with its 'rauhen part' / 'bristly beard' (5), can be so much older than her when they were born at one and the same time. By way of contrast (and as a neat conclusion) the third wonders why hers is so young. There are no answers here: the essence of the salacious humour lies in these maids' foolishly distorted views of their own bodies as expressed through familiar literary tropes.

'Priamel' (fol. 16v): in the third of several short poems concerning female and male private parts the speaker vaunts his ability to satisfy any woman's 'night hunger' ('wenn ein Ffrauen hungert so hart, / So hab ich ein wurst mit einem part' / 'If a lady suffers from terrible hunger, then I have a sausage with a beard' 1–2). If this does not work, if the lady is simply too ravenous (6), then no amount of sausages and sides of bacon (8) will help.

Riddle (nr 39, fol. 35r): a sexually explicit trick question involving bouncing testicles and 'der füd der part' / 'the beard of the quim' (4) is answered 'cleverly' with reference to the process of grinding corn in a mill. As observed by the editor of the text (Kully), it is possible that the ability to solve this riddle depended upon knowledge of millers' slang.[66]

Riddle (nr 68, fol. 44v): the vulgar conundrum of what non-sexual uses a vagina could serve is met with four suggestions. These range from the surreal – hang it around the neck of a stork and it will use it as a pouch for frogs – to the salaciously filthy: 'Nym Sie vnd hencks einem an das maul, Der kain part hat. So hat Er darnach ein feuchten part' / 'Take it and hang it from the mouth of a man who has no beard. And then he will have a moist beard' (7–9). Here the train of 'obscene' thought comes full circle. In an image which proves demeaning to both women and beardless men, the pubic beard of the former is recommended as a disgusting prosthetic for the latter.[67]

The striking thing about this kind of bawdry is that it does not require a moral-didactic framework to exist. At times the collection of Q 565 goes beyond Shrovetide plays in terms of its profanity and unconcealed preoccupation with genitalia. One wonders whether, in spite of all the coarse wordplay, there is an element of titillation to a text like the dialogue of the spinning-maids. Certain norms are of course being upheld here: the primacy of the male sexual gaze; the association of beards with masculinity and hence the absurdity of the notion of female beardedness. However, the emphasis in this codex would appear to be on finding new excuses for repeating the same old vulgar images, with humorous riddles providing one relatively novel means of doing so. Other late medieval beard riddles, we should note, eschew the sexual. The *Straßburger Rätselbuch* of around 1510, containing over three hundred of such micro-texts, includes five more or less innocuous jokes relating to shaving and barbers,[68] and one on the nature of man (nr 289) and goats: 'Ob der bart ee gewesst sey, oder der man ee. der bart ist ee gewesen, dann die geiss vnd ander thier sein vor dem menschen geschaffen worden' / '[Question:]

Did the beard come first or was it the man? [Answer:] The beard came first because the goat and other animals were created before man'.[69]

Heroic antics

The increasing number of references to pubic beards in the course of the fifteenth century should not obscure other kinds of beard-related comedy of longstanding value, as enjoyed by recipients of vernacular literature from as early as the beginning of the thirteenth century (if not earlier). Tweaking by the beard is the prime example of this, a form of assault on another man, more harmful in principle to their honour than to their person, which in the 'real' world of Germanic legal tradition was deemed a crime.[70] This socio-cultural background explains, in part at least, the comic appeal of beard-pulling as a motif in various types of literature which, under certain conditions and to differing effect, play violence for laughs.

One literary tradition which, in spite of many mutations, kept returning to this motif is the medieval (German) heroic epic. Physical comedy, as unabashed as it is unrefined, appears to lie at the heart of antagonistic encounters between heroes and other-worldly beings, both little and large. At one end of the scale there is something intrinsically funny about the beardedness of literary dwarves, a figure type which normally constitutes no physical threat, encapsulating as it does the mismatch between age and body size.[71] One might even say that the imagined proportions of the dwarf's body place exaggerated emphasis on the beard as a primary physical characteristic. Dwarves are further belittled when their beards are pulled by heroes, even when they are, initially, as ferocious as 'wild' Alberich in the *Nibelungenlied*, whom Siegfried must best a second time in a struggle which ends on an unexpectedly light note: 'dô vienc er bî dem barte den altgrîsen man. / er zogt in ungevuoge, daz er lûte schrê' / 'Then he grabbed the old grey-haired man by the beard. He gave it such a mighty tug that it made Alberich scream' (B 495,2–3). The fact that the poet has exaggerated Alberich's strength up to this point (in order to provide Siegfried with a stern enough challenge) leads to the beard-pulling being recast, to no less comedic effect, as a younger hero's act of domination (B 495,4) over an older adversary.

Not all dwarves are envisaged as bearded in this tradition.[72] The dwarf Alberich(!), who is the cunning and capricious orchestrator of so much of the action in *Ortnit* (c. 1230, prequel to *Wolfdietrich*), looks just like a beautiful four-year-old child to Ortnit (version A: 96,1).[73]

This Alberich's rather different appearance cements his central role in the plot, not least when he turns out to be the hero's own father. Beard-pulling in this story takes the form of furious self-harm on the part of the incestuous heathen king (Machorel), whose daughter Ortnit desires to marry: 'Mit paiden seinen henden so rauft er auz den part' / 'With both of his hands he tore at his beard' (275,1).[74] In a later version (D) the comedy latent in such impotent frustration is made even more explicit when Alberich the dwarf turns himself invisible in order to assault the king in exactly the same way: 'Elberich dem kunge den bart vs dem munde brach' / 'Alberich tore the beard from the king's mouth' (387,4). Here the burlesque action derives its full effect from an inversion of the natural order of 'little' being at the mercy of 'large'. In the version of *Wolfdietrich* which follows *Ortnit* A another dwarf appears – in memory of the Alberich figure perhaps – when Wolfdietrich gets closer to the dragons' lair in Ortnit's kingdom. This time, however, the dwarf occupies the marginal position of an increasingly distraught bystander and is characterized far more conventionally: 'das getzwerg begund sich rauffen bey dem har und part' / 'The dwarf began to tear at his own hair and beard' (584,4).

At the other end of the scale, bearded giants, themselves the very embodiment of brutality, are treated mercilessly by the heroes they face in *Virginal* ('Heidelberger' (I) and 'Wiener' (III) versions, c. 1300), in one of a series of weird and wonderful adventures undertaken by Dietrich (von Bern) and his familiar band of warriors. Beard-pulling in this context is more a matter of savage comedy, where grotesquely exaggerated acts of violence are accompanied by provocative direct speech. Thus, Dietleip (one of Dietrich's younger companions) issues a word of mock warning to his huge foe – 'Ris, dir ist nie so lanck der part, / mach dir den kreis czu enge' / 'Giant, no matter how long your beard is, I shall make this circle too small for your comfort' (version III: 664,5–6) – before he grabs the giant's long beard in both fists and rips it out together with his helmet and his throat (664,7–13).[75] Similarly, when Dietleip carries the giant's decapitated head by the beard (665,2) and tosses it into the midst of the other (bearded) giants, he adds insult to injury with his sarcastic words of defiance: 'Secht an, ir starcken man, / wie ich mit rysen fechten kan' / 'Look here, you mighty men, at how I fight with giants!' (665,4–5).[76] Almost from the moment they are introduced into the story these giants are defined by their beards, as first described by old Hildebrand (607,12–13). It is their beards which pique Dietleip's curiosity ('Wo sein si auff gewachssen, / daz si so lange pertte tragen?' / 'Where did they grow up that they wear such long beards?' 609,3–4). And the giant chosen for him to slay is identified for him with reference to the length of his beard (662,10–11). By virtue of these preliminary references the audience has been primed for Dietleip's attack on 'his' giant's beard and most probably anticipates it: by the time the moment of truth comes, everything that the hero says and does to his less than human foe seems entirely logical.

In fantastical narratives featuring the same cast of characters, who – in the post-*Nibelungenlied* tradition – are never really in danger of losing their lives, certain heroes come to be depicted with ironic detachment for a knowing audience. Old Hildebrand, Dietrich's grey-haired 'master', is marked out as a favourite in this context by scenes in which his own beard receives unwelcome attention.[77] In the *Eckenlied* (c. 1230) the young giant Ecke, who is too big to ride a horse, grows so angry with Hildebrand when the latter fails to take his pretensions to knighthood seriously, that he threatens to manhandle him: 'het ich uch bi dem barte / [...] / es wurd u liht ze laide' / 'If I had you by the beard [...] you would certainly come to grief' ((E_2) 47,6–8). This assault never takes place. Instead Hildebrand wisely tries to calm Ecke down. But just for one moment the audience gets to enjoy the possibility of Hildebrand too being subjected to the disrespectful treatment normally reserved for others.[78]

Another epic concerning a giant, *Sigenot* (c. 1280–1300), goes one step further and depicts Hildebrand being slung over his enormous foe's

Figure 5.2 Sigenot the giant holds Hildebrand by the beard (*Sigenot*). Heidelberg, UB, Cpg 67, c. 1470, fol. 80r. Public domain.

shoulder by his beard ('Älterer Sigenot' 20,1–2) (see Figure 5.2). The comic effect of this incident is compounded by Hildebrand's lament (20,11–21,4), even as he is being carried away by the giant, and by his later account of this humiliating experience to Dietrich: 'Den bart er mir do us gelas / sa reht als ainem diebe. / Er het mich sanfter wol getragen' / 'He plucked the hairs from my beard just as if I were a thief. He could easily have carried me more gently' (43,9–11). In the longer version of *Sigenot*, Hildebrand is so traumatized by Sigenot's effrontery that he wishes he had shaved his beard off before leaving Bern ('Jüngerer Sigenot' 158,1–159,1), which represents another idea highly amusing to the text's recipients, for whom Hildebrand simply would not be Hildebrand without his facial hair.[79] Further comedy ensues when Hildebrand yanks at the beard of the dwarf in the giant's service (191,3) in order to compel him to do his bidding. The old warrior thereby does to the dwarf what the giant did to him, the one key difference being that the aggrieved dwarf, unlike the aggrieved Hildebrand, is unable to take revenge for this gross insult.

Like Berchter in *König Rother* and Heimrich in *Willehalm*, Hildebrand occupies a privileged position as a venerable old warrior among younger men, yet in Hildebrand's case this entails being singled out for comedic treatment. Narrative context is a factor. When Hildebrand bursts into tears at Dietrich's cowardly refusal to face Siegfried in a later version of the *Rosengarten* (version D: 1791),[80] such mock-heroic treatment of the 'tearful beard' motif (see Chapter 3) is entirely in keeping with the tongue-in-cheek tenor of this tale as a whole, concerning a tournament hosted by Kriemhild in which Dietrich and his Amelungs are pitted against giants and familiar Burgundian heroes.[81] Nevertheless, the comedy that repeatedly surrounds Hildebrand and his beard may have served more than one poet of 'Dietrich' epic as a means of forestalling recipients' scepticism towards Hildebrand's undiminished fighting prowess in spite of his grand old age. If not quite a signature feature of this tradition, it would appear to be a function of the overtly artificial character of these stories of adventure in which nothing ever really changes.

In *Wolfdietrich* (various versions, c. 1230–1300), Hildebrand provides the template for another redoubtable veteran, Berchtung, who loyally supports the eponymous hero in his struggle against his usurping brothers. When Berchtung speaks up for Wolfdietrich at the royal court in Constantinople, he too suffers the typical insults and threats of abuse: 'du alter zugpart' / 'You old goat-beard!' (version B: 284,1); 'das har von deinem mund hayss ich dir zerren gar!' / 'I shall have all the hair torn from your mouth!' (B 284,4).[82] But somehow the comic effect of these lines is less palpable, perhaps because Berchtung does not enjoy the same high status across numerous texts as Hildebrand. The goat insult is more obviously humorous in a later scene, in the longest version of the text (D), when one of Berchtung's own sons refers to his dead father in the same disparaging fashion in order to get Wolfdietrich, who is beside himself with grief,[83] to stop embracing Berchtung's corpse: 'lont ligen den zigebart!' / 'Leave the goat-beard alone!' (D 2042,1). With the deceased Berchtung, then, this figure type comes to be celebrated in a way that is simply impossible with Hildebrand, who can never be allowed to die. Berchtung's mortal remains are encapsulated by his beard, which in comparison to the fate of his soul no longer seems worthy of the respect of those who care deeply for him. In the extraordinary sequence of events that follows, Wolfdietrich's melodramatic devotion to his 'old master' is rewarded by a miracle when Berchtung speaks to him from beyond the grave before being laid to rest by a suitably inflated number of funeral masses.

Self-parody?

The late medieval heroic epic shows how the abuse meted out to beards could always be rendered more hilarious by including the direct speech of the offended party, as if their voice were needed to complete the spectacle of indignity. The comedic potential of this strategy – first-person expressions of injured pride – was recognized by poets working in other literary traditions too, not least by those who sought to cast courtly, erotic or marital relationships between men and women in an amusing light. Given that for so much of the German Middle Ages youthfulness, and hence beardlessness, was the prized asset of would-be gallants, beards were at best of questionable value when it came to impressing ladies or attractive maidens.[84] At worst, as the stereotypical attribute of husbands and householders, an abused beard in the hands of an unruly wife epitomized marital discord.[85]

The first of these two scenarios is repeatedly evoked by Oswald von Wolkenstein (1376/7–1445), who combined, to an unprecedented degree, literary motifs with autobiographical reference across a wide range of song types in an oeuvre of some 130 songs.[86] In addition to his famous one-eyedness, Oswald's references to his own beard play a significant part in his literary self-projection, as scholars have long recognized.[87] Artistic images of Oswald from within his own lifetime portray him variously as a pilgrim-knight with a long beard (memorial stone (1408) at Brixen Cathedral), as a clean-shaven courtier of some standing (Vienna, ÖNB, Cod. 2777, c. 1425–36) or as a beardless courtly singer (Innsbruck, UB, no signature, dated 1432). But what is really striking is Oswald's readiness to poke fun at his bearded self in a number of songs describing his interactions with courtly ladies and merry wenches.

This strategy occurs in its most concentrated form in (Kl. 21) *Ir alten weib*. Here a call to dance, set against the typical backdrop of nature reawakening after winter, takes the inevitable erotic turn as the singer delights in the prospect of kissing and embracing fine maidens ('freulin zart' 30), revelling in the bucolic scene by virtue of a synecdoche: 'des freut sich mein bart' / 'My beard is overjoyed at this' (38).[88] However, as Oswald is only too aware, in the eyes of younger women, beardedness is hardly equated with attractiveness. Later in the same song he must concede that 'Mein langer bart, der hat mir dick verschroten / vil manchen schmutz von zarten mündlin roten' / 'My long beard has often robbed me of many a kiss from tender little mouths [so] red' (81–2).[89] Indeed, in the sexual fantasy of (Kl. 63) *Wol mich an we der lieben stund* the desired naked embrace seems to depend on Oswald's shaving (23–6). This problem is exacerbated by ageing, the quintessential sign of which is the unwelcome appearance of grey hairs in his beard. These may themselves be read as proof of Oswald's steadfastness as languishing lover over many years as in (Kl. 87) *Rot, weiss, ain frölich angesicht* (24–5). But, as remarked upon in *In Frankereich* (Kl. 12), they do little to impress ladies at court: 'mein dienst, der loufft neur hinden nach, / seit mir die weiss durch braunen bart aufdringt' / 'My service always lags behind since the white hairs started to sprout in my brown beard' (77–8). Distancing himself from such superficial concerns, the singer reveals, in this song at least, that his true hopes lie with the fairest Lady of all, the Virgin Mary (79–84).

Elsewhere, Oswald's beard serves as a touchstone for the success or failure he has experienced in his dealings with women from the highest (royalty) to the lowest (prostitutes) in society. These beard references occur in several songs which allude to memorable episodes in his life as a member of King Sigismund's entourage. Most notably, in (Kl. 18) *Es fügt sich*, the honours bestowed upon Oswald by Margaret of Prades (queen consort of Aragon) involve his beard being decorated (as well as his ears being pierced): 'zu willen raicht ich ir den bart, / mit hendlein weiss bant si darein ain ringlin zart / lieplich und sprach: "non maiplus dis ligaides"' / 'I willingly held out my beard for her. With her white delicate hands she attached a precious ring to it, so tenderly, and said: "Never untie this"' (34–6). Other high-ranking personages, including King Sigismund himself, are shown to be richly amused by Oswald's outlandish appearance (41–8), which suggests that this ceremony is perceived by others to be a little too flamboyant, with Oswald the butt of affectionate ridicule.

Nevertheless, this incident seems to have been a source of some pride on the part of the poet, who alludes to it again in (Kl. 19) *Es ist ain altgesprochner rat,*[90] following it up with reference to another such mock ceremony at the French royal court at the hands of Queen Isabeau: 'die mir den bart von handen / verkrönt mit aim diamanden' / 'who by her own hand adorned my beard with a diamond' (191–2).

Less elevated social company is featured in (Kl. 122) *Wol auf, gesellen*. Here Oswald's (humorous) account of his humiliation in a dance hall in Augsburg centres on the abuse he recalls being subjected to by one particular wench.[91] Having entered the establishment with some confidence – 'ich trug ain part gar wolgevar' / 'I was sporting a very handsome beard' (15) –, he soon finds himself being spoken of in the most unflattering terms: 'si het den sit / vormals mer gesechen nit / wann von der gaiss' / '[She said that] she had never anything of the like before – except on a goat' 17–19). No amount of dancing can rid him of the notion that he would have fared better if he had shaved his beard off completely (25–32). Beards in this song also function as a veiled reference to a man's wealth, hence the opening assertion that only those with a long beard (3), in other words a deep purse, should consider entering such an establishment.[92] This idea is developed further in (Kl. 123) *Der seines laids ergeczt well sein*, which offers a satirical response to the notorious inflation of prices during the time of the Council of Constance (1414–18).[93] The maids of the city, so the singer maintains, are more than adept at 'grazing in men's beards' (6). He himself, he confesses, had all the longer hairs – the coins of larger denomination – plucked from his beard by one such damsel (9–16), so that in the end most of his 'armer part' / 'poor beard' (30) lay strewn on the floor. This same episode is also alluded to early on in (Kl. 19) *Es ist ain altgesprochner rat* as one of several particularly unpleasant experiences Oswald has had, which make the pleasant ones all the more joyful (1–16).

The sure touch, the comic timing displayed by Oswald when recounting past indignities – most obviously in Kl. 122 and Kl. 123 – transform his failings as a hot-blooded male: the wittier he is when it comes to presenting his own mishaps and foibles, the more impressive he appears as a singer. Beard references exercise a fundamental function within this scheme. Oswald's beard, the very first to be immortalized like this in the German tradition of 'Minnesang', may be the proud emblem of his colourful experiences, of the worldly wisdom he has accumulated in travelling far and wide, not to mention a very conspicuous sign of his masculinity, yet time and again this same beard serves him ill in respect of young women, a (comic) frustration which is exacerbated by the symbolic recognition of it by courtly ladies of the very highest social standing.

At about the same time that Oswald was sending himself up as a ladies' man, other poets were entertaining audiences with allusions to their miserable lives as hen-pecked husbands. In *Frauenerziehung*, an early fourteenth-century comic tale by a certain Sibote, the narrator introduces his taming-of-the-shrew narrative by offering it as advice for unhappily married men (7–8), only to confess in his very next breath that he is in desperate need of such help himself (9–15).[94] The ironic praise of his wife's obedience varies across the text's numerous manuscripts. In codex v (c. 1450), for instance, another twenty lines are interpolated in which the narrator grossly exaggerates the tender affections of his 'liebe brüt' / 'beloved bride' (12e). Just as a hawk plucks out a crane's feathers, so she tears the hair from my scalp, he laments, 'Vnd spielte mit mynem barth / Daz vnder wilen vil harth / Dar uß rynnet daz blüth' / 'and so plays with my beard that from time to time the blood runs out' (12g–i). The narrator's bloodied beard, an injury received in the most unheroic of circumstances, provides shameful evidence of the disorder within his own household. The fact that the narrator is foolish enough to make public his domestic humiliation adds to the comedy of the moment. This narratorial role is not maintained throughout the following tale. It represents a particular exordial strategy, by means of which the poet makes his advice more palatable to others by debunking any notion that it is being delivered from a position of superiority. This parody of the bearded self is a provocative means to a rhetorical end.

Redness

Self-parody had its limits. The characteristic of red hair or red-beardedness, to take the most extreme example, was evidently not one that poets were in any hurry to attribute to themselves. With reference to (historical) personages of the highest birth and of faultless reputation, such as Frederick I of Hohenstaufen (Barbarossa), no fault was attached to reddishness.[95] But more often than not, throughout the Middle Ages and well into the Early Modern period, red hair was widely understood to reflect badly on the moral character of the person in question.[96] Red-haired and red-bearded men were consequently easy targets for ridicule across the whole spectrum of medieval literary forms. Any verbal or physical abuse such figures were subjected to tended to be presented as justifiable and laughable rather than cruel. As we have already had occasion to observe, redness could be used as a quick and easy way to stigmatize maligned social types still further.

In the most overtly fictional of contexts, the beast epic, the wickedness of the red-haired is of course epitomized by the fox. 'Reinhart was vbele unde rot' / 'Reinhart was evil and red[-haired]' (2172), observes the narrator of the German *Reinhart Fuchs*, just when the fox poisons the (lion-)king.[97] The idea was so well established by the early thirteenth century that one or two vernacular poets made a point of contradicting it. The status of the red-haired knight Ither in Wolfram's *Parzival* is suggestive of an alternative perspective, as befits an author who habitually uses references to hair and beards to emphasize the humanity of his figures (see Chapter 3).[98] Wirnt von Grafenberg, a proper devotee of Wolfram, goes one step further in his *Wigalois* (c. 1210–20), where the appearance of another Red Knight – 'Im was der bart und daz hâr / beidiu rôt, viurvar' / 'His beard and hair were both red, the colour of fire' (2841–2) – prompts the author-narrator to mount a staunch defence of all such men: 'swie sîn hâr ist getân, / ist et er ein getriuwer man, / diu varwe im niht geschaden kan' / 'No matter what his hair is like, if he is indeed an honest man, its colour can do nothing to detract from that' (2853–5). The course of Wirnt's narrative backs this up: this same noble knight (Hojir) is the first to welcome Wigalois back at Arthur's court, at the end of all of his adventures, in spite of the fact that Wigalois inflicted his first defeat upon him (11468–74).

This enlightened view does not appear to have borne much fruit – with the possible exception of the courtly romance.[99] The poor reputation of red hair persisted. One obvious example of this is Konrad von Würzburg's short (comic) tale *Heinrich von Kempten* (c. 1250–70) – most likely derived from a Latin historiographical source such as Godfrey of Viterbo's *Pantheon* (see Chapter 2) – which concerns a brave but impetuous knight's assault on one Emperor Otto.[100] Heinrich's outrageous attack, which sees him yanking Otto by his long beard across the banquet table (264–73) and tearing the hair out of his chin (295–7), is clearly a last resort. With his own life unjustly at stake he has no choice but to compel Otto to go back on his oath to have him executed. There can be no doubt that the comedic effect of this desperate act lies in the exaggerated significance Otto himself attaches to his facial hair: 'schoen und lanc was im der bart, / wand er in zôch vil zarte' / 'His beard was long and handsome, for he took tender care of it' (4–5). Such loving cultivation of his own beard, such preoccupation with his body as a man, makes his habit of swearing by it (6–7) seem self-congratulatory. But it is the colour of Otto's hair which confirms him as a capricious, even despotic ruler, undeserving of any sympathy: 'er hete roetelehtez hâr / und was mitalle ein übel man' / 'He had red-hued hair and was an utterly spiteful man'

(8–9).[101] And it is thus as 'Der keiser ubel unde rot' / 'The spiteful and red[-haired] emperor' (231) that Otto forces Heinrich's hand. In stark contrast, by the end of the story, when the emperor and Heinrich are reconciled, Otto proves himself affable and capable of making light of his earlier humiliation,[102] and in this context the narrative no longer draws attention to his redness.

By virtue of the detail of red hair Konrad – or his immediate source – creates a composite Otto figure, combining outstanding characteristics of Otto I (accustomed to swearing by his beard) and his son, Otto II ('the Red'), as recorded in chronicles like the *Sächsische Weltchronik* (see Chapter 2).[103] This 'composite' Otto may be a bearded emperor like Karl der Große, but his stature is drastically diminished by comparison. Readers of one fourteenth-century codex (Heidelberg, UB, Cpg 395, c. 1300–25) would have been in a position to appreciate just that, for here a copy of *Heinrich von Kempten* (fols 92v–98r) has been placed immediately after Stricker's *Karl* (1r–92v).[104] The thematic link between the two texts is highlighted by the rubric pertaining to Konrad's text: 'Keiser otto mit dem barte' / 'Emperor Otto the bearded' (92v). In fact this scribe privileges Otto's beard in a way no other (known) copyist of the story does.[105] With the economy afforded by metonymy the text's scribal *explicit* (in the same red ink) narrows down the focus still further, reformulating the title of the work to give beardedness the last word: 'Amen sprechent vil hart. / Hie endet sich der bart' / 'Say Amen most sincerely. Here ends the beard' (98r).

Hostility to red hair, even just in passing, is standard fare in vernacular didactic literature as well. The baseline is set by Freidank's *Bescheidenheit* (c. 1215–30), where the poet singles out for particular praise the short man who is humble, the red-haired man who is good and the tall man who is wise (85,19–22), on the assumption that these virtues go against the very nature of these types of men. A similar message is delivered by the moral tale 'Von zwein gesellen und einem bern', nr 73 in Ulrich Boner's collection of one hundred fables *Der Edelstein* (c. 1320–40), which illustrates the theme of false friends.[106] Here two companions (one with brown hair, one with red) go bear-hunting, only for the red-haired friend to take fright and run off. However, not only does the bear not kill the remaining huntsman, it warns him about the other: 'wan wenne ez gât an rechte nôt, / sô lât er dich, wan er ist rôt' / 'In moments of real peril he will abandon you, for he is red[-haired]' (47–8).[107] The most damning indictment of all comes in *Des Teufels Netz* (c. 1400–50), an extensive social critique in the form of a satirical dialogue between the poet (a monk) and the devil, in the course of which the latter refers to Judas

Iscariot as the embodiment of envy: 'Judas was och der selben art, / Nidig, hässig, mit rotem part'/ 'Judas was of this nature too: envious, full of hatred, with a red beard' (388–9).[108] For all his mendacity the devil was doubtless understood to be a most reliable witness in this matter, given that Judas was 'der helle kind' / 'a child of hell' (394).

Such (ostensibly) historical examples as Otto 'II' and Judas Iscariot legitimized the stigma of red hair in the popular imagination of the later Middle Ages, which was no less 'real' for being merely thought.[109] This detrimental attribute could thus be relied upon by poets to alienate audiences at a stroke. In the European context this strategy is most famously represented by Chaucer's telling description of the (naturally) disreputable miller in the 'General Prologue' of the *Canterbury Tales* (c. 1387–1400): 'His berd as any sowe or fox was reed' (553). As we have already observed, the same rule of prejudicial redness is applied in German texts to social types such as peasants (Heinrich der Teichner; *Großes Neidhartspiel*) and Jews (Jans von Wien).[110] In principle any kind of outsider figure was liable to be treated in this derisive and reductive fashion. The curious blend of fear and pleasure involved in this process is quite evident in Hermann von Sachsenheim's *Die Mörin* (dated 1453), a fantastical first-person narrative in which the poet is abducted and put on trial for crimes against Love. The executioner in attendance looks exactly like what he is, a man debarred from honest society: 'kal beschorn, / Mit ainem roten bart, was dick' / 'with fully shaven head and a thick red beard' (232–3). The more terrified the poet becomes, the more amusing this fictitious face-to-face encounter gets for the text's recipients.

The beards of 'others'

Much late medieval comedy depends on collective identity, on a keen sense of 'us' and 'them', and nowhere more so than in matters of faith and religion. When the social, cultural or ethnic difference at issue is perceived to be so fundamental, poets are given free rein to come up with drastic content. Anti-Jewish sentiment led to imaginative excesses of all kinds with far from harmless consequences.[111] A pernicious comedy of disgust, for instance, lies behind the mock-medical treatment alluded to in the fourteenth-century nonsense poem *Lügenrede*: 'ich trank ab aines juden bart, / daz mir dez ritten wart büß' / 'I drank from the beard of a Jew to rid myself of the shakes' (84–5). This effect is taken in a scatological direction in a fairly typical (Nuremberg) Shrovetide play, (K27) *Das ungleiche Paar*, by an off-the-cuff expression of obvious annoyance:

'Verdruß ein Juden, der im in part schiß?' / 'Is a Jew irked if someone shits in his beard?' (236,5–6). In (K20) *Der Herzog von Burgund* by Hans Folz, a carnival play which subjects Jews to sustained and vicious ridicule,[112] one stage direction suggests that beard-pulling was acted out as part of the entertainment: 'Der narr greift eim juden in part, dicit' / 'The Fool grabs one Jew by the beard, [and] says' (610). That the figure of the Fool should be the one carrying out this action makes it especially demeaning.[113] It does not seem unlikely that when such spectacles of ignominy were performed every opportunity for grotesque misrepresentation was taken in respect of costume, including false beards.[114]

Heathens, or Saracens, also fall into the category of bearded outsider.[115] In bawdier, more profane contexts the narrative consequences of this are more or less inevitable, hence the relish taken in the heathen king's humiliation at the hands of a dwarf in the heroic epic *Ortnit* (see above). Scenarios such as this are far removed from the ideal of shared humanity espoused by Wolfram's *Willehalm* (see Chapter 3), serving as they do the interests of a nakedly hostile attitude. Predictably, the pain of the bearded Muslim 'other' is most gleefully envisaged in yet another Shrovetide play. In (K39) *Des Türken Fastnachtspil* the 'Great Turk' himself is subjected to numerous abusive threats and insults, not least having his beard removed with sickles and his face rinsed with vinegar (297,17–18). Against the backdrop of far-off events of major historical significance, such as the Ottoman conquest of Constantinople of 1453 (alluded to here in lines 299,15–19), the imagined abuse of the Sultan's person is up close and personal, the requisite of vinegar hilariously mundane.[116]

None of this material should deflect from the fact that Christian beards (including those belonging to biblical figures) had very considerable comedic potential too, with some poets being more willing to tease than others. The thirteenth-century amateur historian Jans von Wien, for instance, goes about as far as he can when portraying Noah in his *Weltchronik*:

The traditional biblical account (Genesis 9: 20–21) of Noah's planting of the first vineyard is supplemented here by a preliminary episode in which 'ein boc cluoc' / 'a clever billy goat' (2807) accompanies Noah as he roams the forests. This goat is in fact the first to taste the fruit of the vine. It eats so much of it and gets so drunk 'daz im der wîn ran über den bart' / 'that the wine ran down over its beard' (2810). Far from acting as a warning example of gluttony, the goat's genius is admired (2813–17) by the author-narrator. Indeed, Noah himself takes inspiration from his pet: 'Daz dûht Noê vil guot' / 'This seemed like a very good idea to Noah' (2819).

All the signs are that Noah's drunken goat is a detail peculiar to Jans's version of events following the Flood.[117] It certainly accords with several other amusing animal-related observations made by the narrator in the context of Noah's Ark.[118] Jans's choice of the goat as the one to discover the joys of the grape seems beard-determined, enabling a closer comparison to be drawn between man and beast, or rather between the patriarchal figure of Noah, who was doubtless imagined to be bearded, and his bearded pet. The goat's comic gluttony prefigures that of Noah, its wine-drenched beard necessarily conjuring up the image of Noah's without the poet having to spell it out. Jans's particular interest in this incident is confirmed by wordplay some 19,000 verses later, when Boppard, one of the towns on the Rhine founded by Julius Caesar, is rendered as 'Bockbart' / 'Billy goat's beard' (21162), doubtless in view of its longstanding reputation for fine wine.

The boundaries are pushed further in the 'Schwankroman' *Der Pfaffe vom Kalenberg* (first printed 1473) by Philipp Frankfurter, whose trickster protagonist – a proto-Eulenspiegel, as it were – is a canny village priest who behaves egregiously to get what he wants. When playing host to the duchess of Austria, the priest astonishes his illustrious guest by stoking his oven with wooden figures from his church. These turn out to be all twelve of the Apostles, to whom he speaks with almost vulgar familiarity when picking them up: 'Den anderen nam er pei dem bart: "geseel, du must auch an die fart!"' / 'He seized the second one by the beard: "Matey, you must come along too!"' (1137–8). Audience appreciation of such outrageous behaviour depends to no small extent on their familiarity with the iconographic motif of the 'philosopher's beard' (long, white), which was such a feature of the artistic representation of (almost all) Christ's Apostles throughout the Middle Ages.[119] The iconoclastic humour at work here is indulged further when the priest defends his actions by referring to the figures as 'alte gotzen plindt' / 'old blind idols' (1204), before his true trickster's intent is revealed and the comic effect is reassuringly contained: the priest's ultimate goal is to persuade the duchess to refurnish his church with a new set of Apostles.[120]

The comedic focus on Christian beards tends otherwise to be expressive of lay antagonism towards certain forms of religious existence whose representatives fail to live up to their own codes of virtuous conduct. This thematic interest is quite tangible in several versions of the *Rosengarten*, most notably the printed 'Heldenbuch' of 1479 (version A/II), in scenes involving the hero-as-monk Ilsan, Hildebrand's bombastic brother.[121] Ilsan may be bearded like the other brothers in his monastery.[122] He may even be mocked for it by the ferocious ferryman on the banks of the Rhine: 'du alter zigebart' / 'You old goat-beard!' (219,4). But his beardedness is soon revealed to be that of a formidable warrior (220,2). Later on, having successfully defeated his opponent in the tournament, Ilsan deploys his spiky beardedness as an overtly masculine means of 'taming' Kriemhild, scratching her face terribly when he takes his promised reward of 52 kisses (468,3–469,4).[123] Ilsan's fellow monks are no such men. This is demonstrated beyond doubt upon his return to the monastery, when he chastises them – 'Er knypft in die bert zuo samen vnd hieng sie uber ein stang' / 'He tied their beards together and hung them from a pole' (488,1) – until they agree to help him make amends for his sins. The appeal of this motif can be gauged further from its occurrence in another heroic epic, *Wolfdietrich* (version D), where Wolfdietrich eventually retires to a monastery but is so appalled by the gluttony he discovers there that he resorts to the same drastic measure to get the monks to change their ways (2132,2–3). One and the same woodcut (Figure 5.3) illustrates these twin scenes in the 'Heldenbuch' of 1479 on fols 205v (Wolfdietrich) and 255r (Ilsan).[124] In departure from

Figure 5.3 Ilsan strings up his fellow monks by the beard (*Rosengarten*, in the printed 'Heldenbuch' of 1479). Darmstadt, Hessische Landes- und Hochschulbibliothek, Inc. III 27, fol. 255r. Public domain.

the text(s), however, the cowled figure who punishes the monks in such humiliating fashion is pictured as beardless, which makes the 'otherness' of the bearded monks still more conspicuous.[125]

As far as bearded pilgrims and hermits are concerned, the age-old suspicion that beard length was not always a true measure of piety gives rise, in certain narrative contexts, to extraordinary sequences of action in which both heroes and villains go to extreme lengths to transform their own appearance. In plots which exhibit a sadistic fascination with the beards of others, protagonists (or antagonists) disguise themselves as harmless pilgrims by donning the suitably long and shaggy beards that they have removed from the faces of other men.[126] The false-beard motif is used to get savage laughs in *Salman und Morolf* (composed as early as c. 1190 but surviving only in a mid-fifteenth-century copy). In this burlesque tale of bridal expeditions and abductions – a distant cousin of the *Dialogus Salomonis et Marcolfi* tradition – Morolf, the trickster figure once again, is repeatedly tasked with retrieving the faithless wife (Salome) of his brother, King Solomon. This he duly accomplishes, not least because he is a master of disguise:

In preparation for his first mission Morolf infamously conducts a barbaric operation on an elderly Jew, named Berman, whom he murders and skins from the waist upwards (159,1–162,4).[127] Dressed in Berman's (treated) skin and wearing Berman's beard, Morolf pretends to be a pilgrim as he travels through heathen lands in search of Salome. Numerous escapades later Morolf bamboozles his heathen foes by swiftly changing his disguise from bearded pilgrim to (beardless) courtly musician to butcher. To achieve this, we are told, he carefully gathers together various items, including 'zwene ruche berte' / 'two shaggy beards' (665,4). Where *these* beards come from is never made clear, the emphasis being rather more on the fact that, remarkably enough, he keeps more than one up his sleeve.

The nasty anti-Jewish 'comedy' of the Berman episode, which was not universally popular,[128] would seem to be accentuated by Morolf's deployment of a Jewish beard as a Christian prop together with the other conventional attributes of a medieval pilgrim (rough woollen garments, satchel, staff and palm leaf). Under the cover of this disguise, which only works because the heathens too recognize and respect what a (Christian) pilgrim is supposed to be, Morolf acts with impunity. The journeys he undertakes are arduous in their own way but, as ruthless exercises in tricking, humiliating and killing others, they represent the grotesque antithesis of pilgrimage proper as a means of atonement or spiritual purification. Morolf's transformation into bearded pilgrim is presented as being especially effective in that he is actually a beardless courtier with fair curly locks.[129] Where Morolf runs riot beardedness is no longer a natural symbol for wisdom and piety. Thus, in *Salman und Morolf* the bearded majesty of King Solomon is passed over in favour of the false beards of the cunning arch-trickster.

Conclusion

There is no end to the list of texts in which literary beards were used and abused to elicit audience laughter of one kind or another, most particularly in the later Middle Ages. In this respect Heinrich Wittenwiler's *Ring* is part of a much bigger picture. Examining such features as beard-pulling and comedic violence, on the one hand, and the provocative trope of the female pubic beard, on the other, helps us to appreciate just how similar and how diverse medieval literary comedy could be across numerous text types and traditions. On the whole it seems reasonable to conclude that Wittenwiler's approach to comedy was a relatively serious one, denying the violent and gross peasants he depicts any worth, and eschewing the festive, ludic character of comparably bawdy (or 'obscene') texts. The appropriate frame of understanding for his work is established at the outset by virtue of a comprehensive didactic programme that aims to excoriate moral turpitude. In many of the other texts we have looked at here the broader literary or cultural context makes such an agenda redundant, and the audience's sympathies and antipathies are channelled by their knowledge and enjoyment of a certain tradition, certain plot types and the combination of beardedness with certain other telling attributes.

As in the works discussed in the preceding chapter, humanity, as well as masculinity, continues to feature as a thematic point of reference in texts which render beards, bearded men and just occasionally bearded women laughable. In many instances, we are dealing with acts and utterances that either demean and debase figures of negative identification, or dismantle patriarchal values temporarily by ridiculing other figures commonly perceived to embody such values. By no means all of this material is aggressive and crude – there are affectionate and self-parodic strains too – but quite a lot of it is. For modern recipients this can make for uncomfortable reading, a feeling which may or may not be partially mitigated by bearing in mind that the texts in question are excessive by design.

Notes

1 'He seized one of them by the beard and tore away at it, making him scream.' All translations of Wittenwiler's *Ring* are my own.
2 Odo of Cheriton, *Parabolae* nr 102: 'non vidit locum uiliorem quam barbam pinguedine ciborum perunctam; et ideo in illam conspuebat'; Jacques de Vitry, *Sermones vulgares* nr 149: 'non vidi locum viliorem quam barbam tuam et ideo conspui in ipsam'; Johannes Pauli, *Schimpf und Ernst* E475: 'vnd hab kein vnreiner stat gesehen, dan den bart, da hab ich den wüst auch daryn geworffen'. For an overview see Whitesell, 'Fables in mediaeval exempla', 1947, 358.
3 Much has been written on this topic. For orientation see Bayless (ed.), *Cultural History of Comedy in the Middle Ages*.
4 As discussed in detail by Dimpel, *Zofe im Fokus*, 64–126.
5 Suchomski, *'Delectatio' und 'utilitas'*, 67–202.
6 Goldenbaum, *Krisenexperiment*.
7 Lutz, *Spiritualis fornicatio*, 29–213.
8 Brülhart, *Vexatio dat intellectum*, 98–106.
9 Putzo, 'Komik, Ernst und *Mise en page*', 2009.
10 For the literary transformation of 'obscene' content by virtue of comedy see Haug, 'Die niederländischen erotischen Tragzeichen', 2004, 76–7.
11 See also Lutz, *Spiritualis fornicatio*, 301–5.
12 Lutz, *Spiritualis fornicatio*, 298–301; Brülhart, *Vexatio dat intellectum*, 17–25.
13 Bockmann, 'Literarische Neidhart-Rezeption', 285–9.
14 See also Schmitt, 'Sexualität als Textualität', 133–7.
15 *Renner*: 'Kurzen muot und langez hâr / Habent die meide sunderbar' (309–10).
16 Contrasting hairstyles, for example, are indicative of either Venus's alluring sexuality (2425–8) or the Virgin Mary's chastity (2481–4).
17 Lutz, *Spiritualis fornicatio*, 230–2.
18 Unreliable figures as conveyors of didactic content in the *Ring* are discussed in some depth by Goldenbaum, *Krisenexperiment*, 135–64.
19 The main thrust of Colman's argument at first is that having children leads only to a life of torment and married life is totally incompatible with spiritual concerns (3088–156, 3198–208).
20 The line in question is quoted here on the basis of the manuscript (fol. 20va), transcribed in the edition of the text by Röcke (and Goldmann). In the (standard) edition by Wießner it reads 'greisen palch' / 'grey hide'.
21 In the tradition of the pseudo-Aristotelian *Secreta Secretorum* brown hair indicates good habits and orderly behaviour: 'Prawnes har, ob es mäslich dünne ist, kündet güt sitte und ordenunge des menschn' (in Hiltgart von Hürnheim's vernacular translation of 1282: 76,5).
22 According to Goldenbaum, *Krisenexperiment*, 204, Bertschi gets his proverbial expression wrong. This would certainly add to the comedy of the scene.
23 Anti-didactic interpretations of the *Ring* are spearheaded by Bachorski, *Irrsinn und Kolportage*, 246–52. For an overview see also Hübner, 'Erzählung und praktischer Sinn', 2010, 216–22.
24 Ehlert, 'Gesundheitslehre und Hochzeitsmahl', 1990.
25 Cf. 5571 (pigs), 5718–19 (calf), 5724 (ox), 6090 (wolves). See also Brülhart, *Vexatio dat intellectum*, 148–50.
26 Cf. 6068–70, 6082, 6086. For more on the comedic representation of the 'grotesque' see Velten, *Scurrilitas*, 112–20.
27 Bakhtin, *Rabelais and His World*, 278–302.
28 Lateiner, 'The emotion of disgust', 47.
29 Röcke, 'Drohung und Eskalation', 130–41.
30 Wießner, *Kommentar*: 'eine wohlberechnete Steigerung' (231).
31 Brülhart, *Vexatio dat intellectum*, 184–5, reads this as an allusion to comedic brutality in the heroic epic. The work in question (*Virginal*) will be discussed later in this chapter.
32 Boesch, 'Die Namenswelt'.
33 Note also the name of one of the villages which come out in support of Nissingen: 'Fützenswille' / 'Quim-will' (6964).
34 In the masturbation scene Mätzli's 'futze[n]' (1572) too is compared to a mouth that has been so badly mistreated it is unable to answer her back (1600–2).

35 'Futzenpart' is named for the second time (7264) by a Lappenhausener who shows no signs of finding this name (or any of the others) out of the ordinary.
36 *Deutsche Versnovellistik (DVN)*, ed. Ridder and Ziegeler, IV, 288–9.
37 The same mishap occurs in Wittenwiler's *Ring* (6233–44), only there it causes laughter. Wittenwiler even draws attention to this difference with his knowing remark: 'es was nicht zeit, / Daz sich derheben scholt ein streit' (6245–6). The motif of the broken mirror goes back to Neidhart; see Schulze, 'Grundthemen der Lieder Neidharts', 102–7.
38 For further differences see Ziegeler, *Erzählen im Spätmittelalter*, 405–38.
39 Of the five Nissinger wenches one is spared rape on account of her ugliness (7096–7). Grotesquely, this passage is followed by a dawn song (7098–107) in which clandestine lovers are urged to take leave of one another. See Lienert, 'Das Tagelied', 1994/95.
40 In *Meier Betz* the detail of the grease ('treck' 152) running over the peasants' faces is given not once but twice with reference to their cheeks ('packen' 153) and then to their mouths and beards ('maul vnd der part' 156). Thereafter the uncontrollable laughter of some is prompted by the sight of others burning their mouths on the hot food (157–63). No such connection is made in *Metzen hochzit*.
41 See also Heiland, *Visualisierung und Rhetorisierung*, 75.
42 The counter-courtly world evoked by Neidhart is best elucidated by Müller, 'Strukturen gegenhöfischer Welt'.
43 The final line of one song (WL 36, as preserved in one fifteenth-century manuscript (c)) ends with an archetypal image of anxiety, as felt by the singer when faced with his rustic rivals: 'von in trage ich grâwen bart' (VIIa,10). This represents a variation on Neidhart's more generalized references to turning grey (from fear and loathing) in other songs such as WL 10 (V,2), WL 18 (III,1), WL 22 (IV,6), WL 31 (VI,10) and WL 32 (V,1–6).
44 Cf. also WL 3: VI,6.
45 This is epitomized by the vain peasant Hildemar (as described in WL 29), who prides himself on his fancy headwear, decorated with images of birds, and his long courtly locks (VI,1–VII,8), much to the singer's contempt: 'begrîfents in, si zerrent im die hûben alsô swinde: / ê er waene, sô sint im diu vogelîn enpflogen' (VIII,3–4).
46 See also Bockmann, 'Literarische Neidhart-Rezeption', 283–5.
47 Coxon, 'Punitive laughter', 2012.
48 Grafetstätter, 'Die Neidhartspiele'.
49 Velten, *Scurrilitas*, 222–63.
50 Cf. also the vainglorious bluster of another peasant when, under the mischievous influence of Neidhart, things go awry: 'Jch schluoch durch hyeren vnd durch part' (1911).
51 Velten, *Scurrilitas*, 404–36.
52 Cf. Gregor Hayden, *Salomon und Marckolf*: 'vnd het gestalt nach geisses art. / Auch also was im sein part' (57–8).
53 Velten, *Scurrilitas*, 359–66.
54 Cf. also *Innsbrucker Osterspiel* 688.
55 Dicke, 'Mären-Priapeia', 2002.
56 Friedman, 'Hair and social class', 144–50.
57 Simon, *Die Anfänge des weltlichen deutschen Schauspiels*, 291–348. In this chapter all Shrovetide plays are referred to by their 'Keller-nr' (K) and are taken from the Adelbert von Keller edition of 1853 unless otherwise indicated.
58 Klimczak, *Bildlichkeit und Metaphorik*, 117–233.
59 Not all beard references in these plays are so crude. Other comic beard topoi include: beardedness of goats ((K13) *Buhlerrevue* 119,4–5); pain of having beard torn out ((K16) *Wettstreit in der Liebe* 134,12); unattractiveness of the older man ((K70) *Vom Werben um die Jungfrau* 616,11–12; (K95) *Mädchen und Burschen* 738,6–8).
60 Müller, *Schwert und Scheide*, 60–1.
61 Müller, *Schwert und Scheide*, 74.
62 Müller, *Schwert und Scheide*, 87–8; Klimczak, *Bildlichkeit und Metaphorik*, 156–61.
63 Müller, *Schwert und Scheide*, 121–8; Klimczak, *Bildlichkeit und Metaphorik*, 202–9.
64 Klimczak, *Bildlichkeit und Metaphorik*: 'Bart und Wurst sind semantisch unpassend' (182).
65 *Nürnberger Fastnachtspiele*, ed. Greil and Przybilski, 80, 126.
66 *Codex Weimar Q 565*, ed. Kully, 123. See also Müller, *Schwert und Scheide*, 63.
67 On obscenity, disgust and comedy see Klimczak, *Bildlichkeit und Metaphorik*, 51–9; Velten, *Scurrilitas*, 365.

68 *Straßburger Rätselbuch* nrs 177, 178, 213, 229, 232.

69 Riddles concerning beards and goats were evidently very popular; cf. also Munich, BSB, Cgm 379, dated 1454, fol. 216v: 'welchu creatur hat ein part in muoter leib ee es poren wirt?'

70 See Chapter 1.

71 The bearded dwarf is one of three types described by Lütjens, *Der Zwerg*, 68–72.

72 In the 'Ältere Vulgatversion' of *Laurin*, disparaging reference to the dwarf king's beard in one redaction ('Er hat ein part als ein geis' L_{18} 301) represents a mischievous variation on a different kind of goat reference in another: 'Ez rit eyn ros alz eyn geyz' (L_3 320).

73 Schuler-Lang, *Wildes Erzählen*, 253–62.

74 Cf. also *Ortnit* A 445,2.

75 Brülhart, *Vexatio dat intellectum*, 184–5, finds this deed mirrored in the brawl at the start of Part III of Wittenwiler's *Ring* (6488–90).

76 Cf. also the 'Heidelberger' version (I) of *Virginal* 738,4–13.

77 Dinkelacker, 'Der alte Held', 190–4.

78 The same kind of antagonistic dialogue is a feature of the fifteenth-century ballad-like *Jüngeres Hildebrandslied*, where Hildebrand refers to his own beard as evidence of his age and experience ('dar umb grabt mir mein part' 8,4) only for his son to threaten him accordingly: 'Dein part wil ich aus rauffen – das must du sehen an –, / das dir das plut mussz lauffen und auf dem harnisch stan' (9,1–2).

79 See also Coxon, 'Heroes and their beards', 2018, 44–8.

80 Cf. also *Rosengarten* P 676, C 426,3, F XI,4. Other redactions of this epic do different things with Hildebrand's beard; see Coxon, 'Heroes and their beards', 2018, 37–8.

81 The fire-breathing Dietrich does (of course) eventually fight and vanquish Siegfried.

82 Cf. also *Wolfdietrich* D 369,1, 369,4.

83 'von dem grossen leide rofte er vs sin bart' (1958,5).

84 An unusual scribal note in the codex of the *Rappoltsteiner Parzifal* (Karlsruhe, LB, Cod. Donaueschingen 97, c. 1331–6) plays on this notion too: 'Diz sol nieman vergessen: / ob disem buoche sint fünf jor gesessen / ze tihtende und ze schriben, / hie sol ein ende bliben. / Henselin schriber het ouch vil geschriben heran / und wil noch nüt ein ende han. / er gewan noch nie bart / und ist ouch den vinen vröwelin zart. / der von Onheim ist ein rehter tore, / er trüget die vrowen mit sime growen hore' (fol. 320v).

85 We find this theme in Latin literature as early as the twelfth century. In *Lidia*, a 'comedia' of marital infidelity, the eponymous deceitful wife is required to pluck five hairs from her gullible husband's beard in order to persuade her lover to trust her (267–8). She duly does so under the guise of ridding her husband of unsightly grey hairs (313–24).

86 Spicker, *Oswald von Wolkenstein*, 38–60.

87 See Müller, *'Dichtung' und 'Wahrheit'*, 161–85.

88 Spicker, *Oswald von Wolkenstein*, understands Oswald's beard to function here as 'eine Art Erkennungsmerkmal' (164).

89 This Oswald beard reference is recycled in *Neithart Fuchs* 2962–3. See also Spicker, *Oswald von Wolkenstein*, 167.

90 'dieselbe edle künigin, / zwen guldin ring sloss si mir darin / und ain in bart verhangen, / also hiess si mich prangen' (157–60).

91 See Müller, *'Dichtung' und 'Wahrheit'*, 164–6.

92 Hofmeister, *Oswald von Wolkenstein*, 316 n. 523, dubs this 'pekuniäre Potenz'.

93 Müller, *'Dichtung' und 'Wahrheit'*, 167–75.

94 Text cited in accordance with 'Leithandschrift' K.

95 Cf. the famous *descriptio* of Frederick in the *Gesta Frederici* (IV, 86); also see Chapter 1. Abbot Burchard of Bellevaux (*Apologia de barbis*) asserts with great confidence that King David, no less, was red-bearded: 'et barba illius rufa' (III, 1159–60). Keen on harmony among the lay brothers, Burchard cites this case to refute the wicked jibe so often directed at men with a red beard: 'barba tua rufa infidelitatis est signum' (III, 1154–5).

96 Such prejudice, which may or may not have been rooted in popular superstition, is ubiquitous in the Latin clerical literature of the twelfth century: *Ysengrimus* V, 1040–1; Walter Map, *De Nugis Curialium* II, 31. Cf. also Matthew of Vendôme, *Ars versificatoria*, where a hateful reader by the name of 'Rufus' is repeatedly ridiculed, not least in relation to 'Rufa', the latter's red-haired companion-cum-prostitute (II, 38, III, 5, IV, 48). At the same time Matthew enlivens his discussion of rhetorical colours with humorous sample sentences including proverbial expressions at the expense of the red-haired in general: 'In rufo est prodigiosa fides' (II, 20;

cf. also II, 38, II, 42, III, 14). Earlier evidence of this stigma is famously found in the eleventh-century *Ruodlieb* at V: 451–6, V: 585–VIII: 129.

97 Cf. also *Roman de Renart* I: 731, II: 1068–9, VI: 75.

98 *Parzival* 143,3, 160,27–9. At the moment of his death (at the hands of Parzival) the narrator explicitly praises Ither as 'der valscheit widersatz' (155,11).

99 Cf. Konrad von Würzburg's *Partonopier und Meliur*, where the protagonist is aided by a kindly elderly knight who has grey locks and a bright red beard (13096–9).

100 As comprehensively reviewed by Schnyder (ed.), *Kaiser Otto und Heinrich von Kempten*.

101 Brall, 'Geraufter Bart und nackter Retter'; Beate Kellner, 'Der Ritter und die nackte Gewalt'.

102 The emperor plays a prank on Heinrich by pretending to be still furious with him: 'ir sît ez doch der mir den bart / âne scharsach hât geschorn' (692–3).

103 See also Neudeck, *Erzählen von Kaiser Otto*, 286–93.

104 https://digi.ub.uni-heidelberg.de/diglit/cpg395. Accessed 14 March 2021.

105 In codex Innsbruck, Tiroler Landesmuseum Ferdinandeum, Hs. FB 32001, dated 1456, the *titulus* is much more concise: 'Von chaiser otten' (fol. 84v). However, the opening of the text is accompanied by a miniature which shows an emperor swearing by his long (uncoloured) beard (84v).

106 At least three other versions of this tale, otherwise known as *Die Bärenjagd*, were circulating at this time.

107 Boner concurs with the beast's wise words in his own conclusion: 'Ez süllen vrouwen und man / den rôten gesellen lâzen gân' (49–50).

108 See also Mellinkoff, 'Judas's red hair', 1982. Judas's red hair continued to be alluded to and joked about throughout the sixteenth and well into the seventeenth centuries. Cf. Heinrich Bebel's 'facetia' III, 153, where a red-haired man actually defends the honour of his 'kind' with reference to Judas Iscariot: 'quod Christus deus solius rufi Iudae Iscariotis (quem rufum pingunt) osculo tangi sit dignatus'.

109 Schnell, 'Recht und Dichtung', 2011, 19.

110 Cf. also the *Wormser Passionsspiel* (c. 1325–50), in which the (Latin) stage directions repeatedly place a 'Judaeus rufus' at the heart of the action (711a–1163a).

111 Frey, 'Vergleiche von Juden', 2007.

112 Wenzel, *Juden in spätmittelalterlichen Spielen*, 237–55; Schönleber, 'Antijüdische Motive', 173–81. Text taken from *Nürnberger Fastnachtspiele*, ed. Greil and Przybilski, 171–201.

113 Weis-Diel, *Gewaltstrategien*, 357–65.

114 *Nürnberger Fastnachtspiele*, ed. Greil and Przybilski, 214. The text of K20 is cited in accordance with this edition.

115 Phillips, 'Race and ethnicity'.

116 Ackermann, 'Dimensionen der Medialität', 202–6.

117 Dunphy, *Old Testament material*, 109–18.

118 Toad: plugging the hole made by the devil in the Ark (2575–80). Dogs and cats: domestication goes back to Noah's decision to keep them on board for longer (2752–4).

119 Myslivec, 'Apostel', 1968, 152–3.

120 See also Velten, *Scurrilitas*, 451–2.

121 Hammer, 'Held in Mönchskleidern', 2008; Coxon, 'Heroes and their beards', 2018, 39–40, 44–5.

122 Cf. *Rosengarten* A/II 201,2, 213,1–3, 217,2–3.

123 Cf. also *Rosengarten* A/I, where Kriemhild's face pours with blood (412,4), or version D, where the author-narrator can barely contain his mirth at Kriemhild's discomfort (2250–1).

124 In this collection of heroic epics *Wolfdietrich* (fols 45r–215r) comes before the *Rosengarten* (217r–255v).

125 In preceding *Rosengarten* woodcuts (fols 230r, 234r, 252v, 253r) the belligerent Ilsan figure is, as we might have expected, bearded; on fol. 254v the bearded Ilsan is shown tormenting beardless monks. See also *Heldenbuch*, ed. Heinzle, II, 53–63.

126 This motif plays a prominent role in the German reception of the *chansons de geste*; cf. *Morant und Galie* 3076–87 (villain makes mask out of pilgrim's face); *Loher und Maller* 128,4–9 (hero purchases false beard from fraudster posing as pilgrim).

127 Boyer, 'Murder and morality', 2016.

128 Morolf's notorious ruse is alluded to in the prologue of Der arme Konrad's comic tale *Frau Metze*: 'wie Marolff ain alten juden schant' (3). One of the text's five manuscripts (n^2) offers a gentler alternative: here the trickster's victim is 'ain tierlin' (3).

129 *Salman und Morolf* 261,4.

6
Jesus's beard

> wol getân was Jêsû bart.
> nie schoener mensche geborn wart.
>
> Philipp von Seitz, *Marienleben* 5056–7[1]

Probably the single most important beard in medieval culture belongs to Jesus. As such it merits a discussion all of its own. To come anywhere close to doing justice to this topic would entail analysing a very large number of texts, both Latin and vernacular, far beyond the scope of this more general study. What follows therefore is very selective,[2] although even the briefest of surveys brings to light some extraordinary examples of the principal themes investigated in this book. Abused, ridiculed and crucified in the prime of his human life, so the faithful believed, the Son of God was also perceived to be majestic and wise. Different texts do different things with Christ's beard to emphasize one or more of these aspects.

Evidence, if any were needed, that beardedness was widely regarded as a quintessential feature of Jesus Christ may be found in vernacular works far removed from devotional poetry. At one point in the so-called *Buch von Akkon*, a more or less contemporary account of the fall of Acre (1291) contained in Ottokar von Gaal's *Steierische Reimchronik*,[3] the remarkable appearance of Christian warriors is explained by one heathen to another: 'daz kriuze und den bart / tragent si durch in [Jesus Christ]' / 'They wear the cross and beards for the sake of him [Jesus Christ]' (49726–7). Even the leading Saracens understand the symbols of their enemy, the visual tenets of their faith, as it were. It is thus from an alien perspective that the beards of the Crusaders are presented as being as obvious a marker of their holy mission as the crosses adorning their garments and standards. Elsewhere, in one version of the less than serious heroic epic *Rosengarten*, the rumbustious 'monk' Ilsan is outraged by Kriemhild's objection (on behalf of all of her ladies-in-waiting) to his 'ruchen bart' / 'bristly beard' (D 2237): 'Sulich smehe rede mir nie me erbotten wart. / Den orden trag ich rechte durch den suessen Jhesus Crist' / 'I've never been spoken to in such offensive terms! I wear this [sign of my] order in the name of sweet Jesus Christ' (2238–9). The comedic effect of these lines does not undermine the status of the bearded Christ as a role model (this time for lay brothers); rather, it depends upon the validity of this notion even when it is pronounced by a figure who, anything other than gentle and patient, is interested only in securing a kiss from a beautiful maiden.

The fact of Jesus's beardedness is one thing, its further description is quite another. For this we must look to religious literature proper.[4] Counter-intuitively perhaps, legends concerning 'acheiropoieta' or miraculous 'made-without-hand' images of Jesus's face tend not to be rich sources for specifics.[5] The Early Middle High German Veronica legend (*Dit ist Veronica*) by Der Wilde Mann (c. 1170) relates that the artist commissioned by Veronica tries and fails three times to capture a likeness of Jesus, before Jesus himself presses a towel to his face and presents the image to his devotee as a sign of special favour (183–91), and all of this without a single facial feature being mentioned. It is possible that throughout the Middle Ages the face of Jesus was considered so recognizable to most people that the poets of such legends could depend on their recipients' knowledge to flesh out their narratives. On the other hand, by conspicuously avoiding all such detail the stories lend testimony to Jesus's ineffability, as the Son of Man explains to Der Wilde Mann's luckless artist: 'dine liste inmugen dir nit gevruomen, / iz insule von miner helfe kuomen' / 'Your craftsmanship is of no use to you, unless this is done with my help' (155–6).[6]

One of the most extensive descriptions of Jesus occurs in the *Vita beate virginis Marie et Salvatoris rhythmica*, also known as the *Vita rhythmica*, thought to have been composed around 1225–50.[7] This highly influential account of the lives of Mary and Jesus accords each of these figures a rhetorically polished, set-piece *descriptio* (685–760, 3124–315), which in the case of Jesus serves as a bridge between his childhood and his adulthood and death. From head to toe Jesus is of course a physically perfect specimen, with one or two hints at his miraculous nature thrown in for good measure: the hair on his head, we are told, was black, soft and quite long, and looked after itself: 'Raro compti, nunquam tonsi, tamen non distorti' / 'His hair was seldom combed, never cut, yet not [ever] dishevelled' (3151). As part of this scheme ten lines in total are devoted to Jesus's 'barba' / 'beard' (3220–9). This too is meant to have consisted of soft black hair of rare beauty, its ideal appearance and condition otherwise expressed in terms of the perfect mean: not covering too much or too little of his face, not being too long or too short, too thin or too thick.[8]

By about 1300 the *Vita rhythmica* had already been translated into the vernacular several times. One of the earliest of these German versions was Walther von Rheinau's *Marienleben*, where the description of Jesus, not least the subsection dedicated to his beard, as highlighted by the rubric 'Von dem barte' (6327a), sticks closely to the Latin: 'Sîn bart was swarz und lanc genuoc, / Von lindem schoenem hâre kluoc' / 'His beard was black and just long enough, of soft and fine beautiful hair' (6328–9). The poet's one original(?) flourish comes right at the end of this passage, where a new idea is introduced to convey just how beautifully Jesus's beard grows up to his ears: 'Sam er gemâlet waere dar' / '[It was] as if it had been painted there' (6341). This would seem to be a case of art portraying life imitating art, a poetic device which refutes any notion of Christ's miraculous ineffability. Furthermore, if we understand this line as a nod to painted images of Christ, this background might help to explain why, earlier on in the description, the poet takes the unusual step of departing from his principal source in respect of the colour of Jesus's hair in general: 'Sîns wolgestalten houbtes hâr / Linde was und brûngevar' / 'The hair of his shapely head was soft and brown in colour' (6204–5). Was this an attempt on Walther von Rheinau's part to bring his portrayal of Jesus into line with iconographic norms of the day?[9]

Evasiveness concerning the colour of Christ's hair is more obvious still in another vernacular version, the *Marienleben* of Wernher der Schweizer (c. 1300). Here the description begins faithfully enough: 'Sin har swarcz und linde was' / 'His hair was black and soft' (5801). But it ends on a rather more circumspect note: 'Und etwas in bruner varwe, / Nut alzeswarcz noch grawe' / 'And [it was] somewhat brownish, not too black nor grey' (5811–12). By the time Wernher reaches Jesus's beard he appears to be back on message: 'Och swarzer varwe was sin bart, / Vil minneklich gar und zart' / 'His beard too was black in colour, utterly delightful and soft' (5919–20). By contrast, the portrayal of Jesus in the most widely transmitted German rendering of the *Vita rhythmica*, Philipp von Seitz's *Marienleben*, is quite unequivocal on this point: 'prûn was doch sîns houbtes hâr' / 'The hair of his head was indeed brown' (5013); 'daz kinne und ouch ein teil der wangen / het ein schoener part bevangen, / der was brûn unde reit'/ 'A beautiful beard covered his chin and, to some extent, his cheeks; it was brown and curly' (5052–4). In fact, Philipp von Seitz's description is less fussy and more concise than the others. He devotes a mere six lines to Jesus's beard, seemingly content to reiterate its outstanding beauty: 'wol getân was Jêsû bart. / nie schoener mensche geborn wart' / 'Jesus's beard was delightful. No fairer human being had ever been born' (5056–7). The shift of emphasis is unostentatious but significant. Jesus's beauty, we are meant to understand, was very human and very natural as opposed to miraculous, as stipulated at the very start of the excursus: 'alsô het im ouch gegeben / diu natûre schoenez leben' / 'Thus nature had also given him beauty in this life' (5006–7).

Aside from fixed descriptions of Jesus's appearance, traditions of more dynamic or embedded portrayal developed in the course of the thirteenth and fourteenth centuries as part of the heightened interest in the Passion, in Christ's humanity as rendered manifest by his suffering for the sake of mankind.[10] Not only was this suffering presented in emotionally charged ways, but it was depicted in ever more detail. These late medieval Passion texts went far beyond the canonical accounts found in the Gospels, elaborating on traditional episodes (buffeting, crowning with thorns, crucifixion) with a whole new repertoire of humiliating torments and awful acts of cruelty.[11] References to the Saviour's beard and hair occur in this context in conjunction with other abuses directed at his head and face. The rich iconography of the Passion in the later Middle Ages doubtless played a role in this too.[12]

One of the leading principles in poetic re-imaginings of Christ's suffering is that of beauty defiled.[13] Within this scheme some features of Christ receive more attention than others. Jesus's wondrous, sweet or gentle face, cheeks and mouth are mentioned particularly frequently. Allusions to his beard are a little less common, constituting a special effect which aggravates the indecent assault on Jesus's person.[14] This is illustrated by a work such as the later thirteenth-century *Der Spiegel*, derived from a (Latin) treatise falsely ascribed to St Bernard of Clairvaux, which purports to contain the miraculous revelation of Mary's agonized view of her own son's persecution and death.[15] Here recipients are reminded – by Mary herself – of the gracefulness of Jesus's features even as he is subjected to insult and injury: 'Sin wange minneclich / Vnd sin bart edelich / Zerzarten si im da ze stunt' / 'His delightful cheek[s] and his noble beard were torn to shreds there and then' (G 422a–c).[16] A similar strategy is adopted by Wernher der Schweizer in his *Marienleben*, whose portrayal of the buffeting is expressly phrased in such a way as to bring the earlier panegyrical *descriptio* to mind: 'Sin minneklicher werder bart / Vil schmaechlich gezogen wart' / 'His delightful, adorable beard was plucked most heinously' (9109–10). Where Jesus's beard was conceived of as holy (like the rest of his body), such physical abuse assumed a sacrilegious character.[17]

Defilement goes hand in hand with debasement, as the ubiquitous scene of Christ's crowning with thorns makes clear. To refer to Jesus's beard at this moment in the story of the Passion, as Johannes von Frankenstein does in his *Kreuziger* (c. 1325), evokes the majesty of Christ just when his humiliation appears most grotesque: 'ein durnîn krone ûf daz houbt / wart im gesatzt, dâ von stoub / des blûtes dizen durch den bart' / 'A crown of thorns was put on his head so that a torrent of blood poured [down] through his beard' (7295–7). Majesty, humanity and beardedness are all brought to bear on one another in a Passion song in Frauenlob's 'Zarter Ton' (VIII,207). Towards the end, when Christ the 'künig, der die welte mag erquicken' / '[the] king who can make the world new' (163) is described as carrying his own cross – just before his 'edel menscheit' / 'noble humanity' (169) momentarily fails him and his legs give way –, his wretched suffering is conveyed by the abject condition of his beard: 'auwe der fart! / sein prauner part / stund im von plute naß' / 'Alas! What a journey! His brown beard was dripping with blood' (166–8). The blood implies redness, but still the poet (Pseudo-Frauenlob) insists on the brown of Christ's beard. The same lines, more or less, are recycled in another spurious Frauenlob text (VIII,213), this time to describe Christ after he has been nailed to the cross.[18] This attention to colour, it turns out, is thematically motivated. In several other songs within the Frauenlob tradition the Holy Trinity is indeed colour-coordinated: if the Holy Ghost is white and God the Father is grey(-haired), then Christ the Son has brown hair and a brown beard, no matter what torments he endures.[19]

Abuse of Christ's beard was the kind of detail that could potentially be added to any number of different scenes within the relatively fixed sequence of events of the Passion. In Oswald von Wolkenstein's Passion song, (Kl. 111) *In oberland*, those who arrest Jesus in the Garden of Gethsemane also mistreat him in this way.[20] In the *Passional* (c. 1300), on the other hand, this is one of the nocturnal abuses suffered by Christ in the house of Annas (62,17–18), and, more unusually, in this narrative account Jesus is even dragged along by his beard while carrying his cross (68,87–8). The emergence of vernacular Passion treatises in prose (with no direct Latin source) in the early fourteenth century gave writers the space to depict such torments at greater length.[21] In the earliest known text of this kind, *Christi Leiden in einer Vision geschaut* (c. 1325–50), beard plucking – at the moment of Christ's arrest – turns into something far more brutal as Jesus is thrown back and forth, and cast down and hauled up again by his beard (65,32–66,23). Subsequent depictions go even further in their drastic 'realism'. In Heinrich von St Gallen's *Passionstraktat* (c. 1350–1400) Christ is pulled by his beard so hard 'das im den munt allir zuswollen was' / 'that his mouth became all swollen' (129, p. 27). Other poets explored more refined tortures: 'Sie namen spitze nolden, vnd stachen yme in die luchelin seines bartes' / 'They took sharp needles and jabbed him through the delicate locks of his beard' (*Do der minnenklich got*; c. 1400).[22] However sadistic such narrative detail might seem to be, the attention paid to the minutiae of Jesus's suffering at each stage of his Passion could be understood as one solution to a very particular problem: how to elicit compassion from recipients who knew this story backwards.

Not all depictions of the Passion were designed for quiet contemplation and meditation. Passion plays were performed in front of large crowds over several days and represent a radically different text type which operated with its own quite distinctive modes of representation.[23] The literary tradition of these dramatizations had fully established itself by the second half of the fifteenth century, as evinced by texts such as the *Donaueschinger Passionsspiel* (c. 1470/80). Here too we find multiple references to Christ's beard, for the most part at very familiar points in the action, although, occurring as they do in the speeches of his tormentors, they help to create different – dramatic – effects, posing new interpretative challenges for us. When Jesus is arrested by Pilatus's 'knights' (Ÿesse, Mosse, Israhel and Malchus), reference to Christ's beard takes the form of an imperative, as one figure exhorts others to manhandle Jesus still further: 'Schlachent in den schölmen hart / rouffent in bÿ sinem bart' / 'Beat him hard, the foul wretch! Pluck his beard!' (2167–8). Here as elsewhere speech sustains the action, signalling in this case perhaps a shift, an intensification in the violence being acted out.[24] These lines belong to a speech uttered by an 'extra' figure – 'ein iud heisset ysack' / 'a Jew called Isaac' (2156c) – as the stage directions make clear, and they were doubtless meant to offer tangible evidence *in nuce* of the malign influence exercised by the Jews on the proceedings.[25] At the same time this unexpected intervention may be viewed as a quasi-commentary on the (performed) violence being meted out to Jesus by the other tormentors in this scene, allowing the audience to hear as well as see what was taking place on stage. Other imperatives of this kind are barked out by the soldiers leading Christ to the place of his execution: [Mosse] 'ziechent in bim har vnd bart' / 'Pull him by his hair and beard!' (3123); [Ÿesse] 'vnd ziehent im den schelmen bart' / 'and pull the foul wretch's beard!' (3158). During this phase of the action the hostile speeches of Jesus's tormentors alternate with the lamentations of the several Marys; the scene thus oscillates between diametrically opposed perspectives, setting off cruelty against compassion.[26] The soldiers only speak about Jesus in the third person, effectively objectifying him and making a target of his body parts, whereas the weeping women address Christ directly, fully acknowledging who he truly is: [Mary Salome] 'O Ihesu des lebendigen gottes sün / wie wil man dir vil armen tuon' / 'O Jesus, Son of the living God, what are they going to do to you in your misery?' (3143–4).

In several other scenes, between arrest and crucifixion, Jesus's tormentors speak to him directly about plucking his beard. On two separate occasions these speeches add insult to injury, being linked to stage directions which explicitly write the plucking of Jesus's beard into the play's action. At the house of Cayphas an extended sequence of physical abuses ensues, itemized by stage directions and the words of the perpetrators, under the direction of Mosse who plays the role of a spiteful master of ceremonies. Thus Jesus is duped (by Malchus) into falling to the ground before being hoisted up by his hair; he is blindfolded (by Israhel), slapped (by Mosse), then has a lock of hair torn from his scalp (by Malchus) before yet another brutal prank is played on him:

> *Nu roufft aber israhel den saluator / bÿm bart vnd spricht:*
> Sag mir hie zuo disser fart
> wer het dir zer zerret dinen bart (2282ab, 2283–4)
>
> *Now Israhel once again pulls the Salvator by the beard and says:*
> Tell me then, here and now. Who was it who tore out your beard?!

The scene as a whole is marked by the contrast between the malicious acts and words of the tormentors on the one hand, and Christ's silence and patience on the other. The indignities suffered by Jesus in this way evidently get worse. Beard plucking is the logical next step after hair pulling, and this applies to the other scene in question as well, when the soldiers mistreat Jesus on the way to Pontius Pilate (2545a–49, 2549a–53). The combination of stage direction and mocking speech is significant in a more general sense: at these points at least the performance of degrading violence, including beard plucking, would seem to be carefully choreographed, stylized even, and subject to some control rather than spontaneous. Having said that, the stage direction is formulated in such a way as to suggest that Israhel is not plucking the Saviour's beard for the first time: 'aber' / 'once again' (2282a) hints at a more or less continuous performance of buffeting beyond what is expressly scripted.

Several other references to beard plucking occur in speeches where Christ is ridiculed more wittily, or rather where there is some attempt at wordplay. The comedic effect of such lines would also doubtless have been determined by the accompanying actions of the speakers. The irony in Ÿesse's words of encouragement to Jesus as he is taken to the house of

Cayphas is already quite blatant: 'lieber ertritt mir nit die müss / ich rouff dir anders din bart vss' / '[My] dear fellow, now don't be in too much of a rush, or I shall pull out your beard!' (2257–8). But the effect would surely have been compounded by any concomitant gesture of actual beard plucking. Two further 'witty' threats occur in the context of Jesus's encounter with Herod, an episode in which the *Donaueschinger Passionsspiel* appears to take great delight. First, when Jesus fails to say a single word to Herod, one guard (Zacharias) is moved to say: 'gib antwürt hie zuo diser vart / ich zerzerr dir anders din roten bart' / 'Give an answer here and now, or I shall tear your red beard to shreds' (2696–7). Again one wonders whether the joke is in part a visual one, and depends on Jesus's face being bloodied: the stupidity, or indeed cleverness, of the guard's words would therefore be in treating the wounded Christ with the prejudice reserved for men with naturally red beards, that stereotypical sign of innate dishonesty. Secondly, just as Jesus is dressed in the white robe of a fool and dismissed by Herod, another guard (Salathies) confides in him: 'wer ich nit so von frömer art / So griff ich dir yetz vnd ouch in den bart' / 'If I didn't have such a pious nature, I would grab hold of you by the beard too' (2752–3). Given that Salathies's stated intention of treating Jesus with 'erbermde' / 'mercy' (2750) is quite obviously phoney – he repeatedly calls for Jesus to be scourged – his self-confessed piety is blatantly a sham too. Whether this was meant to be understood as foolish self-delusion or a cruelly ironic prelude to more beard plucking must remain unclear.

The underlying problem with much of this more 'comedic' material is of course working out, if only in principle, who was supposed to be amused by it and to what end. Real audience responses, both collective and individual, are bound to have been unpredictable, spontaneous and thus quite variable. Nevertheless it seems sensible to make a distinction between the grotesque pleasure taken in Christ's suffering by his tormentors on stage, as conveyed by what they do and say, and the amusement felt at any one moment by the spectators, who for long periods of time were otherwise expected to be disturbed and appalled by what they were watching and hearing.[27] The more foolish Christ's tormentors prove themselves to be, even as they are deriding Christ, the greater the incitement to audiences to laugh *at* them from a position of superiority. However witty these guards think they are being, they really do not know what they do. They are totally ignorant of themselves and of Jesus's true nature.[28] By contrast, if and when spectators were ever prompted to laugh *with* the henchmen on stage, this could quite conceivably have served as a pertinent reminder of their own moral frailty and culpability. Performances of the *Donaueschinger*

Passionsspiel were designed to be staged over two days. One wonders whether spectators were being taken on an emotional and moral journey, exposed to fear, horror and the guilty pleasure of scurrilous laughter as they witnessed Christ's Passion (torture of his mortal flesh) before experiencing hope and joyous exhilaration at the Resurrection (revelation of divinity).

The plucking of Christ's beard is to be found in most other German Passion plays of this period, as highlighted by more or less the same kinds of speeches. One notable variation occurs in the *Frankfurter Passionsspiel* (dated 1493), where the guard leading Christ to his crucifixion refers to his beardedness in insulting fashion: 'wir wollen guden schimff mit dir / triben wol auff der fart! / daz nym vor gut, du snoder bart!' / 'We mean to make merry with you as we go along! Be a good sport, you foul-beard!' (2547–9). Elsewhere, in the *Brixener Passionsspiel* (dated 1551), attention is first paid (on a textual level) to Peter's beard, as a means of making fun of him in those moments in which he proves himself most fallible: when unable to contain his rage at Jesus's arrest ('Vnd schwer beÿ meinen graben partt / da werdt Nit lenger angesparrt' / 'And [I] swear by my grey beard, I cannot stand by any longer!' 1218–19), and when recognized for the third time as one of Jesus's followers ('So du mit dem graben partt' / 'You there with the grey beard!' 1340). Subsequently, when Christ patiently endures being abused by a scornful bystander ('ein verspotter') as he is being led to Pilate – 'Peÿt Ich will greÿffen In dein partt' / 'Hold on, I want to grab you by the beard' (1541) – we are reminded both of what unites Christ and Peter and what divides them.

Beyond overtly religious texts, the literary strategy of using foolish figures to mention the unmentionable and do the unspeakable proved ever more popular in the later Middle Ages, as it enabled audiences, listeners and readers to enjoy fictional representations of transgressive behaviour, safe in the knowledge of their own (supposed) superiority. References to God's or Christ's beard crop up in this context too, if somewhat infrequently. In one comic tale (c. 1400), now known as *Von eime trunken buoben*, what begins as a simple story of a drunken knave who is beaten for being too boisterous soon turns into something far more audacious. Nursing his bruises the next morning, the lout launches into an extended parody of the Lord's Prayer, during which he cannot emphasize enough just how terribly he has been persecuted: 'symmer eins bockes bart! / ich hett gar ein swere vart' / 'By a billy goat's beard, I swear I had a terribly arduous path to tread' ((k) 136–7). Bearing in mind that 'bock'/'goat' represents the conventional medieval German substitute word for 'gott'/'God' in exclamations as a means of avoiding blasphemy, its use in the course of a prayer to God is quite absurd.[29] It further characterizes the knave as either misguided (how could God not see through this piece of linguistic camouflage?) or utterly ignorant (he does not know what he is saying). This oblique reference to God's beard, moreover, is part of a bigger joke. The 'swere vart' / 'arduous path' the knave complains about is a drunkard's passion; the manhandling he describes reads like another buffeting: 'ich wart nechtyn sere getunsen / mit dem hare durch die koln' / 'Last night I was dragged by the hair through the coals' (133–4).[30] Unlike the crucified Christ, who prays for his enemies to be forgiven, the knave desires revenge: 'herre vater, ich bijt dich, / laß ez nicht ungerochen' / 'Lord Father, I beg you, do not let this go unavenged!' (170–1).

The most famous late medieval collection of fools is to be found in Sebastian Brant's *Narrenschiff* (first printed in 1494), where the folly of 'verachtung gottes' / 'contempt of God' (chapter 86) is encapsulated in the utterly outrageous act of pulling God's beard, as portrayed in the accompanying woodcut (Figure 6.1).[31] Divorced entirely from the narrative context of the Passion, this demeaning gesture is no longer directed at the suffering Jesus (as man) but at the Risen Christ in his divine glory, offering his benediction with one hand and holding the orb and cross in the other. The fool who sees fit to provoke God in this way is bearded too, most likely to indicate age and the passing of time. According to the three titular verses for the chapter, it is the fool's delusion, should divine punishment not strike at once, that he has the licence to continue to do as he pleases.[32] As the picture shows, however, thunder and hailstones can strike at any moment. In keeping with the work's other chapters, this woodcut offers anyone holding the book (irrespective of their ability to read) a defining image of this particular type of folly.[33] The chapter itself spells out the lunacy of such a contemptuous attitude. Only a fool believes that God, like an ordinary man, will keep his peace 'vnd loß fatzen sich' / 'and let himself be trifled with' (4), tweaking God's beard being the most drastic form of such tomfoolery: 'Dar vmb / das jm gott ettwan spart / Meynt er jm griffen an den bart' / 'Thus the fool thinks to grab God by the beard because he spares him for a time' (16–17). Humorous though this image undoubtedly is, later in the text Brant ensures that the reader does not lose sight of its didactic significance: 'Hör zuo o dor / würd witzig narr' / 'Listen [to me], o Halfwit, come to your senses, Fool!' (20).

The same woodcut is used for the corresponding chapter ('Contemnere deum') in Jakob Locher's Latin rendering of the work, the *Stultifera navis*, produced in collaboration with Brant himself and printed only three years later.[34] The text itself reads somewhat differently, even if

Figure 6.1 Only a fool plucks God's beard (Sebastian Brant's *Narrenschiff*, Basle: Bergmann, 1494). Berlin, SBPK, 8° Inc 604, fol. 115v. Public domain.

the core message is unchanged: just because God does not always rush to punish men's crimes, it does not mean that he is offering his 'foolish beard' to be plucked.[35] The classicizing tendency becomes quite blatant a little further on, when the author-narrator asks the reader: 'De Iove quid sentis, cuius sic vellere barbam / Audes et teneras aures impellere tentas?' / 'What do you think of Jove [God], whose beard you thus dare to pluck and [whose] tender ears you would try to impress?' (8–9). In true humanist style the margin contains the name of a source reference, the Roman satirist Persius, from whose second satire both of these beard references are derived.[36] For recipients with aspirations to the same learning as Locher and Brant, the subtext for the image of plucking God's beard is not the story of Christ's Passion but rather a piece of classical satire mocking those who offer misguided or disingenuous prayers (to the gods). It is not unlikely that Brant was already mindful of this when composing chapter 86 for the vernacular *Narrenschiff*, although the same probably did not go for this work's lay readership.

Notes

1 'Jesus's beard was delightful. No fairer human being had ever been born.' Unless otherwise indicated all translations in this chapter are my own.
2 This also applies to the relevant secondary literature.
3 Lines 44579–53866.
4 For an overview of the huge topic of Christ's appearance in religious art see Kollwitz et al., 'Christus, Christusbild', 1968.
5 Dobschütz, *Christusbilder*, 197–262.
6 Kartschoke, 'Erkennen und Wiedererkennen', I, 17–19.
7 Kemper, *Die Kreuzigung Christi*, 76–9.
8 As the catalogue of Greek and Latin passages compiled by Dobschütz (293**–330**) shows, the description of Jesus's beard varied quite considerably, especially in the earliest known sources. The *Vita rhythmica* represents one of a number of traditions of thought.
9 In the later Middle Ages, perhaps under the influence of the *Epistula Lentuli* (see Dobschütz, *Christusbilder*, 308**–330**), Christ was often pictured with 'nut-brown' hair.
10 Kemper, *Die Kreuzigung Christi*, 1–11.
11 Kemper, *Die Kreuzigung Christi*, 2.
12 Marrow, *Passion Iconography*, 68–76.
13 Dittmeyer, *Gewalt und Heil*, 31–40.
14 Several of Christ's torments, including the plucking of his beard, were thought to have been anticipated by the Old Testament prophet Isaiah, through whom God spoke: 'corpus meum dedi percutientibus et genas meas vellentibus faciem meam non averti ab increpantibus et conspuentibus' (50: 6). See also Marrow, *Passion Iconography*, 68–70; Dittmeyer, *Gewalt und Heil*, 203.
15 Kemper, *Die Kreuzigung Christi*, 64–7.
16 This detail is found in only one of the text's several manuscripts, representing perhaps an addition (by one scribe or another) for the purpose of intensification; see *Unser vrouwen klage / Der Spiegel*, ed. Büttner, XXXIX.
17 Cf. Ludolph of Saxony's *Vita Jesu Christi* (composed c. 1348–68): 'alii manu reversa dulcissimum et mellifluum os ejus percutiebant, [...] alii sanctissimam barbam ejus evellebant' (2: 506).
18 VIII,213: 'sin bruner bart / wart im von blute nass' (48–9).
19 Cf. Pseudo-Frauenlob VIII,219, where 'brun' (36), 'wiß' (37) and 'gra' (39) are the colours attributed to the Son, the Holy Ghost and God respectively. In VIII,201 the singer praises Mary and the miracle of Christ's birth in similar terms: 'von dir wart praun, der sich e selber nante gra' (12).
20 Oswald emphasizes the extent to which Christ the king allows himself to be abused: 'Sein löblich macht / darnach verhieng, das si in viengen, stiessen, / hert bunden, raufften auss den bart, / in wurfn auf die erde' (91–4).
21 Kemper, *Die Kreuzigung Christi*, 144–63.
22 Text taken from Frankfurt am Main, UB, Ms. Barth. 58, fol. 38r. http://nbn-resolving.de/urn:nbn:de:hebis:30:2-12518. Accessed 14 March 2021.
23 Kasten, 'Ritual und Emotionalität'.
24 Eming, 'Gewalt im Geistlichen Spiel', 2005, 8–13.
25 For more on this aspect of late medieval Passion plays see Wenzel, *Juden in spätmittelalterlichen Spielen*, 31–188; Rommel, 'Judenfeindliche Vorstellungen'.
26 For more on the emotive effects of certain structures in this play see Kasten, 'Ritual und Emotionalität', 345–8.
27 See the classic study of this phenomenon by Kolve, *Corpus Christi*, 145–74.
28 See also Kolve, *Corpus Christi*, 201.
29 *Deutsche Versnovellistik (DVN)*, ed. Ridder and Ziegeler, III, 591 (commentary).
30 Cf. *Do der minnenklich got*, where mistreatment suffered by Christ on the first night following his arrest includes 'sie dunsen ÿn durch die kolen' (fol. 37r).

31 Brant's *Narrenschiff* features several other beard references to illustrate various follies: fashion (to shave or not to shave 4: 3–5), gluttony (how Holofernes lost his bearded head 16: 35–6), only a fool emulates another fool (40: a–c), vanity (Emperor Otho shaved and washed cheeks with asses' milk 60: 15–19), boorishness (bearded monk Ilsan 72: 25).

32 'Wer meynt gott well jnn stroffen nyt / Dar vmb das er beyt lange zyt / Den schlecht der tunder dyck noch hüt' (86: a–c).

33 Manger, *Das 'Narrenschiff'*, 62–5.

34 Locher, *Stultifera navis*, ed. Hartl, I.1, 15–19.

35 'Quod deus ad poenas non pronus saeuit amaras / Crimina quodque hominum saepe impunita relinquit, / Non ideo stolidam praebet tibi vellere barbam' (86: a–c).

36 Persius, *Satires* II, 18, 24–9. See also Locher, *Stultifera navis*, ed. Hartl, I.1, 94, 228–9.

Conclusion

Reading medieval literary beards

Reading medieval German texts for beards and, in turn, thinking about what these literary beards can tell us about the texts in which they appear has taken us on a tour of some three hundred years or more of literary history. There will always be a certain amount of serendipity in an endeavour like this. Just as one text led to another in this reader's mind, so other works – and other literary beards – will doubtless have suggested themselves to other readers. Nevertheless, the most basic function of literary beards seems clear enough: to denote masculinity and in doing so to foreground certain male figures and figure types, accentuating the roles such figures play – their relationships both with other men and with women – within broader thematic contexts. The attitudes involved can be affirmative or constructive, and they can be negative and destructive, but the poetic focus on bearded figures is always highly selective.

In addition it has become apparent that images of bearded masculinity were, on occasion, used to epitomize common humanity (between Christians and heathens) and evoke human experiences that were not restricted to men (mortality), with masculinity and humanity (and indeed majesty) converging most dramatically in the bearded figure of Jesus. Female perspectives (as imagined by male poets) and female figures play a role too, although the number of 'conventionally' bearded women portrayed or alluded to in the texts discussed here is very small.[1] Figures such as Markolf's wife Policana necessarily occupy the margins of this study, which takes a closer look at the more obvious but no less significant topic of men and beards. This is not to dismiss other approaches to literary constructions of masculinity which set greater store by reading against the grain, which prize 'effemination', for example. But developing a keener sense for normative masculinity seems like a good thing to do in this disciplinary context too.

Reading for literary beards raises other methodological issues as well. We have seen how medieval texts almost demand to be contextualized in terms of other literary texts. This can and not infrequently does involve comparison with an Old French or a Latin source. However, in respect of late medieval German literature, relatively extensive traditions and chains of works in German must be taken into account as well. To keep the findings of close textual analysis in perspective, especially in relation to just one detail among a plethora of others, it is extremely helpful to get a sense of what other poets have done with the same or similar material. In principle, and as exemplified by our reading of Wolfram's *Willehalm*, this approach can involve working backwards (Old French source material, earlier work by same author) and forwards (so-called *Willehalm* trilogy, later Christian–heathen narratives). Similarly, the uncertainties bedevilling discussions of comedy in medieval texts can be offset – to some degree – through cumulative evidence.

Several other points are worth emphasizing. First, details pertaining to the appearance of (male) figures, not least their beardedness, were evidently conveyed to audiences in a variety of ways, ranging from the full-blown rhetorically polished portrait on the one hand, to fleeting references that are more embedded in the action on the other. However formulaic the relevant passages may be – and they are by no means always formulaic – that does not necessarily diminish their functionality. Even conventional details may accrue significance in the course of a literary work (Karl's beard gestures in the *Rolandslied*). Some kinds of text seem to favour certain strategies over others; some texts feature both extremes. In various versions of the *Marienleben* tradition an extensive set-piece description of Jesus separates the account of his life as a child from that of his experiences as an adult, with further references to Jesus's beautiful features being embedded in the story of his Passion. Equally evidently, certain poets were more creative than others. Wolfram von Eschenbach leads the way in this respect, not least by infusing descriptions of figures – and references to their beardedness – with subjectivity, whether in the form of highly emotional or provocative narratorial interjections or in the speeches of the figures themselves. Voice and perspective turn out to be crucial categories of analysis in a variety of text types from lyric to late medieval drama.

Secondly, these same details, these same techniques, were designed to have an effect of one kind or another on recipients. The neat distinction between the didactic and the comedic upon which Chapters 4 and 5 appear to be based proves deceptive. Very often the two interests go hand in hand, and the differences between works, far from being absolute, are a matter of emphasis and degree. Many didactic works use comedy to make their point stick, Hugo von Trimberg being a master at this. In terms of the social antipathies they rest upon, the fiercely satirical observations of Heinrich der Teichner are quite compatible with Wittenwiler's *Ring*, which itself is an outstanding example of the extent to which the didactic and the drastically comedic can be combined. Even the bawdiest of Shrovetide plays, the crudest mock riddles, exercised a normative effect in respect of gender and sexuality. Bearing in mind that audiences for secular literature were always likely to be mixed, it does not seem *that* unlikely that the respective didactic and comedic effects of beard references varied in their impact: if female listeners identified themselves less readily with bearded figures, this may have detracted from the didactic efficacy of some passages but heightened the comedic effect of others.

The abuse directed at beards, whether verbal (insults) or physical, serves as something of a touchstone in terms of general effect. Audience responses to literary representations of beard plucking or the threat of it most likely depended on the status of the victim in their eyes, on whether they were otherwise encouraged to regard the target of such abuse with sympathy, indifference or antipathy. The greater the perceived pain and shame involved, the more appalling or (basely) entertaining the spectacle becomes. Wittenwiler's rustic world is dehumanized to such a degree that the hurts suffered by Bertschi and others are a matter for derision only. Where comedy takes the form of parody, the literary knowledge of recipients determined whether it served its purpose or not. The harmless fun that was had with the elderly Hildebrand in the later heroic epic evidently became a popular feature of these works, migrating from text to text irrespective of plot. Far more ambiguous are the abuses and torments suffered by Jesus as acted out in plays like the *Donaueschinger Passionsspiel*, where the performance of violence is accompanied by the gleefully demeaning and occasionally witty commentary of his abusers, offering a cue for spectators to laugh against their better judgement.

Thirdly, the literary 'visualization' of beardedness is almost invariably enhanced in manuscripts containing miniatures – not that the relationship between text and image is necessarily a predictable one. It is not uncommon to find apparently contradictory approaches at work within one and the same cycle of pictures, whether they amount to disregard for textual detail, attempted pictorial equivalence, or the inclusion of further detail by drawing on stock iconographic motifs. The miniatures in Heidelberg Cpg 112 (*Rolandslied*) feature all of these tendencies, with a number of images constituting intelligent readings of the narrative sequences they illustrate (Figures 2.1–2.3). Occasionally, we get the impression of artists at work who pay special attention to the beardedness of their figures and exploit their own medium for an effect that greatly exceeds the corresponding passage in the text. Thus, in the Kassel manuscript containing the *Willehalm* trilogy (Figure 3.4) Willehalm may escape captivity disguised as a lady but he retains some semblance of masculinity by virtue of the dots of stubble on his face. In another manuscript of this trilogy (Vienna, Cod. 2670) we even find evidence of artistic (self-?)correction, where beards are added to originally beardless figures (Figure 3.1). In the special case of Thomasin's *Der Welsche Gast*, it is likely that a programme of manuscript miniatures was part of the poet's original design. The beard motifs in the pictures of Heidelberg Cpg 389 may therefore be read in terms of pedagogic function too (Figure 4.1). Hugo von Trimberg's *Renner*, by contrast, accrues an extensive cycle of pictures in the course of transmission, which in one notable instance (Leiden VGG F4) exhibits a veritable gallery of different kinds of beard growth and styles (Figure 4.2; front cover). In the context of literary comedy, the effect of actions and speeches designed to elicit laughter was accentuated by images which captured and prolonged the moment of beard violation (Figures 5.2, 5.3). The extent to which the same picture in a book could summon up different connotations for different readers, and thus quite possibly amuse some more than others, is exemplified by the outrageous image of a fool tweaking the Risen Christ's beard in Sebastian Brant's *Narrenschiff* (Figure 6.1).

Beyond the medieval literary beard

There is no obvious cut-off point in German literary history after which beardedness and beardlessness start to mean more modern things. Vernacular literature continued to develop, of course. The literary text type of the 'Schwankbuch', for instance, became incredibly popular from the mid-sixteenth century onwards. The forerunner of these miscellaneous collections of short prose narratives was Johannes Pauli's *Schimpf und Ernst* (1519), containing almost 700 items, which has its fair share of beard references, ranging from the historical to the anecdotal.[2] But this collection still feels very medieval.[3] Symptomatic of this is Pauli's miracle tale (E656) concerning the corpse of a young man, hanged at the tender age of 18,[4] which sprouts a long grey beard, much to the consternation of all those who pass by the gallows.[5] It takes a priest to explain that by virtue of this astounding event God is showing them just how old this youth would have become if he had not shortened his life by stealing and incurring the curses of his own mother.[6]

Subsequent 'Schwankbücher' recycle medieval material too. Salacious jokes concerning the pubic beards of women continue to be circulated, albeit within more expansive narrative frameworks.[7] Nevertheless, these later works also strive to meet the increasing demand for curiosities and novelties – even news – on the part of their readers, and not just in relation to far-flung lands but also with reference to places and people much closer to home. Hans Wilhelm Kirchhof's large collection, entitled *Wendunmuth* (first volume published 1563), is full of anecdotes of the 'strange but true' variety. In one instance (II, 151) a German prince invites the academic doctors at his court to explain the odd appearance of a peasant who has a black beard but a head of grey hair. Unimpressed by the pseudo-scientific reasons they offer him, the prince calls upon the peasant himself, who evidently still has all the sense he was born with: the hair in his beard, he reveals, is twenty or so years younger than that on his head.[8] With this beard anecdote we get a sense perhaps of something appreciably different, whether it is the bizarreness of the everyday world or the satirical rejection of book learning in favour of the native wit of a (bearded) peasant. God's will is still invoked here by Kirchhof in his rhyming *moralisatio*,[9] but this serves not so much to put an end to enquiry as to legitimize it.

The seeds are sown here for the more elaborate and sophisticated thematization of beards in the later seventeenth century, as found in the works of Grimmelshausen. The second chapter of *Springinsfeld* (1670) contains something of a literary masterclass on the beard as curiosity, this being the outstanding attribute of the redoubtable Simplex, as observed by the first-person narrator, the unemployed secretary Philarchus Grossus von Trommenheim, upon seeing him in the flesh for the first time. The remarkable difference in colour between the pilgrim's older and more recent beard growth (black and white-grey respectively) grabs Philarchus's attention.[10] It is the narrator's ability to work out how this could possibly be the case – the black part of the beard must have grown in a hot climate, the white-grey in a colder one – that recommends him to Simplex and earns him a place at the latter's tavern table. If Simplex's strange beard represents an intelligence test for Philarchus, it testifies more generally to Simplex's experience of the world at large far beyond Germany's borders.

Several years after *Springinsfeld* Grimmelshausen published a ludic study of beards in the form of a mock treatise entitled *Bart-Krieg* (1673) or, to quote the first part of its longer title, 'Des ohnrecht genanten Roht-Barts Widerbellung gegen den welt-beruffenen Schwartz-bart deß SIMPLICISSIMI' / 'Retaliation on the part of the unjustly named Redbeard against the world-famous Blackbeard, Simplicissimus'. Ostensibly composed by a red-bearded individual once mocked for his hair colour by Simplex, this belligerent defence of the red beard and red-bearded individuals past and present represents Grimmelshausen's typically unconventional response to contemporary learned discussions (in Latin) of beards.[11] In true Simplician style the red-bearded 'author' engages in mock-academic argument, combining a wealth of learned allusions and several scurrilous anecdotes, in order to set the record straight. Redbeard is most emphatic, insisting that what pale-skinned, black-bearded melancholics jealously choose to call 'red' is better described as 'golden', and that even if Judas Iscariot did enjoy 'die Zierde seines Goldfarben Barts' / 'the ornament of his golden-coloured beard' (vol. II: 712,24–5) in the company of Christ, the moment he hanged himself his beard turned black. Knowledge of the bigger world is a factor here too. Thus, the 'author' also takes delight in reminding Simplex, his famous addressee, of all the lands Simplex himself has journeyed through and their (black-haired) peoples (Asian, Indian, African), whose relatively sparse beard growth is presented as proof of the deficiencies inherent in black beards per se.[12] In sum, with his *Bart-Krieg* Grimmelshausen mounts a spirited defence of the indefensible, giving characterful voice to a perspective that has never been heard before. It would be a mistake to take Redbeard too seriously. But it is hard to avoid the impression that by virtue of this literary experiment Grimmelshausen was lampooning all those who read too much into the colour of beards, whether red or black. The form and content of the *Bart-Krieg*, the intellectual freedom it exhibits, make this text a milestone, if ever there was one, in the post-medieval literary history of beards.

Notes

1 It has not been possible to include medieval saints' lives in this project, where more evidence pertaining to bearded women may well be found.

2 Langobards: 'Wir lesen in der histori longo barborum der langen bärter' (E231, p. 155); philosopher vomits over king's beard (E475); Emperor Frederick I: 'genant Barbarossa mit dem roten bart' (E511, p. 294); Saint Jerome: 'Mein heilicher bartman' (E636, p. 349). Anecdotes involving barbers and shaving: S195, S565, S601, S602.

3 Cf. Pauli's use of the traditional goat comparison when discussing frivolous fashions, including sporting a long beard: 'vnd wan ein bart ein frum mecht, so wer ein geisz frum' (S175, p. 121).

4 The execution of a beardless delinquent seems to have been considered especially noteworthy; cf. the entry for 21 May 1493 in the Nuremberg 'chronicle' of one Heinrich Deichsler: 'darnach am nechsten tag da hieng man einen jungen gesellen von Bamberg, het nie part geschorn: het vil keten von den wegen auf dem Weinmarkt gestoln, vieng in darauf' (p. 574).

5 'alle menschen verwunderten sich des zeichens das der, der in seinem leben nie kein bart het geschoren, an dem galgen ein bart het vberkumen' (p. 362).

6 'das got durch das zeichen wolt anzeigen, das diser .xc. iar alt wer worden, wan er im selber nit het sein leben gekürtzt durch stelen vnd durch den fluoch seiner muoter' (362).

7 Jakob Frey, *Gartengesellschaft* (dated 1556): nrs 93 (dismayed nun), 130 (neglected young wife); Martin Montanus, *Das ander Teil der Gartengesellschaft* (dated 1560): nr 91 (three witty women answering lewd innkeeper in kind).

8 'daß meine haupt haar viel älter seynd, denn die im barte, die mir allererst zwentzig jar hernach sein hervor kommen' (p. 201).

9 'Und wie vom haupt nicht fellt ein haar, / On gottes willn, so auch keines war / Weiß, schwartz oder sonsten gefärbt' (201).

10 'wurde ich gewahr / daß sein ungeheurer Bart gantz widersinns: das ist / wider die Europaeischen Baert geart und gefaerbt war; dann die Haar so ererst bey einem halben Jahr gewachsen / sahen gantz falb / was aber aelter war / brandschwartz; da doch hingegen bey andern Baerten von solcher Farb die Haar zunegst an der Haut gantz schwartz: und die uebrige je aelter je falber oder wetterfaerbiger zuerscheinen pflegen' (vol. I/2: 166,26–167,1).

11 Breuer, 'Ein Rotbart wehrt sich', 2017; Eickmeyer, 'Wissen vom Bart', 2017.

12 Thus the 'author' poses the rhetorical question of how much more the Chinese would treasure their thin beards ('jhre 17. Schwartze Haar die jhnen die vorsichtige Natur umbs Maul herumber auffs gesparsamst mitgetheilet' 722,3–4), if they were 'Goldfarb' (722,6).

Appendix: A sample of references to Charlemagne's beard

In the epilogue to his *Rolandslied* Pfaffe Konrad claims that he translated the French text into Latin first before rendering it in German.[1] Whatever this process may have involved, it did not have an impact on the poetic strategies governing 'his' beard references; their parameters were undoubtedly set by the Old French source. But there were alternatives, especially when it came to Charlemagne's beard, for the emperor's impressive appearance was also an established theme in Latin works of the twelfth century (if not before). These descriptions purported to be historically authentic but rarely fell short of blatant hagiography.[2]

One detailed *descriptio* is found in the *Pseudo-Turpin* (first composed c. 1140), the renowned and totally spurious eyewitness account of Roland's death and Charles's victory in Spain.[3] Here attention turns to Charlemagne's person in a later chapter (XX):

> And King Charles had brown hair, a red face, a shapely and handsome figure, but a penetrating, threatening look. [...] His face measured one and a half palms across, his beard one palm und his nose about half. His forehead measured one foot across, his eyes shone and flashed like those of a lion.[4]

Perhaps the most unexpected detail in this passage is that of the emperor's brown hair. We get no sense here of the white-haired patriarch as first described in Einhard's *Vita Karoli* (c. 829–36),[5] but are presented rather with the picture of a man in his physical prime, not too dissimilar in fact to various descriptions of Christ (see Chapter 6). The precise measurements of the king's face are doubtless intended to reinforce the ostensible veracity of the account, whilst comparing him to a lion is a more obviously poetic if conventional device.[6] All in all, rhetorically polished descriptions like these were designed to present flawless incarnations of majesty, and as such they were easily transferred from one king to another. It has been suggested that this portrait of Charles is rehashed from an earlier one of Alfonso VI, king of Leon and Castile (d. 1109).[7] In any case, the set-piece description of Charles at this juncture in the text has an important structural function, representing an interlude before the story is told of the annihilation of the Frankish rearguard and Charles's revenge (XXI–XXVI).

In this latter phase of the narrative Charles's facial features are only referred to in so far as they form part of his gestures of despair at Roland's death, whether this be the way he scratches his face or 'tears at his hair and beard' ('barbam et capillos obrumpere' XXV, 8). But however much the Latin work owes to vernacular storytelling traditions, oral or literary,[8] there is a degree of innovation too. In Charles's ensuing lamentation, the emperor addresses Roland not only as his 'right arm' but as the 'barba optima, decus Gallicorum' / 'most excellent beard, crowning glory of the Franks' (XXV, 9). Roland is thus extolled as the perfect embodiment of heroic masculinity, a male symbol of 'national' pride, to which grievous injury has now been done. At this point in the work interest in the beard as metaphor eclipses interest in the beard as physical attribute.

While some strategies appear historiographical, and some epic-heroic, others still set a rather different tone. In the 'Aachener' *Vita Karoli Magni* (c. 1170–80) the legend is told of how Charlemagne brings certain holy relics back from Constantinople, having been called to restore the Patriarch of Jerusalem to his seat of power.[9] The call comes from the Emperor Constantine, who writes of a dream-vision he has had in which Charles was shown to him by an angel:

> And he showed me a warrior wearing greaves and a breastplate [...]; and this warrior was an elderly man, whose face was adorned with a long beard and who was tall in stature, whose eyes gleamed like two stars, but whose head of white hair shone as brightly as the Dog Star.[10]

The dream-vision is a poetic device of very considerable literary pedigree, used widely in medieval hagiography and elsewhere. For us it is significant to register that such moments of extraordinary visualization often contain details pertaining to physical appearance that might otherwise go unmentioned or are taken for granted by both poet and audience. As modelled by two of the most famous works of classical antiquity, male apparitions of this kind were not infrequently characterized by their beards.[11] In the 'Aachener' *Vita Karoli Magni* the image of Charlemagne is of a charismatic warrior-king, old yet tall and strong, and with facial features which make him seem both human (long beard) and superhuman (radiant eyes and brilliant hair).[12] This description is no less rhetorical than the portrait of Charlemagne in the *Pseudo-Turpin*. The key difference lies in its narrative context. The dream-vision marks a moment in the plot when appearances constitute action and are thematically significant, when the specific attributes of an outstanding individual are presented not just as a matter of supposed historical fact but as part of a miraculous or mystical experience.

The influence of twelfth-century Latin historiography and hagiography on later texts concerning Charlemagne is not to be underestimated, and the devices of portrait and dream-vision are to be found in vernacular works too. However, in the wake of the *Chanson de Roland* a tradition of narrative representation develops which is decidedly epic in character. Many Old French epics persist in the same techniques and types of reference to Charles's beard, whether formulaic epithets (not infrequently in the words of other characters), Charles's own habit of swearing by his beard, or the motif of beard display in battle.[13] Charles is the benchmark by which the white-bearded patriarchal status of other figures comes to be measured, whether it be aged vassals such as Aymeri of Narbonne (*Bataille d'Aliscans*, c. 1185; *Les Narbonnais*, c. 1205–10),[14] or heathen foes such as the African king Agolan (*Chanson d'Aspremont*, c. 1180–90), whose bearded head, complete with plaited and braided moustaches, is eventually paraded before Charles on a platter of gold.[15]

These texts all tend to uphold the status of Charles as an ideal king but, as scholars such as Peter Wunderli have pointed out, this agenda is not ubiquitous.[16] Other *chansons de geste* are far more critical and go so far as to present him as wicked or weak or simply ridiculous, and this can have implications for the beard motif too. In *Doon de Mayence* (c. 1250), where a very young Charles is called to subdue the Danes, the king decides to disguise himself as a seasoned war veteran by employing a master barber to glue a white beard to his chin (7421). If this ruse is intended to mislead the Danes, it has limited success. Not only is he repeatedly recognized by the enemy (on account of his proud countenance), but his secret ally, the Danish queen, takes great delight in teasing him in public about his appearance: 'Biau sire, cheste barbe où l'avés vous trouvée? / D'aucun veillart l'avés, chen cuit je, empruntée' / 'Dear sir, this beard, where did you find it? I strongly suspect you've stolen it from some old man' (7921–2).[17] By the mid-thirteenth century the literary tradition of the *chansons de geste* had evidently reached a stage at which the implicit authority of epic diction was weakening and its core motifs could be exploited for parodic effect.

Old French *chansons de geste* were received across Europe and translated, becoming integrated into various late medieval literary cultures, and so the topos of Charlemagne's beard spread far and wide. The Old (West) Norse *Karlamagnús saga* (first version c. 1250), a prose compilation of numerous French heroic epics, is outstanding in this respect. From the early days of his kingship onwards Karlamagnus's white beard is his most important physical attribute.[18] It is referred to throughout the work in standard epic fashion,[19] and we find the familiar hagiographical device of the dream-vision in a final section devoted to signs and miracles: 'He had eyes as fair as the twinkling of a bright star and a white beard which hung down onto his chest' (X: 1, 330). Continual glorification of Karlamagnus does not preclude beard-related comedy either. Part V in particular, concerning the war against the Saxons, plays on the motif of Charlemagne's proud beard display when the Franks build a mechanical statue of Karlamagnus to intimidate the enemy from afar: 'It was also so fitted with clever devices that the man who was in the statue could grasp its beard and shake it, and lift a golden sceptre in its hand and shake it at the Saxons, threatening them' (V: 22, 51). The heathen warriors are duped by this outrageous contraption, of course, and Karlamagnus's audacity is reported back to Guitalin, the Saxon king, at some length.[20] Guitalin himself repeatedly threatens to manhandle Karlamagnus by his beard.[21] But nothing ever comes of it. Karlamagnus's person remains untouchable, and the frustrated Saxon king is made to look ridiculous by comparison.

Karl's beard remains a point of reference in vernacular German literature too throughout the later Middle Ages. This is due in part to the renewed interest in *chansons de geste* at several different courts during the fifteenth century, leading to the translation of further epics in which Karl plays a greater or lesser role.[22] In the prose *Loher und Maller* (c. 1430–40), one of several reworkings of Old French heroic epics associated with Elisabeth von Nassau-Saarbrücken, Karl is a largely peripheral figure, yet it is his banishment of the protagonist at the outset, underpinned by his sacred and self-knowing oath, that sets the chain of events in motion: 'So mir der almechtige got […] vnd so mir die krone, die ich uff han, vnd der bart, den ich in myner hant halten, […]' / 'So help me almighty God […] and by the crown on my head and by the beard I hold in my hand […]' (2,20–5). Several decades later, in *Ogier von Dänemark* (dated 1479), one of three verse translations of *chansons de geste* penned in Heidelberg from Middle Dutch sources, Karl's majesty is repeatedly called into question: not only is he wounded by Ogier in combat so that the blood streams 'Uber den bart' / 'over his beard' (12433), but he sheds so many tears of impotent rage when the banished Ogier is named in his hall 'Das man sinen langen bart / Da mit moehte haben gezwagen' / 'that you could have washed his long beard with them' (15080–1).[23]

Earlier German works continued to be received as well. The grand project of the Low German *Karlmeinet*, a fourteenth-century(?) 'vita poetica' of Charlemagne, amounting to some 36,000 lines of verse,[24] features Emperor Constantine's dream-vision of Karlle (328,53–63) as well as a detailed portrait of him right at the end of the work (538,17–48). References to his hair and beard are notably absent in both passages, however, resulting in images of ageless power and majesty. Karlle's beard becomes a focal point only in the context of the events surrounding Roland's death and Karlle's decisive victory over Baligain (Karlle's final great military achievement), for which the *Karlmeinet* poet drew heavily on Pfaffe Konrad's *Rolandslied*. Roughly half of Konrad's beard references are dispensed with in the process. Conversely, the display of beards in the second battle is explored at greater length (473,46–66), a new emphasis being placed on the sight that thereby presented itself: now Karlle wants to see for himself what his men's beards look like, having shown them what to do (473,48–51). The overall effect is summed up for the text's recipients: 'Ouer de wapen so scheyn / Mench bart vele lutzelich' / 'Many a resplendent beard could be seen over armour' (473,58–9). Although the author-narrator professes to be puzzled by Karlle's instruction to his men, he draws on Pfaffe Konrad when speculating that beards displayed in this way served as a badge of pride, one that was worn in honour of Karlle himself but which also helped to identify the 'French' in battle (473,52–66). This practice provides the definitive image of Karlle's beard in the *Karlmeinet*,[25] and the account of the subsequent trial (of Wellis/Genelun) does not feature any angry beard gesture on the part of the emperor.[26]

Likewise, Stricker's *Karl* served as one of the main sources for a prose life of Karl(us), the so-called *Buch vom Heiligen Karl* (most likely composed in Zurich, c. 1450–70).[27] The unknown author offers a highly condensed version of events; thus many of the references to beards in Der Stricker's text get lost in the process.[28] Nothing is made of Karlus's momentous decision to wear his beard over his armour in the second battle, for example, although we are told that in taking a swipe at Karlus Paligan manages to chop off some hair 'vom houpt und vom bart' / 'from his head and his beard' (80,1); and here too the Christian dead are recognized by virtue of their beards (81,18–19). The *Buch vom Heiligen Karl* also features a detailed portrait of Karlus very near the end of the work (112,17–113,11), which draws quite obviously on the tradition of the *Pseudo-Turpin*.[29] Hence we are not surprised to find that Karlus had the eyes of a lion (112,22) and that 'syn bart was anderhalb span langk' / 'his beard was one and a half spans in length' (112,27–8). More unexpected is the (supposed) colour of his hair: 'Der würdig keyser Karlus ist gesin ein schon hupsch man und hat gehan schwearczes har' / 'The eminent emperor Karlus was a most handsome man and had black hair' (112,17–18). One wonders whether this is variation for variation's sake. Nevertheless, for all the hagiographical tendencies of this work, the image of Karlus which the recipients are left with is of a man at the height of his powers, not the venerable patriarch or the ailing old man worn out by his arduous life of service to God.

Notes

1 'sô hân ich ez in die latîne betwungen, / danne in die tiutische gekêret' (9082–3).

2 The canonization of Charlemagne in 1165 at the instigation of Frederick I is a pivotal event in this context; see Engels, 'Des Reiches heiliger Gründer'.

3 For an overview see Stones, 'Iconography of Charlemagne', 170–3.

4 *Pseudo-Turpin*: 'Et erat rex Karolus capillis brunus, facie rubeus, corpore decens et venustus, sed visu efferus [...]. Habebat in longitudine facies eius unum palmum et dimidium, et barba unum et [nasus] circiter dimidium. Et frons eius erat unuis pedis, et oculi eius similes oculis leonis scintillantes ut carbunculus' (version Ha: XX, 1–4).

5 *Vita Karoli*: 'canitie pulchra' / 'fine head of white hair' (XXII, 6).

6 Jäckel, *Herrscher als Löwe*.

7 *Pseudo-Turpin*, ed. Klein, p. 158.

8 The relationship between the Latin *Pseudo-Turpin* and the vernacular heroic tradition remains uncertain; see Bastert, 'Einleitung', X.

9 This text is based in part on a work from the second half of the eleventh century known as the *Descriptio*, or, to give it its full title, *Descriptio qualiter Karolus Magnus clavum et coronam Domini a Constantinopoli Auisgrani detulerit qualiterque Karolus Calvus hec ad Sanctum Dyonisium retulerit*.

10 *Vita Karoli Magni*: 'Et ostendit michi quendam militem ocreatum et loricatum, [...] et ipse senex prolixe barbe vultu decorus et statura procerus erat, cuiusque oculi fulgebant tanquam sidera; caput vero eius canis albescebat' (II, 6 (148,7–12)).

11 In Book II of the *Aeneid* Aeneas recalls how he dreamed of the slaughtered Hector, bloodied and with 'squalentem barbam' / 'filthy beard' (II, 277). In Ovid's *Metamorphoses* a Roman envoy has a dream-vision of Asclepius, the god of healing: 'caesariem longae dextra deducere barbae' / 'stroking his long beard with his right hand' (XV, 656).

12 This section of the text is taken almost word for word from the so-called *Descriptio*, ed. Deutz and Deutz, p. 341.

13 Cf. *Fierabras* (c. 1190): 282 (oath), 2387 (oath), 2402 (oath), 2408 (oath), 2540a (epithet), 2711 (epithet), 2794 (epithet), 4837–8 (on display), 5310–1 (on display), 5788 (epithet), 5912 (violent threat to Charles), 6193–5 (attribute of Charles as an old man).

14 Cf. *Bataille d'Aliscans* 2255, 2821, 3521; *Les Narbonnais* 26, 61–2, 105, 3506, 3696, 6046, 6201, 6335, 6509, 7977.

15 Cf. 10667–70, 10686–94.

16 Wunderli, 'Variationen des Karlsbildes', 1996, 77–83.

17 See also Wunderli, 'Das Karlsbild', 20.

18 In Part I Karlamagnus swears either by his beard (38, 122; 45, 134) or by his white beard (39, 125; 51, 145).

19 Part III: 2, 241 (oath); 36, 298 (epithet). Part IV: a36, 214 (tears); 64, 238 (smile). Part VI: 1, 113 (outstanding characteristic, curse); 3, 118 (epithet); 23, 157 (epithet). Part VIII: 5, 229 (gesture); 6, 230 (oath); 20, 253 (epithet); 30, 267 (epithet); 37, 279 (gesture).

20 'The greatest wonder is that we know that all the missiles which we shoot at him seem to be of no account to him; and we have seen him grasp his beard and shake it at us, and speak rude words to us, and we heard him make his oath by his beard, swearing by his white beard that you would not have any more of your realm, or more of a host, than is worth a spur' (V: 24, 54).

21 'You shall, rather, be dragged by your white beard out of the castle' (V: 6, 24); 'I shall drag you by those white whiskers you trail after you' (V: 52, 90–1).

22 Bastert, *Helden als Heilige*, 108–13, 368–99.

23 In *Ogier von Dänemark* too Karl swears by his beard in tyrannical rage (2347), and towards the end of this quite convoluted story he is referred to rather disparagingly, by an enemy, as 'Karolo mit dem bart grijse' (15798).

24 Bastert, *Helden als Heilige*, 98–102.

25 A possible last reference to Karlle's beard occurs in one of several prophetic dreams that Roland's wife Alde has, in which an old grey-bearded man (503,46–7) shows her the corpses of both her husband and her brother (503,40–59).

26 In the matter of the judicial combat a certain grey-bearded Duke Naymes (522,22–3) volunteers to fight in spite of his age (522,32–3) but is turned down. During the fight the decisive blow delivered by the weaker Dederich chops off much of Pynabel's face including his beard (529,2–5).

27 Bastert, *Helden als Heilige*, 113–15.

28 There are only two beard references before the second battle: Marsilie's bemoaning of the might of 'Karlus mit dem bart' (59,1), and Marsilie's own expression of sorrow at the death of his men: 'do weinet er und rupft im selben daz har uß uf dem houpt und an dem bart' (60,24–5).

29 Bastert, *Helden als Heilige*, 228 n. 134.

Bibliography

Primary literature

Die Aachener 'Vita Karoli Magni' des 12. Jahrhunderts auf der Textgrundlage der Edition von Gerhard Rauschen unter Beifügung der Texte der Karlsliturgie in Aachen, edited by Helmut Deutz and Ilse Deutz. Siegburg: Schmitt, 2002.

Adalbert of Bamberg. *Adalberti vita Heinrici II. imperatoris*, edited by Georg Waitz, in MGH SS 4, 792–814. Hanover: Hahn, 1841.

Aliscans, edited by Claude Régnier and revised by Jean Subrenat and Andrée Subrenat. Paris: H. Champion, 2007.

Annales Palidenses, edited by Georg H. Pertz, in MGH SS 16, 48–98. Hanover: Hahn, 1859.

Der arme Konrad. *Frau Metze* = DVN 145.

Arnold von Lübeck. *Gesta Gregorii Peccatoris*, edited by Johannes Schilling. Göttingen: Vandenhoeck & Ruprecht, 1986.

Das Auge = DVN 64.

Augustijn. *Der Herzog von Braunschweig* = DVN 116.

Die Bärenjagd I, II, III = DVN 65, 83, 106.

La versione franco-italiana della 'Bataille d'Aliscans': Codex Marcianus fr. VIII [=252], edited by Günter Holtus. Tübingen: Niemeyer, 1985.

Die Bauernhochzeit = DVN 153.

Bebel, Heinrich. *Fazetien. Drei Bücher*, translated and introduced by Manfred Fuhrmann. Constance: Isele, 2005.

Benoît de Sainte-Maure. *The 'Roman de Troie' by Benoît de Sainte-Maure*, translated by Glyn S. Burgess and Douglas Kelly. Cambridge: D. S. Brewer, 2017.

Berthold von Regensburg. Vollständige Ausgabe seiner Predigten, mit Anmerkungen und Wörterbuch von Dr Franz Pfeiffer, edited by Franz Pfeiffer, 2 vols. Vienna: Braumüller, 1862–80.

Boner, Ulrich. *Der Edelstein von Ulrich Boner*, edited by Franz Pfeiffer. Leipzig: Göschen, 1844.

Brant, Sebastian. *Das Narrenschiff. Nach der Erstausgabe (Basel 1494) mit den Zusätzen der Ausgaben von 1495 und 1499 sowie den Holzschnitten der deutschen Originalausgaben*, edited by Manfred Lemmer, 4th, expanded edn. Tübingen: Niemeyer, 2004.

Bremen Stadtrecht von 1433. In *Die mittelalterlichen Rechtsquellen der Stadt Bremen*, edited by Karl August Eckhardt, 187–246. Bremen: G. Winter, 1931.

Brixener Passionsspiel. In *Altdeutsche Passionsspiele aus Tirol. Mit Abhandlungen über ihre Entwicklung, Composition, Quellen, Aufführungen und litterarhistorische Stellung*, edited by Joseph E. Wackernell, 351–431. Graz: 'Styria', 1897.

Bruder Wernher: Sangsprüche, edited by Ulrike Zuckschwerdt. Berlin: De Gruyter, 2014.

Buch vom Heiligen Karl. In *Deutsche Volksbücher aus einer Zürcher Handschrift des fünfzehnten Jahrhunderts*, edited by Albert Bachmann and Samuel Singer, 1–114. Tübingen: Litterarischer Verein, 1889.

Buch vom Heiligen Wilhelm. In *Deutsche Volksbücher aus einer Zürcher Handschrift des fünfzehnten Jahrhunderts*, edited by Albert Bachmann and Samuel Singer, 115–246. Tübingen: Litterarischer Verein, 1889.

Burchard of Bellevaux. *Apologia de barbis*. In *Apologiae duae. Gozechini epistola ad Walcherum. Burchardi, vt videtur, Abbatis Bellevallis Apologia de barbis*, edited by R. B. C. Huygens, 151–224. Turnhout: Brepols, 1985.

Cân Rolant: The Medieval Welsh version of the Song of Roland, edited by Annalee C. Rejhon. Berkeley and Los Angeles: University of California Press, 1984.
La Chanson d'Aspremont: Chanson de geste du XIIe siècle. Texte du manuscrit de Wollaton Hall, edited by Louis Brandin, 2 vols. Paris: H. Champion, 1919–20.
La Chanson de Guillaume (La Chançun de Willame), edited and translated by Philip E. Bennett. London: Grant and Cutler, 2000.
La Chanson de Roland – The Song of Roland: The French corpus, edited by Joseph J. Duggan, 3 vols. Turnhout: Brepols, 2005.
Chaucer, Geoffrey. *The Riverside Chaucer*, 3rd edn by Larry D. Benson and F. N. Robinson. Oxford: Oxford University Press, 1988.
Chrétien de Troyes. *Arthurian Romances*, translated with an introduction and notes by William W. Kibler (and Carleton W. Carroll). Harmondsworth: Penguin, 1991.
Chrétien de Troyes. *Le Chevalier au Lion, ou, Le Roman d'Yvain. Édition critique d'après le manuscrit B.N. fr. 1433*, edited by David F. Hult. Paris: Livre de poche, 1994.
Chrétien de Troyes. *Erec et Enide*, edited and translated by Albert Gier. Stuttgart: Reclam, 1987.
Chrétien de Troyes. *Le Roman de Perceval ou Le Conte du Graal*, edited and translated by Felicitas Olef-Krafft. Stuttgart: Reclam, 1991.
Christherre-Chronik. Text der Göttinger Handschrift 2° Cod. Ms. philol. 188/10 Cim. (olim Gotha. Membr. I 88), transcribed by Monika Schwabbauer. Trier: Trier University, 1991. Online: dtm.bbaw.de/bilder/christh.pdf. Accessed 13 May 2021.
Christi Leiden in einer Vision geschaut: (A German Mystic Text of the Fourteenth Century). A critical account of the published and unpublished manuscripts, with an edition based on the text of MS. Bernkastel-Cues 115, edited by F. P. Pickering. Manchester: Manchester University Press, 1952.
The Poem of the Cid: A bilingual edition with parallel text, translated by Rita Hamilton and Janet Perry with an introduction and notes by Ian Michael. Harmondsworth: Penguin, 1984.
Clement of Alexandria. *The Writings of Clement of Alexandria*, translated by William Wilson, 2 vols. Edinburgh: T. & T. Clark, 1882–4.
Codex Weimar Q 565, edited by Elisabeth Kully. Berne: Francke, 1982.
Dante Alighieri. *The Divine Comedy. Volume 2: Purgatory*, translated with an introduction, notes and commentary by Mark Musa. Harmondsworth: Penguin, 1985.
Dares the Phrygian. *Daretis Phrygii de excidio Troiae historia*, edited by Ferdinand Meister. Leipzig: Teubner, 1873.
Dares the Phrygian. *The Fall of Troy: A History by Dares the Phrygian*. In *The Trojan War: The Chronicles of Dictys of Crete and Dares the Phrygian*, translated with an introduction and notes by R. M. Frazer, Jr, 131–68. Bloomington: Indiana University Press, 1966.
Deichsler, Heinrich. *Chronik, 1488–1506*. In *Die Chroniken der fränkischen Städte: Nürnberg*, edited by Karl Hegel, vol. V, 533–706. Leipzig: S. Hirzel, 1874.
Descriptio qualiter Karolus Magnus clavum et coronam Domini a Constantinopoli Auisgrani detulerit qualiterque Karolus Calvus hec ad Sanctum Dyonisium retulerit. In *Die Aachener 'Vita Karoli Magni'*, edited by Deutz and Deutz, 337–59.
Deutsche Versnovellistik des 13. bis 15. Jahrhunderts (DVN), edited by Klaus Ridder and Hans-Joachim Ziegeler, 6 vols in 7. Berlin: Schwabe, 2020–1.
Das Donaueschinger Passionsspiel. Nach der Handschrift mit Einleitung und Kommentar, edited by Anthonius H. Touber. Stuttgart: Reclam, 1985.
Doon de Maience. Chanson de geste. Publiée pour la première fois d'après les manuscrits de Montpellier et de Paris, edited by Alexandre Peÿ. Paris: Vieweg, 1859.
Ebernand von Erfurt. *Heinrich und Kunegunde von Ebernand von Erfurt. Zum ersten Male nach der einzigen Handschrift*, edited by Reinhold Bechstein. Quedlinburg: Basse, 1860.
Das Eckenlied: Sämtliche Fassungen, edited by Francis B. Brévart, 3 vols. Tübingen: Niemeyer, 1999.
Einhard. *Vita Karoli Magni: The life of Charlemagne*, edited and translated with notes by Evelyn S. Firchow and Edwin H. Zeydel. Dudweiler: AQ-Verlag, 1985.
Ekkehard of Aura. *Ekkehardi Uraugiensis chronica*, edited by D. G. Waitz, in MGH SS 6, 1–267. Hanover: Hahn, 1844.
Eugene of Toledo. *Eugenii Toletani episcopi: Carmina*, edited by Friedrich Vollmer, in MGH Auct. Ant. 14, 231–70. Berlin: Weidmann, 1905.
Fastnachtspiele aus dem fünfzehnten Jahrhundert, edited by Adelbert von Keller, 3 vols. Stuttgart: Litterarischer Verein, 1853.
Fleck, Konrad. *'Flore und Blanscheflur'. Text und Untersuchungen*, edited by Christine Putzo. Berlin: De Gruyter, 2015.

Frag vnd antwort Salomonis vnd marcolfy. In Curschmann, 'Marcolfus deutsch', 240–55.
Frankfurter Passionsspiel. In *Heidelberger Passionsspiel. Mit den Paralleltexten der 'Frankfurter Dirigierrolle', des 'Frankfurter Passionsspiels', des 'Alsfelder Passionsspiels' und des 'Fritzlarer Passionsspielfragments'*, edited by Johannes Janota, 15–571. Tübingen: Niemeyer, 2004.
Frankfurter, Philipp. 'Die geschicht des pfarrers vom Kalenberg'. In *Narrenbuch. Kalenberger, Peter Leu, Neithart Fuchs, Markolf, Bruder Rausch*, edited by Felix Bobertag, 7–86. Berlin: Spemann, 1884.
Frauenlob (Heinrich von Meissen). *Leichs, Sangsprüche, Lieder*, edited by Karl Stackmann and Karl Bertau, 2 vols. Göttingen: Vandenhoeck & Ruprecht, 1981.
Frauenlob. *Sangsprüche in Tönen Frauenlobs. Supplement zur Göttinger Frauenlob-Ausgabe*, edited by Jens Haustein and Karl Stackmann, 2 vols. Göttingen: Vandenhoeck & Ruprecht, 2000.
Freidank. *Fridankes Bescheidenheit*, edited by H. E. Bezzenberger. Halle: Waisenhaus, 1872.
Jakob Freys Gartengesellschaft (1556), edited by Johannes Bolte. Tübingen: Litterarischer Verein, 1896.
Frutolf of Michelsberg. *Frutolfs und Ekkehards Chroniken und die anonyme Kaiserchronik*, edited by Franz-Josef Schmale and Irene Schmale-Ott. Darmstadt: Wissenschaftliche Buchgesellschaft, 1972.
Das gebratene Ei = DVN 9.
Geoffrey of Monmouth. *The Historia Regum Britannie of Geoffrey of Monmouth. Volume 5: Gesta Regum Britannie*, edited and translated by Neil Wright. Cambridge: D. S. Brewer, 1991.
Geoffrey of Monmouth. *The History of the Kings of Britain: An edition and translation of 'De gestis Britonum' ['Historia Regum Britannie']*, edited by Michael D. Reeve, translated by Neil Wright. Woodbridge: Boydell Press, 2007.
Gervase of Tilbury. *Otia Imperialia: Recreation for an emperor*, edited and translated by S. E. Banks and J. W. Binns. Oxford: Clarendon Press, 2002.
Godfrey of Viterbo. *Pantheon*, edited by Georg Waitz, in MGH SS 22, 107–307. Hanover: Hahn, 1872.
Gottfried von Straßburg. *Tristan. Nach dem Text von Friedrich Ranke*, edited and translated with a commentary and afterword by Rüdiger Krohn, 3 vols. Stuttgart: Reclam, 1980.
Grimmelshausen. *Hans Jacob Christoffel von Grimmelshausen. Werke*, edited by Dieter Breuer, 2 vols in 3. Frankfurt am Main: Deutscher Klassiker Verlag, 1989–97.
Das Große Neidhartspiel. In *Neidhartspiele*, edited by John Margetts, 17–100. Graz: Akademische Druck- und Verlagsanstalt, 1982.
Der Große Seelentrost. Ein niederdeutsches Erbauungsbuch des vierzehnten Jahrhunderts, edited by Margarete Schmitt. Cologne: Böhlau, 1959.
Die halbe Decke I, II = DVN 136, 33.
Hartmann von Aue. *Erec*, edited by Manfred Günter Scholz and translated by Susanne Held. Frankfurt am Main: Deutscher Klassiker Verlag, 2007.
Hartmann von Aue. *Gregorius. Der arme Heinrich. Iwein*, edited by Volker Mertens. Frankfurt am Main: Deutscher Klassiker Verlag, 2008.
Hayden, Gregor. *Salomon und Marckolf*. In *Narrenbuch. Kalenberger, Peter Leu, Neithart Fuchs, Markolf, Bruder Rausch*, edited by Felix Bobertag, 299–361. Berlin: Spemann, 1884.
Die Heidin IV = DVN 35.
Heinrich der Glîchezâre. *Reinhart Fuchs*, edited and translated with notes by Karl-Heinz Göttert. Stuttgart: Reclam, 1976.
Heinrich von St Gallen. *Passionstraktat*. In *Altdeutsche Neujahrsblätter für 1874. Mittel- und niederdeutsche Dialektproben*, edited by Anton Birlinger and Wilhelm Crecelius, 1–52. Wiesbaden: Killinger, 1874.
Heinrich der Teichner. *Die Gedichte Heinrich des Teichners*, edited by Heinrich Niewöhner, 3 vols. Berlin: Akademie, 1953–6.
Heinrich von dem Türlin. *Diu Crône. Kritische mittelhochdeutsche Leseausgabe mit Erläuterungen*, edited by Gudrun Felder. Berlin: De Gruyter, 2012.
Heinrich von Veldeke. *Eneasroman. Die Berliner Bilderhandschrift. Mit den Miniaturen der Handschrift und einem Aufsatz von Dorothea und Peter Diemer*, edited by Hans Fromm. Frankfurt am Main: Deutscher Klassiker Verlag, 1992.
Heldenbuch. Nach dem ältesten Druck in Abbildung, edited by Joachim Heinzle, 2 vols. Göppingen: Kümmerle, 1981–7.
Herbort's von Fritslâr liet von Troye, edited by Georg Karl Frommann. Quedlinburg: Basse, 1837; repr. Amsterdam: Rodopi, 1966.
Herger. In *Des Minnesangs Frühling. Unter Benutzung der Ausgaben von Karl Lachmann und Moriz Haupt, Friedrich Vogt und Carl von Kraus*, edited by Hugo Moser and Helmut Tervooren, vol. I, 47–55. Stuttgart: Hirzel, 1977.

Hermann von Sachsenheim. *Die Mörin*, edited by Horst Dieter Schlosser. Wiesbaden: Brockhaus, 1974.

Hildegard of Bingen. *Beate Hildegardis Cause et cure*, edited by Laurence Moulinier, revised by Rainer Berndt. Berlin: Akademie, 2003.

Hiltgart von Hürnheim. Mittelhochdeutsche Prosaübersetzung des 'Secretum Secretorum', edited by Reinhold Möller. Berlin: Akademie, 1963.

Hugo von Trimberg. *Der Renner von Hugo von Trimberg*, edited by Gustav Ehrismann, 4 vols. Tübingen: Litterarischer Verein, 1908–11.

Das Innsbrucker Osterspiel. Das Osterspiel von Muri, edited and translated with commentary and afterword by Rudolf Meier. Stuttgart: Reclam, 1962.

Jacques de Vitry. *The Exempla, or Illustrative Stories from the Sermones vulgares of Jacques de Vitry*, edited with introduction, analysis and notes by Thomas Frederick Crane. London: Folk-Lore Society, 1890.

Jans von Wien. *Weltchronik*. In *Jansen Enikels Werke*, edited by Philipp Strauch, in MGH Dt. Chron. 3.1, 1–597. Hanover: Hahn, 1891.

Johannes von Frankenstein. *Der Kreuziger des Johannes von Frankenstein*, edited by Ferdinand Khull. Tübingen: Litterarischer Verein, 1882.

Der Junge Meißner: Sangsprüche, Minnelieder, Meisterlieder, edited by Günter Peperkorn. Munich: Artemis, 1982.

Jüngeres Hildebrandslied. In *Das Dresdener Heldenbuch und die Bruchstücke des Berlin-Wolfenbütteler Heldenbuchs. Edition und Digitalfaksimile*, edited by Walter Kofler, fols 345r–349r. Stuttgart: Hirzel, 2006.

Die Kaiserchronik eines Regensburger Geistlichen, edited by Edward Schröder, in MGH Dt. Chron. 1.1. Hanover: Hahn, 1895.

Karel ende Elegast und Karl und Ellegast, edited by Bernd Bastert, Bart Besamusca and Carla Dauven-van Knippenberg. Münster: Agenda, 2005.

Karl Meinet, edited by Adelbert von Keller. Stuttgart: Litterarischer Verein, 1858.

Karlamagnús saga: The saga of Charlemagne and his heroes, translated by Constance B. Hieatt, 3 vols. Toronto: Pontifical Institute of Mediaeval Studies, 1975–80.

Karolus Magnus et Leo papa. In *Am Vorabend der Kaiserkrönung. Das Epos 'Karolus Magnus et Leo papa' und der Papstbesuch in Paderborn 799*, edited by Peter Godman, Jörg Jarnut and Peter Johanek. Berlin: Akademie, 2002.

Kirchhof, Hans Wilhelm. *Wendunmuth*, edited by Hermann Österley, vol. 2. Tübingen: Litterarischer Verein, 1869.

König vom Odenwald: Gedichte. Mittelhochdeutsch – Neuhochdeutsch. Mit einer Einleitung zur Klärung der Verfasserfrage, edited by Reinhard Olt. Heidelberg: Winter, 1988.

König Rother. Mittelhochdeutscher Text und neuhochdeutsche Übersetzung von Peter K. Stein, edited by Ingrid Bennewitz (assisted by Beatrix Koll and Ruth Weichselbaumer). Stuttgart: Reclam, 2000.

Konrad (Pfaffe). *Das Rolandslied des Pfaffen Konrad*, edited with a translation and commentary by Dieter Kartschoke. Stuttgart: Reclam, 1993.

Konrad von Fussesbrunnen. *Die Kindheit Jesu*, edited by Hans Fromm and Klaus Grubmüller. Berlin: De Gruyter, 1973.

Konrad von Heimesfurt. *'Unser vrouwen hinvart' und 'Diu urstende'. Mit Verwendung der Vorarbeiten von Werner Fechter*, edited by Kurt Gärtner and Werner J. Hoffmann. Tübingen: Niemeyer, 1989.

Konrad von Megenberg. *Das 'Buch der Natur'*. Volume II: *Kritischer Text nach den Handschriften*, edited by Robert Luff and Georg Steer. Tübingen: Niemeyer, 2003.

Konrad von Würzburg. *Engelhard*, third, rev. edn by Ingo Reiffenstein. Tübingen: Niemeyer, 1982.

Konrad von Würzburg. *Kleinere Dichtungen Konrads von Würzburg. Volume I: Der Welt Lohn – Das Herzmaere – Heinrich von Kempten*, edited by Edward Schröder. Berlin: Weidmann, 1924.

Konrad von Würzburg. *Partonopier und Meliur. Aus dem Nachlasse von Franz Pfeiffer*, edited by Karl Bartsch with an afterword by Rainer Gruenter. Berlin: De Gruyter, 1970.

Die Kreuzfahrt des Landgrafen Ludwigs des Frommen, edited by Hans Naumann, in MGH Dt. Chron. 4.2. Berlin: Weidmann, 1923.

Kudrun, edited by Uta Störmer-Caysa. Stuttgart: Reclam, 2010.

Landfrieden (1152), edited by Heinrich Appelt, in MGH Diplomata (DD F I.) 10.1, 39–44. Hanover: Hahn, 1975.

Laurin, edited by Elisabeth Lienert, Sonja Kerth and Esther Vollmer-Eicken, 2 vols. Berlin: De Gruyter, 2011.

Leges Alamannorum, edited by Karl A. Eckhardt, in MGH LL nat. Germ. 5.1. Hanover: Hahn, 1966.
Leutold von Seven. In *Deutsche Liederdichter des 13. Jahrhunderts*, edited by Carl von Kraus, vol. I, 245–49. Tübingen: Niemeyer, 1952.
Lex Frisionum, edited by Karl von Richthofen, in MGH LL 3, 631–711. Hanover: Hahn, 1863.
Lidia. In *Lateinische Comediae des 12. Jahrhunderts*, translated with an introduction and commentary by Joachim Suchomski (and Michael Willumat). Darmstadt: Wissenschaftliche Buchgesellschaft, 1979.
Locher, Jakob. *Die 'Stultifera navis': Jakob Lochers Übertragung von Sebastian Brants 'Narrenschiff'*, edited by Nina Hartl, 2 vols (I.1: *Untersuchung und Kommentar*; I.2: *Teiledition und Übersetzung*). Münster: Waxmann, 2001.
Loher und Maller. Kritische Edition eines spätmittelalterlichen Prosaepos, edited by Ute von Bloh. Berlin: Schmidt, 2013.
Ludolph of Saxony. *Vita Jesu Christi e quatuor evangeliis et scriptoribus orthodoxis concinnata per Ludolphum de Saxonia*, edited by Jean-Pierre Mabile and Jean-Pierre Guerrin. Paris: Palmé, 1865.
Lügenrede = DVN 139.
The Mabinogion, translated with an introduction by Jeffrey Gantz. London: Penguin, 1976.
Macaire: Chanson de geste publiée d'après le manuscrit unique de Venise, edited by François Guessard. Paris: Franck, 1866.
Maerlant, Jacob van. *Rijmbijbel*, edited by Maurits Gysseling. The Hague: dbnl, 2012.
Mai und Beaflor, edited and translated by Albrecht Classen. Frankfurt am Main: Lang, 2006.
Map, Walter. *De nugis curialium: Courtiers' Trifles*, edited and translated by M. R. James, revised by C. N. L. Brooke and R. A. B. Mynors. Oxford: Clarendon Press, 1983.
Der Marner. Lieder und Sangsprüche aus dem 13. Jahrhundert und ihr Weiterleben im Meistersang, edited by Eva Willms. Berlin: De Gruyter, 2008.
Matthew of Vendôme. *Ars versificatoria*. In Edmond Faral, *Les arts poétiques du XIIe et du XIIIe siècle. Recherches et documents sur la technique littéraire du moyen âge*, 106–93. Paris: É. Champion, 1924.
Matthew of Vendôme. *The Art of Versification*, translated with an introduction by Aubrey E. Galyon. Ames: Iowa State University Press, 1980.
Meier Betz. See *Bauernhochzeit*.
Der Meißner der Jenaer Liederhandschrift. Untersuchungen, Ausgabe, Kommentar, edited by Georg Objartel. Berlin: Schmidt, 1977.
Metzen hochzit. See *Bauernhochzeit*.
Der Mönch als Liebesbote A = DVN 113.
Le Moniage Guillaume. Chanson de geste du XIIe siècle. Édition de la redaction longue, edited by Nelly Andrieux-Reix. Paris: H. Champion, 2003.
Le Moniage Guillaume. Les deux rédactions en vers du Moniage Guillaume. Chansons de geste du XIIe siècle, edited by Wilhelm Cloetta, 2 vols. Paris: Firmin-Didot, 1906–11.
Montanus, Martin. *Das ander Teil der Gartengesellschaft*. In *Martin Montanus. Schwankbücher (1557–1566)*, edited by Johannes Bolte, 255–431. Tübingen: Litterarischer Verein, 1899.
Morant und Galie, edited by Theodor Frings and Elisabeth Linke. Berlin: Akademie, 1976.
Les Narbonnais: chanson de geste, edited by Hermann Suchier, 2 vols. Paris: Firmin Didot, 1898.
Neidhart. *Die Lieder Neidharts*, edited by Edmund Wießner, continued by Hanns Fischer, 5th, rev. edn by Paul Sappler with an appendix of melodies by Helmut Lomnitzer. Tübingen: Niemeyer, 1999.
Neithart Fuchs. In *Narrenbuch. Kalenberger, Peter Leu, Neithart Fuchs, Markolf, Bruder Rausch*, edited by Felix Bobertag, 149–292. Berlin: Spemann, 1884.
Das Nibelungenlied und die Klage, edited by Joachim Heinzle. Berlin: Deutscher Klassiker Verlag, 2015.
Notker der Deutsche. *Der Psalter. Psalm 101–150, die Cantica und die katechetischen Texte*, edited by Petrus W. Tax. Tübingen: Niemeyer, 1983.
Nürnberger Fastnachtspiele des 15. Jahrhunderts von Hans Folz und aus seinem Umkreis. Edition und Kommentar, edited by Stefan Hannes Greil and Martin Przybilski. Berlin: De Gruyter, 2020.
Odo of Cheriton. In Léopold Hervieux, *Les fabulistes latins depuis le siècle d'Auguste jusqu'à la fin du moyen âge. Volume IV: Eudes de Cheriton et ses dérivés*, 2nd edn. Paris: Firmin-Didot, 1896.
Ogier von Dänemark. Nach der Heidelberger Handschrift Cpg 363, edited by Hilkert Weddige. Berlin: Akademie, 2002.
Orderic Vitalis. *The Ecclesiastical History of Orderic Vitalis*, edited and translated with introduction and notes by Marjorie Chibnall, 6 vols. Oxford: Clarendon Press, 1969–80.

Ortnit und Wolfdietrich A, edited by Walter Kofler. Stuttgart: Hirzel, 2009.

Ortnit und Wolfdietrich D. Kritischer Text nach Ms. Carm. 2 der Stadt- und Universitätsbibliothek Frankfurt am Main, edited by Walter Kofler. Stuttgart: Hirzel, 2001.

Oswald von Wolkenstein. *Die Lieder Oswalds von Wolkenstein*, edited by Karl Kurt Klein, 3rd, newly rev. edn by Hans Moser, Norbert Richard Wolf and Notburga Wolf. Tübingen: Niemeyer, 1987.

Oswald von Wolkenstein. Das poetische Werk. Gesamtübersetzung in neuhochdeutsche Prosa mit Übersetzungskommentaren und Textbibliographien, translated by Wernfried Hofmeister. Berlin: De Gruyter, 2011.

Otte. *Eraclius. Deutsches Gedicht des dreizehnten Jahrhunderts*, edited by Harald Graef. Strasbourg: Trübner, 1883.

Otto of Freising. *The Deeds of Frederick Barbarossa by Otto of Freising and his continuator, Rahewin*, translated and annotated with an introduction by Charles Christopher Mierow (with the collaboration of Richard Emery). New York: Norton, 1966.

Otto of Freising and Rahewin. *Ottonis Episcopi Frisingensis et Rahewini Gesta Frederici; seu rectius, Cronica*, edited by Franz-Josef Schmale. Berlin: Deutscher Verlag der Wissenschaften, 1965.

Ottokar von Gaal. *Steierische Reimchronik = Ottokars Österreichische Reimchronik*, edited by Josef Seemüller, in MGH Dt. Chron. 5.1–2. Hanover: Hahn, 1890–3.

Ovid: Metamorphoses, translated by Frank Justus Miller, 3rd edn, revised by G. P. Goold, 2 vols. Cambridge, MA: Harvard University Press, 1977.

Passional. Das Alte Passional, edited by Karl August Hahn. Frankfurt am Main: Broenner, 1845.

Pauli, Johannes. *Schimpf und Ernst*, edited by Hermann Österley. Stuttgart: Litterarischer Verein, 1866.

Persius. *Satires*. In *Juvenal and Persius*, edited and translated by Susanna Morton Braund, 41–125. Cambridge, MA: Harvard University Press, 2004.

Phaedrus. *Fables*. In *Babrius and Phaedrus: Fables*, translated by Ben Edwin Perry, 189–369. Cambridge, MA: Harvard University Press, 1965.

Philipp von Seitz. *Bruder Philipps des Carthäusers Marienleben*, edited by Heinrich Rückert. Quedlinburg: Basse, 1853; repr. Amsterdam: Rodopi, 1966.

Plutarch: Moralia, translated by Frank Cole Babbit, vol. 3. Cambridge, MA: Harvard University Press, 1931.

Pseudo-Turpin. *Die Chronik von Karl dem Großen und Roland. Der lateinische Pseudo-Turpin in den Handschriften aus Aachen und Andernach*, edited with translation and commentary by Hans-Wilhelm Klein. Munich: Fink, 1986.

Rabenschlacht. Textgeschichtliche Ausgabe, edited by Elisabeth Lienert and Dorit Wolter. Tübingen: Niemeyer, 2005.

Rappoltsteiner Parzifal von Claus Wisse und Philipp Colin. Eine Ergänzung der Dichtung Wolframs von Eschenbach, edited by Karl Schorbach. Strasbourg: Trübner, 1888; repr. Berlin: De Gruyter, 1974.

Reinmar von Zweter. *Die Gedichte Reinmars von Zweter. Mit einer Notenbeilage*, edited by Gustav Roethe. Leipzig: Hirzel, 1887.

Der rheinische Merlin. Text. Übersetzung. Untersuchungen der Merlin- und Lüthild-Fragmente. Nach der Handschrift Ms. germ. qu. 1409 der Staatsbibliothek Preußischer Kulturbesitz Berlin, edited by Hartmut Beckers. Paderborn: Schöningh, 1991.

Ritter Gottfried = DVN 123.

The Romance of Reynard the Fox, translated with an introduction and notes by D. D. R. Owen. Oxford: Oxford University Press, 1994.

Le Roman de Renart, edited by Jean Dufournet and Andrée Méline, 2 vols. Paris: Flammarion, 1985.

Le Roman de Thèbes: Édition du manuscrit S (Londres, Brit. Libr., Add. 34114), edited by Francine Mora-Lebrun. Paris: Livre de poche, 1995.

Rosengarten, edited by Elisabeth Lienert, Sonja Kerth and Svenja Nierentz, 3 vols. Berlin: De Gruyter, 2015.

Rüdeger der Hinkhofer. *Der Schlegel* = DVN 34.

Rudolf von Ems. *Der guote Gêrhart*, 3rd edn, edited by John A. Asher. Tübingen: Niemeyer, 1989.

Rudolf von Ems. *Weltchronik. Aus der Wernigeroder Handschrift*, edited by Gustav Ehrismann. Berlin: Weidmann, 1915.

Rudolf von Ems, Weltchronik. Der Stricker, Karl der Große. Faksimile der Handschrift Ms. germ. fol. 623 der Staatsbibliothek Preußischer Kulturbesitz Berlin, with an introduction by Wolfgang Irtenkauf. Stuttgart: Müller und Schindler, 1980.

Rumelant von Sachsen. Edition – Übersetzung – Kommentar, edited by Holger Runow. Berlin: De Gruyter, 2011.

Ruodlieb. Mittellateinisch und deutsch, translated with a commentary and afterword by Fritz Peter Knapp. Stuttgart: Reclam, 1977.

Sachsenspiegel. Landrecht und Lehnrecht, edited by Friedrich Ebel. Stuttgart: Reclam, 1999.

Sächsische Weltchronik, edited by Ludwig Weiland, in MGH Dt. Chron. 2. Hanover: Hahn, 1877.

Salman und Morolf, edited by Alfred Karnein. Tübingen: Niemeyer, 1979.

Saxon Annalist. *Annalista Saxo*, edited by D. G. Waitz, in MGH SS 6, 553–777. Hanover: Hahn, 1844.

Seifried Helbling, edited by Joseph Seemüller. Halle (Saale): Waisenhaus, 1886.

Sibote. *Frauenerziehung* = DVN 45.

Sidonius Apollinaris. *The Letters of Sidonius*, translated by O. M. Dalton, 2 vols. Oxford: Clarendon Press, 1915.

Sigenot, edited by Elisabeth Lienert, Elisa Pontini and Stephanie Baungarten. Berlin: De Gruyter, 2020.

Sir Gawain and the Green Knight, edited by J. R. R. Tolkien and E. V. Gordon, 2nd edn, revised by Norman Davis. Oxford: Clarendon Press, 1967.

Spervogel. In *Des Minnesangs Frühling. Unter Benutzung der Ausgaben von Karl Lachmann und Moriz Haupt, Friedrich Vogt und Carl von Kraus*, edited by Hugo Moser and Helmut Tervooren, vol. I, 38–46. Stuttgart: Hirzel, 1977.

Der Spiegel. See *Unser vrouwen klage*.

Steinhöwel, Heinrich. *Steinhöwels Äsop*, edited by Hermann Österley. Stuttgart: Litterarischer Verein, 1873.

Strassburger Räthselbuch. Die erste zu Strassburg ums Jahr 1505 gedruckte deutsche Räthselsammlung, edited by A. F. Butsch. Strasbourg: Trübner, 1876.

Streitgespräch zwischen Christ und Jude = DVN 117.

Der Stricker. *Karl der Grosse*, edited by Johannes Singer. Berlin: De Gruyter, 2016.

Der Stricker. *Die Kleindichtung des Strickers*, edited by Wolfgang Wilfried Moelleken, G. Agler-Beck and Robert E. Lewis, 5 vols in 6. Göppingen: Kümmerle, 1973–8.

Süsskind von Trimberg. In *Deutsche Liederdichter des 13. Jahrhunderts*, edited by Carl von Kraus, vol. I, 421–5. Tübingen: Niemeyer, 1952.

Des Teufels Netz. Satirisch-didaktisches Gedicht aus der ersten Hälfte des fünfzehnten Jahrhunderts, edited by K. A. Barack. Stuttgart: Litterarischer Verein, 1863.

Thidrekssaga: The Saga of Thidrek of Bern, translated by Edward R. Haymes. New York: Garland, 1988.

Thomasin von Zerklaere. *Der wälsche Gast des Thomasin von Zirclaria*, edited by Heinrich Rückert, with an introduction and index by Friedrich Neumann. Berlin: De Gruyter, 1965.

Trierer Floyris. Gilbert A. R. de Smet and Maurits Gysseling. 'Die Trierer Floyris-Bruchstücke', *Studia Germanica Gandensia* 9 (1967): 157–96.

Ulrich von Etzenbach. *Alexander von Ulrich von Eschenbach*, edited by Wendelin Toischer. Tübingen: Stuttgarter Litterarischer Verein, 1888.

Ulrich von Etzenbach. *Wilhalm von Wenden*, edited and translated by Mathias Herweg. Berlin: De Gruyter, 2017.

Ulrich von Liechtenstein. *Frauendienst*, edited by Franz Viktor Spechtler. Göppingen: Kümmerle, 1987.

Ulrich von Türheim. *Rennewart. Aus der Berliner und Heidelberger Handschrift*, edited by Alfred Hübner. Berlin: Weidmann, 1938.

Ulrich von dem Türlin. *Arabel = Willehalm. Ein Rittergedicht aus der zweiten Hälfte des dreizehnten Jahrhunderts von Meister Ulrich von dem Türlin*, edited by Samuel Singer. Prague: Olms, 1893.

Unser Frauen Ritter = DVN 19.

Unser vrouwen klage / Der Spiegel, edited by Edgar Büttner. Berlin: De Gruyter, 2017.

Valerian. *A treatise vvritten by Iohan Valerian a greatte clerke of Italie, which is intitled in latin 'Pro sacerdotum barbis' translated in to Englysshe*. London: T. Berthelet, 1533.

Virgil: Eclogues. Georgics. Aeneid, translated by H. Rushton Fairclough, revised by G. P. Goold, 2 vols. Cambridge, MA: Harvard University Press, 1999.

Virginal, edited by Elisabeth Lienert, Elisa Pontini and Katrin Schumacher, 3 vols. Berlin: De Gruyter, 2017.

Vita beate virginis Marie et Salvatoris rhythmica, edited by Adolf Vögtlin. Tübingen: Litterarischer Verein, 1888.

Von eime trunken buoben = DVN 102.

Vorster, Johannes. *Der 'Renner' des Johannes Vorster. Untersuchung und Edition des cpg 471*, edited by Henrike Lähnemann. Tübingen: Francke, 1998.

Vulgate. The Holy Bible in Latin Language with Douay-Rheims English Translation. https://vulgate.org. Accessed 12 May 2021.
Wace's Roman de Brut: A history of the British, text and translation by Judith Weiss. Exeter: Exeter University Press, 1999.
Walther von Rheinau. *Das Marienleben Walthers von Rheinau*, 2nd, expanded edn by Edit Perjus. Åbo: Åbo akademi, 1949.
Wernher (Priester). *Priester Wernhers Maria. Bruchstücke und Umarbeitungen*, edited by Carl Wesle. Halle (Saale): Niemeyer, 1927.
Wernher der Gartenaere: Helmbrecht, edited by Friedrich Panzer and Kurt Ruh, 10th edn by Hans-Joachim Ziegeler. Tübingen: Niemeyer, 1993.
Wernher der Schweizer. *Das Marienleben des Schweizers Wernher. Aus der Heidelberger Handschrift*, edited by Max Päpke and Arthur Hübner. Berlin: Akademie, 1920.
Der Wilde Mann. *Die Gedichte des Wilden Mannes*, edited by Bernard Standring. Tübingen: Niemeyer, 1963.
Wirnt von Grafenberg. *Wigalois. Text der Ausgabe von J. M. N. Kapteyn*, translated with a commentary and afterword by Sabine Seelbach und Ulrich Seelbach. Berlin: De Gruyter, 2005.
Wittenwiler, Heinrich. *Der Ring. Nach dem Text von Edmund Wießner*, edited (with translation) by Horst Brunner. Stuttgart: Reclam, 1991.
Wittenwiler, Heinrich. *Der Ring. Text – Übersetzung – Kommentar. Nach der Münchener Handschrift. Mit einem Abdruck des Textes nach Edmund Wießner*, edited by Werner Röcke (and Annika Goldenbaum). Berlin: De Gruyter, 2012.
Wolfdietrich A, D. See *Ortnit*.
Wolfdietrich B. Paralleledition der Redaktionen B/K und H, edited by Walter Kofler. Stuttgart: Hirzel, 2008.
Wolfram von Eschenbach. *Parzival. Nach der Ausgabe Karl Lachmanns*, rev. edn and commentary by Eberhard Nellmann and translated by Dieter Kühn, 2 vols. Frankfurt am Main: Deutscher Klassiker Verlag, 1994.
Wolfram von Eschenbach. *Parzival and Titurel*, translated with notes by Cyril Edwards, with an introduction by Richard Barber. Oxford: Oxford University Press, 2006.
Wolfram von Eschenbach. *Willehalm. Nach der Handschrift 857 der Stiftsbibliothek St. Gallen. Mit den Miniaturen aus der Wolfenbütteler Handschrift und einem Aufsatz von Peter und Dorothea Diemer*, edited (with translation and commentary) by Joachim Heinzle. Frankfurt am Main: Deutscher Klassiker Verlag, 1991.
Wolfram von Eschenbach. *Willehalm*, translated by Marion E. Gibbs and Sidney M. Johnson. Harmondsworth: Penguin, 1984.
Wormser Passionsspiel Das Mittelrheinische Passionsspiel der St. Galler Handschrift 919, edited by Rudolf Schützeichel. Tübingen: Niemeyer, 1978.
Ysengrimus: Text, with translation, commentary and introduction by Jill Mann. Leiden: Brill, 1987.
Zwölf Kräfte des Weins, in *Heinrich Kaufringer: Werke*, edited by Paul Sappler, vol. I, 278–85. Tübingen: Niemeyer, 1972.

Secondary literature

Ackermann, Christiane. 'Dimensionen der Medialität. Die Osmanen im Rosenplütschen "Turken Vasnachtspil" sowie in den Dramen des Hans Sachs und Jakob Ayrer'. In *Fastnachtspiele. Weltliches Schauspiel in literarischen und kulturellen Kontexten*, edited by Klaus Ridder, 189–220. Tübingen: Niemeyer, 2009.
Ashcroft, Jeffrey. '"dicke Karel wart genant": Konrad's *Rolandslied* and the transmission of authority and legitimacy in Wolfram's *Willehalm*'. In *Wolfram's 'Willehalm'*, edited by Jones and McFarland, 21–43.
Bachorski, Hans-Jürgen. *Irrsinn und Kolportage. Studien zum 'Ring', zum 'Lalebuch' und zur 'Geschichtklitterung'*. Trier: Wissenschaftlicher Verlag Trier, 2006.
Bakhtin, Mikhail M. *Rabelais and His World*, translated by Hélène Iswolsky. Cambridge, MA: MIT Press, 1968.
Barthel, Verena. *Empathie, Mitleid, Sympathie. Rezeptionslenkende Strukturen mittelalterlicher Texte in Bearbeitungen des Willehalm-Stoffs*. Berlin: De Gruyter, 2008.

Bartlett, Robert. 'Symbolic meanings of hair in the Middle Ages', *Transactions of the Royal Historical Society*, 6th series, 4 (1994): 43–60. https://doi.org/10.2307/3679214.

Bastert, Bernd. 'Einleitung'. In *Karl der Große*, edited by Bastert, IX–XVII.

Bastert, Bernd. *Helden als Heilige. Chanson de geste-Rezeption im deutschsprachigen Raum*. Tübingen: Francke, 2010.

Bastert, Bernd (ed.). *Karl der Große in den europäischen Literaturen des Mittelalters. Konstruktion eines Mythos*. Tübingen: Niemeyer, 2004.

Bauschke, Ricarda. '*ich wil in alter juden leben mich hinnân fürwert ziehen*: Süßkind von Trimberg – Ein jüdischer Autor in der Manessischen Handschrift'. In *Juden in der deutschen Literatur des Mittelalters*, edited by Schulze, 61–86.

Bayless, Martha (ed.). *A Cultural History of Comedy in the Middle Ages*. London: Bloomsbury Academic, 2020.

Bein, Thomas. *Deutschsprachige Lyrik des Mittelalters. Von den Anfängen bis zum 14. Jahrhundert. Eine Einführung*. Berlin: Schmidt, 2017.

Bertemes, Paul. *Bild- und Textstruktur. Eine Analyse der Beziehungen von Illustrationszyklus und Text im Rolandslied des Pfaffen Konrad in der Handschrift P*. Frankfurt am Main: Fischer, 1984.

Bly, P. A. 'Beards in the *Poema de Mio Cid*: Structural and contextual patterns', *FMLS* 14 (1978): 16–24. http://doi.org/10.1093/fmlsXIV.1.16.

Bockmann, Jörn. 'Literarische Neidhart-Rezeption im deutschsprachigen Raum'. In *Neidhart und die Neidhart-Lieder*, edited by Springeth and Spechtler, 275–90.

Boesch, Bruno. 'Die Namenswelt in Wittenwilers *Ring* und seiner Quelle'. In *Namenforschung. FS Adolf Bach zum 75. Geburtstag am 31. Januar 1965*, edited by Rudolf Schützeichel and Matthias Zender, 127–59. Heidelberg: Winter, 1965.

Bouillot, Carine. 'La chevelure: la tirer ou l'arracher, étude d'un motif pathétique dans l'épique médiéval'. In *La Chevelure dans la littérature et l'art du Moyen Âge*, edited by Chantal Connochie-Bourgne, 35–45. Aix-en-Provence: Presses Universitaires de Provence, 2004.

Boyer, Tina. 'Murder and morality in *Salman und Morolf*', *JEGP* 115 (2016): 39–60. https://doi.org/10.5406/jenglgermphil.115.1.0039.

Brähler-Körner, Isabell. 'Von der Handschrift zum Sammelbild, vom Bilderbogen zum Comic: Die Rolandssage in mittelalterlichen und neuzeitlichen Text-Bild-Kombinationen'. In *Geschichten sehen, Bilder hören. Bildprogramme im Mittelalter. Akten der Tagung Bamberg 2013*, edited by Andrea Schindler and Evelyn Meyer, 49–74. Bamberg: University of Bamberg Press, 2015.

Brall, Helmut. 'Geraufter Bart und nackter Retter. Verletzung und Heilung des Autoritätsprinzips in Konrads von Würzburg *Heinrich von Kempten*'. In *FS Herbert Kolb zu seinem 65. Geburtstag*, edited by Klaus Matzel and Hans-Gert Roloff, 31–52. Frankfurt am Main: Lang, 1989.

Brault, Gerard J. *The Song of Roland: An analytical edition. Volume I: Introduction and Commentary*. University Park: Pennsylvania State University Press, 1978.

Braun, Werner. *Studien zum Ruodlieb. Ritterideal, Erzählstruktur und Darstellungsstil*. Berlin: De Gruyter, 1962.

Brem, Karin. '"Herger"/Spervogel: Die ältere Sangspruchdichtung im Spannungsfeld von Konsenszwang und Profilierung, Konformität und Autorität'. In *Neue Forschungen zur mittelhochdeutschen Sangspruchdichtung*, edited by Horst Brunner and Helmut Tervooren, 10–37. Berlin: Schmidt, 2000.

Breuer, Dieter. 'Ein Rotbart wehrt sich – Zu Grimmelshausens *Bart-Krieg*', *Simpliciana* 39 (2017): 117–30.

Brüggen, Elke. 'Fiktionalität und Didaxe. Annäherungen an die Dignität lehrhafter Rede im Mittelalter'. In *Text und Kultur. Mittelalterliche Literatur 1150–1450*, edited by Ursula Peters, 546–74. Stuttgart: Metzler, 2001.

Brüggen, Elke. '*swie ez ie kom, ir munt was rôt*. Zur Handhabung der *descriptio* weiblicher Körperschönheit im *Parzival* Wolframs von Eschenbach'. In *Literarischer Stil. Mittelalterliche Dichtung zwischen Konvention und Innovation. XXII. Anglo-German Colloquium Düsseldorf*, edited by Elizabeth Andersen, Ricarda Bauschke-Hartung, Nicola McLelland and Silvia Reuvekamp, 391–411. Berlin: De Gruyter, 2015.

Brülhart, Armin. *'Vexatio dat intellectum': Zur Funktion paradoxer Textstrukturen in Heinrich Wittenwilers 'Ring'*. Berlin: De Gruyter, 2014.

Bulang, Tobias and Beate Kellner. 'Wolframs *Willehalm*: Poetische Verfahren als Reflexion des Heidenkriegs'. In *Literarische und religiöse Kommunikation in Mittelalter und Früher Neuzeit. DFG-Symposion 2006*, edited by Peter Strohschneider, 124–60. Berlin: De Gruyter, 2009.

Bumke, Joachim. 'Autor und Werk. Beobachtungen und Überlegungen zur höfischen Epik'. In *Philologie als Textwissenschaft. Alte und neue Horizonte*, edited by Helmut Tervooren and Horst Wenzel, 87–114. Berlin: Schmidt, 1997.

Bumke, Joachim. *Die Blutstropfen im Schnee. Über Wahrnehmung und Erkenntnis im 'Parzival' Wolframs von Eschenbach*. Tübingen: Niemeyer, 2001.

Bumke, Joachim. 'Emotion und Körperzeichen. Beobachtungen zum *Willehalm* Wolframs von Eschenbach', *Das Mittelalter* 8 (2003): 13–32. https://doi.org/10.1524/mial.2003.8.1.13.

Bumke, Joachim. *Höfische Kultur. Literatur und Gesellschaft im hohen Mittelalter*. Munich: DTV, 2002.

Bumke, Joachim. *Wolfram von Eschenbach*. Stuttgart: Metzler, 2004.

Cadden, Joan. *Meanings of Sex Difference in the Middle Ages: Medicine, science and culture*. Cambridge: Cambridge University Press, 1993.

Casagrande, Carla and Silvana Vecchio. *I peccati della lingua: Disciplina ed etica della parola nella cultura medievale*. Rome: Istituto della Enciclopedia italiana, 1987.

Chinca, Mark. 'Konrad's *Rolandslied*: The clerk, the prince and the emperor'. In *Roland and Charlemagne in Europe*, edited by Pratt, 127–47.

Chinca, Mark. 'Willehalm at Laon'. In *Wolfram's 'Willehalm'*, edited by Jones and McFarland, 77–94.

Chinca, Mark. 'Women and hunting-birds are easy to tame: Aristocratic masculinity and the Early German love-lyric'. In *Masculinity in Medieval Europe*, edited by Dawn M. Hadley, 199–213. London: Longman, 1999.

Clark, Laura. 'Fashionable beards and beards as fashion: Beard coats in Thomas Malory's *Morte d'Arthur*', *Parergon* 31 (2014): 95–109. https://doi.org/10.1353/pgn.2014.0006.

Constable, Giles and R. B. C. Huygens. 'Introduction'. In *Apologiae duae: Gozechini epistola ad Walcherum. Burchardi, ut videtur, abbatis Bellevallis Apologia de barbis*, edited by R. B. C. Huygens, 47–150. Turnholt: Brepols, 1985.

Coxon, Peter W. 'Hardy's use of the hair motif'. In *Thomas Hardy Annual No. 1*, edited by Norman Page, 95–114. London: Macmillan, 1982.

Coxon, Sebastian. '*hâhâ, diep Helmbreht!* Punitive laughter and ridicule in Wernher der Gartenaere's *Helmbrecht*', *Oxford German Studies* 41 (2012): 148–61. https://doi.org/10.1179/00787191 12Z.0000000009.

Coxon, Sebastian, 'Heroes and their beards', *ZfdA* 147 (2018): 21–50. https://doi.org/10.3813/ zfda-2018-0002.

Cuadra, Inés de la. *Der 'Renner' Hugos von Trimberg. Allegorische Denkformen und literarische Traditionen*. Hildesheim: Olms-Weidmann, 1999.

Curschmann, Michael. 'Marcolfus deutsch. Mit einem Faksimile des Prosa-Drucks von M. Ayrer (1487)'. In *Kleinere Erzählformen des 15. und 16. Jahrhunderts*, edited by Walter Haug and Burghart Wachinger, 151–255. Tübingen: Niemeyer, 1993.

Curschmann, Michael. 'Wort – Schrift – Bild. Zum Verhältnis von volkssprachigem Schrifttum und bildender Kunst vom 12. bis zum 16. Jahrhundert'. In *Mittelalter und frühe Neuzeit*, edited by Haug, 378–470.

Dale, Johanna. 'Imperial self-representation and the manipulation of history in twelfth-century Germany: Cambridge, Corpus Christi College MS 373', *German History* 29 (2011): 557–83. https://doi.org/10.1093/gerhis/ghr063.

Dicke, Gerd. 'Mären-Priapeia. Deutungsgehalte des Obszönen im "Nonnenturnier" und seinen europäischen Motivverwandten', *PBB* 124 (2002): 261–301.

Diemer, Dorothea and Peter Diemer, 'Die Bilder der Berliner Veldeke-Handschrift'. In *Heinrich von Veldeke. Eneasroman. Die Berliner Bilderhandschrift mit Übersetzung und Kommentar*, edited by Hans Fromm, 911–70. Frankfurt am Main: Deutscher Klassiker Verlag, 1992.

Diemer, Dorothea and Peter Diemer. 'Miniaturen zum Willehalm'. In *Wolfram von Eschenbach. Willehalm. Nach der Handschrift 857 der Stiftsbibliothek St. Gallen. Mit den Miniaturen aus der Wolfenbütteler Handschrift und einem Aufsatz von Peter und Dorothea Diemer*, edited by Joachim Heinzle, 1093–115. Frankfurt am Main: Deutscher Klassiker Verlag, 1991.

Dimpel, Friedrich M. *Die Zofe im Fokus: Perspektivierung und Sympathiesteuerung durch Nebenfiguren vom Typus der Confidente in der höfischen Epik des hohen Mittelalters*. Berlin: Schmidt, 2011.

Dinkelacker, Wolfgang. 'Der alte Held. Belege aus mittelalterlicher Heldendichtung und ihr kulturhistorischer Quellenwert'. In *Alterskulturen des Mittelalters und der frühen Neuzeit*, edited by Elisabeth Vavra, 183–202. Vienna: Verlag der Österreichischen Akademie der Wissenschaften, 2008.

Dittmeyer, Daria. *Gewalt und Heil. Bildliche Inszenierungen von Passion und Martyrium im späten Mittelalter*. Cologne: Böhlau, 2014.

Dobschütz, Ernst von. *Christusbilder. Untersuchungen zur christlichen Legende*. Leipzig: Hinrichs, 1899.
Duggan, Joseph J. *The Song of Roland: Formulaic style and poetic craft*. Berkeley: University of California Press, 1973.
Dunphy, Raymond Graeme. *'Daz was ein michel wunder': The presentation of Old Testament material in Jans Enikel's 'Weltchronik'*. Göppingen: Kümmerle, 1998.
Dutton, Paul Edward. *Charlemagne's Mustache and Other Cultural Clusters of a Dark Age*. Basingstoke: Palgrave Macmillan, 2004.
Easton, Martha. 'Gender and sexuality'. In *Cultural History of Hair*, edited by Milliken, 107–22.
Ehlert, Trude. 'Doch so fülle dich nicht satt! Gesundheitslehre und Hochzeitsmahl in Wittenwilers *Ring*', *ZfdPh* 109 (1990): 68–85.
Eickmeyer, Jost. 'Wissen vom Bart. Grimmelshausens *Bart-Krieg* und barocke Bart-Diskurse', *Simpliciana* 39 (2017): 131–59.
Eming, Jutta. 'Gewalt im Geistlichen Spiel. Das *Donaueschinger* und das *Frankfurter Passionsspiel*', *German Quarterly* 78 (2005): 1–22.
Engels, Odilo. 'Des Reiches heiliger Gründer: Die Kanonisation Karls des Großen und ihre Beweggründe'. In *Karl der Große und sein Schrein in Aachen. Eine Festschrift*, edited by Hans Müllejans, 37–46. Aachen: Einhard, 1988.
Ernst, Ulrich. 'Differentielle Leiblichkeit. Zur Körpersemantik im epischen Werk Wolframs von Eschenbach', *Wolfram-Studien* 17 (2002): 182–222.
Ernst, Ulrich. *Der 'Gregorius' Hartmanns von Aue. Theologische Grundlagen – legendarische Strukturen – Überlieferung im geistlichen Schrifttum*. Cologne: Böhlau, 2002.
Fichtner, Gerhard. 'Christus als Arzt. Ursprünge und Wirkungen eines Motivs', *Frühmittelalterliche Studien* 16 (1982): 1–18. https://doi.org/10.1515/9783110242157.1.
Frey, Winfried. '"Wöllt Gott man hing sie wie die Hund": Vergleiche von Juden mit Hunden in deutschen Texten des Mittelalters und der frühen Neuzeit', *Das Mittelalter* 12 (2007): 119–34.
Friedman, John Block. 'Hair and social class'. In *Cultural History of Hair*, edited by Milliken, 137–51.
Gall, Saskia. *Erzählen von 'unmâze'. Narratologische Aspekte des Kontrollverlusts im 'Willehalm' Wolframs von Eschenbach*. Heidelberg: Winter, 2018.
Gaunt, Simon. *Gender and Genre in Medieval French Literature*. Cambridge: Cambridge University Press, 1995.
Gerhardt, Dietrich. *Süsskind von Trimberg. Berichtigungen zu einer Erinnerung*. Berne: Lang, 1997.
Gerok-Reiter, Annette. 'Der Hof als erweiterter Körper des Herrschers. Konstruktionsbedingungen höfischer Idealität am Beispiel des *Rolandsliedes*'. In *Courtly Literature and Clerical Culture*, edited by Christoph Huber and Henrike Lähnemann, 77–92. Tübingen: Attempto, 2002.
Gerok-Reiter, Annette. *Individualität. Studien zu einem umstrittenen Phänomen mittelhochdeutscher Epik*. Tübingen: Francke, 2006.
Gilbert, Jane. 'Boys will be … what? Gender, sexuality and childhood in *Floire et Blancheflor* and *Floris et Lyriope*', *Exemplaria* 9 (1997): 39–61.
Gjærder, Per. 'The beard as an iconographical feature in the Viking period and the early Middle Ages', *Acta Archaeologica* 35 (1964): 95–114.
Goetz, Hans-Werner. *Geschichtsschreibung und Geschichtsbewußtsein im hohen Mittelalter*, 2nd, rev. edn. Berlin: Akademie, 2008.
Goldenbaum, Annika. *Heinrich Wittenwilers 'Ring' als Krisenexperiment. Erwartung und Störung didaktischer Kommunikation*. Berlin: De Gruyter, 2020.
Grafetstätter, Andrea. 'Die Neidhartspiele'. In *Neidhart und die Neidhart-Lieder*, edited by Springeth and Spechtler, 353–74.
Greenfield, John. *Vivianz: An analysis of the martyr figure in Wolfram von Eschenbach's 'Willehalm' and in his Old French source material*. Erlangen: Palm & Enke, 1991.
Haferland, Harald and Armin Schulz, 'Metonymisches Erzählen', *DVjs* 84 (2010): 3–43.
Hammer, Andreas. 'Held in Mönchskleidern oder Mönch im Heldenkostüm? Zur Wahrnehmung Ilsans im "Rosengarten zu Worms"', *ZfdPh* 127 (2008): 35–49.
Haubrichs, Wolfgang. 'Bilder, Körper und Konstrukte. Ansätze einer kulturellen Epochensemantik in der philologischen Mediävistik', *LiLi* 25 (1995): 28–57.
Haug, Walter (ed.). *Mittelalter und frühe Neuzeit. Übergänge, Umbrüche und Neuansätze*. Tübingen: Niemeyer, 1999.
Haug, Walter. 'Die niederländischen erotischen Tragzeichen und das Problem des Obszönen im Mittelalter', *ABäG* 59 (2004): 67–90.

Haupt, Barbara. 'Der schöne Körper in der höfischen Epik'. In *Körperinszenierungen in mittelalterlicher Literatur. Kolloquium am Zentrum für interdisziplinäre Forschung der Universität Bielefeld, 18. bis 20. März 1999*, edited by Klaus Ridder and Otto Langer, 47–73. Berlin: Weidler, 2002.

Haustein, Jens. *Marner-Studien*. Tübingen: Niemeyer, 1995.

Heiland, Satu. *Visualisierung und Rhetorisierung von Geschlecht. Strategien zur Inszenierung weiblicher Sexualität im Märe*. Berlin: De Gruyter, 2015.

Hellgardt, Ernst. 'Probleme der Bilderkennung und des Text-Bild-Verhältnisses am Beispiel des *Welschen Gastes* Thomasins von Zerclaere'. In *Prodesse et delectare*, edited by Kössinger and Wittig, 102–37.

Henkel, Nikolaus. *Lesen in Bild und Text. Die ehem. Berliner Bilderhandschrift von Priester Wernhers 'Maria'*. Berlin: De Gruyter, 2014.

Hennings, Thordis. *Französische Heldenepik im deutschen Sprachraum. Die Rezeption der Chansons de Geste im 12. und 13. Jahrhundert. Überblick und Fallstudien*. Heidelberg: Winter, 2008.

Hopwood, Hanna Gwen. 'Highlighting hair: What can be revealed from reading hair in Medieval Welsh literature'. DPhil thesis, University of Oxford, 2016.

Hopwood Griffiths, Hanna. 'Self and society'. In *Cultural History of Hair*, edited by Milliken, 37–52.

Huber, Christoph. 'Lehrdichtung. II: Mittelalter'. In *Historisches Wörterbuch der Rhetorik*, edited by Gert Ueding, V, cols 107–12. Tübingen: Niemeyer, 2001.

Huber, Christoph. *Wort sint der dinge zeichen: Untersuchungen zum Sprachdenken der mittelhochdeutschen Spruchdichtung bis Frauenlob*. Munich: Artemis, 1977.

Hübner, Gert. 'Erzählung und praktischer Sinn: Heinrich Wittenwilers *Ring* als Gegenstand einer praxeologischen Narratologie', *Poetica* 42 (2010): 215–42.

Jäckel, Dirk. *Der Herrscher als Löwe. Ursprung und Gebrauch eines politischen Symbols im Früh- und Hochmittelalter*. Cologne: Böhlau, 2006.

Jennings, Margaret. 'Chaucer's beards', *Archiv* 215 (1978): 362–8.

Jolly, Penny Howell. 'Cultural representations: Head and body hair in medieval art'. In *Cultural History of Hair*, edited by Milliken, 153–71.

Jones, Howard and Martin H. Jones. *The Oxford Guide to Middle High German*. Oxford: Oxford University Press, 2019.

Jones, Martin H. and Timothy McFarland (eds). *Wolfram's 'Willehalm': Fifteen essays*. Woodbridge: Camden House, 2002.

Kantorowicz, Ernst H. *The King's Two Bodies: A study in mediaeval political theology*, with a new preface by William Chester Jordan. Princeton, NJ: Princeton University Press, 1997.

Kartschoke, Dieter. '*Der ain was grâ, der ander was chal*: Über das Erkennen und Wiedererkennen physiognomischer Individualität im Mittelalter'. In *FS Walter Haug und Burghart Wachinger*, 2 vols, edited by Johannes Janota, Paul Sappler, Frieder Schanze, Konrad Vollmann, Gisela Vollmann-Profe and Hans-Joachim Ziegeler, I, 1–24. Tübingen: Niemeyer, 1992.

Kasten, Ingrid. 'Ritual und Emotionalität. Zum geistlichen Spiel des Mittelalters'. In *Literarische Leben*, edited by Meyer and Schiewer, 335–60.

Kellermann, Karina. 'Die körperliche Inszenierung des Königs. Ein mittelalterliches Kulturmuster', *KulturPoetik* 1 (2001): 159–81.

Kellner, Beate. 'Der Ritter und die nackte Gewalt. Rollenentwürfe in Konrads von Würzburg "Heinrich von Kempten"'. In *Literarische Leben*, edited by Meyer and Schiewer, 361–84.

Kellner, Beate and Christian Kiening, 'Einleitung: Körper – Kultur – Literatur (1200–1800)', *DVjs* 83 (2009): 3–8.

Kemper, Tobias A. *Die Kreuzigung Christi. Motivgeschichtliche Studien zu lateinischen und deutschen Passionstraktaten des Spätmittelalters*. Tübingen: Niemeyer, 2006.

Kern, Manfred. 'Heiliges Leiden und heilige Leidenschaft. Die Passion Christi als Paradigma des heroischen Affekts'. In *11. Pöchlarner Heldenliedgespräch. Mittelalterliche Heldenepik – Literatur der Leidenschaften*, edited by Johannes Keller and Florian Kragl, 1–18. Vienna: Fassbaender, 2011.

Kern, Peter. 'Bildprogramm und Text. Zur Illustration des *Rolandsliedes* in der Heidelberger Handschrift', *ZfdA* 101 (1972): 244–70.

Kerth, Sonja. 'Wolframs Greise: Alter(n) im "Parzival", "Titurel" und "Willehalm"', *ZfdA* 144 (2015): 48–76.

Kiening, Christian. *Reflexion – Narration. Wege zum 'Willehalm' Wolframs von Eschenbach*. Tübingen: Niemeyer, 1991.

Kinney, Clare R. 'The (dis)embodied hero and the signs of manhood in *Sir Gawain and the Green Knight*'. In *Medieval Masculinities*, edited by Lees, 47–57.

Kleppel, Christoph A. *'vremder bluomen underscheit': Erzählen von Fremdem in Wolframs 'Willehalm'*. Frankfurt am Main: Lang, 1996.

Klimczak, Franziska. *Bildlichkeit und Metaphorik in spätmittelalterlichen Fastnachtspielen des 15. Jahrhunderts – Wie Sexualität von sich reden macht*. Potsdam: Universitätsverlag Potsdam, 2016.

Knapp, Fritz Peter. *Rennewart. Studien zu Gehalt und Gestalt des 'Willehalm' Wolframs von Eschenbach*. Vienna: Notring, 1970.

Knapp, Fritz Peter. *Willehalm: Codex Vindobonensis 2670 der Österreichischen Nationalbibliothek*, 2 vols. Graz: Akademische Druck- u. Verlagsanstalt, 2005.

Knappe, Karl-Bernhard. *Repräsentation und Herrschaftszeichen. Zur Herrscherdarstellung in der vorhöfischen Epik*. Munich: Arbeo-Gesellschaft, 1974.

Koch, Elke. *Trauer und Identität. Inszenierungen von Emotionen in der deutschen Literatur des Mittelalters*. Berlin: De Gruyter, 2006.

Kohnen, Rabea. '*wie têt der wîse man also?* Zur Motivierung des Antagonisten in Wolframs "Willehalm"'. In *Brüchige Helden – Brüchiges Erzählen. Mittelhochdeutsche Heldenepik aus narratologischer Sicht*, edited by Anne-Katrin Federow, Kay Malcher and Marina Münkler, 57–75. Berlin: De Gruyter, 2017.

Kolb, Herbert. 'Nobel und Vrevel. Die Figur des Königs in der Reinhart-Fuchs-Epik'. In *Virtus et Fortuna. Zur Deutschen Literatur zwischen 1400 und 1720. FS Hans-Gert Roloff zu seinem 50. Geburtstag*, edited by Joseph P. Strelka and Jörg Jungmayr, 328–50. Berne: Lang, 1983.

Kollwitz, Johannes, E. Lucchesi Palli, P. Bloch, A. Legner, H. Bauer, P. Gerlach and H. Skrobucha. 'Christus, Christusbild', *LCI* 1 (1968): 355–454.

Kolve, V. A. *The Play Called Corpus Christi*. Stanford, CA: Stanford University Press, 1966.

Kössinger, Norbert and Claudia Wittig (eds). *Prodesse et Delectare: Case studies on didactic literature in the European Middle Ages / Fallstudien zur didaktischen Literatur des europäischen Mittelalters*. Berlin: De Gruyter, 2019.

Kreft, Annelie. *Perspektivenwechsel. 'Willehalm'-Rezeption in historischem Kontext. Ulrichs von dem Türlin 'Arabel' und Ulrichs von Türheim 'Rennewart'*. Heidelberg: Winter, 2014.

Kropik, Cordula. 'Metonymie und Vormoderne. Zur kulturgeschichtlichen Verortung einer Denkfigur', *Poetica* 44 (2012): 81–112.

Kugler, Hartmut. 'Alte Ritter, junge Ritter, Wolframs *Willehalm*'. In *Große Texte des Mittelalters. Erlanger Ringvorlesung 2003*, edited by Sonja Glauch, 127–43. Erlangen: Palm & Enke: 2005.

Küsters, Urban. 'Klagefiguren. Vom höfischen Umgang mit der Trauer'. In *An den Grenzen höfischer Kultur. Anfechtungen der Lebensordnung in der deutschen Erzähldichtung des hohen Mittelalters*, edited by Gert Kaiser, 9–75. Munich: Fink, 1991.

Lähnemann, Henrike. *Der 'Renner' des Johannes Vorster. Untersuchung und Edition des cpg 471*. Tübingen: Francke, 1998.

Lähnemann, Henrike and Sandra Linden (eds). *Dichtung und Didaxe. Lehrhaftes Sprechen in der deutschen Literatur des Mittelalters*. Berlin: De Gruyter, 2009.

Lämmert, Eberhart. *Reimsprecherkunst im Spätmittelalter. Eine Untersuchung der Teichnerreden*. Stuttgart: Metzler, 1970.

Lateiner, Donald. 'The emotion of disgust, provoked and expressed in earlier Greek literature'. In *Emotions in the Classical World: Methods, approaches, and directions*, edited by Douglas Cairns and Damien Nelis, 31–51. Stuttgart: Steiner, 2017.

Lauer, Claudia. *Ästhetik der Identität. Sänger-Rollen in der Sangspruchdichtung des 13. Jahrhunderts*. Heidelberg: Winter, 2008.

Lauer, Claudia. 'Sangspruchdichtung'. In *Handbuch Frauenlob*, edited by Claudia Lauer and Uta Störmer-Caysa, 47–76. Heidelberg: Winter, 2018.

Lees, Clare A. (ed., with the assistance of Thelma Fenster and Jo An McNamara). *Medieval Masculinities: Regarding men in the Middle Ages*. Minneapolis: University of Minnesota Press, 1994.

Lees, Clare A. 'Men and *Beowulf*'. In *Medieval Masculinities*, edited by Lees, 129–48.

Lejeune, Rita and Jacques Stiennon. *La Légende de Roland dans l'art du Moyen Age*, 2 vols. Brussels: Arcade, 1966.

Lienert, Elisabeth. 'Das Tagelied in Wittenwilers *Ring*', *JOWG* 8 (1994/95): 109–24.

Linden, Sandra. *Kundschafter der Kommunikation. Modelle höfischer Kommunikation im 'Frauendienst' Ulrichs von Liechtenstein*. Tübingen: Francke, 2004.

Livingston, Michael. 'Losing face: Flayed beards and gendered power in Arthurian literature'. In *Flaying in the Pre-Modern World: Practice and representation*, edited by Larissa Tracy, 308–21. Cambridge: D. S. Brewer, 2017.

Lofmark, Carl. *Rennewart in Wolfram's 'Willehalm': A study of Wolfram von Eschenbach and his sources.* Cambridge: Cambridge University Press, 1972.
Ludwig, Otto. 'Die Priameln Spervogels', *PBB* 85 (1963): 297–314.
Lumiansky, R. M. 'Benoît's portraits and Chaucer's General Prologue', *JEGP* 55 (1956): 431–8.
Lütjens, August. *Der Zwerg in der deutschen Heldendichtung des Mittelalters.* Breslau: Marcus, 1911.
Lutz, Eckart Conrad. *Spiritualis fornicatio. Heinrich Wittenwiler, seine Welt und sein 'Ring'.* Sigmaringen: Thorbecke, 1990.
Mackert, Christoph. *Die Alexandergeschichte in der Version des 'Pfaffen' Lambrecht. Die frühmittelhochdeutsche Bearbeitung der Alexanderdichtung des Alberich von Bisinzo und die Anfänge weltlicher Schriftepik in deutscher Sprache.* Munich: Fink, 1999.
Manger, Klaus. *Das 'Narrenschiff': Entstehung, Wirkung und Deutung.* Darmstadt: Wissenschaftliche Buchgesellschaft, 1983.
Manuwald, Henrike. *Medialer Dialog. Die 'Große Bilderhandschrift' des 'Willehalm' Wolframs von Eschenbach und ihre Kontexte.* Tübingen: Francke, 2008.
Marrow, James H. *Passion Iconography in Northern European Art of the Late Middle Ages and Early Renaissance: A study of the transformation of sacred metaphor into descriptive narrative.* Kortrijk: Van Ghemmert, 1979.
Matt, Peter von. *... fertig ist das Angesicht. Zur Literaturgeschichte des menschlichen Gesichts.* Munich: Hanser, 1983.
McFarland, Timothy. 'Giburc's dilemma: Parents and children, baptism and salvation'. In *Wolfram's 'Willehalm'*, edited by Jones and McFarland, 121–42.
Mellinkoff, Ruth. 'Judas's red hair and the Jews', *Journal of Jewish Art* 9 (1982): 31–46.
Meyer, Matthias and Hans-Jochen Schiewer (eds). *Literarische Leben. Rollenentwürfe in der Literatur des Hoch- und Spätmittelalters. FS Volker Mertens zum 65. Geburtstag.* Tübingen: Niemeyer, 2002.
Mierke, Gesine. *Riskante Ordnungen. Von der Kaiserchronik zu Jans von Wien.* Berlin: De Gruyter, 2014.
Milde, Wolfgang. *Mittelalterliche Handschriften der Herzog August Bibliothek.* Frankfurt am Main: Klostermann, 1972.
Milliken, Roberta (ed.). *A Cultural History of Hair in the Middle Ages.* London: Bloomsbury Academic, 2019.
Moroldo, Arnaldo. 'Le portrait dans la chanson de geste [Part I]', *Le Moyen Âge* 86 (1980): 387–419.
Moshövel, Andrea. *'wîplîch man': Formen und Funktionen von 'Effemination' in deutschsprachigen Erzähltexten des 13. Jahrhunderts.* Göttingen: V&R unipress, 2009.
Müller, Bruno. 'Die Titelbilder der illustrierten Renner-Handschriften', *BHVB* 102 (1966): 271–306.
Müller, Jan-Dirk. 'Einige Probleme des Begriffs "Metonymisches Erzählen"', *Poetica* 45 (2013): 19–40.
Müller, Jan-Dirk. 'Einleitung'. In *Text und Kontext. Fallstudien und theoretische Begründungen einer kulturwissenschaftlich angeleiteten Mediävistik*, edited by Jan-Dirk Müller, VII–XI. Munich: Oldenbourg, 2007.
Müller, Jan-Dirk. *'Episches' Erzählen. Erzählformen früher volkssprachiger Schriftlichkeit.* Berlin: Schmidt, 2017.
Müller, Jan-Dirk. *Höfische Kompromisse. Acht Kapitel zur höfischen Epik.* Tübingen: Niemeyer, 2007.
Müller, Jan-Dirk. 'Literarische und andere Spiele. Zum Fiktionalitätsproblem in vormoderner Literatur', *Poetica* 36 (2004): 281–311.
Müller, Jan-Dirk. 'Strukturen gegenhöfischer Welt. Höfisches und nichthöfisches Sprechen bei Neidhart'. In *Höfische Literatur – Hofgesellschaft – Höfische Lebensformen um 1200*, edited by Gert Kaiser and Jan-Dirk Müller, 409–53. Düsseldorf: Droste, 1986.
Müller, Jan-Dirk. 'Visualität, Geste, Schrift. Zu einem neuen Untersuchungsfeld der Mediävistik', *ZfdPh* 122 (2003): 118–32. https://doi.org/10.37307/j.1868-7806.2003.01.08.
Müller, Johannes. *Schwert und Scheide. Der sexuelle und skatologische Wortschatz im Nürnberger Fastnachtspiel des 15. Jahrhunderts.* Berne: Lang, 1988.
Müller, Ulrich. *'Dichtung' und 'Wahrheit' in den Liedern Oswalds von Wolkenstein. Die autobiographischen Lieder von den Reisen.* Göppingen: Kümmerle, 1968.
Murray, David. 'Quotation, form, and didacticism: The "Breviari d'Amor", "Der Renner", and the "Vita Nova"'. In *Prodesse et delectare*, edited by Kössinger and Wittig, 261–82.
Myslivec, J. 'Apostel', *LCI* 1 (1968): 150–73.
Neudeck, Otto. *Erzählen von Kaiser Otto. Zur Fiktionalisierung von Geschichte in mittelhochdeutscher Literatur.* Cologne: Böhlau, 2003.

Niesner, Manuela. 'Christliche Laien im Glaubensdisput mit Juden. Eine verbotene Gesprächssituation in literarischen Modellen des 15. Jahrhunderts', *ZfdA* 136 (2007): 1–28.

Ohlendorf, Wiebke. *Das Fremde im Parzifal: Zum Text-Bild-Verhältnis in den Handschriften Cgm 19, Cod. AA 91 und Cpg 339*. Berlin: De Gruyter, 2017.

Oldstone-Moore, Christopher. *Of Beards and Men: The revealing history of facial hair*. Chicago, IL: University of Chicago Press, 2016.

Ott, Norbert. '*Pictura docet*. Zu Gebrauchssituation, Deutungsangebot und Appellcharakter ikonographischer Zeugnisse mittelalterlicher Literatur am Beispiel der Chanson de geste'. In *Grundlagen des Verstehens mittelalterlicher Literatur. Literarische Texte und ihr historischer Erkenntniswert*, edited by Gerhard Hahn and Hedda Ragotzky, 187–212. Stuttgart: Kröner, 1992.

Owen, D. D. R. 'Beards in the *Chanson de Roland*', *FMLS* 24 (1988): 175–9. https://doi.org/10.1093/fmls/XXIV.2.175.

Phillips, Kim M. 'Race and ethnicity: Hair and medieval ethnic identities'. In *Cultural History of Hair*, edited by Milliken, 123–36.

Platelle, Henri. 'Le problème du scandale: Les nouvelles modes masculines aux XIe et XIIe siècles', *Revue belge de philologie et d'histoire* 53 (1975): 1071–96.

Pratt, Karen (ed.). *Roland and Charlemagne in Europe: Essays on the reception and transformation of a legend*. London: King's College London, Centre for Late Antique and Medieval Studies, 1996.

Przybilski, Martin. *Kulturtransfer zwischen Juden und Christen in der deutschen Literatur des Mittelalters*. Berlin: De Gruyter, 2010.

Putzo, Christine. 'Komik, Ernst und *Mise en page*. Zum Problem der Farblinien in Heinrich Wittenwilers "Der Ring"', *Archiv für das Studium der neueren Sprachen und Literaturen* 246 (2009): 21–49.

Rasmussen, Ann Marie. 'Fathers to think back through: The Middle High German mother–daughter and father–son advice poems known as *Die Winsbeckin* and *Der Winsbecke*'. In *Medieval Conduct*, edited by Kathleen Ashley and Robert L. A. Clark, 106–34. Minneapolis: University of Minnesota Press, 2001.

Reuvekamp, Silvia. 'Hölzerne Bilder – mentale Modelle? Mittelalterliche Figuren als Gegenstand einer historischen Narratologie', *Diegesis* 3 (2014): 112–30.

Richter, Horst. 'Das Hoflager Kaiser Karls. Zur Karlsdarstellung im deutschen Rolandslied', *ZfdA* 102 (1973): 81–101.

Richter, Horst. *Kommentar zum Rolandslied des Pfaffen Konrad. Teil I*. Berne: Lang, 1972.

Röcke, Werner. 'Drohung und Eskalation. Das Wechselspiel von sprachlicher Gewalt und körperlicher *violentia* in Heinrich Wittenwilers *Ring*'. In *Blutige Worte. Internationales und interdisziplinäres Kolloquium zum Verhältnis von Sprache und Gewalt in Mittelalter und Früher Neuzeit*, edited by Jutta Eming and Claudia Jarzebowski, 129–43. Göttingen: V&R unipress, 2008.

Rolland-Perrin, Myriam. *Blonde comme l'or: La chevelure féminine au Moyen Âge*. Aix-en-Provence: Publications de l'université de Provence, 2010.

Rommel, Florian. '*ob mann jm vnrehtt thutt, so wollenn wir doch habenn sein blutt*. Judenfeindliche Vorstellungen im Passionsspiel des Mittelalters'. In *Juden in der deutschen Literatur des Mittelalters*, edited by Schulze, 183–207.

Rostek, Markus. *mit selher jugent hât minne ir strît. Die Bedeutung von Jugend, Ehe und Verwandtschaft für die Entwicklung der Titelfigur im 'klassischen' mittelhochdeutschen Artusroman*. Munich: Meidenbauer, 2009.

Ruff, Ernst. *Der Wälsche Gast des Thomasin von Zerklaere. Untersuchungen zu Gehalt und Bedeutung einer mittelhochdeutschen Morallehre*. Erlangen: Palm & Enke, 1982.

Saurma-Jeltsch, Lieselotte E. *Spätformen mittelalterlicher Buchherstellung. Bilderhandschriften aus der Werkstatt Diebold Laubers in Hagenau*, 2 vols. Wiesbaden: Reichert, 2001.

Schanze, Christoph. *Tugendlehre und Wissensvermittlung. Studien zum 'Welschen Gast' Thomasins von Zerklaere*. Wiesbaden: Reichert, 2018.

Schmidt-Lornsen, Jutta. 'Der Griff an den Bart – wikingerzeitliche Bildzeugnisse zu einer bekräftigenden Gebärde'. In *Sprache und Recht. Beiträge zur Kulturgeschichte des Mittelalters. FS Ruth Schmidt-Wiegand zum 60. Geburtstage*, 2 vols, edited by Karl Hauck, Karl Kroeschell, Stefan Sonderegger, Dagmar Hüpper and Gabriele von Olberg, II, 780–96. Berlin: De Gruyter, 1986.

Schmitt, Kerstin. 'Sexualität als Textualität. Die Inszenierung von Geschlechterdifferenz und Sexualität in Heinrich Wittenwilers *Ring*'. In *Schwierige Frauen – schwierige Männer in der Literatur des Mittelalters*, edited by Alois M. Haas and Ingrid Kasten, 129–52. Berne: Lang, 1999.

Schneider, Christian. 'Textstruktur und Illustrationsprinzipien im 'Welschen Gast' des Thomasin von Zerklaere', *PBB* 139 (2017): 191–220.

Schnell, Rüdiger. 'Gefühle gestalten. Bausteine zu einer Poetik mittelalterlicher Emotionsbeschreibungen', *PBB* 138 (2016): 560–606.
Schnell, Rüdiger. 'Kulturtheorien und Lektürepraxis in der germanistischen Mediävistik', *ZfdA* 145 (2016): 421–58.
Schnell, Rüdiger. 'Narration und Emotion. Zur narrativen Funktion von Emotionserwähnungen in Chrétiens *Perceval* und Wolframs *Parzival*', *Wolfram-Studien* 23 (2014): 269–331.
Schnell, Rüdiger. 'Recht und Dichtung: Funktionen und Fiktionen. Beobachtungen zur höfischen Literatur des Mittelalters', *LiLi* 41 (2011): 18–41.
Schnell, Rüdiger. 'Text und Kontext: Erzählschemata, Diskurse und das Imaginäre um 1200', *Poetica* 40 (2008): 97–138.
Schnyder, André (ed.). *Kaiser Otto und Heinrich von Kempten. Abbildung der gesamten Überlieferung und Materialien zur Stoffgeschichte*. Göppingen: Kümmerle, 1989.
Schönleber, Matthias. '*der juden schant wart offenbar*: Antijüdische Motive in Schwänken und Fastnachtspielen von Hans Folz'. In *Juden in der deutschen Literatur des Mittelalters*, edited by Schulze, 163–82.
Schramm, Percy Ernst. *Die deutschen Kaiser und Könige in Bildern ihrer Zeit 751–1190*. New edition by Florentine Mütherich. Munich: Prestel, 1983.
Schuler-Lang, Larissa. *Wildes Erzählen – Erzählen vom Wilden. 'Parzival', 'Busant' und 'Wolfdietrich D'*. Berlin: De Gruyter, 2014.
Schultz, James A. 'Bodies that don't matter: Heterosexuality before heterosexuality in Gottfried's *Tristan*'. In *Constructing Medieval Sexuality*, edited by Karma Lochrie, Peggy McCracken and James A. Schultz, 91–110. Minneapolis: University of Minnesota Press, 1997.
Schultz, James A. *The Knowledge of Childhood in the German Middle Ages, 1100–1350*. Philadelphia: University of Pennsylvania Press, 1995.
Schulze, Ursula. 'Grundthemen der Lieder Neidharts'. In *Neidhart und die Neidhart-Lieder*, edited by Springeth and Spechtler, 95–116.
Schulze, Ursula (ed.). *Juden in der deutschen Literatur des Mittelalters. Religiöse Konzepte – Feindbilder – Rechtfertigungen*. Tübingen: Niemeyer, 2002.
Schulze, Ursula. *Das Nibelungenlied*. Stuttgart: Reclam, 1997.
Schwarzbach-Dobson, Michael. *Exemplarisches Erzählen im Kontext. Mittelalterliche Fabeln, Gleichnisse und historische Exempel in narrativer Argumentation*. Berlin: De Gruyter, 2018.
Sears, Elizabeth. *The Ages of Man: Medieval interpretations of the life cycle*. Princeton, NJ: Princeton University Press, 1986.
Sherwood-Smith, Maria C. *Studies in the Reception of the 'Historia Scholastica' of Peter Comestor*. Oxford: SSMLL, 2000.
Shoaf, R. Allen. 'Dante's Beard: Sic et Non (*Purgatorio* 31.68)'. In *'Magister Regis': Studies in Honor of Robert Earl Kaske*, edited by Arthur Groos with Emerson Brown et al., 171–8. New York: Fordham University Press, 1986.
Short, Ian. 'Roland's final combat', *Cultura neolatina* 30 (1970): 135–55.
Sieber, Andrea. 'Gender studies'. In *Literatur- und Kulturtheorien in der germanistischen Mediävistik. Ein Handbuch*, edited by Christiane Ackermann and Michael Egerding, 103–40. Berlin: De Gruyter, 2015.
Simon, Eckehard. *Die Anfänge des weltlichen deutschen Schauspiels 1370–1530. Untersuchung und Dokumentation*. Tübingen: Niemeyer, 2003.
Spahr, Gebhard. *Weingartner Liederhandschrift. Ihre Geschichte und ihre Miniaturen*. Weissenhorn: Konrad, 1968.
Spicker, Johannes. *Oswald von Wolkenstein. Die Lieder*. Berlin: Schmidt, 2007.
Springeth, Margarete and Franz Viktor Spechtler (eds). *Neidhart und die Neidhart-Lieder. Ein Handbuch*. Berlin: De Gruyter, 2018.
Steger, Hugo. *David rex et propheta. König David als vorbildliche Verkörperung des Herrschers und Dichters im Mittelalter, nach Bilddarstellungen des achten bis zwölften Jahrhunderts*. Nuremberg: Carl, 1961.
Stevens, Sylvia. *Family in Wolfram von Eschenbach's 'Willehalm': mîner mâge triwe ist mir wol kuont*. New York: Lang, 1997.
Stock, Markus. 'Figur. Zu einem Kernproblem historischer Narratologie'. In *Historische Narratologie – Mediävistische Perspektiven*, edited by Harald Haferland and Matthias Meyer, 187–204. Berlin: De Gruyter, 2010.
Stones, Alison. 'The *Codex Calixtinus* and the iconography of Charlemagne'. In *Roland and Charlemagne in Europe*, edited by Pratt, 169–203.

Suchomski, Joachim. *'Delectatio' und 'utilitas'. Ein Beitrag zum Verständnis mittelalterlicher komischer Literatur*. Berne: Francke, 1975.
Tervooren, Helmut. *Sangspruchdichtung*. Stuttgart: Metzler, 2001.
Urban, Felix. *Gleiches zu Gleichem: Figurenähnlichkeit in der späthöfischen Epik. 'Flore und Blanscheflur', 'Engelhard', 'Barlaam und Josaphat', 'Wilhalm von Wenden'*. Berlin: De Gruyter, 2020.
Velten, Hans Rudolf. *Scurrilitas. Das Lachen, die Komik und der Körper in Literatur und Kultur des Spätmittelalters und der Frühen Neuzeit*. Tübingen: Narr Francke Attempto, 2017.
Vetter, Angila. *Textgeschichte(n). Retextualisierungsstrategien und Sinnproduktion in Sammlungsverbünden. Der 'Willehalm' in kontextueller Lektüre*. Berlin: Schmidt, 2018.
Vetter, Ewald. 'Die Handschrift und ihre Bilder'. In *Der Welsche Gast des Thomasîn von Zerclaere. Codex Palatinus Germanicus 389 der Universitätsbibliothek Heidelberg*, 69–190. Wiesbaden: Reichert, 1974.
Vogt, Dieter. *Ritterbild und Ritterlehre in der lehrhaften Kleindichtung des Stricker und im sog. Seifried Helbling*. Frankfurt am Main: Lang, 1985.
Volfing, Annette. '*Parzival* and *Willehalm*: Narrative continuity?' In *Wolfram's 'Willehalm'*, edited by Jones and McFarland, 45–59.
Vollmann, Justin. 'Wolfdietrich und die wilden Frauen', *JOWG* 14 (2003/2004): 243–54.
Wachinger, Burghart. *Sängerkrieg. Untersuchungen zur Spruchdichtung des 13. Jahrhunderts*. Munich: Beck, 1973.
Wachinger, Burghart. 'Wolfram von Eschenbach am Schreibpult', *Wolfram-Studien* 12 (1992): 9–14.
Wallace, Lewis. 'Bearded woman, female Christ: Gendered transformations in the legends and cult of Saint Wilgefortis', *Journal of Feminist Studies in Religion* 30 (2014): 43–63.
Weichselbaumer, Ruth. *Der konstruierte Mann. Repräsentation, Aktion und Disziplinierung in der didaktischen Literatur des Mittelalters*. Münster: LIT, 2003.
Weigand, Rudolf Kilian. *Der 'Renner' des Hugo von Trimberg. Überlieferung, Quellenabhängigkeit und Struktur einer spätmittelalterlichen Lehrdichtung*. Wiesbaden: Reichert, 2000.
Weis-Diel, Alexandra. *Gewaltstrategien. Codierung und Inszenierung von Gewalt im vorreformatorischen Nürnberger Fastnachtspiel*. Wiesbaden: Reichert, 2018.
Wenzel, Edith. *'Do worden die Judden alle geschant': Rolle und Funktion der Juden in spätmittelalterlichen Spielen*. Munich: Fink, 1992.
Wenzel, Franziska. *Meisterschaft im Prozess. Der Lange Ton Frauenlobs – Texte und Studien. Mit einem Beitrag zu vormoderner Textualität und Autorschaft*. Berlin: Akademie, 2012.
Wenzel, Horst. 'Hören und Sehen. Zur Lesbarkeit von Körperzeichen in der höfischen Literatur'. In *Personenbeziehungen in der mittelalterlichen Literatur*, edited by Helmut Brall, Barbara Haupt and Urban Küsters, 192–218. Düsseldorf: Droste, 1994.
Wenzel, Horst. 'Repräsentation und schöner Schein am Hof und in der höfischen Literatur'. In *Höfische Repräsentation. Das Zeremoniell und die Zeichen*, edited by Hedda Ragotzky and Horst Wenzel, 171–208. Tübingen: Niemeyer, 1990.
Wenzel, Horst. *Spiegelungen. Zur Kultur der Visualität im Mittelalter*. Berlin: Schmidt, 2009.
Werthschulte, Leila. 'Erzählte Männlichkeiten im *Nibelungenlied*'. In *Genus & generatio. Rollenerwartungen und Rollenerfüllungen im Spannungsfeld der Geschlechter und Generationen in Antike und Mittelalter*, edited by Hartwin Brandt, Lina K. Hörl, Anika M. Auer, Johannes Brehm and Diego De Brasi, 269–94. Bamberg: University of Bamberg Press, 2011.
Whitesell, Frederick R. 'Fables in mediaeval exempla', *JEGP* 46 (1947): 348–66.
Wießner, Edmund. *Kommentar zu Heinrich Wittenwilers Ring*. Leipzig: Reclam, 1936.
Wolf, Gerhard. *Die Kunst zu lehren. Studien zu den Dialoggedichten ('Kleiner Lucidarius') der 'Seifried-Helbling'-Sammlung*. Frankfurt am Main: Lang, 1985.
Worstbrock, Franz Josef. 'Wiedererzählen und Übersetzen'. In *Mittelalter und frühe Neuzeit*, edited by Haug, 128–42.
Wunderli, Peter. 'Das Karlsbild in der altfranzösischen Epik'. In *Karl der Große*, edited by Bastert, 17–38.
Wunderli, Peter. '*Speculatio Carolina*. Variationen des Karlsbildes in der altfranzösischen Epik', *Vox Romanica* 55 (1996): 38–87.
Wyss, Ulrich. 'Der Schatten des Körpers des Königs'. In *Körperkonzepte im arthurischen Roman*, edited by Friedrich Wolfzettel, 21–31. Tübingen: Niemeyer, 2007.
Yao, Shao-Ji. *Der Exempelgebrauch in der Sangspruchdichtung vom späten 12. Jahrhundert bis zum Anfang des 14. Jahrhunderts*. Würzburg: Königshausen & Neumann, 2006.
Ziegeler, Hans-Joachim. *Erzählen im Spätmittelalter. Mären im Kontext von Minnereden, Bispeln und Romanen*. Munich: Artemis, 1985.

Index

Page numbers in *italics* are figures.

www.ingramcontent.com/pod-product-compliance
Lightning Source LLC
LaVergne TN
LVHW052017300826
846742LV00020B/83